Any resemblance to anyone living or dead is exactly the way I remember what I saw, or what I heard, or what I was told by acquaintances that are identified herein.
I am certain that many of my enemies wish my memory was not so accurate.

ACKNOWLEDGMENTS

My nieces Danielle Griffin and Robin Reach were especially helpful, my cousin, Ann Womack spent many hours helping me, for which I am eternally grateful.

To Hon Addison -
Good Hunting
Good Teaching -
Good Luck -
I hope you enjoy my stories

815 - 2023

BEFORE I FORGET

A Country Lawyer from Livingston Parish,
Louisiana's Memories of the Civil Rights
Era, Politics, and Fishing and Hunting

Table of Contents   Page

Book 4 HUNTING AND FISHING 1950's THROUGH 1990's

BOOK 1 CIVIL RIGHTS ERA

Chapter 1. Growing up in the Segregated South 1950 - 1959

Chapter 2. Helping Black Citizens Register to Vote in Livingston Parish Louisiana 1960 - Local Judges Election – 1961

Chapter 3. Congressional Race, March from Bogalusa Through Livingston Parish to Baton Rouge August 10-20, 1967

Chapter 4. 1968-1969 Ku Klux Klan At Livingston Parish Fair, Concordia Parish, Democratic Convention in Chicago

Chapter 5. First Civil Rights Lawsuits - District Attorney's Race

Chapter 1. Growing up in the Segregated South 1950 - 1959

My mother, who was the only pharmacist in the small town of Springfield encouraged her black cook to bring her small son to our home where he and I played together while our mothers worked. My mother took me to the Black Methodist Church to hear gospel music when I was a small boy. A giant black man with a deep bass voice was a featured singer, and my mother's black friends always told her when there was going to be a service where we could come and hear Big Boy sing.

My first experience with integration occurred when I won a trip to Chicago to attend a 4H club convention in 1955. We traveled on the Illinois Central Railroad from Hammond Louisiana on a train called the Panama Limited which was segregated. When we arrived in Chicago the hotel, restaurants, and movie theaters were all integrated. On the trip home we rode a train called The City of New Orleans which was integrated, and I shared meals in the dining car and the club car with black-and-white passengers until we reached Memphis, Tennessee when the black riders had to move out of the dining and club cars for the rest of the trip.

My father had developed subdivisions in Baton Rouge in the 1920s and worked for the Federal Land Bank during the depression in the 1930s. Immediately after World War II he recognized that there would be a market for small tracts of land to sell to soldiers who were returning home and starting families. He purchased land right outside the city limits of the small towns of Albany and Springfield Louisiana where he built gravel streets and divided the property into 50' x 120' lots. In Springfield he purchased about 50 acres, part of which bordered a black community on one side of the highway and the rest on the other side bordered whites.

Everything was segregated in the early 1950s when he started this development and there was no land that Blacks could purchase to build homes on and no banks that would lend them any money to buy land. I worked with black laborers clearing the land, digging ditches, driving stakes to mark the lots for the surveyors and building waterlines and drilling shallow wells to provide water. We began selling lots on credit to Blacks in the black subdivision and to Whites in the white subdivision for $200 each on terms of $20 down and $10 per month. The sales were on bond for deed contracts providing for transfer of title when the land was paid for. Many older Blacks encouraged their older children to purchase lots from my father and I would accompany him to their houses each month to collect the payments. He was a Notary Public and many of the poor Blacks sought his advice if they had problems and he always tried to help them and never charged them any money.

I continued to follow this practice after I came back from the Army and developed friendships with the vast majority of the black community in our area. Very few of them were registered to vote.

I graduated from a white segregated high school in 1956, served in the U.S. Army in 1957-1958 and graduated from Southeastern Louisiana College, a white segregated college in 1963.

When I joined the Army in 1957 it was completely integrated, and I had no problem with that whatsoever. I did my basic training at Fort Chaffee Arkansas at the same time the schools were integrated in Little Rock. I met soldiers who were protecting the schoolchildren from the rioters at Little Rock High School before I was transferred to Fort Devens, Massachusetts.

Several of my cases during my first years after finishing law school in 1966 were representing School Board employees and parents who felt that their children had been mistreated in the schools. I went before school boards in Livingston and Tangipahoa in cases involving integration which was very very unpopular with the lily-white school boards in those parishes. I didn't care what the school board members thought, I believed they needed to follow the law and I paid dearly for it.

10

Chapter 2. Helping Black Citizens Register to Vote in Livingston Parish, Louisiana 1960- Local Judges Election 1961

In 1958 I had just come out of the army which was fully integrated, so I didn't have the same mind set as many of the people in my area. I was absolutely convinced that the black people had the right to vote.

Julius Foster, the local police juror needed those votes to get re-elected and they weren't registered. He asked me if I would help register those black people to vote. Many of them were illiterate and could not read or write, and the new administration of Governor Jimmy Davis had passed laws saying not only did you have to be able to read and write, but you had to interpret the constitution to be able to register to vote. Well, I was in college, I had gone one year to LSU was in my second or third year at Southeastern, so I knew a little bit more about the constitution than the register of voters or anybody else that had any say so about registering people to vote.

In 1960 my wife and I separated and went to court before Judge Fanny Birch in Livingston Parish for our divorce.

The trial took place in January 1960 and Judge Birch took the matter under advisement, leaving custody of my 18-month-old son with me. Months went by without her making a final decision. When I talked to my lawyer he said we would have to wait for the judge to decide. In the meantime, former Judge Warren Comish qualified to run against Judge Birch for election in the fall of 1960. In March I called Judge Birch's office and asked for an appointment to talk to her and she agreed to see me. I had just made 21 years old in February and was not registered to vote. When I went into her office I asked her why she couldn't give me my divorce since the evidence was clearly in my favor. She told me that we should try to get back together and added that as long as she was Judge I did not have to worry about her taking my son away from me. I told her that she may as well go ahead and rule against me because I was going to do everything I could to make sure she was

11

defeated for reelection and that I would appeal her decision if she ruled against me.

The next day I drove to Livingston to the Registrar of Voters office and registered to vote myself. During the next 90 days after the offices at the courthouse were closed in the afternoon and on Saturday's I personally carried between 80 and 90 black citizens to the Registrar of Voters office in Livingston Parish and helped them register to vote. This occurred in 1960 while the Ku Klux Klan was trying to suppress black voters' registration. I also contacted dozens of my white friends and asked them to vote against Judge Birch.

A few days before the election I met with local officials, Police Juror Julius Foster, Springfield Mayor Harold Abels, Assessor Bubbie Abels and some of their supporters to make plans to get out the vote on election day. We obtained a list of voters, made several copies on a primitive copier one of the schoolteachers used after classes and marked each person on the list that was for us, against us or undecided. Drivers, including myself, were assigned which of our supporters were to be given rides to the polls.

We had poll watchers at every voting precinct who had a list of the voters and checked off the name of each one who voted. The poll watchers' list was periodically taken outside to another worker who updated the master list showing which of our voters had not voted. Telephone calls were then made to each one to remind them to come vote, and if they needed a ride, drivers were sent to pick them up.

Our side was better organized than our opponents who consisted mainly of Ku Klux Klan members who gathered in a group outside the polls and tried to intimidate our voters. When the polls opened at 6 AM I arrived with my first carload of newly registered black voters, and personally escorted them past the Klan members into the school gymnasium where voting took place. After they voted I drove them home and picked up another load. As the morning progressed the crowd of Klansmen grew larger as did a group of men on our side who heard the others making threats against me after I left.

12

Well, by about 10:00 in the morning as I drove up there with my fifth or sixth load of voters, 4 or 5 at a time, Bubbie Abels and Julius Foster and a couple of other men that were on our side stopped me and Bubbie told me, "Boy," he said, "Look it's too damn dangerous what you're doing. Let's just give one of those blacks some money and let them haul them in." I said, "Bubbie they may not make damn sure that these folks vote right." I said, "I took them to the court house and registered them to vote, they trust me and I'm gonna make damn sure they get to vote." And with that I took out my 38-caliber pistol which was underneath the seat of my car and laid it on the dash where everybody could see it. A group of Ku Klux Klan members, that were for Ms. Birch, were standing at the door. They saw me put that pistol in my pocket and walk right on in the polls with those folks to help them vote. I was ready to use that pistol if anybody would have tried to stop me. I got cussed, I got discussed, and I got criticized about being a "N" lover and a whole lot worse than that. I had a cross burned in front of my house and in front of some of my Black friends' houses. We won that election by less than 200 votes and I personally put in more than 70. After that I was in the middle of every election they had in Livingston Parish for years and years. When I finished law school I started a practice in Springfield. Many of the blacks that I had helped register to vote and later their children and now their grandchildren and their great grandchildren still use me as their lawyer, and it all goes back to that. I didn't stop just with the blacks when I registered people to vote. I also registered lots of semi-literate poor white people.

It was illegal then and it is illegal now to use public funds on private property. Julius Foster had a different philosophy. He felt like that if you lived off the road and had a driveway coming back to your house and you had people, your friends, your neighbors or the mailman or anybody else that came on your property that was for the public's benefit, and if the public's grader went on the road to grade the holes out of it, this was a service not to you individually but this was also a service to the public who used that road to visit you or to bring you services or to benefit from your farm produce or whatever else came across that driveway and if you needed to keep the ditches from being blocked so you and your neighbor would have drainage you needed a culvert and a public culvert would benefit the public by having better drainage for all, and also to allow transport across that land.

In those days vote buying, though illegal, was a common practice on both sides of many elections. Before the invention of voting machines, when paper ballots were used, a scheme was developed to guarantee that a person who was paid to vote for a candidate actually cast his vote for that candidate.

When the polls opened a supporter of one of the candidates would come to the polls, obtain a paper ballot from a commissioner, go in the booth behind the curtain and mark the ballot for his candidate. He then folded the ballot which was to be placed in a slot in the locked ballot box in the presence of the commissioners.

The first voter would have a blank piece of paper the same size as the ballot already folded in his pocket when he went behind the curtain. After marking his ballot, he would put it in his pocket, walk outside to the commissioners and deposit the folded blank piece of paper in the ballot box.

When a person agreed to sell his vote, he would be given the previously marked official ballot to put in his pocket then pick up a new ballot from the commissioners. After going behind the curtain, he would fold the blank ballot, put it in his other pocket come out and deposit the marked ballot in the ballot box. He would then come outside the polls and exchange the unmarked ballot for the money agreed upon. The political supporter would then mark the new ballot for the next person selling his vote. At the end of the day a different political supporter would take the previously marked ballot into the polls when he got his ballot and deposit both folded ballots in the voting box. When the boxes were opened, and the votes counted the commissioners and poll watchers could always tell if illegal vote buying had occurred by the presence of the blank papers in the ballot box, but they could not do anything about it. This was called a floating ballot.

14

In the election in 1960, voting machines were used and there was no way to be certain a person who had received money to cast his ballot would actually vote as instructed unless he was registered to vote as needing assistance due to age, disability, or being illiterate. Each voter when registering to vote was given an identification card to be presented to the commissioners before being allowed to cast his vote. Anyone could ask for assistance from a commissioner to enter the voting machine and help him cast his ballot. People who were registered as needing assistance were issued a blue card rather than a standard white card. These voters could select a friend or relative to go into the voting machine with them to help them cast their ballot. In that case the person buying the vote could actually pull the lever of the machine.

I personally observed vote buying in the election between Judge Comish and Judge Birch. One of Judge Birch's main supporters was a restaurant owner from Manchac in Tangipahoa Parish. He came to the polls in Springfield about the middle of the day when I was standing outside talking to Elliott Foster, the owner of a local bar who was a brother of police jury member Julius Foster. The supporter of Judge Birch walked past us and met with the group of Klansmen standing nearby.

About that time an army veteran with his Philippine war bride approached the polling place and Elliott walked over and talked to him. After their discussion Elliott told me that he had offered the man $10 for he and his wife to vote for Judge Comish. The couple then walked towards the polling entrance and stopped to talk to the other man, and then entered the polls. A few minutes later they returned from voting and I moved closer to where Judge Birch's supporter was standing and saw him put his hand in his pocket bring it out and shake hands with the man who just voted. I moved back next to Elliott as the couple approached and told him what I had seen. He told me not to worry about it, he knew the man and he had promised to vote for Judge Comish. When the man got to us Elliott handed him a $10 bill and I heard the man say, "keep your money the other side paid me $20 for our vote."

15

Chapter 3. Congressional Race, March Through Livingston Parish to Baton Rouge August 10 -20,1967

In 1966 I graduated from Loyola Law School, we had a congressman named Jimmy Morrison who had been in office for almost 20 years. He had probably the most efficient staff of any member of Congress. When people wrote letters requesting information or favors there was an immediate response and he had no serious opposition after he was first elected. He was a Democrat and supported the National party without question. In 1962, before President Kennedy was assassinated in November 1963 he voted to enlarge the House Rules Committee to dilute the power of members who supported segregation. In 1965 he supported the Voting Rights Act, although the white people in our district overwhelmingly were for segregation and denial of voting rights for blacks. Despite this, Jimmy voted for the act.

Schools were being integrated in New Orleans and other places in the South and there were news reports of white protest on television every day. The Ku Klux Klan became active in the sixth Congressional District and in the Feliciana parishes a judge named John R Rarick openly displayed a Confederate flag in his courtroom.

Judge Rarick ran against Jimmy on a segregationist ticket and was endorsed by all the right-wing organizations. Jimmy had not had to campaign for reelection for many years, but he recognized the need to get out his vote.

He put on a campaign reminiscent of the times when he ran in the 1940s and 50s going from town to town and making speeches. He made the critical error of recognizing his opponent by name. The great majority of the voters had never heard of John Rarick. Jimmy repeatedly made his speeches about the things he had accomplished for the people over the years and finished by stating "nobody but the frogs are for John R Rarick".

Rarick supporters began to go to the Morrison speeches and interrupt them with chants of "Rarick, Rarick, Rarick!" Imitating frogs. This tactic along with the segregationist position of the majority defeated

Jimmy Morrison. I heard many seasoned political observers state that if Jimmy Morrison had stayed in Washington and never made a speech he would have been overwhelmingly reelected despite his votes for the voting rights act and other Kennedy sponsored bills.

There was much agitation between black organizations supporting the Civil Rights Act sponsored by President Johnson and members of the Klan in South Louisiana at this time. Black citizens in Bogalusa Louisiana sought equal employment from Crown Zellerback Corporation in 1966 and many cross burnings and acts of violence by the Ku Klux Klan occurred. A Black Organization called the Deacons for Defense was organized to protect black citizens from the Klan with their weapons.

Actress Jane Fonda attended meetings with the civil rights groups which resulted in the organization of a March to the state capital in Baton Rouge Louisiana to meet with Governor John McKeithen to address their grievances.

The March was led by a huge black man named A. Z. Young in July 1967. Whites gathered along the roads to taunt the marchers. The governor called out the state police to protect them. When the marchers reached Livingston Parish Senior police officer Rudolph Ratcliff from Livingston Parish was on a white horse and state police trooper "Black" Freddie Piazza, whose dark complexion distinguished him from state trooper "White" Freddie Piazza both of Italian decent, from Tangipahoa Parish joined the other policeman guarding the marchers.

On August 12, 1967 when the marchers reached Satsuma, a small all-white community, a gang of Klan members and their supporters attacked the marchers and State Troopers. The police retaliated with billy clubs and tear gas and arrested the attackers who were placed in the Livingston Parish jail. Some were hospitalized for their wounds inflicted by the troopers.

A couple of days later the marchers reached Denham Springs, Louisiana where a large crowd had gathered. A large white redneck man spied Trooper Piazza and shouted out "It's not bad enough that we got the niggers marching through Denham Springs. We got the Dago's marching on the side of them." This infuriated Trooper Piazza and he chased the man through the crowd, but couldn't catch him.

A day or so later Frank Brent McCarroll and Dick Cogley were at Mike Erdey's OK bar and got in an argument with Mike about the March. Mike, a World War II combat veteran told them he didn't care if the blacks marched up and down the road. His bar was segregated serving whites in the front and blacks in the rear in a separate room. The men went outside the bar and Mike was shot and killed. Both McCarroll and Cogley were charged with murder.

Barbee Ponder represented McCarroll and Ossie Brown represented Cogley. I was fresh out of law school and did some abstract work for Art Macy, a Hammond attorney who was contacted by Dick Cogley's family to prepare a mortgage on their property, so they could borrow money to pay Ossie.

I had never met Ossie before but had read about him in the newspapers. He was a flamboyant criminal attorney from Baton Rouge. I was in court in Livingston when he appeared on a motion day before the murder trial. He was dressed in a red and white suit that looked like a checker board. He had on a red shirt, white tie, red shoes, and white socks. A few weeks later I saw him at another hearing in Livingston and this time he was dressed in a Kelly-green suit, light green shirt, dark green tie, dark green shoes, and light green socks.

When he started to leave the courtroom, I followed him outside and asked why he dressed that way. He told me to follow him back in the courtroom and as we stood near the rear door looking at the judge and other lawyers in the front of the courtroom who were all dressed in dark suits said," look at those guys, do you know them?" I said "I knew one or two but not the others. He said," the public don't know any of them but when I walk in the courtroom everybody knows me."

I quickly realized that I needed to find me a gimmick so that when I walked in the courtroom everybody would know me, or at least know I was not like the other lawyers, but I sure wasn't going to wear checkerboard suits or green shoes. That's when I started wearing western cut suits, cowboy boots and a bolo tie. I have been wearing this type of

18

clothing for more than 50 years, and when I walk in any courtroom from Benton Louisiana to New Orleans everybody in the room notices me.

The District Attorney made a deal with Ossie for his client to testify against McCarroll but Barbee picked a jury with teetotalers and Klan sympathizers. He painted Mike as a bar owner who ran gambling games and sold liquor to blacks. He told the jury that his client was innocent, and the killing was done by Dick. Frank Brent McCarroll had remained in jail for about a year before his trial and was found not guilty.

Chapter 4. 1968 - 1969 Ku Klux Klan at Livingston Parish Fair, Concordia Parish, Democratic Convention in Chicago.

From the time I was in junior high school, I loved to go to dances and listen to music. Before there was rock 'n roll, there were a few stations that played Rhythm and Blues on the radio late at night. Some of the artists I listened to were Bo Diddley, Little Richard, Chuck Berry and Fats Domino. However, there was also country music on the local radio stations every day. When I came home from the Army and began taking courses at Southeastern, Johnny Horton, Webb Pierce, Lefty Fresnel, Patsy Cline, Johnny Cash, Willie Nelson, Waylon Jennings, Loretta Lynn, and Conway Twitty were the artists I listened to on the radio and the jukeboxes in the local bar rooms.

A friend of mine from Walker, Louisiana, named Lloyd Hodges, opened an establishment featuring big-name country singers called The Old South Jamboree. Many local and not so famous entertainers would provide music to the audience before the top acts would perform. No alcohol was served in this bone-dry part of Livingston Parish at that time, and I did not attend the shows on a regular basis. On the other hand, James Pate, who did not drink, took his family to almost every show and got to know many of the local entertainers.

Brother Pate, as he was universally known, became one of my clients shortly after I started practicing law. The Livingston Parish Fair was held each year in early October at the fairgrounds in Livingston. Like the schools, it was completely segregated, and no Blacks were allowed to attend except on one day that was set aside for them. In 1968, a group of Blacks decided they were going to go to the fair on a day that was reserved for Whites. A group of Ku Klux Klansmen quickly assembled at the fairgrounds and attacked the Blacks. Sheriff's deputies who were at the fair called for assistance and, using billy clubs, subdued the Klansman and put them in jail. The wife of one of the Klansmen, a young woman in her 20s, verbally attacked chief Deputy Odom Graves

20

because he had arrested her husband. When she continued her tirade and charged towards Odom, he hit her on the bosom with a large flashlight causing a large bruise but didn't put her in jail.

The next day, Brother Pate and Mack McCaffery, a leader of the Klan in the Springfield area came to see me about getting them out of jail. When I arrived at the courthouse, there were a large group of men at the door and deputies had prohibited any of them to go upstairs to the jail. The men told me they thought the deputies had seriously injured the Klansmen they arrested and were demanding to see their friends in jail. The deputies told me there was no way they were going to let that gang in their jail or, for that matter, in the courthouse itself.

I knew all the deputies and the sheriff, and they all knew me. They also knew that I represented a lot of Blacks in the area and that anything I was doing for the arrested men was strictly as a paid attorney. Tom Kent Stewart, one of the deputies, and I hunted wild turkeys together and were best friends. I told the Klansmen that I was going to see the sheriff, and I would ask permission to meet with the men who were arrested. If they needed medical assistance, I would try to get it for them. When I asked Tom Kent to let me see the men in jail, so I could tell their friends they were not hurt badly, he talked to Odom and Sheriff Taft Faust, who quickly agreed. When I met with the prisoners, none of them were seriously hurt. I came back down stairs and told the Klan members their friends were okay and to go home, which they did.

The next day, Brother Pate and McCaffrey brought the injured wife to my office, and she explained she had a large bruise where she had been struck. I told her I needed to see it and take a picture if she was going to have a case against Odom Graves for hitting her. She reluctantly opened her shirt which revealed a yellowish green bruise on her breasts, but she insisted that Pate and McCaffrey look the other way.

I told Tom Kent Stewart she may have a civil case against Odom and the Sheriff's Department because he hit her but didn't arrest her. I knew I could probably get the charges dropped against all of them if I told the sheriff there would be no lawsuit, but I told Brother Pate and McCaffrey they were going to have to make sure their friends, who they got me to represent, were going to do what I told them. About three weeks later, the Klansman were to appear in court for arraignment, and when I arrived, the only ones there were Pate and McCaffrey. I met with Erlo Durbin, the assistant district attorney, and Judge Warren Comish, and they told me that my clients didn't need me anymore because they had dropped all the charges. I never got paid and never represented any Ku Klux Klansmen again.

In early 1968 I had been working as an attorney for the Louisiana Department Revenue for two years. Lyndon Johnson was becoming more and more unpopular because of the Vietnam War. There was much speculation about who would oppose him for the Democratic presidential nomination at the national convention that summer. Robert Kennedy, the late president's brother was rumored to be a candidate. I was watching a speech by President Johnson on television on March 31, 1968 when he unexpectedly declared that he would not be a candidate for reelection.

Five days later Martin Luther King Jr. was assassinated in Memphis Tennessee and riots broke out all across America resulting in large areas of Detroit Michigan and other northern cities being burned down. Young people from the north were coming to the southern states to help Blacks register to vote. The Ku Klux Klan, and their supporters including some police officers violently opposed these volunteers, resulting in beatings and sometimes murders.

During that time my job required me to supervise collection of past due taxes from small businesses all across the state of Louisiana. When a business failed to file sales tax returns or purchase occupational licenses the local revenue office would attempt to collect the money owed to the state. When they were unsuccessful the businesses were reported to my office in Baton Rouge where warrants for distraint were issued authorizing the seizure of assets belonging to the delinquent taxpayers. When payments were still not made I would travel along with senior agents working under me to the business location to either collect the taxes or seize the business assets.

Early one morning I and two agents got in my car in Baton Rouge and traveled to Concordia Parish to make several seizures. Ferriday, Louisiana was a small Delta community on the Mississippi River surrounded by large cotton and soybeans farms. It had a large black population and there were several black-owned shops and bar rooms in the community that had not obtained occupational licenses and paid sales taxes.

I had heard rumors of civil rights workers being beaten by law enforcement officers In Concordia Parish in the past and the FBI was making an investigation. When the other Revenue agents and I drove into the black section of town to the location of a delinquent business I noticed a Sheriff's office vehicle following us. We went into the business to talk to the owner and had him sign an agreement to pay his past due taxes. I waved penalties, so he could continue to operate and generate funds for the state. When we went back to our car I noticed Sheriff's deputies were parked down the street watching us. We proceeded to another location to meet another taxpayer and were followed by the deputies. After we finished talking to that black taxpayer we started to another location with the deputies continuing to follow us. One of the agents working for me was a former state policeman, so when we stopped at the next location he and I walked over to the deputy's car and asked them why they were following us.

They had already ran my license plate which revealed who I was and where I lived in Livingston Parish, but they had no idea who I worked for. When we showed them our Louisiana State Department of Revenue badges, the two white deputies said they thought we might be civil rights workers who were trying to stir up trouble with the Blacks and apologized for interfering with our business. I believe if we had not been on official business for the state, we would probably have been taken to the Sheriff's office for questioning and possibly been arrested on some trumped-up charges.

After President Johnson made his announcement, Senator Robert Kennedy announced his candidacy for president, as well as Senator Eugene McCarthy. On June 6, 1968 Senator Kennedy was assassinated.

At the revenue office in Baton Rouge where I worked, a young law student from North Louisiana named Ralph Long came to work with Herman Stuart in the legal department. Ralph had a friend named Carson Killen who also worked at the capital and they had a connection through Congressman Gillis Long to Vice President Hubert Humphrey who was also considering a run for the presidency.

Ralph told me that he could get us some hotel rooms near the convention headquarters of the Democratic National Committee in Chicago, if we wanted to attend. I had ran for the Democratic State Central Committee from Livingston Parish in 1967 against a long time conservative incumbent and was narrowly defeated. I figured the trip to Chicago would be a step in the right direction for me to achieve my future political goals, so I went along for the ride.

Ralph got the room reservations at a discount rate a couple of blocks away from the Conrad Hilton Hotel. It was located on Michigan Avenue at the lakefront where Governor John McKeithen and the rest of the Louisiana delegation were staying.

When we arrived at O'Hare airport, there were several welcoming groups seated at tables with signs offering free rides to the delegates going downtown. Although we had no official designation we quickly assumed the titles of delegates and alternates and took advantage of the offers. After securing our hotel rooms we went to the lobby of the Conrad Hilton Hotel where other tables had been set up and manned by volunteers to welcome the delegates.

We introduced ourselves as being alternates from Louisiana and were advised that some of the Democratic officials would like to interview us about our observation of the support Vice President Hubert Humphrey could be expected to receive in Louisiana.

I readily agreed to the meeting and was taken to a nearby room and introduced to Gore Vidal, an author who I had never heard of before. He had a British accent and questioned me at length about politics in Louisiana. I told him I'd attended law school at Loyola University in New Orleans with fellow students from all over Louisiana that were active in the Democratic Party. I also told him that Hubert Humphrey's

24

best chance to carry Louisiana would have the open support of Governor John McKeithen.

During our conversation he made some witty statements that I later wrote down. For instance, he told me "Style Is knowing who you are, what you want to say, and not giving a damn." He also said "Half the people have never read a newspaper. Half have never voted for President. One hopes it is the same half." And his final advice to me was "Never pass up the chance to have sex or appear on television." After I returned to Louisiana I read some of his books and considered myself lucky to have had the conversation with him.

Before we left for Chicago I had read in the newspapers about the possibility of antiwar demonstrations occurring at the national Democratic Convention. I correctly figured that if something like that happened the first thing the police would do was shut down the bars and liquor stores. To prepare for such an eventuality I brought an extra suitcase with me with a half-dozen bottles of Jack Daniels inside it.

The Governor's suite was on the third floor of the Conrad Hilton Hotel facing Michigan Avenue. While we were there I brought a couple bottles with me, and I was talking to my friend Representative Bobby Freeman who had attended Loyola Law school with me and later was elected Lieutenant Governor. The large windows were open, and we heard the crowd outside on the street began to shout antiwar slogans. We walked over to the window and watched as police approached with billet clubs and began to attack the demonstrators. Soon the air was filled with tear gas some of which rose up to our open windows and affected everyone in the room. The hotel stopped serving liquor or selling bottles, and I became the most popular man in the room with my Jack Daniels.

Chapter 5. First Civil Rights Lawsuits - District Attorney's Race

A lawsuit had been filed in federal court seeking to integrate the Tangipahoa Parish schools when I was approached by two school bus drivers from Ponchatoula one black and one white. At that time school bus drivers were required to purchase their own buses and were paid $350 per month as compensation. This money was paid by the State of Louisiana.

The Tangipahoa Parish school board decided that the local high schools could make more money if they purchased school buses and hired their own bus drivers at a cheaper rate. These two drivers who came to see me were both being underpaid. The white driver was being paid $150 per month, and the black driver, who was doing the same amount of work was being paid $75 per month. The high school was getting the rest of the money.

I contacted Superintendent Ed Newman and demanded that both drivers should be paid equally at the same rate of all other bus drivers who were doing the same work. The school board refused my demands and I filed a suit on behalf of my clients and all other school bus drivers in Tangipahoa Parish that were being underpaid.

The school board was represented by District Attorney Leonard Yokum and Assistant District Attorney Joe Simpson. There were about 20 school bus drivers that were driving buses for various schools that were being underpaid and Yokum and Simpson figured I was trying to make the school board pay me attorney fees for representing all of them.

Each bus driver was called in to the school principal's office and told to sign a statement that they did not want me to represent them in my lawsuit or else they would be fired. All of them, with the exception of my two clients from Ponchatoula had never heard of me and didn't want to lose their jobs, so they signed the paper prepared by Joe Simpson.

I asked for a status conference with the federal judge in New Orleans Louisiana and met with Yokum and Simpson at that conference.

26

When the federal judge saw the school board was violating the law he told them my clients were entitled to equal pay of $350 per month. When Joe Simpson presented his affidavit from the other drivers the judge asked me how I could represent them. I told him I did not expect to be paid by those employees or the school board and he told Simpson and Yokum to tell their client the Tangipahoa Parish school board he was ordering it to pay all of bus drivers in Tangipahoa Parish at the same rate of pay.

When the Tangipahoa Parish schools were ordered to integrate by the federal court in 1969 school board members decided to close some small schools and demote and replace tenured teachers and principals of black schools with whites.

Many of the black teachers and principals were not as well qualified as the whites, but under state law their salaries could not be cut if they were moved to a lesser position. The Tangipahoa Parish School Board chose to ignore the law.

Fred McCoy was a Black US Army veteran of the Korean War and went to school at Southern University taking educational courses to become a teacher. He began teaching in Tangipahoa Parish and took additional courses to qualify him for higher positions in the school system. He did not have a master's degree which would qualify him as a principal, but when an opening occurred at the black school in Amite the board appointed him anyway. He served in that position for more than three years and became tenured.

When white children were assigned to the formerly all-black high school where Fred was principal the school board decided they needed someone with better qualifications and replaced Fred with a white man. They then demoted Fred to the position of janitor of the school and reduced his salary accordingly.

At the same time the school board closed a small all-white grammar school in Chesbrough and demoted the elderly white female principal, Mrs. Sarah Dantone, to a teaching position at another school and reduced her salary.

Mr. McCoy and Ms. Dantone had heard of my fights with the Livingston Parish School Board and asked me to represent them. I filed suit against the board in the 21st Judicial District Court in Amite, Louisiana. The school board was represented by District Attorney Leonard Yokum and Assistant District Attorney Joe Simpson. I won those cases, and obtained judgments ordering my clients salaries to be increased to the level they had previously been paid by Judge William M Dawkins, who had been a schoolteacher before he practiced law.

The school board insisted that the District Attorney appeal the decision, and he and Joe Simpson did not tell them they couldn't win on appeal. When they appealed to the First Circuit Court of Appeal in Baton Rouge Louisiana, The Judges affirmed Judge Dawkins decision, and ordered the board to pay court costs.

The school board then appealed to the Louisiana Supreme Court which also affirmed the decision. Several years had passed from the time I first filed suit until we obtained the final decision, and the school board had to pay interest on money it had to pay my clients. In Fred's case the total sum was more than $20,000.

After the judgment had become final I called Joe Simpson and asked him when I could expect to have my client's money. He told me that the board was thinking about it and I would just have to wait. I then obtained a court order for the sheriff to seize the desk, chairs and other furniture as well as pictures on the walls of the office of the Tangipahoa Parish Superintendent of Schools, Ed Newman to satisfy the judgment, and sent a copy to the newspapers.

This made national news, and Ed Newman received calls from Superintendents from all over Louisiana some of whom offered to send him some empty crates that he could use for a temporary desk and substitute for his chair. Sheriff Frank Edwards personally went to Ed's office to inform him of the seizure. The next day I received a call from one of Ed's assistant superintendents who told me I could come by their office and pick up the check. I told him that they could bring the check to my office or I would proceed with the seizure. Within two hours Fred McCoy and Mrs. Dantone's checks were delivered.

When he got his money, Fred McCoy bought a brand-new black and white Cadillac and placed metallic signs on each door stating, "Paid for by the Tangipahoa Parish School Board". He drove that car to the school each morning until he retired years later.

My wife and I had attended Southeastern at the same time. I graduated a year before she did, went to New Orleans and taught school, in the daytime and went to law school at night, while she was in her senior year at Southeastern. When she graduated in 1964 we got married and she got a job teaching in Jefferson Parish, where there was a shortage of teachers at the time. I got a job with the State, so I could go to day school at Loyola Law School. While I was going to law school and working, she took night courses at Loyola working on her Master's degree, and also took special courses in counseling. In the summers when I was in summer school, she completed more Masters' degree courses. She graduated with her Master's degree in counseling and got certified as a teacher and counselor.

When I finished law school and came back to Springfield our local school board members Carew Foster and Johnny Ratcliff recommended Loretta be hired as a teacher in Livingston parish. The local principal at Springfield High School was Bray Sibley, who had been a counselor at other schools. Loretta continued her post graduate studies at Southeastern at night and summer school, and he hired her as a part-time counselor and English teacher. She worked in the Springfield school for three years. When the schools were integrated I was among the men that actually guarded the school with rifles at night to prohibit any radical Ku Klux Klan members from burning it down as they threatened to do.

I, as well as Carew Foster, my friend, who was School Board Member was threatened by Klansmen for following the law and keeping the schools open when they wanted to have them shut down. When the schools were integrated in Livingston Parish, the majority of the board members were from the western side of the parish. Most of those areas had few or no Blacks whatsoever. There was a black school between Springfield and Albany, East Livingston High School, and a black school in Walker, West Livingston High School. The schools were inferior to the white schools with old buildings, old books, desks, and old buses. In fact, when the school board bought new desks for children in the white schools they would take the old desks and put them in the black schools. The school board was told by the federal court they couldn't do anything about the integration of the schools, so they decided they would build new school buildings for the Blacks on each side of the parish. They built a brand-new school at East Livingston and used it as a black school for one year. Then the federal judge ordered the school board to integrate all students into white schools, or he would order bussing of white students some 30 miles to black schools and black students some 30 miles to white schools. The school board held a public meeting to discuss the issue. And decided to avoid the bussing they would close the new black schools and move the black students to the overcrowded white schools near their homes. And the brand-new black school at East Livingston was closed. The school Superintendent, Warren Curtis and school board members had gone to the judge and told him that the black school was inferior, and they would have to put all of the children in the white schools, many in temporary buildings.

The judge did not care that there was a brand-new school sitting there empty. The Ku Kluckers made it well-known that they didn't want their white children going to that black school and sitting in the desks the black children had used and eating in a lunchroom that the black children had eaten in. Therefore, it was better to close down a brand-new school than to let their white children go to that school.

I was contacted by parents of both black and white children about the situation, so I went to the school board and made a demand that they reopen the school. They laughed at me and said the judge made his decision and that was it. The judge that made the decision was Judge E Gordon West from Baton Rouge, who had jurisdiction over Livingston parish. When he issued the order to close the school I filed an intervention in the lawsuit by parents of both black and white children. The Judge denied my intervention, and I took an appeal to the Fifth Circuit Court of Appeal in New Orleans to have the school reopened. The judges on the Court of Appeal set a status conference and I

30

appeared, along with the Superintendent of schools Mr. Warren Curtis, the president of the school board, the District Attorney Mr. Leonard Yokum, and his assistant Mr. Joe Simpson.

Before I went down there for the conference I got a local photographer to accompany me to the school and with the help of Board Members Carew Foster and Johnny Ratcliff we were allowed to go inside the school where he took pictures of the brand-new desks, the brand-new lunchroom, and all the other brand-new equipment that was unused. I also got a copy of the plans for the new school when it was built, and a map of the property. Mr. Yokum, Superintendent Curtis and the President of the School Board told the Judges the school was dilapidated and had to be closed. After they told that lie, I produced my evidence and asked the Judges to allow the children to use the new school that the taxpayers paid for. The appellant judges quickly sent the case back to Judge West, who was very embarrassed by the lies the school board had told him about the school being old and dilapidated. He had no choice but to order it reopened. He did that with Mr. Yokum and the school board president and Superintendent Curtis at a so-called hearing in Baton Rouge, without giving me notice to attend, and gave me no credit for having them reopen the school. The school board made an announcement that they had decided to reopen the school on their own. Of course, the local people knew about what happened. Well the school board decided to pay me back and pay me back they did.

They placed a black man who lived in Baton Rouge that had served as counselor in West Livingston school as counselor at Springfield. They placed a Black principal from Walker who had been principal at West Livingston school as principal at Springfield, and they placed another black man from Denham Springs who had been principal of a black junior high school in Walker as principal of Albany. So suddenly Springfield had a black counselor and black principal. Albany had a black principal and a black counselor, and all the rest of Livingston parish had white principals and white counselors. In addition, they took Loretta's job. The white principal at Springfield, Merlin St. Cyr who was made a co-principal with the black principal that year, changed

31

assignments for my wife from counselor to English teacher. This was a violation of the teacher tenure laws in Louisiana as she had been counselor for more than three years. So, we filed suit to overturn the school board's position, so they attempted to transfer her to Holden High School as an English teacher. I got Art Macy along with a young lawyer in his firm named Duncan Kemp to represent Loretta. We had a hearing in the local court before Judge Grover Covington who ordered the school board to reinstate Loretta as the counselor in Springfield. They countered by attempting to fire her because she refused to go to Holden to be an English teacher. The school board saw they were about to lose so they went back to their friend Judge Gordon West, the federal judge in Baton Rouge and he issued a stay order summarily denying our suit and keeping the status quo and Loretta lost her job.

I decided it was time for some payback for me, and I went to see Leonard Yokum. I told him, "This whole thing can be settled very easily, you're the advisor for the school board, why don't you tell them to give Loretta her job back as guidance counselor and that will take care of it. I know the school board members hate me because I made them reopen that school that was closed down, but you know that was the right thing to do," and he agreed with me about that. I said, "you're backing the school board, and if they're wrong, they are wrong." He said, "I've got to represent the school board." I suggested that he could tell them to compromise. He said "No, I represent the school board and I'm going to back them up on the what they want to do." I said "Let me ask you something Leonard, "Your election is coming up in the next few months. The deadline for filing qualifying papers has been set within 30 or 40 days. How many people on that school board are lawyers?" He said "None" I said, "How many of them can run against you?" He said "None, I said "you are looking at a son of a bitch that is a lawyer, can run, and is gonna run and beat your ass if I'm able." "Well you can't get anywhere." he said. I was mad, and I told him, "Well you watch me." I had talked to Art Macy about running a year before, and he had encouraged me to go Duncan Kemp, the young lawyer working for him. Duncan's daddy had been district attorney and died in office a couple

32

years before, and Yokum had been appointed District Attorney by the governor and had never been elected. Young Duncan told me he was going to run for that office and other lawyers and I had agreed to back him and to change the system. Duncan instead ran for the Senate and got beat, but he still said he was gonna run for district attorney in the election in September 1972.

A group of young lawyers and I met with Duncan and he agreed he would announce his candidacy in November 1971. He did not announce and told me he would announce in January 1972, when January arrived he did not announce. I told him "Hell Duncan if you are going to run, you better get going". He told me he was going to run, but when March arrived he still had not announced. Qualifying day was set for April or May and he still didn't announce. That's when I had my conversation with Mr. Yokum. Duncan didn't run, and I did.

I called an old friend of mine, Vic Anderson, who was Seventh Ward Marshall in Tangipahoa Parish and he gave me advice on how to run. He said you got to go everywhere to get known. You know you can't win, but that's what you got to do. There was a Police Juror named Aswell Robertson from Tangipahoa Parish who didn't like Leonard Yokum who helped me, and Julius Foster from Livingston who, along with some other police Jury members in Livingston who also liked me. Red Bridges was the sheriff of St. Helena Parish for many years and was in the produce business. He bought almost all the produce from small truck farms in St. Helena Parish. The main cash crop there was vegetables. People would raise pole beans and peppers and tomatoes, and other vegetable crops. When they brought produce to Mr. Bridges he paid the black, and the white poor farmers $0.10 a bushel more than anyone else. When he got elected he served as Sheriff for 40 years. I first met him was when I was running for district attorney, Art Macy contacted the sheriff and he said he wanted me to come talk to him. Art told me to go up to the jail to meet the sheriff at 7 o'clock one night. I made it my business to be in St. Helena parish that day to meet people all over the parish. At 7 o'clock when I arrived at the jail, I expected to be going to his office to talk to the sheriff. Instead, I was escorted to the jail, and when I walked in, the first cell I came to was open and it contained a cot and a chair. The sheriff was sitting on the cot, and I sat down in the chair. He reached underneath the cot, pulled out a bottle of Jack Daniels whiskey, and asked if I wanted a drink. I liked Jack Daniels whiskey but during the campaign I didn't hardly drink at all. He insisted I join him, so we shared a drink straight out of the bottle and talked about my campaign. He was very noncommittal about helping me or not helping me. I told him if I got elected, I would work with him as District Attorney and we had no conflicts after the election. Later when I talked to Art Macy about it he said "Well you know the sheriff sleeps in that jail, that's where he lives, his wife and him don't get along. At the jail they cook for the prisoners and they cook for him, he eats his meals there.

To make a long story short, I went for 20 hours a day and put 18,000 miles on my car in that six weeks' time. I came within 750 votes of beating Leonard Yokum. That was one of the best things that ever happened to me, because lawyers couldn't advertise in those days and I got known for being a fighter and bucking the odds. My name got heard enough that I started to get lots of new clients.

BOOK 2. PREPARATION FOR A LIFETIME CAREER

Chapter 1. Growing up in a Small Southern Town

Chapter 2. Local Politics, Marriage, Cold War Army Service

Chapter 3. Shaping my Legal Philosophy

Chapter 1. Growing up in a Small Southern Town

I was born in the little town of Springfield, Louisiana. My father dealt in real estate and timber, my mother was a pharmacist. In the early 1940's we lived in an apartment behind the drug store in the town, which had a population of maybe 100. The drug store served an area encompassing the southeast side of Livingston Parish and the Southwest side of Tangipahoa Parish. My parents were somewhat better off than a lot of the local farmers and laborer's in that my mother owned the property where the drug store was located.

Some of my earliest memories are about growing up as a kid in the town. I started school when I was 5 years old. My Aunt Doris Coats was a first-grade teacher at Springfield School and that helped me to enter a year earlier than most other children. Due to my Momma's insistence, I got a head start on the other children. The school had no lunchroom, everyone brought their lunch to the school, mine usually consisted of a sandwich but many of my friends would only bring a baked sweet potato, instead of any other kind of lunch. When recess took place, I got in the usual scrapes and fights and all the other things that kids did during that time. One of our main type of games was to play marbles, which I was not especially adapted to, but I usually would manage to win about as many games as I lost.

Another game we played was tops. We would draw a circle in the ground and throw our top in that circle. Then while it was spinning the other children would take their top and throw it in the circle and try to hit your top and knock it out of the circle. If your top was spinning and knocked the other child's top out, you won that top and of course if they knocked your top out, you were sunk, and they took your top. There was always competition, and this is what I grew up with my whole life.

When I was in grade school in the late 1940's and early 1950's, Springfield had one general merchandise store which sold everything from shoes to horse collars to hog feed. It had been in operation since before 1900 by the Settoon family whose current proprietor was Mr.

John, assisted by his elderly employee Albert Traylor, and his teenage nephew V E "Son" Settoon.

Mr. John, whose father had been a State Senator in the late 1890's and early 20th century, worked in his store his whole life. He once told me that he had gone to Baton Rouge to attend LSU in the early 1900's but only stayed a semester or two and then decided to come back to Springfield to operate the store.

Across the street his sister, Miss Ethel Tanner, had a little store where she sold sewing supplies and notions, as well as cloth to make clothes. Next door was a mechanic shop that specialized in repairing wagons, farm tools, and automobiles that was owned and operated by Little Charlie Schenks. As a barefoot 10-year-old I would hang around the mechanic shop and look at the calendar which had a picture on it of a beautiful young woman with her breasts exposed.

On the other corner was the Springfield Methodist church which had a front porch and a large front lawn where I got in my first serious fight when I was 13 years old. This was the church where my mother took me to Sunday school and church every Sunday until I was a junior in high school.

Across the street from the mechanic shop were other businesses; Kennedy's grocery, owned by Claude Kennedy, one of several brothers who came from Mississippi to pick strawberries during the great depression, and Patterson's restaurant operated by Hazel Kinchen Patterson.

Mrs. Patterson's father had been killed around 1930, and after a trial the killer was convicted and sentenced to Angola where he served more than 10 years in prison. When I was in grammar school that man, having been released from prison, stopped in that restaurant without knowing that the daughter of his victim worked there. She recognized him and got a gun to try to kill him for killing her father. My uncle Ernest Coats, a former deputy sheriff took the gun away from her and saved the man's life.

Also located in the same block was the post office, a small two room wooden building, my uncle Roy Coats's meat market, where his employee Tucker Richardson worked, my mother's drugstore, which also sold fishing supplies, and the Springfield Texaco filling station owned by my uncle Ernest Coats. It was operated by Hollis Hagg, an elderly man who had a crippled leg. In the next block was Calvin Fayard's Gulf filling station and his residence where he lived with his wife Ms. Catherine Abels Fayard, a schoolteacher, and son Calvin Junior who was a few years younger than I.

Across the street from the drugstore where my parents, my sister and I lived, there was a large gravel lot between Mr. Johns and little Charlie Schenks that had a flowing well with a concrete water trough which was used to water animals before anyone had automobiles. Next to the gravel lot a huge oak tree stood festooned with hanging Spanish moss were colorful Baltimore Orioles nested each year. The small birds attempted to drive small boys armed with BB guns away from their nest with their pop, pop calls, and were assisted by Miss Grace Rounds, the elderly postmistress who worked across the street. Next to the tree, stood a small one room wooden barbershop operated by Gassee Kemp, a small man who combated the oppressive summer heat in his little building by putting a window fan in the single window. The fan would pull air from the outside in through a screened container filled with Spanish moss that had water from the flow well dipping through it that cooled the temperature inside at least 10°.

Between the barbershop and the gravel lot Henry Felder, who had recently returned from the war, had a used car lot consisting of no more than four or five automobiles. A homeless man named Ollie Kinchen who was an alcoholic army veteran and existed doing odd jobs, used to sleep in Henry's unlocked vehicles. In the early morning when Henry arrived and found Ollie in one of his cars you could hear them cursing each other all over town.

One of Ollie's employers was Judge Warren Comish who loved to fly fish for bass on the local rivers. On mornings when the judge had no court they would rent a boat at one of the local landings, and Ollie would paddle the boat while the judge fished. Both old men were short tempered, and you could hear them shouting at each other up and down the river as the judge insisted Ollie bring the boat closer or farther away from the bank and Ollie would tell the judge where he should try to place the bait.

Next door to the barbershop was Henry Wall's business which purchased strawberries and other vegetables from farmers to ship to northern markets. A small café was also operated by Mr. Henry. Next door was the residence of Mr. Marcus Carter Rownds, an attorney who lived with his daughter Annie Laurie and grandson Marcus Carter Russell, who was a couple of years older than I and my best friend.

My distinct memories of the 1940's as World War II dragged on was hearing my parents and other elderly citizens in the town talking about faraway battles, and how we couldn't have sugar cookies because sugar was rationed. Candy was not obtainable in Mr. Johns store, and I never tasted bubble gum until I was at least seven or eight years old after the war ended.

Carter had been in the store when a truck arrived with supplies, among which was a large box of Fleer's double bubble gum. Mr. John opened the box and Carter purchased the first bubble gum in Springfield at the price of two pieces for a penny.

We were both dressed in our usual summer attire, short pants, no shoes, and no shirts when he approached me and gave me my first piece of bubble gum. He gave me instructions on how to blow bubbles after I had chewed the gum a while. I went inside my mama's drugstore and asked for nickel to buy some gum, but she only gave me a couple pennies. Carter had no more money and it looked like the other kids were going to buy the rest of Mr. Johns bubble gum.

It was late afternoon and Carter told me he had a plan to get the money to buy the whole box of bubble gum which would cost us a couple of dollars. To me, getting that much money was as impossible as getting one million dollars. I knew that I could get a nickel or two from my daddy when he got home, but that was my limit. Carter told me we had to go see his Paw, who was sitting in his rocking chair by his coal burning fireplace drinking whiskey, which he usually did every afternoon. When we entered the darkened room, the old man had been drinking for several hours and Carter told him he needed some money. The old man gave Carter a quarter and told us to go play. Carter told him he wanted more money than that, and the old man insisted on knowing the reason for the need of the funds. I figured the jig was up and there was no way old man Carter Rounds was going to give us that much money to buy bubble gum.

Carter was the old man's favorite grandson and he knew just exactly how to get what he wanted from him when he was drunk. Carter told him that if we bought all the bubble gum for two pieces for a penny we could sell some to the other kids for three pennies each, get the money back and still have lots of gum for ourselves. The old man reluctantly gave us the money and we went back to the store and bought the whole box. We never sold any of that bubble gum to any of the other kids and old man Carter never questioned us about returning his money from our proposed sale.

My sister, Jane was two and half years younger than I. She was named for my father's sister, Lela Jane Moore, who with her husband, my Uncle Earl, lived in Rayville, Louisiana. Their home was more than 100 miles away, and due to gasoline rationing and two-lane roads during and shortly after World War II we only saw them once every year or so.

My Aunt was a large woman who had no children and was crazy about my sister and I. She loved to cook, and made sugar cookies, cakes, pies and especially divinity, heavenly hash and chocolate fudge candy, which she would wrap and send to us in a large cardboard box for Christmas every year. This was a real treat for small children who could not buy candy due to the war rationing of sugar. I remember my mother tried to make some divinity candy one year which was tasty but was soft and sticky instead of the consistency of Aunt Lela's. She told my mother her secret of making good candy was to wait until a cold front had passed through, and cook the candy on a clear, cold winters day.
I had no understanding at that time that high atmospheric pressure had an effect on candy making.

During our infrequent visits Auntie, as she was called, took my sister and I into her arms and smothered us with hugs and kisses.

She wore lots of powder and cologne, which had its own distinctive smell, when she pulled us to her ample bosom. The fragrance of the powder did not completely mask the smell of tobacco smoke on her breath. She was the first woman I ever saw smoking cigarettes, and the only person I ever saw who would moisten the end of the cigarette with her tongue before she put it in her mouth and lit it.

Each year my mother would reciprocate for the Christmas gift my Aunt Lela sent us by sending her a box with her special brand of powder, powder puffs, cologne, soaps, and other goods from the drugstore.

As we grew older my sister Jane, affectionately called Sister by all my family was the favorite niece of my old bachelor uncle, Ernest Coats. He and my old maid aunt, Alma, and my divorced uncle Clark lived in the old family residence that they were born in, where my mother lived until she married my father.

Uncle Ernest never drank alcohol nor smoked and strongly disapproved of any of his sisters who did. When my aunt Myrt, one of his old maid sisters who lived in New Orleans, worked in the customs house as a secretary, and chain-smoked cigarettes, came to visit she would have to go outside the house to smoke.

In 1946 a book written by William James was made into a movie named Smokey about a cowboy who tamed a wild horse. My mother took my sister and I to see that movie and my sister was enthralled with the horse. She told my uncle Ernest about the movie, and the next time he went to the auction in Baton Rouge where he bought and sold cattle and other livestock he took us with him in his pickup truck.

It was a warm spring day in May and the schools were closed for early vacation, so the children could pick strawberries on their parent's farms. We traveled from Springfield on the gravel road to Albany, then turned on US Highway 190 which was a paved two-lane road to Baton Rouge. When we crossed the Amite River bridge at Denham Springs into the East Baton Rouge Parish, the road right-of-way was expanded to several hundred feet to make room for future lanes of traffic. When the right-of-way was cleared, all the large magnolia trees and live oak trees were left. And the rest of the undergrowth was mowed.

41

The pickup truck had no radio and to entertain ourselves we would count the number of white magnolia flowers we saw in the trees as we slowly proceed to the livestock auction. Before the sales began my uncle, Ernest took my sister and I through the auction barn to look at the cattle and horses that were to be sold. The smell of fresh hay, manure, and grain filled the air and the sound of the animals and the cracking whips by auction employees driving individual animals to the sales arena were fascinating to my sister and me. We went to the pens that contained horses and my uncle closely examined a dappled gray stallion that was to be sold. He was a large gentle horse and my sister immediately fell in love with him.

Before the auction began my uncle took us to the cafeteria to purchase sandwiches for lunch. We then went to the arena and took our seats to watch as the animals were brought into the ring, made to run around so all the potential buyers could see them, and the auctioneer began his chant to conduct the sale. My uncle did not bid on any of the cattle, but we were entertained by the men in the ring popping their whips. This infuriated some of the semi-wild Brahman cattle, who chased them out of the open ring and made them climb the fence to escape the animal's wrath.

When the dapple-gray stallion was brought into the ring, my uncle started the bidding and purchased him. The horse was loaded in the back of the pickup truck and we brought him home. When we unloaded the horse, my sister told my uncle to name the horse Smokey, and that was that.

My uncle trained Smokey to stretch out, so he could easily step into the saddle when he mounted him. And he always rode the horse when the cattle were rounded up each spring and fall from the open woods and swamps where they ranged.

During these roundups my cousins and I, many of whom were pre-teenagers, became real cowboys for a day. We would get on the horses early on a Saturday morning and ride several miles through the woods toward the swamps surrounding Lake Maurepas. When we heard the sound of a cowbell, which was strapped around the neck of an old cow, it would lead us to the herd that was feeding in the open woods. When we heard the bell ringing as the old cow walked around, my uncles

42

would begin to call in a loud voice, Whoo cow, Come on, Whoo cow! When the cattle heard this the old cow would let out a bellow and start towards us in a run, leading the entire herd.

My uncles and older cousins each rode their own horses. My younger cousins and I would ride bareback, two or three at a time, on an old mare who had a protruding backbone which was quite uncomfortable. We made no complaints, however because we were allowed to be 10 or 11-year-old cowboys. We had no cowboy boots and rarely wore shoes on these expeditions.

After the cattle were rounded up, we drove the herd out of the woods and passed neighbors houses and farms until we reached my uncle Ernest's pasture. We put them in a pen next to the barn where they could be driven into a chute, so we could separate the cows from the calves, and yearlings which needed to be castrated, vaccinated, and branded.

The chute was made of heavy boards and was divided into two runs, one of which had an elevated floor that allowed us to back a pickup truck or cattle trailer to its gate, so the cattle could be easily loaded.

When we separated the cows from their calves, so we could brand them and castrate the males, the semi-wild cows began to bellow and tried to rescue their offspring.

I learned how to catch, throw down, and tie the legs of the calves so they could be branded. Also, how to heat the branding iron and apply it to the yearlings so they could be properly identified as belonging to my uncles, whose brand was the number 18.

When we castrated the male yearlings, my uncle Grafton would save the testicles, wash and split them open. He then would put a frying pan on the coals of the branding fire, put a piece of fat back in the pan and cook them. Each boy was invited to share the feast with my uncles and older cousins. Some of us were uncomfortable with this table fare, but none of us wanted to take the chance of being laughed at by our companions for refusing to eat what my uncle called a delicacy. After the spring round-up some of the older cattle were taken to the auction which was held every Monday morning in Baton Rouge and sold.

Next to the loading pen, my uncles had dug a dipping vat about 6 feet deep, and 20 feet long which they filled with water. A chemical

43

which killed ticks was added to the water in the dipping vat and the remaining cattle were made to swim through the dipping vat before being returned to the woods for the summer. In the fall the process was repeated, and fat yearlings as well as older cattle that might not live through the winter were also sold at auction.

After World War II, manufactured goods could be purchased again, and my mother bought one of the first chest type deep-freezers in Springfield. She made a deal with her brother, my uncle Ernest, that she would buy the deep-freeze and pay butcher fees to cut and wrap beef if he would supply the beef for both families. After that every few months we would take a yearning to a nearby slaughterhouse to have it processed. The animal would be killed, skinned and hung for several days to age, before being cut and wrapped to be put in the deep freeze. I would usually go to the slaughterhouse when the meat was being cut and packaged so I could make sure the fat steer that we delivered for processing was the same one that we picked up and not switched for a less desirable animal.

My cousin, Sonny Womack, showed me how to do this so the butcher could not deny I had identified the animal hanging in the cooler as being one I had brought to slaughter. After the animal had been killed and skinned as I watched, I would go to the carcass that was hanging in the cooler and make a cut into the meat under the front shoulder. A few days later when I went to pick up the meat I would examine the carcass and make sure my mark was on the one that was being prepared for butchering.

During World War II the Livingston Parish draft board contained a majority of the members who were pastors at various churches. Men between the ages of 18 and 40 were required to register for the draft to supply manpower for the Army. Men who were over 40 and had families were required to join the state guard.

The southeast part of Livingston Parish allowed the sale of beer and liquor, while the northwestern part of the parish was dry. Many bar rooms and taverns were located in the wet area, but the majority of their customers came from the dry wards next door, whose residents had voted to outlaw the sale of liquor.

Before the war efforts had been made by the preachers to vote the wet wards dry but were unsuccessful. After the war began the preachers on the draft board made sure that every male bar owner was drafted into the army.

Elliott Foster and his wife Hazel owned and operated a small bar room near the Rome Ferry bridge on the Tickfaw River where they also had fishing boats for rent. They had no children, and Elliott was one of the first man to be drafted even though it was over 40 years old. His wife Hazel continued to operate the bar while he was in the service.

Sugar was rationed after the war started and the Coca-Cola bottling company arbitrarily stopped selling its products in small bar rooms in rural areas. Customers in the bars were forced to mix water with their liquor or drink it straight, but they kept on drinking. When the war ended Hazel called the company that distributed Coca-Cola and requested several cases. The company refused to sell to her while selling the product at nearby grocery stores. After a few months a Coca-Cola truck arrived at her bar and begin unloading cases. When the driver came in the door she told him to put the Coca-Cola back on the truck and she never purchased Coca-Cola again.

While visiting Mr. Johns store I often saw members of a family of imbeciles, who lived right past the city limits, on the road to Albany. The family consisted of a brother named Mike Duffy, his sister Ida Lee and their son Bobby who was about my age. They lived in a shack on a 20-acre tract of land belonging to Inez Brown's father, Mr. Davis. Across the street Stanley Hutchinson, a self-taught mechanic, lived with his wife, a still beautiful, middle-aged woman who gave piano lessons.

Stanley and his wife had no children. They lived quietly next to his mechanic shop. I asked my mama why Mr. and Ms. Hutchinson were the only family in Springfield who had no kids. She told me that their father and mother were brother and sister, and since they were first cousins their families refused to allow them to marry because any children they had might be retarded. They promised their parents that they would never have children, so they could live with each other.

Mike Duffy was a large man who could not speak clearly. He had the mind of a five-year-old and did odd jobs for Stanley, Mr. John, and other residents. He wore overalls and I never saw him wear a pair of

45

socks. In the winter he wore a flannel shirt and ankle high brogan shoes that he purchased from Mr. Johns store. In the summer he was barefoot and rarely wore a shirt under his overalls. He cut firewood to burn in the shack for heating and cooking. He never combed or cut his hair and as he grew older he wore a heavy feed sack on his head.

The only blacktop roads in the area where the two main streets within the city limits of Springfield and the road to Ponchatoula in Tangipahoa Parish, which were built when Huey Long was governor. My uncles told me that Mr. Johns father, who had been in the legislature, had blocked the paving of the road to Ponchatoula for years because he felt he would lose business in his store if the people could easily drive the 7 miles to Ponchatoula to purchase goods which were cheaper.

In the summertime the temperature often exceeded 100°, and my friends and I who were barefoot, would have to walk along the gravel shoulder of the street to keep from burning our feet on the hot asphalt. We often saw Mike Duffy walking on the road and laughed at him when he burned his feet on the pavement.

In the 1950s the police jury adopted an ordinance prohibiting cattle to range at large in the sixth ward of Livingston Parish. The owners of the cattle, some of whom were my uncles, banded together to build fences to keep them off the roads and out of town. My cousins and I helped build some of the fences. We cut and split oak trees to make fence posts, and when we found old heart pine logs we used them also.

Mike Duffy watched us work along the road near his house and shouted gibberish at us to try to stop us from proceeding. We ignored him, and put our posts in the ground, with plans to string wire the next day. The next morning when we arrived at the job site, we found Mike Duffy had pulled up the heart pine posts and was cutting them up for kindling. When my uncle and the other men tried to stop him, he threatened them with his double bit ax. Stanley Hutchinson, who was much smaller and older than Mike heard the commotion and came out of his mechanic shop. When he saw what was happening he cut a small switch, walked up to Mike Duffy who was still brandishing his ax and told him to go home or he was going to give him a whipping. Mike immediately turned tail and hurried across the road in the direction of his shack. We completed the fence as Mike watched us from across the road mumbling to himself.

Stanley Hutchinson and Son Settoon helped the Duffy's get welfare assistance. When the check came in every month they would take it to Settoon's store and pay for the groceries and other supplies they had purchased. Often, I watched Mike, barefooted and wearing his sack on his head standing in the middle-of-the-road trying to direct traffic. The locals paid no attention to him, but out-of-towners who did not know him, would often stop to ask him questions when he swung his arms gesturing to them and speaking gibberish that they could not understand.

My uncles were all farmers; all of them had cattle and raised various crops. My Uncle Eugene specialized in strawberries, and he had seven or eight children who harvested those berries and planted and harvested other crops. Even though my parents had no farm and did no farming, all of us kids would pick strawberries in the spring of the year. We were paid approximately three cents per pint for picking these berries, and we picked them in hand carriers that held six pints or eight pints. I always tried to pick a six-pint carrier because I was paid 20 cents for the six-pint carrier. If I had an eight-pint carrier, I was paid twenty-five cents, so I got an extra nickel, but had to pick two extra pints of berries. We picked for various farmers, and the farmers would pay us with tickets. We had to keep the tickets for two weeks before we could cash them in with the farmers.

The reason for this was that most of the farmers would sell their berries to associations, which would pay a reduced price for the berries, or they could be shipped to the market on the railroad trains to Chicago or to other markets in other parts of the United States. When the farmers sold these strawberries on consignment through the associations, the shipping costs were calculated and paid, then the strawberries were sent to the Northern markets, and they usually got a bigger price for the berries. But they always ran a chance that they might not get as much as if they had sold them for cash.

Anyway, most farmers took the chance on paying the shipping cost, but there was a delay of a couple of weeks for them getting their money, and they, in turn, waited until they got their money to pay their pickers. For that reason, they used the ticket system to keep track of wages due the laborers. My Uncle Eugene was not wealthy, and he had all those kids. His kids would pick the berries, and their mother, my Aunt Alice, would issue the tickets. Each child's tickets were kept in a separate envelope and kept by their mother. They didn't get paid money for those tickets as everybody else did after the two or three weeks wait. Their tickets were held until the end of the strawberry season, about two or three months. When the berry season was over, my Aunt Alice would calculate how much money was due each child. And this was for kids who were five or six years old to teenagers. Instead of giving them their money, she took them to the store and bought their clothes. All their clothes were paid for out of the money they earned picking berries, and then they might have been given a nickel or two extra for candy or a cold drink when they went to the store.

Beside the strawberries, my Uncle Grafton mainly raised pole beans. These pole beans were the prime type of bean that was for sale back in those days, and he got top dollar for them. While all the other farmers were raising berries, Grafton would have his pole bean patch. In the early spring, he took his two boys, Babin and Shug, and I out into the neighboring woods. All of us were close to the same age, and we would go with Uncle Grafton and cut poles for the bean patch. We'd load them onto a horse drawn wagon and bring the poles back to the field. Grafton would plow the fields and make up the rows, fertilize his ground, then plant the beans, and we would stick the poles by each bean plant, so the vines could grow up on the poles and keep the beans off the ground. Grafton used a special process he had discovered, so he'd have bumper crops of pole beans each year.

In the early 1950s, the first chicken farms were started in our area of Louisiana, Egg and Chicken Processors would contract the farmers and finance the building of vast chicken houses, so the chickens could be mass produced as they are today. They'd raise thousands of chickens in those big houses, and the feed was supplied by the processors. The chickens were taken to slaughter when they reached a certain age. Eggs were harvested by some farmers and the companies that financed the process and provided the feed would pick up and market the eggs. That many chickens created a huge amount of manure. Every so often, it was necessary to go into those chicken houses, usually right after a big lot of chickens had been harvested and right before a new bunch of bitties were put back in for the next crop and clean all the manure off the dirt floors. That was a job for Grafton, my cousins, and me. We would go in those chicken houses with a pickup truck, take shovels and load the pickup truck with chicken manure. It was old and dried and had been deposited for months or years, so there was no danger of putting fresh manure on plants and scalding, burning, and killing them. We would take that chicken manure into the bean field before the beans were planted and spread it on the tops of the rows, and Uncle Grafton would cultivate the manure for fertilizing the plants into the ground. After a period of a month or two, we would go ahead and work the rows again and prepare the seeds for planting. This was Grafton's special process.

All my uncles raised two kinds of corn. They had what we called sweet corn and field corn. Sweet corn was the type you buy in the grocery store today, which is primarily roasting ears to eat as soon as they matured. The plants grew much shorter than the tall field corn, and the corn was harvested when it was young and tender, so it could be roasted in the shucks or could be boiled in water. Field corn was primarily raised to feed the chickens, cattle, and hogs that all my uncles raised, and this corn was not harvested until after the stalks had dried and the corn got hard. Sometimes some of the corn was taken to a mill, and the corn was ground into corn meal, although by the 1950's few farmers did that anymore, since the massed produced corn from other states was ground into corn meal and sold in the stores. Still, they raised the corn for their livestock. After the corn had matured and dried on the stalk, we would pull the corn off, leave it in the dried husks, load it in wagons, and take it to the corn crib. Every farmer had a corn crib, and we would fill up the crib with that dried corn. Most cribs were something like 12 feet by 12 feet and 10 feet high. We would fill the corn crib up to the ceiling with freshly harvested corn. This usually lasted from one year to the next. About the time the new corn was maturing and ready to be picked, most the corn in the corn crib had been used, and the corn that had been packed to the ceiling had been reduced down to approximately a foot deep. When that happened, all us kids would go to the corn crib with some sacks and pick up the remnants of the last years corn off the floor. We would put it in sacks, so the corn crib could be cleaned out for the new crop. As we removed the last of the corn, the rats, which had lived in that corn crib for the whole year, had less and less room to hide. When we walked into that corn crib, we would see rats darting around, but they'd dive underneath the corn cobs and corn shucks on the floor and disappear into the pile. When we got all the rest of that corn put in sacks, there was no other place for them to hide. And you could imagine five or six kids, each armed with a stick of stove wood, going after those rats when the rats had less and less places to go. Rats would be darting everywhere; everybody would be swatting at them with the stove wood, and the rats really had no place to escape, except for a very few that could get outside the corn crib which was in the open yard, and there were always two or three kids ready to swat any rats that managed to get to the outside of the crib. The bigger kids would try to hit the rats that ran up the walls and rafters near the ceiling to try to escape. There were rats darting everywhere, and there were kids swinging everywhere, and that's what we used to call an old-time rat killing.

When I was in the fourth grade, my mother arranged for me to go to school in Ponchatoula, Louisiana, which had one of the most advanced grammar and junior high schools in the state. It was called a pilot school. And because of her influence in the area she managed to pull whatever strings were necessary to allow me to cross the parish line, from Livingston Parish to Tangipahoa Parish, to attend that school. I used to walk about a quarter of a mile down the road from Springfield cross the Natalbany river bridge to Tangipahoa Parish, and catch the school bus that was driven by my uncle, Gerald Coats, at the intersection of the Springfield-Ponchatoula road and the Pumpkin Center Road.

When I attended school there the principal was Mr. Charlie Van Rankin. He seemed a huge man to a little boy, actually standing well over six feet tall and probably weighing more than 200 pounds. He was a strict disciplinarian for children who were bad kids like I was on occasion. If you went into a class room, your teachers, would insist on strict discipline. Any breach of the discipline would condemn you to go into the hall and await further instructions. Every hour Mr. Charlie would start at the bottom of the two-story building at one end of the hall and walk down that hall and any kid he caught in the hall for disciplinary purposes was severely punished and sent back to the room. Excuses made no difference. Mr. Charlie would tell you "if you are in the hall, you should not be there. You should be minding your teacher and do not come back out" depending on the severity of your offense, you were instructed to bend over and receive a pre-determined number of licks from Mr. Charlie's a paddle. He would raise it high over his head and bring it down smartly on your rump. The crack of that paddle could be heard from one end of the hallway to the other, from the top of the second floor down to the first floor and one of the most terrifying things that I can remember hearing and anticipating was Mr. Charlie's footsteps walking down the hall towards me from the bottom floor to the second floor where I was. He periodically stopped, and you heard another crack when he popped some kid on the bottom who had been misbehaving. The closer he got to me the louder the pops sounded and the more terrified I was. By the time he got to me, I could just anticipate how much that was going to sting when he popped me, and I would imagine that this big man when he swung that paddle across my backside was going to lift me completely off the ground. Of course, that didn't really happen, but the anticipation was worse actually than the blow. I only got spanked a couple times in my several years of attendance at that school, but it was probably some of the best discipline I had ever had because of the anticipation of the matter while the actual physical torment was not nearly as bad as I imagined.

The other thing about it was, even though the tears would come to my eyes, and I wanted to cry, I knew I had to be too much of a man at age 9 or 10 years old, and not be seen crying or make a sound that my classmates could hear inside the classroom. When I got whacked I had to bite my lip and come back in the classroom and not let my classmate know how badly I was hurt or embarrassed, so they could laugh at me.

The school had one of the best libraries in the State of Louisiana for a grammar school/junior high school. I was a bookworm, while I played all sports, football, baseball, track and the usual physical educational during that time, I was fascinated with books and by the time I was in the seventh and eighth grade I would spend my recesses not on the playground but in the library reading books. Many times, I was so engrossed in some of the books I was reading, that I didn't hear the bell

51

ring to go to classes, and the librarian, Ms. Susie Dufreche, would come and tap me on the shoulder and tell me I had to put the library book down and go back to the classroom. I read almost every book in that library by the time I finished junior high school in the eighth grade of school in Ponchatoula.

I remember specifically the books about the Vikings, the Romans, the Greek Gods, Science Fiction about astronauts and space travel, and all types of fiction as well as history, and I couldn't get enough of it. By the time I finished the eighth grade I was actually reading Shakespeare plays, not necessary the play itself but the interpretation of the plays which gave the story rather than the actual language used by Shakespeare himself. I didn't really understand some of the old English prose, but the story of the Taming of the Shrew, of Julius Caesar, and many of the other writings by Shakespeare were fascinating to me.

I didn't know anything about I Q's at that time, but I took all the I Q tests in those years and was told later that I had one of the highest I Q 's in that school. I'm not saying this to brag because while I knew things that a lot of other kids didn't, I didn't make straight A's. I excelled in courses I liked and in courses I didn't like such as Math and Science and English composition I made B's and C's and I studied only enough to get by. But in History, Literature, and everything I liked I made straight A's.

When I was in the ninth or tenth grade at Ponchatoula High School at the age of 15 I had already acquired a liking for cigarettes and Miller High Life beer. On a weekend night one or two beers was my limit, and I didn't really like the taste, but I drank it because my friends did, and it was the thing to do. In my junior year I decided to go out for spring training on the football team. I did this mainly to prove to myself I could, and how tough I was. Actually, I was athletic but not very tough. Many of the young girls in my classes looked up to boys that played football, especially the older boys that played football. My problem was I had started school at age 5 and in today's world I would not be able to attend until I was six and a half. My birthday being in February, so I was not as big and strong as the other boys in my class. My Daddy told me before I started spring training, that he did not think it was a good idea for me to play football but that if I was gonna do it I damn sure wasn't going to quit, and that was the exact words he told me.

Well, I started, and was proud to put on the pads, and the uniform, and do so the calisthenics, and do the plays, and do the practice, but in two days or three I knew that I was not going to be a football star. I wasn't fast enough to be a running back or pass receiver or one of the star type of players that I dreamed of. Nor was I big enough to play effectively as a guard or a linebacker or one of the other offensive players on the team. One of my earliest memories of football was being on the field with all the other kids. The first day of football practice I weighed about 120 pounds. A new coach named Bill Johnson had just stated to coach there. Bill was a big, rough, and tough type of fellow who weighed over 200 pounds. He had been in WWII and after coming back from the war he went back to college, got his degree and was a first-time coach at Ponchatoula. At the first meeting with the coach all of us in our new uniforms were placed in a circle with everybody clasping their hands behind their backs. The coach got in the middle of the ring with a football in his hand and was talking about the things he expected us to do and what he was going to teach us and so forth. And without any warning he took that football and struck one of the guys a couple feet away from me in the belly and bowed him over. That gave me just enough warning to know I was pretty well going to be next, and when he hit me, the wind went out of me. I lost my breath and I felt excruciating pain, tears actually came to my eyes, but I bit my lip and would not say anything and did not cry out. I caught my breath and he hit me again, I still didn't say anything, after that he left me alone.

I came home and told my Daddy, I had enough of this and did not want to play football. He said, "I told you, you had your opportunity, now you started it, you will stay with it." During the next five or six weeks after school every evening we would go out and do the calisthenics, run, and scrimmage, but I never made the team during that spring training. I did get to play two plays during the final scrimmage, on defense as a tackle, when I made a single tackle on the star running back, Mickey McLauren, who was the quarterback for the team. It was so easy when I hit him, all I did was just catch his ankles and tripped him. I got a big pat on my back from the couch and some of the other players.

When I started football practice, I was just a skinny little kid but during that spring season I gained about ten pounds in a period of a few weeks. It was amazing, every day after football practice, I would get on the school bus and ride back to Springfield, and immediately walk to the home of my Aunt Alma an old maid, who lived on the old family homestead with her old maid sisters and old bachelor brothers. She would warm up some beans or peas and rice. or mustard greens, and cornbread and sausage or ham, whatever it might be that they had left over from dinner and at five o'clock in the afternoon I would sit down at her table and sometimes eat three plates full of food. My appetite was just ravenous after doing all that exercise. I always had a good appetite anyway but during that time it was really something.

By the end of that spring football practice, I was about fifteen, starting to really notice girls, and realized that I was not going to be a football star. I liked to drink that beer and liked to smoke cigarettes and decided it was a whole lot better for me to try to use my head instead of my brawn and body to attract girls and to have fun and do things I wanted to do. So, my football career only lasted about six weeks. Fortunately, I came through it without any injuries or disabilities, but a whole lot wiser in the ways of the world.

During that same time, I, like all the other kids in the area, picked strawberries in the spring. There were many strawberry farmers in the area, and always looking for someone to pick their crops. The school started in July and let out in March, so the children would be able to harvest the strawberries rather than the normal school term of September through May. At that time strawberries were picked in what we called hand carriers of either six pints or eight pints. We were paid 25 cents for picking an 8-pint carrier, and 20 cents for a 6-pint carrier of those berries. It didn't take me long to figure out that I made more money picking 6-pint carriers than 8's but the farmers had a lot more of the 8-pint carriers than the 6's. It was feast or famine in those day with the berry crops, my friends, my uncles, and my family that raised berries would go through the entire season of preparing the land, planting the berries, picking up sticks in a pine thicket, raking straw to place around

54

the berry plants to keep the berries off the ground and kill weeds, fertilizing and chopping the grass out of the middles of the rows. Farmers didn't make any money at all for several months, from the time they planted berries in November until they finally started picking in March. I decided that I wanted to raise strawberries myself, because I saw my uncles and other farmers I picked strawberries for getting paid five and six dollars for twenty-four-pint crates of berries. As a picker I would get only seventy- two cents for my labor.

Right next to my house, I picked out an area that had been farmed by my grandfather. It consisted of about a half an acre. I went to the woods near my home with a cross cut saw and my cousins helped me cut down post oak trees. Post Oaks were hardwood trees that usually had very few limbs on the lower part of the trunk. They didn't get to be very large in diameter but usually we could cut a tree down, trim it up and cut it into about an eight-foot length. Then using a sledge hammer and wedge as well as a double bitted ax, we split the tree into four or six posts, hence the name of post oak. We cut the trees, split the logs into posts, and hauled them from the woods to the site where I planned my strawberry patch. I dug the post holes with a post hole digger by hand, set up the posts, put the dirt around them, packed the dirt in with the handle of a hoe and then strung the wire around the fence. The lower part of the wire was made of what we called chicken wire to keep rabbits and opossums and other animals from being able to get in and get to my crop, I used my uncle's tractor to plow the ground and make the rows.

My Daddy told me that he didn't think it was a good idea for me to raise those strawberries. Raising a vegetable garden was fine, my mother always had a garden, behind the drug store and my Daddy grew up on a farm in North Louisiana. Everybody in my family always liked fresh vegetables and all I really needed to do was just raise a vegetable garden. I insisted on strawberries, so my Daddy told me, "You're in the 4-H club, you need to have that strawberry farm as a 4-H project." In 4-H we were taught how to keep records, but my daddy told me I was going to keep very good records on this. He got a ledger book and made me keep track of all the time that I worked on that strawberry farm. I don't think I put down the time that I actually used for sawing down the trees, splitting the posts and actually building the fence, but I wrote down

55

everything else I did each afternoon I got in from school. When I used the tractor to plow the ground to make the rows, put down fertilizer, picking up sticks out of the pine thicket, raking the pine straw, set out berry plants, and everything else I did, I marked it down in the ledger. I listed the type of work I was doing and the time it took me to do it. I purchased the straw berry plants and planted the rows. Later I came back with a hoe and scraped the weeds and grass from around the plants, put the straw on top of the newly scrapped row, and went back and opened the pine straw away from the berries and pulled it tight around them. After a few weeks I put down extra fertilize along the side of the row and worked it into the ground. Just before and during the time the strawberries were harvested, I used a hoe to cut all the weeds and grass out of the middle of the rows. I also listed the time it took to go get the crates and the pints that the strawberries were put in. I diligently kept records of all I did on the strawberry crop that year and I made a bountiful crop, for a fifteen-year-old kid, totaling about four hundred dollars. When you consider the minimum wage for an able-bodied man was fifty cents an hour, this was a lot of money. My Daddy financed my crop. He put up the money for the strawberry plants, fertilizer, the crates and the containers for the strawberries to go in and covered all my other expenses. When I finished, I paid him back the monies that he put out, something less than a hundred dollars, and I had more than a three hundred profit. I thought this was the greatest thing in the world. I didn't have to pay my Momma to pack the berries which is normally an expense and I didn't put any charge on the actual picking of the berries, which would have also been an expense, but I still made all that money and I told my Daddy "I think I'm going to do this again". He said "well, let's look at what you did. Let's get the books." I got the books and he had me add up all the hours that I worked from November through April on that strawberry crop. After I totaled the hours and the amount of money I had, I learned I had made the princely sum of twelve cents an hour. He then told me "do you want to be a strawberry farmer?" and I said "not no, but hell no." One of the best lessons I ever had in my life was taught to me by my Daddy in a way that really came home to me, because he made me keep the records and I found out just exactly what I had accomplished.

56

My daddy loved to fish and during World War II he and my mother operated Coats Pharmacy where my mother was a druggist. We lived in an apartment behind the drugstore where we had a shallow well behind the store and the water never stopped flowing. There were switch canes growing in the backyard as well as a garden for vegetables. My daddy built a small swimming pool that was about 3 feet deep by 20 feet x 30 feet in size when I was about four or five years old and that's where I learned to swim.

There are three rivers near Springfield, the Natalbany, Blood, and Tickfaw Rivers which flow into Lake Maurepas. The rivers all are subject to tidal flow except during the early spring rainy season. There were no sporting goods stores in the area and my daddy sold fishing tackle at the drugstore. He also cut canes and dried them to make fishing poles to sell, and He built a minnow pond to keep live bait for sale to white perch fishermen. He used a seine to catch the bait in the shallow water of the river north of Springfield. He regularly caught white perch in treetops that had fallen into the rivers and took me fishing with him from the time I was five or six years old.

He also used a fly rod to fish for bluegill during their spawning season in early spring. His favorite bait was a black gnat tied behind a silver spinner which he pulled across the bream beds a few inches under the water. He also used popping bugs with white heads and black or yellow feathered tails to catch them on top of the water. He and I would rent a wooden flat boat and paddle down the river in the early morning and catch 100 or more bream within two hours. We would often do the same thing late in the afternoons after I finished school.

Each year beginning in mid-February there was a spawning run of small striped bass that proceeded up the rivers from the lake. These fish usually were from 8 to 12 inches long but had very small mouths. The migration only lasted a few weeks but when they were running we would catch wash tubs full of fish between the time I got home from school about 4:30 PM until near dark at 6 PM.

The favorite bait that we used were tiny grass shrimp that we impaled on a very small long shank hook. We purchased the bait from an old man who had flooded some low ground next to his house, and planted water grass in the pond and stocked it with grass shrimp. We would rent a boat from a man who lived on the river and paddled about 100 yards to a bend in the river where the water was about 10 feet deep. We would use cane poles with braided line tied to the tiny hook, with a split shot sinker placed about five or 6 inches above the hook. We then baited the hook with a grass shrimp and dropped the line into the deep water. The sinker would go all the way to the bottom and the line would go slack. We would then lift the pole until the slack went out of the line causing the bait to move off the river bottom, and usually a fish immediately took the bait. These fish traveled in schools and when you caught one you could catch four or five more before the school moved on up the river toward the spawning grounds. Then we would continue fishing until the next school came along and we would catch several more.

When I was in grade school at Ponchatoula my father told me we would go fishing when I got home. School ended at 3:10 PM and I rode the school bus to Springfield. My father had the cane poles and the fish bait ready when I got home and we together with his friend Buster Dudley drove to Killian on Tickfaw River. We rented a boat from Lucky Rogers who lived in a small shack on the river. There were no ice chests in those days and we brought a washtub with us to put our fish in. Before dark we had filled the tub to the brim, came home, cleaned the fish and my mama cooked all we could eat.

My uncle Ernest Coats had worked as a deputy sheriff in Livingston Parish during the 1920's and 30's and also raised cattle and vegetables for sale. In 1940 when Sam Jones, an anti-Long candidate, was elected governor my uncle became a game warden. He served in that position for eight years until Earl Long was elected governor and he was dismissed. In 1945 at the end of World War II, my father purchased a Scott Atwater 7 ½ hp outboard motor for my uncle to use as a warden. That motor on a small flatboat made it one of the fastest boats on the river, and he used it to patrol for game violators. After he lost his job he gave me the motor in about 1954.

In the early spring my father and I would put the motor in the trunk of his car and drive about 40 miles east to Lacombe where the Bayou emptied into Lake Pontchartrain. We would rent a boat at the lake and buy shrimp for bait. We each used a rod and reel with a leader tied to the line. We would attach a sinker on the end of the leader and had two hooks attached to lines approximately 12 inches long tied above the sinker. Each hook was baited with shrimp. We would arrive at the lake at daylight and proceed about a mile from the shore where the water was about 4 to 6 feet deep. We would then cast our baits out into the water and let them sink to the bottom then slowly reel in. If we didn't get a bite, we would go further into the lake until we started catching croaker. The action was usually fast and furious, and we often caught two at a time.

Usually when we fished here the water in the lake was slick with no waves when we first arrived. As the morning progressed a slight breeze would begin to blow and after a couple of hours clouds would appear on the horizon from across the lake. I paid little attention to the clouds until my father asked me if I could smell the rain. I looked around and out across Lake and saw no rain whatsoever, but I could smell the scent of fresh rain and the cooling air. Fish were still biting, and I was in no hurry to leave but my father told me that we had to go back to the landing because a squall was coming. I pulled up the anchor got the motor running and we started back to the bank. Before we got to the mouth of the Bayou the waves were rising and when we reached the landing about a half-mile from the lake the rain had started. We loaded up fishing gear, fish, and the motor and started home, stopping for lunch at a seafood restaurant near the lake, and as we drove back home the rain was moving from the place we had been fishing westward all the way home.

In the late spring of 1954 when I was 15 years old and just got my driver's license, I had a cousin, Shug Coats, who was my age. Shug was the youngest son of my aunt and uncle Mary Lou and Grafton Coats. When we started school in 1944, Springfield had no lunch room until after Governor Earl Long was elected and began a free lunch program for schoolchildren. Before then all the kids had to bring their lunch, which was usually a sandwich, but often just a cold sweet potato, to school each day. Aunt Mary Lou always put Shug's lunch in an empty bag that had contained sugar. She made him bring the bag home each day, so it could be reused. He was the only kid in school whose lunch had the word Sugar on it. The nickname stuck, and everyone called him Shug except his mama, who called him Sugar.

Strawberry season usually lasted from early March until May each year when school was recessed so the children could pick strawberries. After strawberry season that year we had about a month before school started again and we decided that we would try to make some money catching catfish.

I had a little wooden flat boat that we used to fish for bream, sac-a-lait, and small striped bass, I also owned the 7 1/2 horsepower Scot Atwater motor I got from my uncle Earnest Coats.   Uncle Earnest had been a game warden from 1940 through about 1948 and he had been a good one. He was a terror for people that outlawed game and fish, but he backed the wrong candidate for governor. When Earl Long got elected governor in 1948, there was no civil service and my Uncle Earnest was one of the first to get fired, and someone else who was on the right political side took his job. Without the job Uncle Earnest went back to full time farming, raising peppers and cattle. He really didn't have any use for that outboard motor, so he gave it to me. Shug and I bought us some trot lines which in those days were just regular cotton lines. If you put them in the water, they would last only a few months before they would begin to rot and soon break. We saw an advertisement in a magazine and purchased a preservative treatment for our trot lines. We took the cotton trot line and put it in the preservative solution and soaked it for a couple of days, then let it dry. When we did this the preservative caused the line to turn green.

We took our small wooden boat and my 7 ½ hp motor and tied it to the bank of Blood River at Calvin Kitchen's landing. Mr. Kinchen had a small store and cabins for rent to fisherman who came from Baton Rouge and Mississippi on weekends. He also built a swimming pool and charged us ten cents each to use it. Since we were his swimming pool customers he did not charge us for leaving our boat at his landing.

We put several lines across Blood River and Lizard Creek and hung about a dozen limb lines along the bank. Each trot line had drop lines about 18 inches long with a single hook tied approximately 4 feet apart called staging's. We tied a couple of bricks to longer drop lines on each side of the river to make our trot lines sink deep enough so no passing boats would cut them with their propeller's.

Each morning before daylight, we left home for the river and ran and baited our lines. Most of the fish we caught weighed about 1 to 3 pounds, but sometimes we caught 10 to 15-pound catfish. We soon discovered that a small catfish, when hooked, would swim in circles until it twisted the drop line around the main trot line and the hook would come out of its mouth. To stop the loss of fish we put swivels on the drop lines above the hooks.

When we got home we used fish pliers to skin and clean the fish which we sold to our relatives and our parents and friends. Then it was time to catch some more bait. We hardly made enough money to cover our expenses.

One Saturday morning when we got to the river and started running our lines, I noticed a limb line was missing from the place it had been tied. On close examination I found someone had cut the line and taken it leaving a small piece near the knot. The next two lines were also missing but a new untreated white limb line had been placed nearby. We rounded a bend in the river and I saw another white line tied to the same limb one of my missing green lines had been tied to.

We pulled up to the white line and I pulled it up out of the water. About a foot under the water one of my missing green lines had been tied to the white line. After that we checked each of the new white lines and found our green lines tied to all of them. We removed all of our stolen lines and reset them, then came back to Mr. Kitchen's landing and went into his store. I told Mr. Kinchen that we were going to get our shotguns and come back to the river and guard out lines day and night to catch whoever was stealing our fish and our fishing lines. I also told him I was pretty sure the culprits were from out of town, probably renting cabins from him, and if we caught them, we would shoot them. We never lost another line after that. We would get up at daylight and be on the river running our lines, taking the fish off and baiting the lines. We would come home with maybe ten to twenty pounds of fish and clean them. Then we would go sell the fish to neighbors or to relatives who bought most of them. After that we would take our dip net and buckets and go to all the roadside ditches to catch crawfish to bait the lines. After that we went back to the river before dark in the evening to bait up the lines and maybe pick up a few more fish, come home, clean those fish and get up the next morning and go again. After about a month of this, Shug and I determined that we weren't making enough money to pay for the gas for the outboard motor and the gas for the car. We gave up on our commercial fishing enterprise very soon, and I learned another valuable lesson. That I didn't ever want to grow up to be a commercial fisherman.

I told my daddy I need a different kind of job. He had bought a small tract of Pine Timber from one of my aunts who lived in New Orleans and made a deal to sell the logs to a sawmill. He told me that he would pay Shug and I to cut the trees into logs, and bunch and load them on trucks to take to the mill. We would be paid by the thousand feet of logs we cut for our labor. We had a crosscut saw, a double bit axe, sledge hammer, and wedges that we used to cut firewood for my aunts and uncles. When cutting pine, the sap from the trees would stick to the saw blade and make it impossible to cut. To remedy this, we got a Coke bottle, filled it half full with coal oil, put pine needles in the mouth of the bottle and shook the coal oil on the saw blade, which removed the sap. Uncle Ernest had a small Ford tractor that I used to help him plow his pastures and to cultivate our garden. He agreed to let Shug and I use the tractor to bunch and load the logs.

Every day after school and on Saturday's, we cut down the trees. We then cut then into logs and bunched them together to load on the trucks. We were paid much more than we would have made if we had been paid the current rate of twenty-five cent an hour. The work was hard physical labor and when we finished that job, we had no more timber to cut. Shug quit school the next year and went to work for a seismograph crew in Southwest Louisiana.

In 1955 I began my senior year at Ponchatoula High School. I had learned to smoke cigarettes a couple years before and drove a 1953 Ford that belonged to my mother back and forth to school. I kept my cigarettes in a hidden compartment underneath the dash board.

One day my father had to have his car repaired and used the car I had been driving to school. I thought about my cigarettes all day long. My father picked me up at school that afternoon and I drove us back home. When I got in the car, my pack of cigarettes was on top of the

62

dashboard. I was shocked that I had been caught by my dad. He asked me if they were mine and I admitted that they were. He told me that he had been traveling over a rough road hit a bump and the cigarettes fell out of their hiding place. He said he was glad to know they were mine and that my mother had not taken up smoking. He told me to put them in my pocket and never hide to do anything in the future.

During that year my father and I traveled to courthouses to check land titles on property he was interested in buying. Many times, we would not return home until after dark. I was 16 years old and I usually did the driving. As I drove along in the evening my father and I would talk about all sorts of things and we became best friends as well as father and son. He knew that when I went out with my friends to the football games and dances I would drink beer and sometimes mixed drinks such as sloe gin and 7-Up. When we were together late in the evening, he would often have me stop at a bar room, so we could have a drink.

The bars we stopped at catered to older people and rarely had teenagers visit them. Since I was with my daddy and he paid for the drinks from the bartenders he knew, they never questioned my age and did not strictly follow the law and refuse to serve me. We never drank a lot, usually one or two small beers, and on rare occasions a drink of strong liquor. I specifically remember when he introduced me to scotch and soda.

We had been checking the title to some property in St. Tammany Parish at the courthouse in Covington Louisiana, and on the way home stopped at a small bar in Madisonville. He introduced me to the bartender and ordered two shots of Cutty Sark and soda. It tasted vastly different from the Seagram's Seven and seven up or coke that I drank on weekends when my friends and I would go to dances. I didn't particularly like the taste of Scotch whiskey and almost never drank it again until I went on my first sheep hunt in Canada, many years later, where you couldn't buy Jack Daniels.

Chapter 2. Local Politics, Marriage, Cold War Army Service

I had several girlfriends in high school but never got serious about any of them until December 1955 when I met Kathy. She was a year behind me and attended Hammond High School. I went to a party as a guest of one of my friends, Freddy Anderson, who was going steady with Hazel Kinchen and she had invited Kathy to the party.

She came on to me like no other girl I had ever met, and I was greatly attracted to her. I asked her for a date the next night and we engaged in very heavy petting. While she let me touch her breasts, caress and kiss her, she would not go all the way and have sex with me on the first date. When I took her home, I asked her to go out with me the next night and she agreed. All day long all I could think about was having sex with her. I was no virgin, but my sexual encounters had been very infrequent and usually one-time encounters.

Kathy quickly changed all that. She was hotter than a two-dollar pistol, and like me, she just couldn't get enough. Over the next year and a half, I saw her almost every day. When I would pick her up at her parents' house, before we got to the movies, party, or wherever we were going we would first stop at a secluded place and have sex in my car. After the movie we would stop on the way home and do it again.

All she could talk about was getting married and having kids. She wasn't interested in going to college and as soon as she finished high school she got a job as a telephone operator. When I finished high school in early 1956 she and I were going steady. My parents didn't like this situation and had plans for me to go to college at LSU. My daddy bought me a car after I finished high school. It was a 1947 Cadillac that he had purchased from an old widow. The old car was in very good shape with very few miles on it. It was one of the largest Cadillacs made at that time and was a dark green color. It had innovations that were not to be seen on Fords and Chevrolets that were 10 years newer. I could push the knob on the radio and the antenna would go up or down. I drove the old car back and forth to LSU during the time I attended in 1956 and 1957.

I bought Kathy a small diamond solitaire engagement ring at a jewelry store in Baton Rouge for Christmas in 1956. My parents gave me an allowance while I was in college of $20 per week. I stayed in a dormitory and paid my own expenses for food and drink. I had saved a little money and paid about $30 down on the ring and agreed to pay five dollars per week on the balance. I finished paying for it a week before we drove to Mississippi with her mother and one of her mother's friends and got married in April 1957. The preacher refused to marry us until the friend of her mother told him that she was my mother and she signed as such to allow me to marry.

I kept the marriage secret from my parents until I finished the second semester of college. I thought that I would be able to get a job, so I could have a place to live with Kathy and hopefully go to school part-time. The problem was, there were no jobs available for young unskilled men. I had no trade and no chance to get in an apprentice program with a union or obtain other training for a job. One of Kathy's cousins husband worked as a welder at a shipyard in Madisonville and he volunteered to teach me how to tack weld. I had no idea about the skill needed to become a welder. I went to his house several nights and he showed me how to operate the welding machine. I then went to the shipyard in Madisonville and applied for job as a welder's helper. They took my application and told me they would let me know when they had an opening. I never heard from them again.

I next went to Chalmette Louisiana to the Kaiser aluminum plant on the Mississippi River and applied for a job there and was told they were not hiring. I next went to Venice Louisiana and applied for a job as a deck hand, welders' helper, or general laborer in the offshore oil fields, and was told by all that they were not hiring. Kathy and I were living with her parents, my parents were distraught that I had ran off and got married and apparently given up on seeking an education. Kathy's father was a disabled World War II Army veteran, and many of my uncles and cousins had served in the Army, Marines, or Air Force so I started to check into joining the Army. Kathy greatly encouraged me. She wanted to move out of her parents' home where she would be unsupervised.

The woman who had posed as my mother at my marriage was married to a career Army Sgt. who had been in the service for many years. I talked to him about joining the Army and asked his advice as to which MOS I should seek. He told me that if I could qualify, one of the best jobs I could obtain would be in the Army Security Agency, which primarily dealt in espionage. To get in the agency you had to complete basic training, obtain a top-secret security clearance and complete special training in espionage against the Russians and Chinese.

At that time, you could volunteer for the draft and be required to serve two years. If you did this, you had no choice as to what part of the Army you would serve in. If you volunteered in the regular Army you were required to serve three years, but you could choose which school or division of the Army you would like to serve in after you finished basic training. Then you had to complete your training in order to obtain the MOS you sought.

The United States and Russia were engaged in a Cold War in 1957. The fighting had stopped in Korea but there was fear that fighting could break out in Germany, the Middle East, or Korea again. I wasn't interested in being a front-line soldier in the infantry or artillery. The sergeant told me if I got in the Army Security Agency I would probably be sent overseas to Germany or Japan. If this happened, I could probably bring my wife with me and live off base while I worked. Kathy was all for this, she wanted to get away from home, and Europe sounded wonderful to her.

I told my parents that I was going to join the Army about two days before I left. My mother was heartbroken, and my father was very disappointed, but I had made up my mind and there was no turning back.

I went to New Orleans with two of my friends, Goose Niehaus and Teddy Kraft from Ponchatoula, who also couldn't find jobs. They were told they could not be hired at the chemical plants because they would have to undergo expensive training for the jobs but would still be subject to the draft and could be required to leave their jobs and enter the service. They therefore decided to volunteer for the draft for two years and after having served their time they could come back home, apply for their factory jobs and probably be employed since they would then be veterans.

We went to the customhouse in New Orleans where we were sworn in. The next day I was placed on an airplane for the first time in my life and sent to Fort Chaffee Arkansas for basic training.

During basic training I gained weight, got tougher physically and mentally and tried chewing tobacco while on the firing range. I swallowed some tobacco juice and got sick at my stomach but couldn't do anything about it but suffer. I never chewed tobacco again. While on the firing range we were issued blank ammunition for our weapons as well as live ammunition to shoot at targets. When we left the range, we were supposed to turn in any extra rounds we did not use. I kept one blank round when we returned to our tents. The next night I was on guard duty and placed the blank round in my rifle.

As I was marching my post a black soldier from another company came into my territory and I told him to halt and identify himself. Instead of obeying my order he began to run through the camp with me right behind him yelling halt. When he didn't stop I pointed my rifle at him and pulled the trigger. The blank round exploded about 6 feet from him and hit him in the buttocks leaving a painful but not serious burn on his ass. He let out a scream and fell to the ground and I thought I had killed him.

He immediately jumped up and attacked me. I hit him with my rifle as we fell to the ground fighting each other. At the sound of the shot the whole camp was awakened and other guards rushed to my assistance. When we were separated, a captain who had been roused from a deep sleep, came to investigate the disturbance. After questioning, the other soldier was treated for his wound and we were sent back to our tents. The next day an informal hearing was conducted, and I got a verbal reprimand for having the blank round in my rifle but was congratulated for stopping the intruder. My buddies in my company considered me a hero. Many told me I should have killed the SOB.

After I finished basic training I had about a week's furlough home. I was then sent to Fort Devens, Massachusetts to await the granting of my top-secret security clearance so I could enter the Army Security Agency's spy school. I spent the winter there and finished second in my class. As a reward I was allowed to choose my duty station overseas where I would serve. The choices were Germany, Korea, Japan, and Turkey. The time of service at each station varied from 2 ½ years in Germany and Japan to one year in Turkey. I had talked to Kathy about going overseas and she had wanted me to choose Germany where she could go with me. We had been living in an apartment off the post while I was attending school and she had an opportunity to meet people including other soldiers while I was gone every day. By the time I finished the school in early spring our marriage was deteriorating. I decided the best thing for me was to do my service for the shortest possible time while Kathy would be staying with her parents. Therefore, I chose Turkey.

We returned home in April 1958, and the temperature in Louisiana was 50° warmer than in Massachusetts. After about a two week furlough I flew to Fort Dix, New Jersey to await shipment overseas. While there I met about a dozen other soldiers who were going to Turkey. Some were career soldiers that had previously served in the security agency in Korea and in Ethiopia.

U.S. Army Sinop, Turkey 1958

We flew on a two-engine military air transport service airplane with about 75 other military personnel to Newfoundland Canada then to Ireland and then to Frankfurt Germany where we stayed for about a week. Many of the buildings still showed damage from bombs and artillery fire from WWII more than 12 years before. While there I was introduced to some fraulines and beer gardens. We then were put on a commercial airline with stops at Vienna, Austria, and Istanbul before arriving at Ankara, Turkey where we were housed in an Air Force facility for a few days. The rest of my buddies I had traveled with were put on a 2 ½ ton truck that transported supplies from Ankara to our radar base near Sinop, an ancient walled city located on a peninsula on the Black Sea. A couple of days later I was placed in a small two-seater airplane and flown to that base. It took my friends about 12 hours to make the trip by truck over the gravel roads through the mountains. My flight took about two hours.

Our base was located on a high plateau overlooking the Black Sea almost directly across from the Russian's missile facility on the other side, where missiles were being tested, which happened infrequently, I would be on call 24 hours per day. All other times I had to check in my duty station for an hour or so each day since I was the only man on the post with my type of MOS.

I felt I had the best job in the Army. The mess hall served 4 meals each day to facilitate soldiers who did eight hour shifts 24 hours per day. We slept in Quonset huts that had eight beds each and due to the shift work, some of us would be sleeping while others were working. While we were not on duty we were confined to the post except on weekends when we could get a six-hour pass to visit the wine shops and restaurants of the small town. We were under strict orders not to speak to any of the women in the town and most of the older women covered their faces when we were present.

The post had an officer's club restricted to the officers and an enlisted men's club for all the rest of us. We could drink beer but no hard liquor and play card games each night for pay day stakes. We would keep records of our games during the month and when we got paid we would pay or collect our winnings and losses. After the club shut down

70

each night we would go to mess hall and have a midnight breakfast before going to bed.

Every two or three months we would be eligible for a pass in the city of Ankara. Three or four of us would get permission to catch a ride in a 2 ½ ton truck which went for supplies every couple of days. Each would buy a case of beer and bottle of liquor from the EM Club and pick up sandwiches from the mess hall for the 12-hour ride.

We were paid in United States dollars and would convert them to Turkish lira for use in the city and villages we passed through. The legal rate was five lira per dollar but on the black market you could get 12 to 15 lira per dollar. The soldiers who drove the trucks had a lucrative side business where they could sell dollars for 20 lira each in Ankara and then sell lira to the rest of the soldiers for 15 lira per dollar in Sinop.

In Ankara they had nightclubs with entertainers from Germany and other parts of Europe who would perform and mix with the soldiers. They also had a government run brothel consisting of three-story buildings in a walled compound with one entrance. It was guarded by Turkish police who searched all American soldiers for weapons when we entered. We would walk around the streets of the compound and look at the women who were seated in the windows of their rooms inviting us inside.

The women were required to have regular medical checkups and the entire operation was run by the Turkish government. Each woman was required to shave her pubic hairs. Due to the language barrier each encounter was all business and very brief. Afterward we would leave the brothel and return to our barracks.

After serving several months in Turkey I was told by a friend of mine in communications that my father had a serious heart attack several days earlier and was not expected to live. Regular mail took about a week to arrive from the states and I had no way of knowing if my father was dead or alive for about two weeks until I was finally officially notified that he had been hospitalized but was expected to live. When I asked my superior officer why I had not been officially notified of my father's illness he told me that since I had a critical MOS and was the only one on post doing my job I would not have been allowed to return home for his funeral if he had not survived.

71

My mother wrote me a letter explaining my father's condition. His doctor said he would probably be permanently disabled and could not conduct his timber and real estate business. My younger sister was still in high school and I was needed at home to take care of his business.

He had been in the timber business and bought a lot of timber, and when he had that heart attack he wasn't able to supervise his business and he lost thousands of dollars due to the action of his partners cutting the timber. For every four loads of logs that were taken to the mill he probably got paid for one load. My mother went to congressman Jimmy Morrison who had been in office many years and interceded with him to try to get me a hardship discharge to come back home to help my daddy. I was about 20 years old and my daddy was 58 years old when he had that heart attack.

I knew the Army would be in no hurry to replace me since there were less than 20 men in the world serving with my MOS. I applied for a hardship discharge and begin training another soldier to take over my duties. In November 1957 I left Turkey for the return flight to the United States.

The first leg of the flight was from Ankara, Turkey to Tripoli, Libya which at that time was governed by a king who had leased an airbase to the United States. After a two-day layover I boarded a MATS flight as the sun rose over the Sahara Desert. We flew from Tripoli across the Mediterranean Sea and over Spain, and Portugal, on a 4-engine prop plane and landed in the Azores Islands about dark to refuel. After about an hour on the ground we took off and arrived in Bermuda in the predawn hours to refuel again, where we got out to stretch our legs. Shortly after we began the last leg of the flight to Charleston, South Carolina where we arrived about noon. I was so tired of flying I didn't care if I ever got on a plane again.

When I got off the plane in Charleston I had two choices to travel and I took the wrong one. The right choice would have been to check in with the Military Air Transport Service, to find out when a plane would be flying out from Charleston toward Louisiana. I could have hopped a plane and gone to Atlanta or Jackson, Mississippi or possibly all the way to New Orleans. Instead I got on a Greyhound that supposedly was an express to New Orleans. Well it was an express alright. In those days

72

there were no interstates when the bus pulled out. As it went down the road for a number of miles there was no stop until we got to the next town, where the driver took the express sign off. After that the bus stopped at every crossroads that anybody would be standing by to pick up additional passengers or let other passengers out; not at the terminals, just anywhere people were standing along the road. The stop and start drug that ride out to a day and a half. I got in New Orleans about midnight two days later and I never rode a bus again until I chartered one from Hammond to Mexico for a fishing trip 50 years later.

After spending a couple days at home, I flew to Fort Chaffee, Arkansas where I was discharged from the Army in early December 1958. I immediately began working in my father's business and enrolled In Southeastern Louisiana College in January 1959.

In 1959 and 1960 my father had partially recovered from his heart attack but was restricted in his physical activity. Every day when I was not in school I drove him to inspect his property which included timberlands as well as subdivision lots. I met all of his friends and acquaintances and he and I were inseparable. In the afternoons and early evenings, I often took him to his old friend Joe Kiss's bar to play cards with his friends. This left my wife, Kathy with lots of time on her hands, and she began a relationship with one of my friends, a Korean war veteran who was four or five years older than I. He had been a POW, who was alleged to have collaborated with his North Korean captors and lived down the street from us with his parents. I trusted her completely and was shocked when I came in one night and she told me she was leaving with him. I begged her to stay but told her if she left she could never expect me to ever take her back. A little while later he knocked on my door and told me he had no way to take her. I told them to get in my car and I drove them to the Greyhound bus station in Hammond and gave them five dollars and told her don't ever come back to me. She left our infant son with me and I almost lost my mind.

Within a week she returned to her parents' house and wanted to meet me. I talked to her on the telephone and she swore she had not had any sexual relations with her boyfriend while they stayed in a motel in Baton Rouge after she left. I was still in love with her and after a couple months I agreed to meet her. When she got in my car I had no idea some

73

of her relatives were following us. She suggested we go to a motel where we could talk. I readily agreed since I had not touched her since she left, and she was a very desirable woman. We spent an hour or so in a motel in Baton Rouge and I took her back to her car. I did not trust her and had no intention of having a reconciliation at that time. Within a week I got served with a petition for divorce.

I had never met Louis Ourso, who was a sole practitioner from Hammond who I figured was getting some extra benefits from Kathy besides his fee. He came after me like a tiger, alleging that Kathy and I had a reconciliation, that I was at fault following the reconciliation and that she was entitled to custody of our son, alimony, and child support, despite the fact that I had the child with me from the day she left with her boyfriend. I went to my friend Tom Matheny, a young attorney, who was in the DeMolay organization with me and asked him to represent me. He told me he didn't believe in divorces but his law partner Iddo Pittman would represent me. He filed a reconventional demand for divorce in my favor and the case was allotted to Judge Fanny Birch who had defeated Judge Warren Comish five years earlier.

The trial took a day and a half with allegations on both sides. Kathy did not deny that she had left with her boyfriend and spent several days with him but that we had a reconciliation. I denied the reconciliation.

After the election, Judge Birch ruled against me on her last day in office, I appealed and won the appeal. Kathy moved to Ohio and I didn't see my daughter until she was 10 years old.

Working part-time and going to school part-time and getting a divorce and finding new girlfriends and hunting and fishing took up enough of my time that I didn't finish college until 1963. During my years at Southeastern I renewed acquaintance with one of my best friends, Howie Nichols who I had first met when I joined the DeMolay's when I was 12 years old. Howie finished college before I started and got a job teaching history at Southeastern. I enrolled in every course he taught while I was completing the 160 or so hours I earned credits for by the time I graduated. I then went to Loyola University School of Law.

During the time I was going to school at Southeastern and helping my Daddy run his real estate business around Springfield, he decided to build some spec houses in the subdivision we developed. The powers that be on the Western side of Livingston Parish had a monopoly on financing houses. The law was established to protect local homesteads in each parish and other homesteads could only lend money to finance houses in the parishes where they were located.

Tangipahoa Parish had Ponchatoula Homestead, and Hammond Building and Loan. They had lots of money to lend and they also offered financing to contractors to build houses for sale, but only in Tangipahoa Parish. When I approached them to lend money on houses in Livingston they simply said, "go see the Livingston Parish Savings and Loan." I did that, but it was located in Denham Springs, and they frankly told me that they had all the business they needed around Denham Springs, Walker, Livingston, and the western parts of the parish. So, we had absolutely no way to finance the homes in the eastern part of the Parish.

Well, my Daddy decided to build some houses anyway. There was a crying need for people who were poor to have housing. They couldn't afford large brick homes. We were selling our lots for about two hundred to three hundred dollars apiece and my Daddy figured if we could build houses at a cost of about $2,500.00 we could easily sell them with two 50' X 120' lots for five, six, or seven thousand dollars and make some pretty good money. After I finished the Spring Semester at SLU one summer, he made a deal with a lumbar supplier in Amite and bought an eighteen-wheeler truckload of lumber to build three two-bedroom houses. He hired an old man, who was a semi-retired carpenter, who had bought some property from him and built his own house in the subdivision, to build the houses. He also hired my cousin Buster Coats and I to be carpenter's helpers.

I knew nothing about finished carpentry work but had grown up helping to build sheds, barns, and things like that on my Uncle's and Aunt's property and I was eager to learn. I couldn't get a job anyway during the Republican Eisenhower Administration and summer school was out. My Daddy agreed to pay us the minimum wage, which was seventy-five cents an hour. He paid the old man, who actually laid out and supervised the building, about a dollar and a quarter an hour. That summer we started building three houses a one time. By the end of the summer we had them built.

75

Andy Berthelot had been in the Marine Corps at the same time I was in the Army and he got discharged shortly after I came back from overseas. He had served with the Marines in Lebanon while I was with the Army in Turkey. His grandfather, Mr. Milton Anderson, one of my father's best friends, had taken Andy in since his mother and father had divorced when he was a small child and she went to work in New Orleans during WWII. He and his wife raised Andy since he was very young. Andy and I became the best of friends. Mr. Milton drove a school bus and spent the middle of the day at Charlie Schenk's bar drinking wine and talking to his friends. Andy got a job working as an assistant to Willie Schliegelmeyer, who was a local electrician and plumber. My Daddy made a deal with Mr. Schliegemeyer to do the plumbing and electrical work on the houses that we built.

Our day generally started at seven in the morning and we would work until twelve and take a half hour off for lunch, I usually managed to get about a fifteen-minute nap on the floor of one of the houses that we were building after we got a sandwich and drank our water for lunch. We then went back to work in the broiling heat from one to three thirty p.m. to make our eight hours. After that Buster, Andy and I would go directly to one of the local bars and get a cold beer, then usually go back home and clean up and make the rounds of the local bars.

Some bars were strictly for old men, and others that were for younger people and mixed crowds. Most of the bar rooms in Springfield and Albany area also doubled as grocery stores. That way if you were in the bar drinking and you got hungry, you could get the bartender to make you a sandwich from food that they also sold. One of the bars I frequented was called the OK Bar and Social Club. It was run by a Veteran of WWII named Mike Erdey, who was of Hungarian decent. The bar was built in two sections, the front section was for whites only and the back section was for blacks only. All the blacks would come to the back of the building and come in through the back door, and they had their bar room and their bartender. The front part of the building was for whites only, mainly frequented by older people, and also sold groceries. I never actually went into the black part, which was usually frequented by men. Although it was mixed with women to some extent.

The white part of the bar room also had a poker room. A group of men in the area had poker games there on a weekly basis.

My Daddy was part of that group that met on weekly occasions to play poker. The way they did it, one week they would have a game at Mike Erdely's place. The game would generally start about seven thirty or eight O'clock on a Wednesday or Thursday night and would sometime go all night long. Around midnight they would take a break and have a big supper which was provided for by the host of the poker game. Of course, the host of the poker game made a great deal of money for his business because he would cut the pot, allegedly to take care of the cost of the supper, providing a place for the game, and providing the cards and chips and he also sold drinks. The next week the game would probably meet at Elliott Foster's bar on Tickfaw river at Rome Ferry. And the next week they would go to Joe Kiss's bar in Albany. On rare occasions the game would go to one of the other player's homes.

I remember many times being at the bar room watching those poker games until the wee hours of the morning. In fact, one morning I had gone to an early class at Southeastern at 7:00 a.m. When I finished I came back through Albany towards Springfield and noticed a crowd of cars parked in front of the OK Bar at about 8:30 that morning. I stopped out of curiosity and found the poker game was still going on. It had reached an impasse, the players had a huge pot of money on the table and Elliott Foster, the owner of the place at Rome Ferry was in a standoff with Vercey Smith, a trucking company owner originally from Mississippi. The players had cards on the table, and Mr. Smith had made a huge bet, at least fifteen hundred or two thousand dollars which was like twenty-five to thirty thousand dollars today. When Elliott called the bet, Vercey told him to put up his money, and Elliott was short by about one thousand dollars. They got in a big argument, about whether Elliott had the money to back up his bet. When I walked in, Elliott, who was an old man in his sixties, saw me. I was twenty-two or twenty-three years old, but I had known him since I was a boy. He called me over to the table, said he had a check made to cash for two thousand dollars and told me to go to the bank in Albany and bring him the money. The bank opened at nine o'clock. I did as I was told and when I got to the bank I realized the check wasn't for two thousand dollars, it was for four thousand. Well, I went in to see Mr. Wild, who was the president of the bank there and told him Mr. Foster had given me that check to cash. I told him that he could call the OK bar, and Mr. Foster would verify it. Mr. Wild called Mr. Foster, who authorized me to cash the check and gave me the four thousand dollars in one hundred-dollar bills. I brought it back and gave it to him. He then immediately called the bet and raised Mr. Smith an extra thousand dollars. Smith grumbled about the raise, but he was backed up and he counted out his thousand dollars. The pot probably had more than ten thousand dollars in it at this time. When they laid the cards down Elliott Foster won. I don't remember what the cards said but he won the money and that broke up the game.

I was always fascinated by the political elections that occurred in South Louisiana and in my local area from the time I was in high school. In those days state politics consisted of two factions of Democrats who were divided between the people who supported Earl Long and those who opposed him. The Republicans were a minor party. The Long organization led by Governor Earl Long, Huey Long's brother, had supporters in legislative, judicial, and parochial offices. Many of the local offices such as school boards and police juries had members who generally supported one faction or the other but were bitterly opposed to each other in their local races for election.

After World War II a new group of young men returned from the war and entered politics opposing the older officials who had governed during the war years and shortly thereafter. Small towns were incorporated, and new leaders emerged to seek improvements to roads and infrastructure that had been neglected while the country had been at war. One such town was Albany Louisiana and in the late 1950s a young man maned Grady Stewart became his it's first mayor at age 21. Grady was very ambitious, had graduated college, and was a schoolteacher.

While serving as mayor he decided to run for Louisiana House of Representatives from Livingston Parish against a former incumbent, Jim Brignac from French settlement. Both men were in the Long faction. A vacancy for the house seat occurred when representative Mack Dawkins resigned to accept an appointment to be assistant District Attorney in Livingston Parish and Grady won the election.

Earl Long had been elected as governor in 1948 and served until 1952. He was prohibited by law from succeeding himself and in 1952 Robert Kennon of the anti-Long faction was elected governor. He instituted reforms such as statewide civil service for state employees and was generally more conservative than Earl Long.

Governor Kennon, who had ran on an anti-gambling ticket promised to rid the state of illegal slot machines, and hired Francis Grivenburg, a veteran Army officer as superintendent of state police. He along with state policemen raided nightclubs, restaurants and gambling halls and destroyed hundreds of slot machines using sledgehammers.

One of my aunts, Gertrude Halbert, a widow with two teenage sons and 2 daughters had operated a restaurant and bar with my uncle in Tangipahoa Parish before his death. They had purchased slot machines for their establishment and also placed some in other businesses in Livingston Parish as well as Tangipahoa. She was in competition with larger organizations who had machines.

When the news reports came out about the state police raids she had her oldest son pick up all of the machines she owned. She asked her brother, Gerald Coats, who was a respected school bus driver, to store them in his garage where he parked the school bus. The plan did not work because the state police found out where those machines were and seized and destroyed them. My aunt falsely accused my mother, her sister, of reporting the location of the slot machines to the authorities because my mother opposed gambling.

I remember talking to my uncle, Grafton Coats about that situation between his two sisters and the placing of the machines at his brother's residence when I was about 13 years old. He said that my aunt should have talked to him and he and I could have put those slot machines in a wagon and used his horses to pull them deep in the woods near a swamp where they could have been safely hidden from the state police.

In 1956 Grady Stewart ran for re-election and was opposed by Jim and others. Grady and Jim were in the second primary against one another when Grady made a deal not to run it off and Jim became the representative from Livingston Parish. At the time there was much talk about Grady giving up and I thought his political career was finished.

79

What nobody knew was that Governor Long and other politicians had reached an agreement that Grady would run as the Long candidate for the state Senate in our district of Livingston, Tangipahoa and St. Helena parishes in the next election in 1959.

Grady was elected to the State Senate and became a floor leader for governor Jimmy Davis in 1960. In that position Grady was a party to all important conferences with the Governor making decisions affecting the state of Louisiana. On his way home from Baton Rouge Grady would usually stop in the afternoon by a bar room, owned by Joe Kiss, a close friend of my father.

I was attending Southeastern Louisiana College and helping my father in his real estate developments at that time. The Livingston Parish School Board provided a school bus to take college students from their homes in Southeast Livingston Parish to and from college at Southeastern Louisiana College in Hammond Louisiana. I rode the bus daily to school and would often get off the bus at Joe's bar in the afternoon to meet my father. Grady would tell us about his conversations he had with the governor. In 1960 John F. Kennedy was elected President of the United States in a very close election with Richard Nixon. Before the electoral college voted there was a movement to change electoral votes in Louisiana and other Southern states to prohibit Kennedy from being elected and throw the election into the United States House of Representatives.

Grady told us that he was with the governor and a group of legislators and other state leaders on a conference call with Democratic leaders in Washington including United States Sen. Lyndon Johnson.

Segregation had been declared illegal by the United States Supreme Court and schools were being integrated and laws were being passed by the Louisiana legislature to make it more difficult for black citizens to register to vote. Grady had benefitted from the black vote but walked a narrow line because he also had supporters who belonged to the Ku Klux Klan and his Senate district had a large white majority.

During the conversation with the governor, Louisiana officials and the Democratic officials in Washington, Kennedy's support of Martin Luther King and voting rights was discussed. Grady admitted that he, during that conversation which was very heated at times, had stated "the

80

only blacks Jack Kennedy knows are the ones who have on a white jacket with a towel across their arm serving drinks" later on he was told that President elect Kennedy had been at the meeting in Washington when he made that remark and after the call had asked "who is that smart ass from Louisiana who thinks he knows it all?"

Another time Grady came by that bar and told us that he had just left the governor's office. He said that when he went to the door he was stopped by state troopers who were guarding the governor. A group of men were standing outside the door being denied access by the troopers. As the governor's floor leader Grady was allowed inside the office by the officers. When he walked in Governor Jimmy Davis was lying on the couch on his back with a damp towel across his face. Grady said, "Governor there's a lot of very important people outside your door and you need to talk to them right away." The governor answered "Grady, that's the same bunch that drove Governor Bob Kennon to drinking and ran Earl Long crazy. They'll be back there long after I am gone".

Chapter 3. Shaping My Legal Philosophy

In 1968 I had been practicing law for two years and was still working for the revenue department. I traveled all over the State of Louisiana and gained some invaluable experience from judges and lawyers and people that were very different from the local people in Livingston and Tangipahoa Parish where I grew up. I was beginning to attract more clients in my private practice. When I first got out of law school I did a lot of abstracting for a Hammond law firm called Reid and Macy. The Reid's, from Tangipahoa Parish, included several Judges dating back to the 1800s. Another attorney, named Art Macy, became a member of the firm in the 1950s, he was my role model in those days.

I had actually done some abstract work for him while I was in law school. I learned abstracting and land titles from my father when he was in the timber and real estate business. In those days there was no central index for the mortgage and conveyance records in Livingston, Tangipahoa, or St. Helena Parishes. Each deed and each mortgage was copied from the original into large books and until the early 1900s this was all done by hand.

In the 1900's typed copies of the records began to be placed in the books. Each book had an index in the back, with a list of the names of the people who bought and sold land, together with the dates of the sales and a brief description of the property showing the Section Township and Range where it was located. To do the abstracting in those days you started off with the name of the person who was selling the land together with the description. You read that description showing the starting point of the survey which was a certain distance from the section corner, then the direction and length of the property lines surrounding the tract of land, making sure the description matched the map.

You then started working backwards in time looking in the indexes to find where the person who was selling the land had purchased it and from whom. To do this you had to start at the current book and pick up book by book all the way back at least 51 years to establish the chain of title. You had to look in each index to find that name under Vendee's to determine when it was purchased. Then you looked in the Vendor's index to find out who the seller had purchased the property from, then switch back over to the Vendee index again to find out where that person had purchased it.

The books were not nearly as voluminous as they are today, but it was a long tedious process. You had to check all those records to find out the history of the property which was called an abstract. After you checked it all the way out to find each name of whoever owned that property, then you had to double check the description when they had sold it to somebody else. Many times, you would see a tract was purchased by one person who kept it for a while, sold part of it, then sold the rest of to someone else. Each sale had to be noted. I had learned this method from my father before I went to law school and had traveled to all of the courthouses in the area. I went to Greensburg in St. Helena Parish, Amite in Tangipahoa Parish and Livingston in Livingston Parish and got to know all the clerks of court. When I began to practice law, I had a head start on everybody else getting out of law school, because I already knew how to abstract, which wasn't taught in school. The clerks and some of their employees would give me assistance if I needed it. In fact, when I started to practice in 1966 Alsay Addison, the Clerk of Court for Livingston Parish who had served for several terms gave me a key to the clerk's office at the courthouse. That allowed me to get up at 5 o'clock in the morning or after hours at night and check the conveyance and mortgage records to do my abstracting work, rather than have to wait until the courthouse opened at 8 o'clock in the morning. I often had finished two hours work before court started at 9:00a.m. and be that much ahead of any other lawyer doing that type of work.

The first criminal lawyer I met when I was just a boy, was Marcus Carter Round. He was a brilliant man and handled many criminal and civil cases. I later heard many stories about some of his more famous trials that I was too young to witness at the time. One of the more interesting cases Mr. Round handled occurred during prohibition when it was illegal to purchase whiskey. Lots of people found it very profitable to make wine from strawberries and blackberries and other types of fruit and to make whiskey or white lightning from corn. One of my uncles, Clark Coats loved the taste of whiskey and when the government prohibited the big distilleries from making whiskey and selling it, he made his own. It must've been pretty good because he soon had many customers that wanted to buy some of his wares.

The federal government hired officers to enforce the liquor laws and sent revenue agents into the rural areas to try to apprehend the people who were breaking them. The whiskey makers also had people who let them know who the government agents were or at least their physical characteristics so they could avoid getting caught. The way my uncle Clark operated, according to the tales I was told, he made his whiskey at his still in the woods, put it in bottles, and then brought the bottles to an area close to his home where he placed them in a hollow log. Anybody who wanted to buy his whiskey would come to his house, or to the general store where he worked for Breckenridge Lumber Company and tell him they needed some whiskey. They would make the deal on the price and he would go get the whiskey and bring it back to the purchaser. He was warned that there was a new government man searching for whiskey makers and he could be identified because one of his thumbs had been cut off, so he only had one thumb. The revenuer came to my uncle and made a deal to buy a bottle whiskey from him. When my uncle got the whiskey and handed it to him the revenue agent pulled money out of his pocket and my uncle realized he had only one thumb. Before my uncle Clark could escape he was arrested, and later spent six months in jail in New Orleans.

Mr. Carter Rounds represented people who made whiskey and was often paid in bottles of their merchandise instead of cash. A sheriff's deputy had arrested one of his clients for making whiskey in Livingston parish and seized the whiskey as evidence. Mr. Carter came to see his client in the jail and got him out on bond before the trial came up. On the morning of the trial Mr. Carter went to court, and being friends with the sheriff, his deputies, the judge and the district attorney, he had quite a lot of leeway to examine the evidence. Before court began he went to the district attorney's office and said he wanted to see the evidence. The District Attorney told him to go down to the Sheriff's office and have a look. He went to the Sheriff's office and told the deputy in charge that he wanted to see the evidence against his client. The deputy opened the safe and pulled out a pint bottle half full of whiskey and handed it to Mr. Carter. Mr. Carter turned his back to the deputy with the bottle of whiskey in his hand, opened the bottle and drank the whiskey down. He then handed the deputy the empty bottle and told him "Where is your evidence now?" The case got thrown out real quick.

As I grew older I actually saw some of the trials that took place. One of the lawyers that was practicing in Livingston parish at the time was Erlo Durbin. He was a flamboyant criminal defense lawyer and also had a civil practice. Erlo quickly gained a reputation of being crooked because he won a lot of his cases for his clients who had been charged with violating the law. If you represented a lot of crooks, you had to be crooked yourself, or at least that's what the general population thought.

In Tangipahoa Parish the most prominent criminal attorney was Barbee Ponder, a brilliant man who was also a miser. It was said Barbee was so tight he squeaked, but he became very rich because he was very successful in the defense of persons charged with crimes. When it came to keeping criminals out of jail, or in capital cases saving someone from getting hung, his fees were very high. If you killed somebody in Tangipahoa Parish in the late 1930s 1940s and 1950s you hired Barbee Ponder. He would save your life from hanging, and later the electric chair, and often he would save you from doing any time in jail. But, if you had any money or land, when you got through with your trial, you had no more land and no more money, because Barbee got it all.

My father told me about one of Barbee's trials in Amite, Louisiana. when he represented a black man for murdering another black man. The Judge was Warren Comish, the District Attorney was Joe Sims and Barbee was the defense attorney.

My father told me that he was at the courthouse when the trial was going on and they picked the jury to try the man for murder. After the jury had been picked and the trial began there was testimony that the victim had been at the residence of the accused. At least two eye witnesses testified that they saw the victim run out the door of the house with the accused in pursuit shooting at him with a gun. The victim was hit several times as he was chased around the house, where he fell to the ground and died. After the testimony, which took place before noon, Joe Sims, the District Attorney, rested his case, Judge Comish recessed court, and they all went over to Ardillo's restaurant to have lunch. My daddy went to the same restaurant with these men who were all his friends and had lunch with them. During the meal Judge Comish told Barbee "Well, we are going to hang him, the evidence shows the man's guilty. Did you get all your money?" and Barbee told him "I got part of it" the Judge says "you ain't gonna get no more because they are going to convict him." Joe Sims agreed with the Judge and they poked a lot of fun and Barbee, telling him "this is one time you're not gonna win and you ain't gonna get paid, Barbee." Barbee just looked at him and laughed and said, "we will see." They all went back to the courthouse, and when it came time for Barbee to put on his case, he didn't call any witnesses. Or have his client testify. Judge Comish and Joe Sims were astounded. There was just no sense to this, nobody could figure out what Barbee was doing.

Well, when you finish a trial, the District Attorney makes a summary of the charges in the case and gives his argument for conviction and then the defense attorney gives his argument for the defendant. In his argument, Barbee told the jury "you all heard the witnesses say that my client shot this man, my client ran him out of the house and ran around shooting at him and he fell and he died. And you can certainly all say that he probably killed the man, but you have to give him the benefit of reasonable doubt. Do you know whether or not he died from that gunshot?" The District Attorney forgot to put a doctor or coroner on the stand who could testify that he died from a gunshot wound. Barbee continued "Hell, he could've died from eating green persimmons." The jury found the man not guilty. These were some of the brilliant things that the best attorneys used. I made it my goal to try to emulate them and to use my wits as well as common sense to mix with the law to save my clients when they were charged with crimes, and to try to win my civil cases when my clients had suffered injustice or injury.

I didn't have many customers for abstracting, but Reid and Macy did lots of sales and mortgage work for banks and businesses. Mr. Macy would hire me to do the abstracting in Livingston Parish. He also told me practical things about the practice of law from his standpoint that almost nobody else realized. I had grown up in Livingston parish and had followed court proceedings with interest. I heard stories of criminal cases as well as civil cases and heard from many people talking about

86

those cases. I had met almost all the civil and criminal lawyers that practiced in the district when there were really only a few from Livingston parish.

Art Macy was the first true liberal politician that I had ever met. He was an integrationist in the 1950s when all the schools, busses, hotels and everything was segregated. Art Macy was against that.

Art Macy wound up in Hammond Louisiana after being born and raised in Massachusetts, he taught school in California after he finished college, and joined the Army during WW II. He never did talk to me much about his army experiences other than he was in World War II. When he was discharged, the G.I. Bill was passed in Congress, providing veterans money for education. This gave him the opportunity to go to law school. He was a brilliant man, but his family was very poor. The G.I. Bill entitled him to go to LSU which was cheaper than places like Harvard and Yale or other Eastern law schools. One of his best friends at LSU Law School was Hubert Humphrey who also came to Louisiana to study law at LSU because it was cheaper than to go to school in Michigan where he lived. Because of his brilliant career in law school, Art was recruited by the Law Firm of Reid and Reid to come to Hammond and practice with them. A lot of their business was representing banks, Insurance Companies and Businesses, and he quickly proved his worth to the leading businessmen in Tangipahoa Parish, where he had a long career in law and in politics. When I first began my practice, I did some abstract work on a part-time basis for Art who had represented my father and Leonard Kinchen in many of their business transactions. We became very close personal friends and often discussed politics. He became my role model and gave me advice which shaped my personal philosophy. In fact, he encouraged me to help Black people register to vote and stand up for all people's rights against anyone and any public body who tried to walk over them.

DON'T GET MAD, GET EVEN

Art Macy

"You have entered a new profession, and you have certain standards you will be expected to maintain, you will be criticized for many of the things you do and you will be called names and accused of improper actions by dissatisfied clients and people you oppose, you must not let the criticism and accusations affect you. You must let it run off you like water on a duck's back and proceed to your next case. A lawyer should be like a lightning rod, let the criticisms be made against you. It's better for people who are in legal disputes to blame the lawyers rather than to hate one another" he told me. Then he asked me "Who are the crookedest lawyers in our area?" "That's easy I said. Everybody knows that Barbee Ponder and Erlo Durbin are crooks."

Art stopped me, and said "Well, let me tell you something, both those attorneys have represented many clients accused of committing crimes, and many have been convicted, and they have won acquittals for many more. Both have made a lot of money representing their clients, but that doesn't mean they are crooks.

I'll give you an example, he said "If you enter an agreement with an attorney like Burrell Carter, who has a reputation in his parish of making lots of money, you better make sure that you put it in writing, because if you don't he will later conveniently forget his agreement and use it to your detriment. On the other hand, if you have an agreement with Barbee Ponder or Erlo Durbin, you can take it to the bank. They will do exactly what they say they will do and will not take advantage of you by telling lies about what was agreed to." I was astounded, but later found that what Art had told me about Burrell Carter was believed by many people.

Some of the so-called pillars of society would use any kind of underhanded trick that they could to win. Burrell Carter, who later became a District and Appellate Judge on the Court of Appeals earned a reputation in his later years of being a greedy, untrustworthy man who many said worshiped money rather than God. Erlo Durbin and Barbee Ponder felt that their word was their bond.

On September 28, 1982 a train derailed in Livingston Louisiana causing the entire town to be evacuated for more than a week due to chemical explosions. I was one of nine local lawyers who filed one of the first-class action lawsuits in Louisiana against the railroad. We represented more than 3000 people who were exposed to chemicals, suffered property damage, and loss of business. After several years we settled the case for approximately $39 million. The trial court judge was Judge Gordon Causey.

We had contingency fee contracts signed by our clients for 33 1/3 percent and had personally signed notes with banks to help cover court costs and expenses of $867,682. While we were working on the case Burrell Carter was a judge in the 21st Judicial District, and his son Robbie was attending law school at LSU.

Judge Causey told me and the other attorneys representing the people of Livingston that Judge Carter had approached him and

89

suggested that to avoid criticism by the public he should appoint a Special Counsel to do research and submit a Memorandum on Class Action Attorney Fee's. It should contain recommendations for the amount of attorney's fees to be approved by the court, and the best person for that job would be his son, Robbie Carter, who had just finished law school in 1984.

Judge Causey followed that advice, and after a couple of weeks Robbie Carter prepared his memorandum on attorney fees. In any contested case that goes to trial attorneys on each side will prepare memorandum pointing out cases that support their position for the judge to consider before making a decision. Often a reply memorandum is submitted pointing out cases that detract from the position of their opponents.

A special counsel appointed to research and prepare a memorandum is expected to review all similar cases covering opposing positions of both sides.

In the railroad case the steering committee had recommended attorney's fees to be set at 33 1/3%, presented testimony of an expert class action attorney supporting their position and citing cases in their favor.

In his memorandum Judge Burrell Carter's son Robbie cited seven cases, four of which set the amount of attorney's fee awarded at .036 percent, .08 percent, 5.5 percent, and 16 percent. The other three cases he referred to did not reveal the amount of the settlement or the amount of attorney's fees. No cases whatsoever were cited revealing larger awards of attorney fees although others existed.

Judge Causey, had indicated to the other steering committee members and I, that he intended to award the 33 1/3% fee to the attorneys who did the work, put up the money, and assumed the risk before Judge Carter stuck his nose in the case. He later told me that he would have to cut our fee from $11,596,884.00 to $7,928,202.97 or face real criticism due to the biased memorandum submitted by Judge Carter's son.

When Robbie Carter submitted his bill for $25,000 for his few weeks work it became obvious that the only reason Judge Carter made his suggestion to Judge Causey was out of jealousy for our success and hard work, and his greed to have his son get some of our money.

Judge Burrell Carter's philosophy was just the opposite of Leonard Kinchen's. I represented Leonard Kinchen, one of my father's old partners in the timber business. He got me to check land titles and help him close some land deals. Before he died I would go with him to meet working people he was purchasing property from who lived in all parts of South Louisiana. I would prepare the deeds and we would drive to their homes at night to get their signatures and those of the witnesses, I notarized the papers, and filed them at the courthouse for him.

Leonard Kinchen had helped a lot of people and he dealt with politics all the time. He could call any judge after hours at night and get him to set a bond, so he could get them out of jail. When election time came he remembered all the people he had helped, and they voted for the politicians that Mr. Leonard was supporting. As I was riding with him at night, he would tell me stories about his family and some of the things he saw and heard back in the 1920s and the 1930s. Many of them were not exactly legal.

One of the wisest things he told me was: "Pardue, you know people are very jealous when they see somebody succeed. I'm different than that, you are my friend, I want to see you prosper, and it's a selfish thing on my part. If you prosper, and I get in trouble you can help me, but if you don't prosper, and I pull you down, or don't do anything for you to help you prosper, and I get in trouble, you can't help me." He said, "You should always make sure you help your friends prosper." Some people that I've known over the years have rose in prominence and grew very wealthy, but they, like Burrell Carter, operate just the opposite of what Leonard Kinchen did.

BOOK 3 MY LEGAL PRACTICE AND POLITICS

Chapter 1. Livingston Parish Local Politics

One of my best friends was Judge Sam Rowe. Sam and I had attended Southeastern Louisiana College as undergraduates together. Sam was working for one of the insurance companies as an adjuster and attended school at Southeastern while I was in the Army. When I returned from the Army and went back to school at Southeastern, Sam who was a Marine Corp veteran, and I actually had classes at the same time, but didn't really know each other very well. When I finished Southeastern and moved to New Orleans, Sam, like me, had to work his way through Loyola Law School. He graduated a few years after I did in 1966.

Sam's family lived in St. Helena Parish, when he married Representative Bumbo Alford's oldest daughter. Bumbo ran a little grocery store at the crossroads in Easleyville. When I started turkey hunting in the late 1960s and early 1970s I hunted in St. Helena Parish and in southern Mississippi around Gillsburg. Every two or three years I'd be lucky enough to kill a turkey. In those days the interstate was not completed, and we would drive the back way between Gillsburg and Springfield. When anyone of our group killed a turkey, we would always stop at Bumbo's store to have the turkey weighed on his scales.

After Sam finished law school, he moved down to Livingston Parish and established himself as an attorney in the town of Livingston. There were no other lawyers living in the town when Sam started his private practice and he quickly developed a following. Sam became the town attorney and later town attorney for Albany and French Settlement, where I served after I first got out of law school. I also was town attorney for Springfield and was paid $25.00 per month. We often crossed swords, representing different sides of domestic cases and disputes involving real estate. The relationship we had was very cordial and we became very good friends.

After a couple years Sam took on a partner named Reggie McIntyre and changed his sign and cards to read Rowe and McIntyre. Shortly after that they split up and Sam took in another young lawyer and changed his sign again. This partnership didn't last either, and he soon did it again.

94

After a couple more times, I told Sam since he couldn't get along with any of his partners, he should run for Judge.

Odom Graves was elected sheriff after Taft Faust retired. Taft had been sheriff from 1948 through 1976. Odom had been chief deputy during his last two terms and was picked as the heir apparent to succeed him.

Any sheriff's who's been in office for 15 to 20 years is going to pick up a lot of enemies during that time. The sheriff's job is to put criminals in jail. If you put somebody in jail, whether they're right or the wrong, their family and friends are gonna resent you putting their kinsman in jail, and those families will vote against you in the next election. As time goes by you pick up a solid opposition to your regime. The key to staying in office is to make friends with those friends and relatives of the people you put in jail. You treat them cordially, realizing that they can't help their kinfolk or friends that break the law, and the only people that need to be punished are the people that actually break the law. Odom believed when he arrested somebody, and put them in jail, unless it was a very serious case such as murder, you assisted them. You helped their relatives and friends to post bond to get their kinsman or friend out of jail. Even though their property may have been valued less than the amount of the bond, the sheriff could approve the bond. I have seen many cases where someone, who owned property that was worth only $10,000 and owed probably $5000, was allowed to sign a $20,000 bond to get their son, nephew, or brother out of jail on charges of theft or fighting.

Odom was elected for the first time in early 1976. I had known him since he was first hired as a deputy, and we were very good friends.

I ran for district attorney in 1972 and I'm certain Sheriff Taft Faust voted for me, but he would not publicly endorse me against and the incumbent District Attorney that I was running against. I carried Livingston parish although I got beat in St. Helena and Tangipahoa. When Odom ran in 1978 he wanted my support especially, since I had ran and won in Livingston where I had made lots and lots of friends. Another young man who was a close personal friend of mine named Dudley Arledge, wanted to be Sheriff. Dudley had been a police office in the city of New Orleans at the time when I was going to law school,

95

teaching at Kenner and going to school at night. He served as a police officer for two or three years and then got a job as a probation officer back in Livingston Parish, where he had been born and raised in Walker Louisiana. He and I met when I was representing people that he was supervising on probation and we became very close friends. When I ran for District Attorney, Dudley came to see me and told me he was going to get all his family and everybody he could to vote for me. This surprised me, because I didn't really know Dudley that well, but I was very grateful for his support. I had no idea that Dudley had any political ambitions whatsoever at the time.

Before Odom announced he was running for sheriff, Dudley came to see me and told me that he wanted to run for Sheriff. I told Dudley, since he had voted for me, that I owed him a vote and would vote for him. I told him I wasn't going to make a firm commitment on how far I would go until I knew who else was gonna run. Then Odom announced he was going to run. Well, it was a foregone conclusion that Dudley Arledge was not gonna beat the chief deputy in Livingston, who had many friends, but did not have the same enemies of the old sheriff had, and he had the old Sheriff's support.

In other words, you couldn't blame Odom for what other deputies had done over the years, while working for Taft, just because Odom later worked for Taft. Odom had the backing of many people who had money to spend in politics. He also had the backing of the politicians on the police jury, the school board and the towns. While Dudley had a large family in the Walker area he had virtually no kin people in the eastern part of Livingston parish where I was from, and not too many people in the Denham Springs area on the western side of the parish. The more telling thing was that Dudley didn't have any money and he didn't have any political organization.

The opposition to Odom was opposition that Taft had accumulated over the years and these people were looking for a strong candidate. In addition to Dudley Arledge, there was another candidate named Rudolph Ratcliff. Rudolph Ratcliff was the brother of Otis Ratcliff who had been a police jury member from the 10th ward of Livingston parish in Killian which is right down the road from Springfield where I live. Otis had fooled with politics his whole life. He was very active in the campaign

96

for governors Earl Long and Jimmy Davis and, later supported Gillis Long who ran third behind John McKeithen and DeLesseps Morrison from New Orleans in 1963. In the second primary he backed John McKeithen who was elected. Partially through Otis and mainly through a lot of hard work and well-deserved promotions Rudolph Ratcliff had risen to be the Superintendent of the Louisiana State Police. He ran for Sheriff of Livingston parish at the same time that Odom and Dudley ran.

Rudolph was straight arrow law and order, Otis was a politician that wanted to win and wanted his brother to win. My side of the parish, the east and south part, was mainly more liberal than the conservative Bible Belt Baptist part around Denham Springs, Walker, Watson and Livingston, where there were no barrooms or package liquor stores. Many many people from that area of the parish would come to our side of the parish which was a wet area, to party and get drunk on weekends. The state of Louisiana had a law prohibiting barrooms from opening on Sundays, but that law had been ignored by Taft Faust as long as he was sheriff. The barrooms were open seven days a week in French settlement, Port Vincent, Maurepas, Whitehall, Bear Island, and Springfield, and to some extent in Albany and Holden.

Otis told me of a rally he attended in French settlement at a restaurant and bar called the Y, operated by Merlin Brignac, that was very popular at the time. Hundreds of people came there for suppers and dances on weekends. In those days the way to draw a crowd was to have a free meal, booze if you were on our side of the parish, and lots of soda pop if you were on the other side of the parish. To get the votes of the crowd you needed to feed them, make speeches, and tell them what they wanted to hear. Otis engineered the meeting and brought his brother to the barroom for the speeches. Rudolph made his speech and a couple of Cajuns from that area came up to the podium and told him they wanted to ask him a question. The question was "Mr. Ratcliff, when you get to be Sheriff, you gonna close these barrooms down on Sunday?" And Rudolph being honest, straight and true, and not a very good politician at all told them the exact truth. He said his whole life he had been a law enforcement officer and if the law said it was required they be closed on Sunday he would enforce that law and they would be shut down. The crown was stunned. Otis told Rudolph it was time for them to go. They got into Otis's car to take Rudolph home and Otis told him, "you just lost the election, I got these people over here that like to party, like to drink, and like to have a good time. They're not bad people, they don't go out and commit robberies and mayhem and things like that anymore than other people do in other parts of the parish, but they do like to have their parties. And you have lost all of their votes," which proved true.

Otis was a man who didn't drink very much at all, the only times I ever saw him drink anything at all was maybe at a Christmas party at his house, and that was only one drink or a glass of wine. He knew politics, and he knew people that drank, and he knew what it took to get them to vote for you and he knew what would happen if they did not agree with you. In any event the election between Odom, Dudley, and Rudolph was steaming up and got red-hot. Odom called me in to see him at the Sheriff's office. When I met with him, he told me, "I want you to help me get elected" and I told him, "Odom when I ran for District Attorney a couple years ago you didn't do anything for me, and I'm not gonna ask you if you voted for me, but I don't believe you did. I know your boss voted for me and some of the other deputies voted for me but then some of the deputies were openly against me. I promised Dudley Aldredge that I was going to vote for him." Dudley, who had little money, had given me a few dollars, which meant more to me than some that gave $1,000.00, and got the rest of his family and a few friends to help me. He came to me on his own without me asking and said he wanted to help me any way he could. I felt I owed him my vote. I also said, "I know that Dudley cannot win, and I'm not gonna do anything against him but I don't want to see Rudolph Ratcliff elected Sheriff instead of you." He said, "that's good enough for me, if you hear something that I need to know, just contact me and were going be friends and there won't be any problem." I heard a few things he needed to know when it came to the second primary between him and Rudolph Ratcliff and Odom got elected Sheriff. Odom immediately started to do what became his standard method of politics. He began to go to people who were openly against him and told them that he wanted to be their friend. He was elected Sheriff and any way he could help them he would try to do it. If they had any problems, he wanted them to come see him, his door was open and he would be glad to try to help. Now he didn't tell them that he was going to help them second, because he was going to help us first, but he didn't have to.

Within four years Odom Graves was the most powerful politician in Livingston Parish and remained that way for 20 years, as long as he was sheriff. He became more popular every year as time went by. His whole philosophy was to help people. I remember an occasion where some lowlife individual who was probably drunk and fighting, with a prior criminal record, was arrested by Odom's deputies and taken to jail. I don't remember the name of the person but there was an incident at the jail where the guy tried to fight the deputies and they beat the hell out of him. This was standard procedure all over South Louisiana during those years in any jail. Some of the man's family heard about it and went to the jail to check on their relative. The deputies at the jail told them they didn't have to tell them anything and they could leave. These people went to Odom and told him what happened. This enraged Odom, and he called a meeting of all his deputies the next day. He went to the jail and at that meeting he told them "Everybody that's in this jail are my people, because no matter what they do, they have parents, brothers, sisters, cousins, sons, and daughters who haven't done anything wrong and I will not stand for you to punish these other people for something someone does in this jail. If I ever hear of anybody working for me who doesn't treat the relatives of the people who are in jail with the utmost respect and give them whatever information that can be given and help if necessary, you may as well go ahead and turn in your resignation right now, because you will be fired when I find out about it. The way you operate a jail won't get you elected, but it certainly can beat you." To my knowledge none of that ever happened again and Odom became more and more popular.

In 1978 Judge William Mack Dawkins retired as judge. Judge Dawkins was born and reared in North Louisiana came down to Livingston Parish where he taught school and became principal at Live Oak High School. He served in the Army in WWII then went to LSU Law School on the GI Bill and opened his office in Denham Springs where he began his practice. Judge Dawkins was an Anti-Long candidate for State Representative in 1952 and was elected at the same time as Judge Robert "Bob" Kennon who beat the Long candidate, Judge

Carlos Spaht for governor. Judge Dawkins served two years as representative, and in 1954 Duncan Kemp Jr. from Amite, Louisiana ran for District Attorney and defeated the incumbent Joe Arthur Sims from Hammond, Louisiana, who was a very close friend of Earl K long who became governor again in 1956. When Duncan Kemp got elected he hired Mack Dawkins as his Assistant District Attorney for Livingston Parish. Judge Dawkins served as Assistant District Attorney, and in 1960 ran for Judge when Judge Horace Reid was elected to the Court of Appeals. At that time there were only 2 judges from Livingston, St. Helena, and Tangipahoa Parishes. When the vacancy occurred, Judge Dawkins ran from Livingston, Barbee Ponder ran from Amite, and Ben Tucker ran from Hammond, Louisiana. Judge Tucker had the backing of the conservative establishment in Tangipahoa Parish. Barbee had a reputation as a criminal lawyer and just that reputation attracted the outlaw vote. The good solid citizens of Tangipahoa Parish in the district tended to vote against anybody who was backed by outlaws. Judge Dawkins had the support of almost all the solid citizens from Livingston parish. Problem was, in those days Tangipahoa Parish had almost twice as many votes as Livingston did. The runoff occurred between Judge Tucker and Barbee Ponder, and in the runoff Ben Tucker, was elected, while Judge Dawkins continued to serve as Assistant District Attorney.

Judge Dawkins and his supporters made a deal to support Judge Tucker in the run-off in exchange for his support in the legislature to create a third Judgeship for the 21ST Judicial District. There was an understanding among the lawyers that this was going to be a Livingston Parish seat, and Judge Dawkins won the election to the District Court, being the only candidate from Livingston Parish to run. He had no opposition from Tangipahoa and became judge. He served through 1977 when he retired, and an election was called to fill his seat.

When he retired, Odom Graves was sheriff, and he called a meeting of all the lawyers from Livingston Parish. At that time there were only about 8 or 10 of us total, and out of that there were only 7 or 8 who were actually qualified to be Judge, because you had to have practiced for 5 years before you could be elected. There were two or three young lawyers that hadn't practiced that long and weren't invited to the meeting. The meeting took place at one of Odom's favorite hangouts, a restaurant and bar in Baton Rouge called the Galley. Many times, when I finished court in Livingston, especially if court got through around noon, I would drive to Baton Rouge and meet with Odom and some of our friends and have lunch. If we didn't have any other kind of appointments, we would stay on after lunch and have drinks in the adjoining lounge of that restaurant. When Odom called the meeting that was the place we met. Every lawyer from Livingston Parish that could possibly be elected judge was invited and everyone who had any interest in being judge attended. The oldest lawyers in Livingston Parish at that time were Erlo Durbin, from Denham Springs who was in his 60s and had been Assistant District Attorney, and State Representative and was semi-retired, Jim Cudd who did nothing but abstract land titles and do notary work, Jerry Bunch, also from Denham Springs who was two or three years older than me and had no political ambitions whatsoever, Doug Neeson and Bob Mellon, law partners who had no personal political ambition. Mr. Neeson was a part of the Long political organization and had business interests with Senator Russell Long, Congressman Gillis Long, and some of the other politicians in the area. His firm specialized in personal injury cases, and had two attorneys who worked for him, Carl Cavanaugh, who was absolutely apolitical and Robert Tillery who was an aggressive trial lawyer and had no political ambitions. None of these showed up. The ones who did show up were Judge Raymond Bennett from Denham Springs who the year before had been elected to the newly created Seventh Ward City Court for Denham Springs and the surrounding areas. The others attending were me, Calvin Fayard, Sam Rowe and Hayden Berry. Odom called the meeting to order and told us that we were going to have the selection for judge. He said this was a Livingston parish seat and we needed to have somebody from Livingston parish get elected, and the surest way we could get beat was for two or more candidates from Livingston parish to run. If that happened, he was certain that one candidate from Tangipahoa Parish would run and since Tangipahoa had more votes than Livingston the Tangipahoa man would get in the second primary and then would be elected. We needed a Livingston parish judge, so the only way to do that was for everybody to pick one man and everybody get for him. It made a lot of sense to me and like it or lump it everybody agreed that was the

101

thing to do. Odom told us were going do this absolutely fair. We are going to start off with the lawyers that have been here the longest. He said Erlo Durbin had been here the longest, but he doesn't want it, Jim Cudd had been here the second-longest and he don't want it. He asked Raymond Bennett, the new City Judge of Denham Springs City Court do you want it? Raymond said "no I don't. I have just exactly what want, I can serve as Judge and keep my real estate practice and I do not want to be District Judge." Then he turned to me and said "Hobart, you are next in seniority, do you want it?" If I had said yes, I would have been elected judge, but I'd ran for District Attorney before and I knew something about politics, but also when I ran I got the best advertisement in the world for a lawyer by running a good race. I got beat but still got a lot of votes. I made a lot of contacts, a lot of new friends, and for the first time in my life I started making money from all these new friends and people I met during that campaign. Lawyers could not advertise at that time so when I ran for office I had the opportunity to gain lots of new clients. Of course, it wasn't my inclination anyway to be a judge and I told him so real quick. I said "There's two reasons I won't run for judge. Number one I can't afford to be a judge because I make more money than a judge would, and number two, I'm not a referee, I'm a fighter. If I'm in a fight I will pick sides, I can't sit up there be a referee. I don't want it." Odom says okay the next one on the list was Calvin Fayard. Calvin was a couple years behind me in seniority and he practiced basically the same law I did, except he didn't do a lot of criminal work. After my run for District Attorney against Leonard Yokum and Erlo Durbin retired, Calvin was offered the Assistant District Attorney's job from Livingston. He called me, and I encouraged him to take it. It was a job I certainly didn't want. Calvin was one of my best friends and I was tickled to death to see him get it. Calvin had learned about personal injury cases and how to make more money. He wasn't interested in being a judge because of the money part of it and he quickly told Odom that he had what he wanted. Then it got to be Sam Rowe's chance. Odom said, "Okay Sam do you want it?" Sam said, "Yes I want it." The meeting ended, and Sam was the candidate for Livingston Parish.

Chapter 2. Law School and Politics

I entered Loyola School of Law in the fall of 1963. I had finished Southeastern Louisiana College with a BA degree and a teaching certificate. I made an application for a job with the New Orleans Police Department and with the Jefferson Parish school board as a teacher of social studies and history. The school board paid more than the police department, so I took the job that paid the most, $300 a month.

I was hired to teach at Kenner Junior High School in Kenner, Louisiana, which is located about 15 miles from the law school. The first year I taught school from 8 AM until 3 PM and went to law school at night. I then got a job with the Louisiana Department of Revenue and went to school in the mornings and worked in the afternoons. I met students from all over Louisiana with all kinds of backgrounds. Almost all were interested in politics, and later many were elected to various state and local offices.

Jud Downs from Shreveport was the son of a Police Commissioner of that city. His uncle Sammy Downs, a State Senator, from Rapides Parish, was a floor leader for Governor John McKeithen. Jud met his wife when she was attending Loyola University. They got married, when he was a senior at law school, in Palm Beach Florida where her grandfather lived next door to President Kennedy's father's home. Jud and his family were hard-shell Baptist and Kathy and her family were liberal Roman Catholics.

Jud invited me to stand in his wedding in Palm Beach. My wife and I traveled to Florida, and for the first time in my life, I experienced the home and lifestyle of the super-rich. We were invited to Kathy's grandfather's house for a rehearsal dinner before the wedding. The food was exotic, instead of silverware the knives and forks were gold. The dishes were inlaid with gold. We were served key lime pie which I had never eaten before, and three different kinds of wine.

Jud's family insisted that he be married in a Protestant church and Kathy's family insisted that she be married in the Catholic Church. With the wedding at a stalemate they decided to have two ceremonies one after the other and we went to the Baptist Church and immediately after the ceremony a Catholic priest married them again.

After he graduated Jud and Kathy moved to North Carolina where he practiced law, then was elected judge and served for many years until his retirement.

Bobby Freeman was from Iberville Parish and often wore his deputy sheriffs' uniform to night school at Loyola. He was aligned with Sheriff Jessel Ourso who had just been elected Sheriff and had been opposed by long-term assessor Joe DuPont. Joe's son, Joe DuPont Jr. attended law school in the daytime. While they were bitter political enemies both were friends of mine. Bobby was elected State Representative after he graduated and became a floor leader for governor John McKeithen and later was elected Lieutenant Governor of Louisiana. Joe was elected City Judge of Plaquemine, Louisiana.

The DuPont and Ourso factions remained political enemies until the death of both men. Both were re-elected every time they ran but neither could defeat the other for their respective jobs. When Old Joe DuPont died Sheriff Jessel Ourso went to his wake, walked up to the casket, reached into it and grasped the corpse by the arm and shook it. The spectators were shocked, and when someone asked "Sheriff, why did you do that?" He answered, "I just wanted to make sure he was dead."

Eddie Knowles was from Avoyelles Parish in North Louisiana, and had married his wife Jeanette, while we were in law school. He returned home to Marksville and later was elected District Attorney, where he served for more than 20 years. His wife was elected to the Court of Appeals and later to the Louisiana Supreme Court.

Paul Hardy from St. Martin Parish returned home from law school and was elected to the Louisiana Senate and later Secretary of State. He ran for Governor against another of our classmates Louis Lambert who was a State Senator from Ascension Parish and later Public Service Commissioner. Paul nearly missed the runoff, and he endorsed Louis's opponent Dave Treen who was elected and gave Paul a job in his administration.

Harry Lee was one year behind me at Loyola. His father operated one of the largest Chinese restaurants in New Orleans. We had a professor at Loyola named Bill Redman, who had never ran for political office. When Bill decided to run against a long time Judge from New Orleans, my classmates and I enthusiastically supported him for that office. I was working for the state Department of Revenue in the Louisiana state office building next door to City Hall in New Orleans. Just about every employee in that building had got his job through politics as I had. I took Bill through the entire building and introduced him to almost every employee. Most of them had never met anyone running for Judge and did not have any reason to support one of the other of the candidates.

To help raise money for Bill, Harry got his father to agree to have a fundraiser at his restaurant. The food that was served was hot dogs. Others of my classmates went door-to-door canvassing voters and giving out campaign material. Bill did not win but ran a very close race. After the race Governor John McKeithen hired Bill as one of his top aides and after couple of years appointed him Judge on the Court of Appeal.

Harry was appointed as Attorney for Jefferson Parish after he graduated and also served as United States attorney. During the time he represented Jefferson Parish, he made headlines when a newspaper reported he had visited the camp of Carlos Marcello, a reputed mafia leader in Grand Isle. Harry made a joke of it, saying they cooked dinner together.

Shortly after this Harry ran against longtime Jefferson Parish Sheriff, Alwyn Cronvich and defeated him. He later considered running for Governor but remained Sheriff until shortly before his death many years later.

Louis Lambert from Gonzalez was very active in local politics in Ascension Parish. He had served as a page in Washington DC for Congressman Jimmy Morrison when he was in high school. When he entered Loyola Law School he was working as a levee inspector for the local Levee Board. That job required him to drive up and down the levee of the Mississippi River when the water got high to look for leaks. This only occurred once every few years during the spring. The rest of the time he just got a paycheck. Louis was very ambitious and his lifetime goal was to become governor. Since my parish of Livingston joined Ascension Parish and we both had political ambitions, we became very close friends. Louis decided to run for the Louisiana State Senate from Livingston, Ascension and St. James Parishes, and he was elected at the same time Edwin Edwards was first elected governor. Louis later ran for and was elected to the State Public Service Commission, and from that office he ran for governor, got in the second primary and then was defeated by Dave Treen.

Tony Guarisco from Morgan city was elected to the Louisiana House of Representatives, and later ran for Congress but was defeated. He, Jud Downs, and I studied for the bar exam in 1966 in the law office of Philip Casio and Alwyn Cronvich, where Tony worked part time. Phillip was elected to the New Orleans City Council, and Alwyn became Sheriff of Jefferson Parish after we finished law school.

In the fall of 1963 John McKeithen, from Columbia Louisiana was on the Long ticket, defeating former New Orleans Mayor Chip Morrison. Morrison had the overwhelming support of the New Orleans political factions but could not overcome the support of the northern part of the state for his opponent. I had been on the side of John McKeithen from the beginning of his race, as had been Pippi Bruneau, one of my classmates who was very conservative and lived in New Orleans. Shortly after graduating from law school, Pippi was elected to the House of Representatives where he served for more than 30 years.

Ben Baggart, another classmate also was elected to the Louisiana Senate and served for many years. Jim Donelon, from Jefferson Parish was the nephew of the parish president and got a job with the parish while he was attending Loyola. He later was hired by Governor Edwards as his Executive Council then served in the legislature. He then was elected Louisiana Commissioner of Insurance for several terms. Other members of my law school class were elected to judgeships across the state.

Chapter 3. Andy Berthelot

Andy Berthelot was about my age, but we didn't really get to know each other until I came home from the Army and he came home from the Marine Corps in the early 1960's. He graduated from Springfield High School and I graduated from Ponchatoula where I had attended since the fourth grade.

His grandfather Milton Anderson had several children. Mr. Milton spoke with a heavy cajun accent he acquired from his parents who lived in the Whitehall area. His wife, Andy's grandmother was a Richardson from Springfield. Their home was on Blood River Road near Lizard Creek right outside Springfield. Andy's mother was still in high school when he was born, his father was a truck driver for Baumer foods in Metairie Louisiana. When his father went in the Army his mother got a job in New Orleans, but there was no way she could work and take care of a small baby, so Mr. Milton and his wife raised Andy.

Mr. Milton and my father were very close friends who often had drinks together in the late afternoon in the bar rooms at Springfield. Mr. Milton had given part of his property to two of his sons, Albert who was married to a schoolteacher named Nell, and Joe who everyone liked and had two boys and a girl about my age. When Andy came home from the service, Mr. Milton decided to give him 6 acres of land adjoining his home and the land he had given to Albert.

When Albert returned home after serving in World War II he was appointed as local service agent for Livingston Parish by the veteran's department to assist veterans in obtaining benefits. He also operated a small grocery store near his home.

He and his wife strongly objected to his father, Mr. Milton's donation of part of the family homestead to Andy, which my father as Notary Public had prepared. Andy, who was working as a plumber and electrician's helper decided to build a small house on his land. He had little money and I helped him build a one bedroom, kitchen and dining room, 16' x 32' shack with a wood-burning heater/stove. We also used shovels to build a short 25-foot-wide dirt driveway from the parish road to the house. His uncle Albert and aunt Nell objected to our building the driveway which crossed some of Mr. Milton's property. Mr. Milton then got my daddy to draw up a right-of-way for Andy to use the road.

Shortly after that we had an election and Julius Foster was elected police juror. Andy and I, who had just registered to vote, went to see Julius and asked him to put some gravel on the driveway. I had helped Julius in the election registering people to vote and bringing them to the polls and he told us he would help Andy. A few days later the parish road grader and a truck loaded with gravel and a culvert arrived and the parish road crew-built Andy a road to his house.

Albert and Nell were furious, and she made a complaint at the police jury office about public funds being used to build Andy's road. The police jury ignored her since all the members helped their constituents all over the rural part of the parish with culverts which improved drainage and gravel for the driveways, which any member of the public could use. Andy and I used his house to entertain our girlfriends. We placed a blue light in the front window that Albert and Nell could see from their house, which we turned on when either one of us arrived. We also played rather loud music when we were entertaining.

In those days anyone who wanted to open a bar room had to place an advertisement in the Denham Springs News, the parish official journal of their intent to apply for an occupational license to sell alcoholic beverages. The police jury then had to vote on the application. When this happened, most of the police jurors, being influenced by preachers, teetotalers, and do-gooders who sat in the Amen corners of the local churches would vote to deny the license. When I began practicing law I filed many lawsuits against the police jury, and obtained judgments ordering it to issue the applicants licenses.

Andy and I decided to pay back his uncle Albert and aunt Nell for messing with him, so I placed a classified advertisement in the Denham Springs News that read as follows "We are applying to the Livingston Parish Police Jury for a permit to sell beer and liquor at the following address: Andy's Go Go Joint, Albert Anderson Rd., Springfield, LA." Of course, Andy had no intention of actually making the application much less turn his home into a bar room, but Albert and Nell didn't know that, and they went ballistic about having a bar next door to their residence.

After the notice was published many people asked Albert if he was planning on opening another bar room in Springfield, which further infuriated he and his wife. After a few weeks' things had cooled down, so we placed another classified ad in the paper which said "Dancers wanted, apply at Andy's Go Go Joint, Albert Anderson Rd., Springfield, LA. An equal opportunity employer."

Nell almost had a stroke, since at that time all public facilities including schools' restaurants and churches were segregated in Livingston Parish, and the new Civil Rights Act was working his way through Congress in Washington DC. Of course, many of her fellow teachers, and Albert's friends, acquaintances and kinsmen were asking them if they had anything to do with bringing black female strippers to a white bar room near their home.

The controversy between Andy and his uncle Albert and aunt Nell continued. Sometime after we had ran the newspaper ad, Albert and some of his friends were rabbit hunting with beagle dogs near Andy's property and he heard Albert driving the dogs. Nell also heard Albert shouting at the dogs but was too far away to determine what he was saying, and thought he was calling for help.

Andy was walking past her house when she ran outside in an old faded see-through nightgown, stopped him and asked him to go rescue Albert. At the time she was in her 60s, a slender old woman who Andy described as having tits that were about as big around as a quarter and about 10 inches long like a zucchini squash, or maybe a milk cow. Andy went to the woods, found Albert was not in trouble, and returned to find Nell. When he told her Albert was okay, she fell to the ground crying "And I had to stop old Andy. "

During this time alligators were on the endangered species list and could not be harvested for their meat and hides. The lack of a market caused a population explosion of the animals in the nearby swamp. Many of Nell's students and former students held grudges against her. Andy told me he saw the carcasses of seven large alligators lying in her front yard one morning with Nell's name painted in red on their white bellies. Of course, Andy got the blame.

Andy also told me about an incident that happened when he was three or four years old while he lived with his grandparents. During

World War II there were bands of Gypsies who traveled through the southern United States and allegedly kidnaped small children and raised them as Gypsies.

While Andy's grandfather was away at work he was alone with his grandmother, when a pair of men dressed as Gypsies with red bandana's approached their house. When Andy's grandmother saw the Gypsies, she grabbed Andy and started inside. When the men followed her, the grandmother's collie dog attacked them and drove them away saving Andy from becoming a gypsy.

I have told Andy on more than one occasion, that they must've put a hex on him, because after five wives, six or seven divorces, at least three times jumping over a broomstick with a girlfriend, and learning numerous trades, while residing in several states, he certainly resembles a gypsy.

Chapter 4. Revenue Job in Law School

In 1963, we had an election for a new Governor and John McKeithen and his running mate, Mayor Ashton Mouton from Lafayette, held a rally in Denham Springs, Louisiana, they were allies of former Governor Earl K. Long. Julius Foster's brother, Carew, had been elected school board member from Springfield, after Julius had been reelected police juror. Julius and Carew had seen to it that while I was in Southeastern taking teacher training courses, that I got hired as a substitute teacher at schools in Maurepas and Springfield on days when a regular teacher was absent. The meeting in Denham Springs was the first time I met John McKeithen and Ashton Mouton. Carew and I went over there and got to shake hands with them. We saw many of the local politicians, candidates for Senator, Representative, Sheriff, Assessor, Clerk of Court, and Police Jury members. All of them coming up for election at the same time. At that meeting instead of standing in line to talk to our candidate for Governor, I spied the man running for Lieutenant Governor who was not quite so busy shaking hands, so I went over and introduced myself, and had a private conversation with him. I told him I was going to do everything I could for him, I told him about registering all those voters and that we would turn them out for him and for Governor McKeithen, but I wanted something from him. He said, "well sure son, what is it?" I said "I'm down at Loyola University in New Orleans and I'm teaching school in the daytime at Kenner Junior High and I'm going to law school at night. If I keep doing it that way it's gonna take me four years to get though law school because I can't take but so many courses at night, but when you get elected, I want you to give me a job. I don't care if I have to work at night, that's fine with me, and I don't care what it is. I can work part time, so I can go to school in the daytime. I can take more courses and I can save myself a years' time in school." He said, "I'll do that." I didn't see him again until after the election. In the first primary he got beat, but he continued to support John McKeithen in the run-off with DeLesseps Morrison, who was the former mayor of New Orleans. I took all of my annual leave and sick leave from my teaching job and came back home to register voters and get out the vote on election day, in the second primary, and John

McKeithen won. When John McKeithen took office, he had a swearing in ceremony on a Wednesday, and it was announced in a newspaper that Ashton Mouton had been appointed the Collector of Revenue and was going to take office the next day. The next morning when they opened the door of the Collector of Revenue's office I was standing in the hall outside dressed in my best suit and tie. When the doors opened, I walked in and approached the secretary sitting at her desk. She was an old woman that had worked there for many years as secretary for the Collector of Revenue no matter who it was. She most certainly had her politics right being for Governor John McKeithen instead of Delesseps Morrison, because she still had her job.

I came up to her desk and told her I needed to see Mr. Mouton. She asked me "son you have an appointment?" I said, "no ma'am I just need to see him for just a few minutes, it won't take but a minute of his time." She said, "Well, if you don't have an appointment, you're not going to be able to see him." I said, "Well I want to talk to him," she said, "you can sit down over there but I don't know what time you'll get to see him or if you'll get to see him." I said, "Well I'll wait." I sat there from seven-thirty in the morning until noon. During that time, there must have been twenty or thirty people that went through that office and were taken on back to Mr. Mouton's office which was connected to hers. I recognized some of them, Senators and Representatives, whose pictures I'd seen in the newspapers. I got a giddy feeling to see all these politicians and famous people. I sat there for that length of time, and finally two or three men came in together, who I recognized as being Legislators who were talking about going to lunch when they went back to the Collector's office. A few minutes later they came back out, and Mr. Mouton came out with them. When he walked out the door of his inter office into the room I was in, I got up and walked over and faced him. I said, "Mr. Mouton I'd like to speak to you just a minute if you've got the time, I've been waiting here all morning." I don't think he really recognized me, but he said, just being the kind of man, he was, "Well come on in here son, let's talk." He made everybody else wait and we stepped back in his office and I reminded him of our meeting at Denham Springs. I'm sure he didn't remember that, but I told him "I'm the one who asked you about a job during that election. I did everything I could do for you and I continued to do everything I could for the Governor. Am I going to be able to get that job, so I can go to school full time and save that year of extra schooling?" He looked at me and he laughed. He said "when do you want to go to work?" This was on Thursday and I said, "tomorrow morning," he said How about Monday?" I said, "That will be great." He wrote down the name of the head of the revenue department in New Orleans. The fellow's name was LeBarre and he told me, "You be down there at eight o'clock Monday morning and you will meet Mr. LeBarre and tell him I said to show you what kind of work you need to do." I said, "yes sir." Then I had to scramble, because I had been living in Kenner where I taught school, but I had given up my apartment because I didn't know if I was going to continue teaching after the spring semester. Loretta and I had just gotten married when she finished college. She was going to go to work in Jefferson Parish as a teacher, so we had to find an apartment. We went down to New Orleans and found an apartment, and got our stuff moved, which wasn't much more than just clothes.

On Monday morning I was at the Revenue Department in New Orleans and found the boss who had been working for the Revenue Department for a long time. He was not for John McKeithen during the election, but had been for Delesseps "Chep" Morrison, the Mayor of New Orleans. Just about everybody else, in that office, also was for Morrison, and here I am a new kid, green behind the ears, in my early twenties and I'm going to work there.

I came straight from Baton Rouge from the "Big Boss." Well, they didn't know anything about me, and they figured I was a spy to come down there to see how they were running things, so I could go back and tell Mr. Mouton what was going on. Well, I did keep my eyes and ears open and if I saw something he needed to know I damn sure let him know it.

First off, they put me at the very bottom. I did everything you can do in a revenue office in those times. I started selling license plates, then they sent me out to collect sales taxes, and that was interesting in itself. The City of New Orleans had its sales tax collectors and the State had theirs. The City of New Orleans required all the businesses in the city to register and purchase occupational licenses and collect city taxes. The

113

State had a separate list of businesses which also had to purchase occupational licenses and collect state sales tax.

Well, one of the brilliant things that the state did to collect more taxes was to make a deal with the City to exchange the lists of the businesses. Real simple, but in the past New Orleans had theirs and the state had theirs and they didn't get along very well and didn't do anything for each other. When I got there, books were printed with the names of all the businesses that were registered with the State and a copy was furnished to the City. In exchange the City gave the State it's list of businesses, showing all the places that were registered. When we compared them, they were hundreds of businesses, anything from snowball stands to bar rooms, to Mom and Pop stores, that were registered with the City but weren't registered with the State. These businesses were collecting sales tax money on goods they were selling but were not paying taxes to the State at all. At the same time there were dozens of places that were registered with the State and weren't paying the City taxes.

A group of employees were assigned to go to these different locations and get these people registered so the State could start collecting the taxes. They put me in that group and two older agents started training me. The first thing they did was show me the big books where I could find the names and addresses of these businesses registered to the City but not the State, and then took me with them to see the taxpayers. We would knock on the door and tell them we were State Revenue Agents and they had to buy an occupational license and pay sales taxes to the State. We had the information from the City on the amount of City sales tax the taxpayer had paid for three years, so it was easy to determine the amount of State tax they collected but hadn't paid.

Well, we had a lot of leeway and we could cut deals. We would tell the taxpayer we would waive the penalty and interest and all they had to do was pay the taxes, and we would even give them time to pay it in installments. If you owed Four Hundred Dollars, you could pay Fifty Dollars a month for whatever time it took to get caught up, but you had to keep on paying regular taxes from here on out. Everybody I talked to that way liked the fact that they were not getting penalized and weren't being put out of business. It worked good for the State because we were

114

able to give them something while we were taking something away from them.

The Revenue Agents in New Orleans that worked for the State, got an expense account and were paid mileage wherever they went, on State business. When they started training me, I got in the car with them and we would start in one part of town and we would go see a taxpayer in another part of town. At the office we would mark our mileage in our log, and then we would drive from there three or four miles to the other side of town and see another taxpayer and mark that millage. When we got through with that one then we would drive three or four miles to another part of town and see another one. The way they showed me, you would see maybe three to four people all day as you went from one place to another and you were running up maybe thirty or forty miles a day. This was great for the expense account, but it wasn't very damn efficient.

After two or three days of that, I told my supervisor "Okay, I know how to do this, now let me go." He told me I was on my own. The first thing that morning, I sat down at the desk where those big books were and got me a map of the City of New Orleans. I'd been down there a year going to school and I knew part of New Orleans, but I didn't know it very well. I went through that list of names and I picked out addresses that were all in the same neighborhood, so instead of crisscrossing all over town I would go in one area, say the uptown area, around St. Charles Avenue to see delinquent taxpayers. I spent all day in that one area and I might visit fifteen businesses. Next day I might go to the French Quarter and spend all day there or maybe two or three days, but I stayed in the same area and I saw more people. The more taxpayers I saw, the more money I was collecting. Within the first month, I collected more money than all the rest of the Agents put together, and I got called in. Old man LeBarre, told me, "you are not doing this right." I said, "What do you mean I'm not doing it right?" "Well look," he said, "you got the other people complaining, other members on the team that you are on." I said "Hell I can do better than that if you give me a percentage of what I collect" but there was no way to do that, it wasn't legal, and I knew I couldn't do it. I said, "I'm just doing my job." He said "Well you gonna have to quit that, go zig zagging across town and it will benefit you because you'll get an expense account. "Well, that didn't sit very well with me, so I kept on doing what I did and that's when they moved me to selling license plates. In September 1964, I was back in school at Loyola and some of the Judges on The Supreme Court would come in and sit in on some of our classes, to pick up new things that the Law Professors were talking about. I got to meet them that way, but I also got to know them because The Supreme Court Office was right next door to the Revenue Office, on Loyola Avenue.

My immediate Supervisor, Albert Rose, was an Attorney for The Department of Revenue with his office in New Orleans. He introduced me to those Supreme Court Judges in their offices next door to his office. If any of the Judges needed a special license plate number, or other assistance, we took care of it.

I made detailed notes of the professor's lectures when I was studying law at Loyola and I would bring them home after class each day and Loretta, who had her typewriter in our apartment, would type them up. The next day I was in class I'd have these notes from the day before all typed up and if I got called on I had the answer where I could read it and it made sense. One of the Supreme court Judges sitting next to me in that class saw the notes that I had, and he asked me "how did you do that?" I told him I just made notes and my wife typed them and offered him a copy. He said he'd love to have copies of them. I said well I think I can handle that, I work for the Department of Revenue and they have a copy machine, which was a brand-new thing in those days. That afternoon when I arrived at the office there was not much going on, so I make my copies and I got to doing it every day.

Somebody made a complaint, and old man LeBarre called me in. By this time, I had been working for The Revenue Department for close to a year. He told me that I couldn't use that copy machine, it was costing the state 1 quarter cent a page, I was wasting money, and I couldn't do it anymore. I told him very nicely that the only reason I made the copy was for the judges over there at the Supreme Court. He said, "Well I don't care you can't make any more copies." I said "Okay, I'm going to take a day's leave tomorrow." "What's going on?" he asked. I said, "I'm going to Baton Rouge." He said, "What are you going to Baton Rouge for?" I said, "I'm going to see the Collector." Well, he knew that

116

got that job the day after our Collector got sworn-in, but he didn't know how close I was to Mr. Mouton. He got scared, and told me, if I was going up there to Baton Rouge to see the Collector. I could take a sack of mail to Baton Rouge and bring another back and get paid for my time and put the mileage on my expense account. I said, "Well that's fine, thank you."

Before I went up to Baton Rouge, I called ahead of time and got an appointment with Mr. Mouton, and when I got there he was tickled to death to see me. We visited awhile, and he wanted to know what was going on and I told him about how I made the tax collection's without running all over town and he agreed with me, that was the way to do it instead of having people wasting all the time and money on unnecessary mileage. I also told him about making the copies for the judges, and Mr. LeBarre order for me to stop. He got on the phone and he called LeBarre right then and I heard him say "if you want to keep your job you leave that boy alone, he can make any damn copies he wants and anything else he wants. I don't want to hear anything different from you." I had never seen anybody do that before, but he popped that whip and when I got back to New Orleans it was like I was in a new place. Nobody messed with me at all, and it all came back to politics. After I got out of law school, I made it my business to keep up with the politics on everything. When my son was born in 1966 I named him Ashton.

Chapter 5. Harold Picou

I first met Harold Picou after I returned home from the Army. I was living in Springfield and attending Southeastern Louisiana College and working with my daddy developing subdivisions and a trailer park and building houses.

Harold just returned from serving in the United States Marine Corps to his hometown of Maurepas. Harold was the second youngest of five brothers and one sister. He took up boxing during his military service and was known for his fights in local barrooms. Maurepas, like Springfield, was a rural community mainly populated by strawberry farmers, trappers and construction workers. Harold's father made his living growing flowers. He was the only person in the area to supply flowers for people who put them on graves for All Saints Day. Harold and his whole family spoke with a French accent.

After he came home from the service, he became a construction worker and later specialized in laying carpets and installing flooring for new and renovated houses. Harold married and had several children, later he separated from his wife who divorced him. Harold's wife lived in Ascension Parish and had a cousin who had lost his arm, then went to law school and became an attorney. His nickname was "Nubb" Kling. Nubb spent many years trying to make Harold pay child support but was mainly unsuccessful because Harold moved from Livingston to Tangipahoa parishes to elude being arrested for non-support.

I would see Harold in various barrooms during our younger days and we got to be good friends. Later on, while I was in law school, Harold started dating Mickey Kinchen, the daughter of Mr. Leonard Kinchen, who was a wealthy landowner and logger from Tangipahoa Parish.

The town of Springfield which had been incorporated in 1832 had ceased to exist as a registered municipality around 1900. In the late 1950s the grandson of the last mayor, Harold Abels, was instrumental in reviving the town charter and was appointed mayor by Governor Earl Long. Mayor Abels was in his early 20s and his brother-in-law Calvin Fayard Sr. was elected Marshall. The town had very little money, but it acquired an old Nash automobile, whose top sped was about 60-70 mph, to use as a police car. Calvin ran a Gulf service station and visited Charlie Schenk's bar every afternoon. He didn't believe in writing tickets and putting people in jail for speeding and if he did write a ticket to anybody who was local he would take it to his brother-in-law the mayor the next day and tell him to fix it.

The local board of Alderman and mayor decided the town needed some revenue, and the best way to get some was to start having tickets written and collected from out of town motorists. Marshall Fayard didn't write many tickets while he was sitting at that barroom, so the mayor and aldermen decided to hire a private detective agency from Tangipahoa Parish to work weekends and catch speeders, so the town could make some money. The private detectives were made special deputy policeman and given the old Nash car to use to chase speeders. The old car wouldn't run more than 70 miles per hour, but that was enough to stop most violators of the 35 mile-per-hour speed zone in town.

The second weekend after the new policemen went to work, along came Harold Picou and his girlfriend Mickey. It was about 2:30 p.m. on a Sunday afternoon and Harold was driving about 45 miles per hour through town in the 35-mph speed zone. They were observed by the police who turned on the siren and gave chase. Harold had been drinking beer since about 8:00 a.m., as he usually did on Sundays, and saw no reason to stop for an old worn out car operated (he thought) by old Marshall Fayard. Harold's old car wouldn't run much more than 70 miles per hour, as they speeded on down the road towards his home in Maurepas. The chase continued for several miles past the Springfield city limits. Finally, the frustrated young policeman started shooting at Harold's car and luckily no one was hit. At this juncture Harold stopped, got out the car and went to the policemen and knocked the hell out of one of them. The policemen called for assistance and Harold was soon handcuffed together with his girlfriend Mickey and taken to jail. A call to Mickey's father Mr. Leonard quickly resulted in their release on bond.

This occurred in the mid-1960s after the assassination of President Kennedy in 1963 and the resulting investigation by District Attorney Jim Garrison from New Orleans, who attempted to convict a businessman named Clay Shaw of conspiracy to murder the president. Mr. Shaw hired

119

a defense attorney from New Orleans named James Diamond who won an acquittal for his client and made newspaper and television headlines around the world.

Mr. Leonard was furious that these part-time police officers had shot at his daughter and her boyfriend, but he correctly realized that no local attorney would file suit against a town that had no money and had a strong case. He therefore made an appointment to see Mr. Diamond at his office in New Orleans. Mr. Leonard always wore a ring with a large diamond on it, overalls, an old black hat, and always looked like he needed a shave. When he and Harold arrived at the lawyer's office before entering Mr. Leonard turned his ring around, so the diamond didn't show. He told Harold to explain what had happened and that Harold wanted to sue the Town of Springfield for he and his girlfriend.

Mr. Diamond agreed to represent Harold and Mickey for a 50% contingency fee but told Harold he would have to put up $500 to start with and possibly more money later. Harold borrowed the $500 from Mr. Leonard and the suit was filed. When they left the law office Mr. Leonard told Harold that he had saved Harold $1500 by turning his diamond ring around, so the lawyer would think he was just a broke old man. The next couple of years Harold would tell all his friends and acquaintances how he was going to get rich collecting money from the town of Springfield.

Springfield's attorney that time was young lawyer named Tom Matheny from Hammond. He filed pleadings and had the case put off for several years. When I finished law school, I became the town attorney. Harold and I were good friends and I had represented him on several cases including keeping him out of jail for non-support. I told him that Springfield had no insurance to pay him and Mickey for false arrest, he was damn lucky that nobody got hurt, and the case needed to be dismissed. Mr. Leonard agreed, and attorney Diamond, who had already got paid certainly didn't want to pursue a loser. So, I obtained a dismissal for my client.

Not long after that Harold, who was working as a carpet installer in Baton Rouge, was on his way to work when he came into a construction zone where someone had removed the barricade. He crashed into an open pit where new construction of a sewer line was located. I heard

120

about the accident a few days later and was certain he would come see me to handle his case.

Mr. Leonard Kinchen also heard about the accident and mentioned it to Jimmy Morrison, his good friend who had just got beat for re-election to Congress. Jimmy had not tried a case in court in 20 years, but he knew a high-powered lawyer in Baton Rouge and got Mr. Leonard to bring Harold to sign up with Jimmy who immediately referred the case to the guy in Baton Rouge, so Jimmy could get a fee. I was aggravated because I didn't get the case, but I learned some useful tactics that helped me in the future.

When the defense took Harold's deposition, Harold's lawyer told him beforehand to testify that he could no longer use his knees to stretch carpet. Before the accident when stretching carpet, Harold used a special tool that gripped the carpet and Harold would get on his hands and knees and kick with his knee causing the carpet to become tight.

Harold had been hospitalized after the accident and had a knee operation. His doctor testified that it would not be unreasonable for Harold to experience extreme pain if he continued in his occupation and the case was settled for more than $100,000 which was a huge sum in those days.

Harold's lawyer charged him about 50% plus expenses plus loans advanced over the two-year time he was out of work and Harold wound up with about $35,000. After a new car and some high living including running a bar room where he provided lots of free food and too many unpaid bar tabs for his friends, Harold was busted. So, despite his painful knees Harold went back to laying carpets for the next 40 years.

Harold loved to eat crawfish and entered crawfish eating contests each year which were held in various South Louisiana locations and soon won the championship for the number of pounds of boiled crawfish he could consume in a short period of time. He held the title of world champion for several years.

After my father died in 1968 I remodeled his house to include an office and waiting room for my law practice. I hired Harold to do the carpet work. He ran a one-man business and would bring carpet samples to his customers, so they could pick out what they wanted. He would then calculate the price of the job and have his customer pay him at least enough to pay for the carpet which he purchased in New Orleans. He would always tell his customer the carpet would cost more than he would actually pay for it and then he would collect the rest of his money when he completed the job.

Many times, when Harold collected the money to go purchase the carpet he would spend it before he went to New Orleans, and the supplier of the carpet would not give Harold any credit. When this happened Harold would have to hustle up another job to get paid enough to pay for the first order.

In the early 1970s I built a hunting camp near Woodville Mississippi and hired Harold to help with the construction and do all the floors. At this time, I had an employee named Willie Hughes who worked for me as an investigator, handyman, and bodyguard on occasion. Willie, a black man, whose nickname was Slim, was about 6'6" tall and weighed about 250 pounds which was almost all muscle. He had very little formal education but was very intelligent and absolutely loyal to me.

When I got ready to order the carpet for the floors of my camp, Harold told me the cost would be about $120, but it might be more, so I should give him $150 so he could go to New Orleans and get the carpet. I knew the carpet would really cost no more than $100 and he was going to pocket the extra $50, so I told Harold that I was going to send Slim with him to get the carpet. He told me that he didn't need no Negro to help and I should just give him the cash. I told him that if he wanted to do the job Slim was going with him. He reluctantly agreed, and I gave Slim the $150 for the carpet. Harold was furious, but he knew that this was the only way he was going to get the job.

When they got to New Orleans Harold told Slim to give him the money. Slim refused, insisting that I had instructed him to pay only the supplier. When they went inside the building to get the carpet Harold tried to talk to the salesman by himself, but Slim would have nothing of that. He would not let Harold get out of his sight and heard all discussions with the salesman. When the purchase was made Slim paid the man $95. When they got back with the carpet Slim made it a point to count the change in front of Harold and give it to me. For the rest of the day Harold was muttering under his breath about the smart-ass helper of mine.

Harold's second wife was in her early 20s and he was at least 10 years older than her when they married. He was working steady and she insisted on saving money to buy a house. Harold had judgments against him for failing to pay child support and for failing to complete some jobs that he had been paid for. Harold figured that the best way to beat the judgments was for them to put the house in his wife's name, and he did this without talking to me beforehand.

Harold built that house with the help of some of his friends and his brothers and soon had it paid for, when his wife unexpectedly died. Her brothers and sisters who didn't like Harold opened her succession and took the house away from him.

His first wife's cousin, attorney, Nubb Kling. garnisheed Harold's wages for the past child support so he quit his job and went to Dulac, Louisiana where his brother Irvin lived, and got him a job on a shrimp boat where he was paid cash.

Harold came home to visit his family, ran in to me at a local bar, and told me where he was working. This was in late August and Harold told me about seeing hundreds of teal ducks in the marsh. There was a special teal season set in September and I asked him if he would set up a hunt for me and a doctor friend of mine named Herb Plauche`. He agreed, and we traveled to Dulac when the season opened.

I had never hunted in that area before and brought my bass boat with me. Harold made arrangements for us to borrow a pirogue to hunt out of. We pulled the small boat behind the bass boat down a bayou to a shallow pond then got into small boat and push poled across the pond to a clump of cane. When daylight came we shot a couple of ducks and sometime later decided to return to the Bayou.

When we started to push our boat back across the shallow pond we discovered the tide had gone out and we were stuck in the mud. We only had one push pole and we couldn't get anywhere. I finally got out of the boat and went to my waist in the mud. With the help of Herb using the push pole and me pushing the boat we finally managed to get back to the Bayou where I jumped into the water to wash the mud off.

After we returned to the camp we hooked up a small shrimp trawl to my bass boat and along with Harold tried to catch some shrimp. We found no shrimp, but we caught a small cooler full of squid and made a meal of them when we got back to camp. For years after that anytime Harold came to my camp he would talk about the time we caught what he called "squibs".

Chapter 6. Bilbo and Moochie

In the 1950s and continuing for 20 some years thereafter, the southeastern part of Louisiana where I live consisted of Piney Woods country and Cypress Tupelo swamps. My uncles raised cattle, which ranged free in the company owned woods. Many other residents also owned free ranging cattle and hogs. There were no stock laws to prohibit the animals from free range, and it was up to other residents to fence them out rather than the owners to fence them in.

At that time most of the state roads were gravel, and 95% of the parish roads were gravel or dirt. In the summertime the cattle were attacked by flies and mosquitoes, and the owners often built fires with green trees and bushes to make smoke to protect the animals from the insects. Often, herds of cattle would gather in the smoke at night seeking relief from the insects. During periods of dry weather cattle would bunch up along gravel roads in certain areas at night, seeking relief from the insects in the dust caused by passing automobiles.

As a teenager I would accompany my cousins from Springfield to Bear Island, Maurepas, and Head of Island to dances held at bar rooms where beer and whiskey could be purchased without the requirement of proof of our age. We would travel the gravel roads at high rates of speed, knowing exactly where the herds of cattle would be gathered to avoid mosquitoes in the dust. We might be traveling 45 to 60 mph on the straight stretches, but we knew to slam on the brakes and slow down to 20 or 25 mile-per-hour when we approached the herds of cattle.

When I started practicing law in 1966 I was hired by two cousins from Centerville whose relatives owned cattle that were free range. Moochie and Bilbo Efferson worked with cattle, and also worked on construction jobs, and in the woods as teenagers and as young men.

Moochie was about 6 feet two inches tall and weighed about 240 pounds, Bilbo was much shorter and not quite so heavyset. Both of them loved to hunt wild turkeys and went to the southwestern part of Mississippi every spring for their turkey hunts. They would take a tarpaulin, tie a rope between two trees, and make a tent for shelter, sleeping on the ground. They hunted along with other Livingston Parish men in the national forests and also trespassed on private property of the

125

native citizens on a daily basis. While they were turkey hunting, if they came across some hound dogs they would quickly steal them and bring them back to Louisiana.

My first dealings with Moochie was shortly after he broke the middle finger of his right hand while working on a job in Baton Rouge. He did not immediately go to the doctor and the finger healed with an upward curve. I saw him in a store and watched him try to put his hand in his pants pocket, but the middle finger stuck outside the pocket instead of going in the pocket with the rest of his fingers. I asked him what was wrong with his finger, and he told me about getting it hurt on his construction job. I told him I could get him Worker's compensation benefits and make the insurance company pay the doctors' bills to fix his hand. This was just before turkey season opened and he asked me if I could get him the compensation, so he could get paid while he was hunting.

In those days if you got hurt on the job there was a schedule of payment based on the injury and any disability. Attorney's fees were set at 20% of the weekly benefits. I took Moochie's case, sent him to the doctor, who re-broke his finger and put a cast on it so he could put his hand in his pants pocket again and made the Worker's Compensation insurance company start to pay him, Moochie drew his weekly check of about $40 less my eight dollar fee all through turkey season.

A few weeks later, Moochie and Bilbo were arrested for cattle rustling. Livingston Parish, at that time, had a local chapter of the Louisiana Cattlemen's Association which had lobbied the legislature to pass a bill which made cattle rustling a felony, the penalty of which was mandatory jail time without probation.

The president of the Livingston Parish Cattlemen's Association, Kelly Howze, checked on all arrests for cattle rustling in the parish, and when he heard of Bilbo and Moochie's arrest, he went to the sheriff and district attorney and insisted that they be sent to the penitentiary in Angola.

When Moochie and Bilbo got out of jail on bond, they came to me to represent them. I found out that they had driven a car along a gravel road to the place where the cattle were trying to stay in the dust to avoid the mosquitoes. When they arrived, Bilbo would take a rope and sit on

126

the front fender of the car and Moochie would slowly drive the car among the cattle, so Bilbo could slip a noose around the neck of a young calf and catch it.

After they caught three or four, they would take them to the auction in Kentwood, Louisiana, and leave them for sale in a fictitious name, and later go back to pick up the check. This went on many times, until one night they took some caves that belonged to some of their neighbors, and one of them happened to be at the auction the next day and recognized his cattle that were being sold.

There was no way that I could get them out of the trap they were in, but I did persuade the judge to sentence them to the minimum amount of time, and both went to Angola where Moochie was made an inmate guard. In the meantime, the workers comp insurance company continued to pay for Moochie's injury, but he had the checks sent to my office rather than to the prison.

Chapter 7. My First Criminal Case

In the spring of 1967, I showed up one Monday morning at the courthouse and I ran into "Uncle" Dillard Stewart. He was a deputy for Sheriff Taft Faust and he had been there 20 years. He and my daddy were good friends, and I knew his boys, who were my friends. "Uncle Did" told me, "Boy, I got a fellow here that needs a lawyer, and he's got some money in his pocket." Now that was the kind of words I loved to hear. So, I met the fellow right there at the courthouse, and we struck a deal. I was going to charge him $500, and he gave me $400 right then. I figured I had it made because I was hired that morning. I said, "So, when are you going to court?" He says, "I'm supposed to be in trial today." Well, I looked at "Uncle Did" and says, "There ain't no way I can be ready to try this case, be hired this morning and pick a jury today." He said, "Don't worry about that, boy. You just go ahead and go up there and tell that judge you just got hired and he'll put it off for you and you can get some time to get ready for it." Well, being green as grass, I think I had been out of law school maybe six months, I figured that was good advice. So, I walked in the courtroom and announced to Judge Comish and Erlo Durbin, the DA, that I was going to represent Mr. Stafford who's charged with theft. And he was supposed to be tried today and I needed a continuance because I wasn't ready to try the case. I just got hired. Well, being green as grass, I didn't know that I had a big stick, if I would use it, because I quickly learned after that when the judge tried to make me try a case quick, all I had to do was get up there and put on the record that I am not prepared and that stopped the trial right there. But, I didn't know it that day, and I asked for that continuance and Judge Comish says, "Well, certainly boy. It's 10 o'clock this morning. We're going to continue it to 1 o'clock this afternoon and we'll start picking that jury." I didn't even know how many challenges I had on a six-man jury and had to go quick and look up a book to find out how many I had, which was six. I looked at the jury list, and in those days, it seemed like many, many people were called on the juries over and over again, so I recognized some names on there, and I quickly issued subpoenas to some witnesses to have them in court the next day, and naturally, the sheriff's department, consisting of about four or five deputies, found it impossible to find any of my witnesses even though one was in jail. The case was about a scheme set up by Jessie Reed Martin and at least one other fellow, and allegedly my client, Stafford. Well, they had a young lady whose name was Betty Bob, and they got Miss Betty Bob to go over to some of the bar rooms in Baton Rouge and Port Allen by the Old Mississippi River Bridge, and look pretty, and smile, and dance, and pick up men. The requirements she had were to make damn sure they had a wedding band on, were reasonably well dressed and had some money. Well, after the dancing and the smiling, and the conversation, she was easily persuaded to take a ride with the mark who had picked her up. And, if he suggested maybe going to a motel, she would say, "Well, no. We'll go over to my trailer which is right across the line over in Livingston Parish and you can save the money for the motel". So, she and the mark would ride to Livingston Parish. Unbeknownst to the mark, Jessie Reed and one of the other guys were watching them leave and followed them, parked down the road, and watched the mark and Betty Bob go into the trailer. They gave them just about enough time to get partially disrobed, or maybe entirely disrobed. Betty Bob was pretty good at getting the fellow's clothes off him pretty quick, while she wasn't completely undressed. And, at that time, the door would bust open, and Jessie Reed and one of the other guys would come in and tell the astonished mark that one of them was Betty Bob's husband and they were going to kill him or just maybe beat him half to death for fooling around with the wife. But, if he had some money, they might relent, and let him out with his scalp. And usually, he had some money, which they quickly relieved him of, and sent him on his way. It was a scheme that was almost foolproof in those days because the mark, being married, didn't want to file charges or be involved in an investigation because then his wife would have found out that he was fooling around with other women. So, many of the times that this happened, there was no report. However, after a period of time, and many pickups by Betty Bob, three different men from parishes other than Livingston decided that they were going to ask the sheriff for an investigation and make charges against Betty Bob and her accomplices. Jessie Reed was the first to be arrested and having been a resident of Angola before, he figured the best thing for him to do was cut the best deal he could cut, and he, without

129

having a lawyer, managed to get his sentence reduced from five years to eighteen months, and he was in the jail in Livingston waiting to be sent to Angola when this trial came up.

I first found out about the scheme as Erlo made his opening statement and I found out about Jessie Reed's involvement after the trial, because the sheriff's office couldn't find Jessie Reed to have him there as a witness for my client. I made the best effort I could. I argued that my client was not one of the ones who did the robbing. Betty Bob was not at the courthouse, nor was Jessie Reed Martin, and one of the marks could not clearly identify my client as being one of the conspirators, but another was certain it was him. So, it came down to a dispute over which one was telling the truth, and which one was lying. Well, with me having no time to research, and no time to get witnesses, and no time to really scientifically pick the jury, the jury came in with a guilty verdict. Judge Comish set the sentencing and Erlo set the next trial at the same time, in about sixty (60) days, for the second victim of the scheme. Then Erlo told me when he got through convicting my client the second time, they would try him the third time, so the best thing I could do was just go ahead and plead him guilty to the other two charges, and he would get five years in the penitentiary, instead of fifteen. My client was adamant about the fact that he was innocent. He told me he did not do this, and he was not guilty of the charges against him. This time, I had 60 days to get myself ready. I immediately went to the Clerk of Court's office, found out who was on the jury list for the next trial coming up in 60 days, and made certain I knew the background on every potential juror who was to be called, among which was a client of mine, B. G. Sartwell, Jr., who Erlo had tried for DWI, and I had managed to get the charges reduced down to a reckless operation charge. B. G. wasn't happy about that, because he considered himself entrapped when he was stopped by the police and he certainly didn't have any likings for Erlo Durbin. When we came back to court for the second trial, I knew in advance that they were going to use the same witnesses, use the same tactics, the same arguments that they had used in the first trial, and I was loaded for bear. Mainly though, I picked the jury, and on that jury, I had B. G., who wound up to be the foreman of the jury. Erlo had forgot that he had convicted him of the driving offense and accepted him, as well as two or

130

three ringers, men who had little respect for the law, or the deputies, or the sheriff, or Erlo, or the judge, and a few people who had convinced me from their answers to my questions that they would have an open mind and give my client the benefit of the doubt. The second trial began with Erlo opening, using the same statement, and me, better prepared, making a little more sense about my client's innocence and this time I had my witness. After Erlo had put on his case, I called Jessie Reed Martin, who was in jail and was my number one defense witness, and asked Jessie Reed about his part in the scheme. He readily admitted, since he had already plead guilty and was serving time for it, that he had engineered the scheme, recruited Betty Bob, and recruited another man who he only referred to as "Bill," but he absolutely denied that Mr. Stafford had anything to do with it whatsoever. Jessie Reed said he was present when the robberies took place, and Mr. Stafford was not there. Erlo got his chance to ask him, under cross-examination, a few questions, which were: "Your name is Jessie Reed Martin?" "Yes." "You are a convicted thief?" "Yes". "You are in Angola serving time for robbing these people?" "Yes." "You have been convicted before for thieving and robbery?" "Yes, sir." "Well, why should this jury believe you, as a convicted thief, in this case, Jessie Reed?" "I might be a thief, but I ain't no liar." The jury all just got a big laugh out of that deal. The next witness I called was Betty Bob, who was not there. I made a big issue of the fact that I had subpoenaed her to be there, and the State had not. I knew when I issued that subpoena that she was not going to be found and was not going to show up, and she certainly didn't show up. This time, however, I had issued that subpoena at least a month before the trial, and I lambasted the sheriff's office from one end to the other about not finding my witnesses and trying to put an innocent man in jail. I said the sheriff's office didn't want to go find Betty Bob and bring her in there, so she could testify, and I said the DA's office didn't try to get Betty Bob in there to testify. Well, their case suddenly fell apart, and the jury came in six to nothing, not guilty. I saw something then that I had never heard of happening before, and in the last fifty years, have not seen it happen again. Erlo turned red as three beets and stomped out of the courtroom. Ole Judge Comish was so mad, he got up and he told that jury, "You all are a disgrace to Livingston Parish to let this outlaw go

131

when you know he's guilty, he was guilty, and he should be put in the penitentiary." The jury, of course, didn't have anything to say to the judge, and I certainly kept my mouth shut.

Chapter 8. Brent Dufreche

When I first got to be a lawyer, I went to the court house with my daddy and visited Alsay Addison, who was the Clerk of Court. Alsay had only one arm, and he was a very pleasant fellow who ran a very efficient clerk's office. He and my daddy were good friends. My daddy did a lot of abstracting of land records, and bought and sold timber, timber land, and lots, and he taught me how to abstract at the court house. When I got my law degree and went to see Alsay with my daddy, he presented me with a key to his office where the conveyance and mortgage books were kept. That allowed me to go out there at night or early in the morning to do my abstracting before court started, on whatever case I was working on. No matter how early I got there, five o'clock in the morning to six o'clock in the morning, I almost always ran into Brent Dufreche. Brent was an older lawyer from Ponchatoula, and he also had a key to Alsay's office. Not many lawyers had those keys, just a few selected local lawyers, and some of the local lawyers who weren't selected according to Alsay's standards couldn't get in there, unless a clerk's employee was there to make sure they were watched. Brent was very trustworthy as I was in Alsay's eyes, and he did much of his research for his primary business, which was real estate and business transactions early every morning, then he would go back and open his law office around 8 o'clock or 9 o'clock, and either go to court or make his appointments at his office. The thing I remember about Brent, who was a very good friend of mine and later got to be a judge, in those days was the fact that almost every morning that I showed up at the court house to do that early morning research, one of the employees who worked for Alsay, a very attractive young lady, was frequently at the court house when Brent was there. I never saw anything improper about the coincidence that they were often at the court house for a couple hours early in the morning, when no other employees or anyone one else was there, but there was speculation of a dalliance that I suspect occurred.

Brent later was appointed a special prosecutor in the city court in Hammond where Judge Leon Ford was the judge. Leon was a good man. I've often said that Leon's, only problem was that he had never got drunk, he had never got in a fight, he had never chased other women, and he didn't understand people who did.

Brent was a man of the people, he was one who would say what he meant, he would speak his mind, and he'd tell it like it was. In court, when he was the prosecutor, he would ask very embarrassing questions to defendants and prosecution witnesses alike. In that city court misdemeanor atmosphere, people were charged with fighting, getting drunk, and petty theft, as well of having civil disputes over of a limited amount of money. When I started to practice law, every time I got a chance I would go to the city court in Hammond and watch Brent put on a show before Judge Leon Ford with the prosecution of people, often black people, who had been in fights or had disputes with one another and were arrested by the police. A typical cross examination of a witness by Brent Dufreche would be something like this:

"All right, you charged your boyfriend with assault and battery, and he charged you with assault and battery so that means y'all got in a fight?"

Answer "Yes sir, see he beat me up."

"Ok, what did you do to him?"

"I didn't do nothing."

"Ok, what'd you say to him?"

"I said to him not to be going around with Sally Brown."

"Ok, and was he going around with Sally Brown?"

"Yeah that mf was going around with Sally Brown."

Judge Ford would roll back his chair, and he'd cough like he disapproved of this kind of talk and this kind of questioning, but he wouldn't say anything, and Brent would say,

"What exactly did he say?"

"Well, he called me an mf."

"What does mf mean?"

The witness would just be trembling and wiggling and trying to keep from saying the terrible words. Judge Ford would just scowl down his nose at the witness and at Brent, and the witness wouldn't want to talk, and Brent would say "Judge order the witness to answer the question."

And Leon didn't really want that show in front of that whole crowd that he was backing Brent's line of questioning, but there wasn't anything he could do about it, and he'd gruffly say, "Answer the question."

And the witness would say "He called me a mother fucker."

Brent would come back

"And what did you call him?"

She'd say, "I called him a sob."

"What is a sob?"

"Well you know, sob."

"Judge ask the witness to answer the question."

"The witness will answer the question."

"Well, I called him a son of a bitch."

"And what did you do?"

"That's when I knocked the hell out of him."

The crowd in the court room would be roaring with laughter. This didn't happen just every once and a while, it happened just about every day Brent had court in the city court of Hammond with Judge Ford as the judge. And it continued until Judge Ford ran for and was elected to the District Court and Brent ran for and was elected Judge for the City Court Judge in Hammond. Brent ran a tighter ship than Leon did because when he was judge, the assistant district attorneys didn't use Brent's tactics to liven up the court room. And Brent wouldn't interject from the bench the orders to answer questions exactly like he had tricked Judge Ford into making the witnesses answer. After serving as City Court Judge for a couple of terms Brent Dufreche then ran for the District Court and was elected. After he had been elected to that position, he told me that he had made a terrible mistake. You see a City Court Judge can actually practice law, not in the city court, but in the District Court. And can handle any kind of case other than criminal cases. This allowed Brent to continue his real estate and business practice while drawing his salary as a judge and having the duty and powers of a judge. Once he got elected to the District Court he could no longer practice law and his income was cut considerably. He told me after that he had the best job in the world to start with and gave it up misguidedly to be a district judge.

Chapter 9. Bobby Moore

The first time I heard anything about Bobby Moore was when I was in junior high school in Ponchatoula. Bobby was about my age but a year behind me in school. One of my best friends was Jerry Mitchell, and Jerry was a nonviolent type of kid, just kind of average, he played football and he was pretty doggone intelligent. Somehow or another he and Bobby got crossways. Bobby actually stabbed Jerry, with a Case knife, but luckily it wasn't life-threatening. They had to take Jerry to the hospital and sew him up, but it was only just one stab wound, and was not terribly bad. Bobby got suspended from school and that was the talk among the kids for a few weeks. It wasn't too much longer after that Bobby dropped out of school. He was in the 9th or 10th grade.

I never saw him again for at least 10 years. I heard about him a little bit. He had gone to work as a carpenter's apprentice and became a member of the carpenters' union. This was real real hard to do, because it was a closed shop where you had to be related to somebody or have a lot of stroke with the union officers to be able to get into that program. Bobby was very intelligent. He wasn't too good at reading or writing, but he was an excellent carpenter and a really tough kid. He got into lots and lots of fights, and by getting in the fights he got in trouble with the law. On a lot of occasions, he spent a little time in the local jails but his daddy, who was a school bus driver, had lots of friends and managed to keep him from doing any hard time. Bobby loved to deer hunt and he discovered hunting in North Louisiana a little bit before I did.

There was a wildlife refuge in Tensas Parish where people could hunt on public land. Bobby and a group of Livingston and Tangipahoa Parish hunters would take their tents and camping gear and go up to there, camp out in the National Forest and hunt deer with dogs. If a deer came by them, they killed it, regardless if it was legal or not.

When Bobby was about 21 or 22 years old he went on a hunt with a bunch of his friends. An unfortunate bear managed to come running through the woods in front of the dogs and Bobby killed it. He didn't have to kill the bear, and it was a protected species. Bear hunting was absolutely against the law in Louisiana, but that didn't bother Bobby any. To compound his problem after he killed the doggone thing, he decided he was gonna bring it home. He had it in the back of his pickup truck where he could show it off as they were coming back from Tensas Parish. Somebody saw it, called the game wardens, and Bobby got arrested. In the normal course of things, Bobby would've probably spent no more than 30 days in jail and pay a fine of a few hundred dollars, but it didn't work that way.

This was Tensas Parish, 200 miles from Pumpkin Center, Louisiana where Bobby lived, where his friends were, and were his daddy's friends were that could protect him. The Judge and the people in Tensas Parish didn't have any love for the outlaws from Livingston and Tangipahoa Parish, who would come up, invade their hunting paradise and kill their game. Bobby was arraigned in court in Tensas Parish and thought he was going to be out of jail shortly, but an old judge up there gave him a one-way ticket to Angola.

Angola at that time was one of the worst prisons in the United States. Bobby's daddy had some connections there and Bobby had it not quite as bad as everybody else, but it was bad. Bobby told me later the only good people at Angola were the guards, and the free people, everybody else was bad. Of course, Bobby was a strong tough fighter and not too many people wanted to mess with him. His first job was in the mess hall where he worked as an assistant to the cooks. His main job was washing pots, pans, and steel trays that the prisoners ate from, and serving the prisoners their meals. The job was much better than working in the fields. While he had to get up at 2:30 or 3 o'clock in the morning to prepare the food for breakfast, after the food was served and all the pots and pans and everything was cleaned up, he had the opportunity to go back over to the bunkhouse and get an hour or so of sleep.

He told me he made the mistake of not remembering everything. One day when he was on the line serving, one of the inmates told Bobby to give him another scoop of food. Bobby told him "just get your ass on down the line and shut up" and refused to give him the extra spoon of food. Later the next day Bobby had his daily siesta and was laying in his bunk on his back with his arms across his face. He said he didn't hear anything, and suddenly felt a terrible blow to his face. The prisoner who he had refused to feed had created a weapon which consisted of two metal locks in a sock. He slipped up behind Bobby as he was asleep and

137

hit him in the face with those locks cutting him severely. Somehow, Bobby did not lose consciousness and managed to get up and defend himself, but he was groggy, and the other prisoner ran and got away. When the guards found Bobby and asked him what happened, he said "well I fell down and bumped my face." The code of the prison, at Angola was never tell anything on anybody. When Bobby's family found out about what happened, they pulled some strings and had Bobby moved out of the area for his own protection.

Bobby was sent to an area in Angola where they trained the dogs to chase escapees. This fit Bobby to a T, because during the time before he went to prison he, owned and trained packs of Walker hounds, a breed of hunting dogs to chase deer. In Angola the dogs were bloodhounds which were trained to hunt men. He told me how they would take certain items of his clothes, such as socks or underwear, and let the dogs smell them to get his scent, Bobby would then leave 30 to 40 minutes ahead of the dogs and run for 2 or 3 miles through the woods on the prison grounds. The dogs would then be turned loose to chase him. He told me about how he crossed creeks on logs and waded in the creeks to try to throw the dogs off his scent. When the dogs found him, they would be given treats as a reward. He served approximately six or eight months in that capacity. The warden and the guards liked what he was doing because the dogs were well-trained. When a real escape happened, Bobby was with a group of guards chasing the men who escaped and controlled the dogs when they caught the escapee. After being released from Angola, Bobby came home and began to work again as a carpenter. He also got into the used car business. About that time, I finished law school and saw Bobby for the first time in many years when he and Frank Brent McCarroll came to my little cubbyhole Law office one Saturday morning. He wanted me to notarize a bill of sale on a vehicle that they got from somewhere and were going to sell to somebody. Neither the seller nor the buyer was there but they wanted me to notarize signatures of the so-called seller and the so-called buyer. I told them that there no way in hell I would do something like that, and they left my office pretty indignant. I hadn't had any dealings with Bobby, but I knew Frank Brent McCarroll's family. I knew Frank Brent's daddy and his brothers, and they were a rough bunch. Frank Brent and Bobby later brought one of their friends down to see me who'd been in an automobile accident. I readily took his case and was successful in getting the injured man a good settlement.

Bobby and Frank Brent were two of the roughest characters in our area. They went from barroom to barroom and would fight anybody that messed with them and some who didn't. They would take off and go hunting at the drop of a hat. They would go to any location that they thought that they might be able to kill a hog or kill a deer and they didn't care a whole lot about the laws they broke while doing it.

Lots of my clients visited the same barrooms in the area that I visited while I was in high school and later in college, so it kind of became natural for me to be in some of those same bars and honky-tonks Bobby and Frank Brent frequented. I got along real good with them and they made damn sure nobody messed with me because I was their lawyer and I could help them if they got in trouble. They would also help me by sending me clients where I could make some money.

I loved to hunt, and I located a place in Concordia Parish that was state owned land where we could hunt without having to pay to lease it and we could hunt out of our tents, the way Bobby and his group had done for years. Since I was in the early years in my practice of law I had a lot of time on my hands that I could use to go on hunting and fishing trips. I had hunted and fished all my life, but I learned a whole lot of new things from Bobby Moore, such as how to catch frogs the easy way.

When I was a boy we used to go in the swamps in the spring of the year and bull eye frogs with a headlight. We caught them with our hands because it was illegal to break the frog's skin when you caught one. I had a patch of switch canes where I could cut, trim and dry them to use as fishing poles. I figured out the best way to catch frogs in the shallow water when they were sitting on lily pads and water grass. If you try to wade up to the frog and grab him with your hand, by the time you got close enough. The water would be rippling, and the frog would dive under. Rarely did you see a frog on a log or on the bank. Most of them were in the shallow water. You couldn't use a frog grab because the frogs had to be sitting on something solid for the grab to work, otherwise the frog would escape.

139

The way I caught them was to take a green cane pole about 8 or 10 feet long and wade up to the frog who was floating in the water. When I got within 8 or 10 feet from him, I would whack him real hard with that cane pole. The frog would not be killed but would be stunned, then I could pick them up and throw them in a sack.

I went frogging with Bobby one time in North Pass at Manchac between Lake Maurepas and Lake Ponchatrain. He had a friend that had a camp down there and a boat we could use. We went one night in February when it was unseasonably warm. The frogs had just came out of the mud where they hibernated all winter, and we were ahead of anybody else in the frog catching business. We went out that night in the boat and I had my cane pole. We were having problems getting close enough to the frogs because of the water grass and lily pads in the shallow water. It seemed they always wanted to dive before we could get close enough to catch them. Bobby quickly showed me how to not waste any more time with all this. He produced a 22 rifle with 22 short bullets and when we would see a frog, Bobby would shoot at it from 20 or 25 yards away. Rarely were those frogs actually killed by the 22 rifle. Usually when he shot at the frog he aimed right in front of it. The bullet would strike the water right next to the frog, which stunned it without breaking its skin. We then picked them up and threw them in our sack. Needless to say, our take that night was far beyond the normal limits of the frogs we would usually catch, and I was introduced to some of the best fried frog legs that I think I ever ate. It wasn't like in the old days where I only caught 4 or 5, this time we could eat all we wanted.

Of course, your chances of getting caught shooting a rifle at night with a headlight were pretty doggone good if you were out when the game wardens were patrolling or on weekends, and certainly anyone who heard those gunshots would call the game wardens. Bobby would go frogging, during the week, not on the weekends when everyone else was off work and at their camps. He also waited until 3 or 4 o'clock in the morning to lessen the chance of his getting caught.

Bobby had some enemies. He was known for his fights, and few people would actually take on Bobby because he was a big man and very very quick. It didn't seem to matter how hard you hit him or how hard he got hit, he could take any kind of pain and any kind of blows and dish out twice as much as he could take. Bobby and I were good friends and he frequented many barrooms in the Springfield area. One of his main hangouts was Schenk's bar where he and Jackie, his girlfriend, and later his wife, would go on a daily basis after he got off from work. When Bobby was 11 or 12 years old he, like myself and most of the other kids did not having any swimming pools. We used to swim in the creeks and rivers of the area. About 1950 he and some of his friends were swimming in Ponchatoula Creek which ran between Ponchatoula and Hammond. Almost nobody had swimsuits in those days. We went to the creek, stripped off, and went skinny-dipping. Bobby and a couple other 12-year-old kids were swimming in the swimming hole when Milton Blount, who also had a reputation of being bad and fighting all the time, and couple of his friends who were three or four years older than Bobby, came down to the swimming hole and discovered the younger kids in the water. They immediately stole the younger kids' clothes and told them they would have to walk home naked. Bobby didn't care that Milton Blount outweighed him by 20 or 30 pounds and was three or four years older than him. Bobby tore into Blount, but it was a one-sided fight. Milton, being older and stronger, bloodied Bobby's nose and face and beat him pretty badly. I didn't even know about that incident until at least 20 years later.

In the early 1970s I decided to try to sell a piece of my property on the Natalbany River. From the town, down the river, and to Lake Maurepas, the river was deep enough and wide enough for large boats to navigate. Further up the river to my property only small boats could travel through the shallow water.

One of my acquaintances was Milton Blount, a couple of years older than I who had attended school with me in Ponchatoula. Milton lived a few miles east of the town. He was named after his grandfather Milton Avery Blount, who had been convicted of murder, and hung in the early 1900s. Milton told me that his grandfather's last words just before his execution were "it's a good day to kill a turkey."

Milton was in the real estate business, and when I told him about my property he told me he thought he could sell it for me to someone from New Orleans. Milton had broken his lower leg a few weeks before and was in a walking cast, so we decided to look at my property from my bass boat.

We drove to the property and I explained to him that we could get in a boat and go from the property which was north of Springfield on the Natalbany River and go all the way to Lake Maurepas, Milton was more familiar with the Tangipahoa River and Bedico on the east side of Ponchatoula where he lived and not the Natalbany on the west side where I lived. After we looked at the property from the land, he came back by my house. We got my boat and launched it at Pitcher's Landing and I took Milton up the river to my property. I then drove all the way down the river to the lake. When we got back to Springfield just before dark, we brought my boat on back to my house and we decided we would go get a beer before Milton went back to Ponchatoula. Milton had his vehicle and I had mine when we drove up to Schenk's bar. He didn't have a walking cane, but he was walking with a pronounced limp when we walked into the bar. There were probably 8 or 10 people there, as well as Lloyd Schenk's wife Hazel, who was tending the bar. Bobby Moore and his girlfriend Jackie were sitting at the bar when I walked directly up to Bobby, and Milton walked with me. I reached the bar between Bobby and Milton, and I offered to buy Bobby a beer. Bobby had been drinking heavily all afternoon and was in a belligerent mood. When he saw Milton Blount, he turned to me and said "what are you doing with that son of a bitch" I didn't know what he was talking about. Bobby got off his bar stool, turned to Milton Blount and said "you're the son of a bitch that beat me up when I was a kid, let's see if you can do it now. Let's both of us go outside and get naked and see who the best man is." Bobby was a lot bigger than Milton at that time and Milton had that injured leg. I stepped between them as Milton moved toward the door and told Bobby "leave him alone, the man's got a bad leg." Bobby grabbed me and gave me a push and I went spinning across the whole barroom and crashed into the jukebox. When I started to get up I saw the crowd going towards the front door of the barroom behind Milton and Bobby. By the time I got to the door the fight was on.

Milton was trying to get away from Bobby and started out when Bobby caught him from behind right in the doorway and started to hit Milton. Milton had a little penknife in his pocket, the blade was only 2

142

inches long, but it was sharp as a razor. He started to cut and stab Bobby, and the only reason Bobby didn't die right then was because the knife blade was too short and did not get deep enough to hit a vital organ. But he cut him and cut him. When he cut Bobby's face, Bobby grabbed Milton's right hand which held the knife, but Milton was so quick that he got the knife in his left hand and use it to cut the top of Bobby's hand that was holding his right hand. He severed the tendons which caused Bobby to lose his grip and then Milton cut him four or five more times in the chest. He then got away from Bobby and got into his vehicle and left.

I got outside the door about the time all this was happening, and Bobby yelled at me, "Hobart he's cut me to pieces, help me." Bobby's girlfriend was screaming and there was four or five men standing around. I said, "somebody help me get him in my car, so I can take him to the hospital." Nobody did anything, so I grabbed Bobby and with the help of his girlfriend we got him in the backseat of my car, and she jumped in with him. The distance from that barroom to the nearest hospital was about 7 miles, I made it in five minutes. On the ride Bobby was bleeding profusely and his girlfriend couldn't stop it, somehow, I managed to rip my shirt off and give it to her, and she used that shirt to try to stop the bleeding. I pulled into the emergency room and ran inside. A nurse met me at the door of the emergency room and I told her had a man that was cut real bad. She told me to take him to Lallie Kemp Hospital which was 15 miles further away. She said, "we can't handle it." I said, "well you're gonna handle it, I'm not gonna let him die in my car and he can't live to make that trip." I grabbed a gurney and the nurse by her arm and went to the car. We got Bobby out of the car and on the gurney and I wheeled him inside that hospital toward the emergency room. The nurse had broke free from me and ran back in and kept saying to take him to Lallie Kemp or take him to somewhere else, do not bring him in here. A young nurse's aide, Rowena Effler, who was maybe 16 or 17 years old was on duty that night. I had represented her daddy in a Worker's Compensation accident, so she knew me, and she came over and said, "I'll help you Mr. Pardue" and we rolled Bobby into the emergency room where a doctor started to work on him. It took more

143

than 300 stitches to sew up his wounds. He was scarred for life, and he died with the scars on his face many many years later.

Many stories were told about that fight, Bobby never would admit that he had started it, he always said that there was another friend of Milton's involved, and that both of them jumped him but it didn't happen that way. It happened just the way I saw it. I doubt seriously there's anybody alive today, more than 40 years later, that can dispute my version. Milton Blount later claimed Bobby came after him with a knife, but I never saw that happen.

There's more to this story though, after Bobby had partly recovered and the Sheriff's investigation of the fight was finished, the Sheriff told Bobby they would arrest Blount and charge him with aggravated battery. Bobby told him no, he would not file any charges at all, he would tend to it himself.

Frank Brent McCarroll, Bobby's friend and later his brother-in-law, and some of Bobby's other friends, took up the fight with Blount. Blount received all kinds of threatening phone calls. Telephone calls were made to his mother telling her that she needed to buy black dress because there was going to be a funeral for her son, Milton Blount. And this went on for some time. Milton had, an uncle named Aswell Robertson, who was a very popular Police Juror from the Robert area of Tangipahoa Parish, and a very good friend of mine. An election was coming up and a meeting was held at Little Johnny's bar and restaurant between Ponchatoula in Hammond by Mr. Robertson and several candidates for state and local offices. The parties were trying to make up a ticket to elect various political candidates to offices. Milton was part of that organization and was scheduled to be at that meeting.

Bobby, who had recovered from his wounds, Frank Brent McCarroll and others decided they were going to catch Blount at the meeting and kill him. They armed themselves with shotguns and went to Little Johnny's soon after the meeting started, Blount was late for the meeting, and Bobby and Frank Brent and the others came into the restaurant. When they spied Blount's uncle Aswell and the other politicians they held them at gunpoint, demanding the whereabouts of Blount. They told them they would keep them there until Blount arrived, so they could kill him. During the altercation somebody put a shotgun to Aswell's stomach

144

and threatened to blow him apart. Luckily no shots were fired, and nobody was injured. Blount drove up to the restaurant and bar while the altercation was going on inside and wisely left without going in. Bobby and Frank Brent and the others were arrested and placed in jail in Amite in Tangipahoa Parish. They were held without bond for a few days until their bonds were reduced. Eventually they were sentenced to jail time in Tangipahoa Parish. One of Frank's brothers went to trial, he was represented by Barbee Ponder and was found not guilty.

Frank Brent and Bobby frequented a bar between Springfield and Albany called the Old Tomb Bar and this was one of their regular hangouts. The phone calls kept coming to Blount's mother, girlfriends and associates about how Blount was going to be killed. some said with a knife, some said with a gun. Before he died, Milton Blount, talked to a newspaper reporter from Ponchatoula and gave his story of the knife fight and what happened at the Old Tomb Bar. Milton said he had his girlfriend bring him to Springfield in the backseat of her car. While the girl was driving, he had a shotgun loaded with buckshot. He claimed that he picked up the wrong gun that day. He said he usually used a gun that had a full choke barrel, but this one had a scatter barrel. Frank Brent was in the bar when Blount's girlfriend drove him up to the bar and parked outside. When Frank Brent walked out the door, Blount shot, but only one pellet in the shot gun went through the bridge of Frank Brent's nose. Milton and his girlfriend drove away. He was not arrested, and no charges were made. Rumors were put out; the attack was done by members of the Teamsters Union. No other revenge was taken by either side. But shortly thereafter Milton Blount got into a completely unrelated fight with someone else and wounded that person badly, Milton was arrested and tried for attempted murder and aggravated battery.

I don't remember who his attorney was but the jury found Milton not guilty by reason of insanity. Milton testified at his trial that he had received all these death threats and it drove him completely insane. He said that he snapped when this other person and he got in a confrontation. At that time if you were found not guilty by reason of insanity they sent you to an insane asylum. Milton Blount was very very intelligent, and he played the system to the hilt. Frank Edwards was

145

Sheriff and Frank did not have much use for Milton and did like Bobby. Milton Blount was a very handsome man with coal black hair and he was very proud of his semi-long hair and his appearance. When he was arrested for the assault on the other individual, the Sheriff's office decided they would delouse him, and they shaved his head. When Milton Blount was tried his head was still shaved.

After a few months Milton Blount was released from the Insane Asylum in Jackson, Louisiana.

Chapter 10. Grover Covington

In the late 1960s Grover Covington practiced law in Kentwood Louisiana, where he resided and had made one run for political office, which was for school board member in northern Tangipahoa Parish. He was unsuccessful in that race, and few people thought he had any political future. He had some very powerful political friends in southern Tangipahoa Parish however, including Judge Warren Comish and Leonard Kinchen. Judge Comish decided to retire in 1969 when Governor John McKeithen was in office and had the power to appoint his successor. Leonard Kinchen had been a supporter of the governor, and he and Judge Comish went to Baton Rouge to meet with him about appointing Grover as the new judge. In those days the governor could appoint someone to fill a vacancy and then call and election to be held a few months later for that office. In that case, anyone who had received the appointment had a tremendous advantage over any other candidate in the election.

I hardly knew Grover, having seen him at the courthouse in Tangipahoa Parish one or two times, but I had done title work for Leonard Kinchen for over five years since I finished law school and had known him, and his children from childhood. There was no advance publicity about Judge Comish's retirement or Grovers' appointment to succeed him and it appeared that Grover would have no opposition in the upcoming election.

My wife Loretta taught school in Jefferson Parish while I was in law school and she attended classes at night and summer school to obtain her Masters degree in guidance counseling. When I graduated in 1966 we moved back home where she got a job at Springfield High School as an English teacher and guidance counselor. By 1969 she had obtained tenure in those fields and according to state law could not be demoted from that tenured position without a formal hearing before the school board.

In my early practice of law, I had represented parents, teachers, and school bus drivers in disputes with the Livingston Parish school board, and many of the board members did not like me. In 1969 the federal courts ordered the schools in Livingston Parish integrated and the first step the school board took was to close former black schools and move students and teachers to the remaining former white schools.

The majority of the school board members who were from the western side of Livingston Parish did not want black principals, or guidance counselors in their schools so they transferred them to Springfield and Albany, and transferred Loretta to Holden, Louisiana where she would be demoted from guidance counselor to English teacher.

The teacher tenure law clearly prohibited this action, and I got a friend of mine to file suit against the Livingston Parish School Board to prohibit this illegal action. The case was assigned to Grover Covington. The school board's attorneys filed a summary proceeding to allow her transfer and Grover ruled in favor of the board without doing any legal research.

The election for Grover's judgeship was to be held in about three months, and no one had expressed any interest in opposing him. He had ruled against my wife on a Monday. On Friday afternoon about 4:30 PM I drove from Springfield 45 miles to the Mississippi state line. Five miles north of Grovers' hometown of Kentwood, Louisiana there were two large nightclubs located across the street from each other. I had been to those nightclubs only once or twice in my life and knew no one there.

When I arrived at the first bar room, Skinny's, I walked in the bar ordered a beer for myself and for the several customers who were there. I introduced myself and told them I was running for Judge against Grover Covington and asked them to vote for me. After a few minutes I told them I had to see other voters and walked across the street to the other barroom, The Pines, and did the same thing again. After that I headed down Highway 51 South, to Roseland, where I stopped at Benny Tates bar and repeated the process. By 10:30 PM I had visited almost every bar room on Highway 51 in Tangipahoa Parish from Amite to Ponchatoula.

About 5:30 AM the next morning I heard someone knocking on my bedroom window. I got up and got dressed and found Leonard Kinchen standing at my door. I invited the old man in and offered him a seat. He demanded that I tell him what I was doing talking about running for Judge against Grover Covington. I explained to him what Grover had

148

done for the school board against my wife and told him I was going to make him pay for it, since he was completely wrong according to the law.

Mr. Leonard told me that the judge had probably made a mistake, but I didn't need to be running against him after all the work he had done to help him get appointed. I told him I was sorry about that but that didn't change anything as for as the case was concerned.

He told me that he would set up a meeting for me to go see Grover at his office in Amite Monday morning and try to work things out. I told him that I would talk to Grover, but he would have to come to my office in Springfield. He told me that Grover had court on Monday morning and I needed go to him. I told him that Grover was the judge and he could cancel court to come see me. The old man told me I was being unreasonable, and he was sure that we could work things out. I told him that I would come to the courthouse in Livingston at 8 o'clock Monday morning and meet with him and Grover, and Grover could then go to his court hearings.

When I arrived at the courthouse in Livingston the old man met me in the lobby and we walked to the judge's office where he told me to go inside and work things out with Grover. When I went inside Grover told me that he had made a mistake and would grant a rehearing on the case. I told him that all I wanted was a fair ruling according to the law without any favor being given to the Livingston Parish school board just because they were just a bunch of politicians. We made our peace and became very close friends for the rest of his life. I told him that I was very glad that we came to an understanding because the last thing I wanted to be was a judge.

A few years later an opening for Judge of the First Circuit Court of Appeals came up and Grover called me asking for my help to get him elected to that position. I told him I would do anything I could to help him achieve his goal. He asked me if I knew a judge from Franklinton, Louisiana named Hillary Crain who had been talking about running for the same position on the Court of Appeals. I told him I didn't know Judge Crain, but I would go talk to him.

I had very few cases in Washington Parish, but I knew they had a rule day every Friday where most of the lawyers would come to get

149

uncontested divorces and minor rules heard by the judge. I had my secretary call to make sure that Judge Crain would be there that morning and find out what time he started court. I arrived about an hour before court started and went to the judge's office and asked his secretary if I could talk to him. She had me sit down while she went in the back, then returned shortly and invited me in to see the judge. I had never formally met him before, but he had heard of me and apparently thought I was coming to see him about supporting him for the Court of Appeals seat.

I told him I came to ask him not to run against Grover and that if he didn't I would support him and do everything I could do to keep any other lawyer or Judge from the 21st Judicial District from running against him at the next opening for Court of Appeals Judge. He must've thought that I was very impertinent by making such a request, but I told him that if Grover had no opposition I was sure we could get the support of three Sheriffs, Assessors, Clerks of Court and the District Attorney of the 21st Judicial District when he ran for the next opening. He told me that he thought he could probably beat Grover if he ran and that he was considering it. I then told him that I would make him a promise that I would do everything I could for him as I had stated if he did not run at this time, but if he did run and was elected Judge on the Court of Appeal within 10 years he would be up for reelection and every 10 years thereafter. Then I said, "If I am alive and practicing law and I cannot find someone else to run against you, then I personally will run against you every time you come up for re-election."

Judge Crain decided to wait, and Grover was elected to the Court of Appeals, without opposition. Several years later another opening occurred on the Court of Appeals, and Judge Crain announced that he was running. I got in touch with Sheriff Odom Graves from Livingston Sheriff Ed Layrisson from Tangipahoa, and Sheriff Eugene Holland from St. Helena as well as the assessors, clerks of court and many other elected officials from the 21st Judicial District Court to attend a large rally at the Bear Creek restaurant in St Helena Parish, to pledge their support for Judge Crain, and he won without opposition.

I don't believe I ever won a case before Judge Crain, after that, but I always respected him, and now consider his son, Judge Will Crain, who sits in the Court of Appeals one of my closest friends.

Chapter 11. Judge Ben Tucker

Judge Ben Tucker, who had presided at the Cogley and McCarroll trial was upset by the verdict and had a reputation for being tough on criminals. He was also ultraconservative in awarding civil damages. I had opposed Judge Tucker when he was first elected, and he never forgave me for it. Art Macy who represented insurance companies said Ben Tucker still thought he was working for Travelers Insurance Company after he got to be judge.

When Judge Tucker decided to run for the Court of Appeals I enthusiastically supported him. When I asked Frank McCarroll and Bobby Moore to vote for Judge Tucker they asked me if I had lost my mind. I told them that there was no way we could beat him if he ran for reelection as District Judge and the only way to get rid of him was to move him up to the Court of Appeal. I firmly believe that a majority of the outlaws in our district voted for Judge Tucker for that reason.

Before Judge Tucker was elected to the Court of Appeals, my friend Charlie Abels, was a state trooper assigned primarily to Livingston Parish. His daddy Bubbie Abels had been Assessor of Livingston Parish since 1948 and had plans for Charlie to someday succeed him in that office.

Charlie had a mind of his own and was dedicated to getting the drunk drivers off the roads. He knew the location of all the bar rooms and he patrolled that area every weekend as well as during the week when he was on duty. As a result, he got the name of Super Trooper for the number of DWI arrests that he made. While this activity on Charlie's part didn't hurt his daddy, he told him that he could never get elected if he kept on putting people in jail. Charlie didn't care he just kept on arresting people.

One night while patrolling between Springfield and Albany Louisiana, Charlie stopped a black man for DWI. He had a black passenger named Brooks who lived in Killian, La. near Charlie's home. Brooks asked Charlie to give him a ride home and Charlie told him to get in the police car with the man who was arrested and after he took the arrested man to jail in Livingston, he would then bring Brooks home. On the way to Livingston Charlie saw a vehicle in the ditch on the right-hand side of the road. He stopped on the shoulder and got out to investigate and arrested that driver for DWI. There was not much traffic on this rural road at that time of night, and it was never determined whether Charlie had turned on his flashing lights before he got out of the car to arrest the second driver. As Charlie returned to his car with the second man a third car came up behind Charlie's car and ran into it. Charlie discovered that Brooks had apparently got out of his car while Charlie was investigating the car in the ditch and the third car struck and killed Brooks when it crashed into Charlie's car.

Brooks widow, who had two small children, hired me to represent them in a claim for wrongful death. Brooks also had a grown daughter who hired a young lawyer from New Orleans to represent her.

The driver of the automobile that struck and killed Brooks had no insurance and the only way for me to get compensation for my clients was to prove that Charlie was partially at fault. Charlie maintained that he had his emergency lights flashing before the accident, but he admitted that he had allowed Brooks to get in the police car after he made the first stop. I maintained that if Charlie had not done that Brooks would not have been at the location where he was killed.

The two men who had been arrested by Charlie for DWI and a passenger in the third car swore there were no emergency flashing lights on Charlie's car at the time of the accident. The other attorney for the state police argued those witnesses were drunk and their testimony was not reliable. We tried the case and the local judge found Charlie and the State Police partially liable and awarded me a judgment of about $120,000 and the other daughter about $10,000.

The state police appealed to the First Circuit Court of Appeals where Judge Ben Tucker sat. As luck would have it my case was assigned to Judge Tucker and two other judges. When I appeared at the Court of Appeals in Baton Rouge my case was about third or fourth on the docket. Before court started the lawyer for the State Police, Bob Van Derworker, an older very experienced defense attorney, told me that he had authority to settle the matter for $60,000. I told him I would have to think about it and went back in the courtroom sat down listening to the other cases. As I sat there I noticed Judge Tucker looking at me and it was obvious to me that he was pleased to find me before him. The more

I looked at him and he looked at me I became convinced that he would probably vote to reverse the District Court and give me nothing. I therefore walked over to Bob and told him to come outside the courtroom where we could talk. I tried to get him to come up with some more money, but he stated he had no further authority than the $60,000 and I accepted the settlement. The young New Orleans lawyer was not part of the deal and he went ahead and argued his case before the Judges'. That night, Judge Tucker, died of a heart attack and the other two judges who heard the other lawyer's case later rendered a judgment affirming the findings of the trial court, Judge Tucker cost me $20,000 in fees on the day he died.

Chapter 12. District Attorney's Race

When I was a teenager in the 1950's, before Bob Kennon got elected governor, every bar room in the state had slot machines. In the southern part of Livingston Parish where I grew up, there were about five bars for every church. By the time I finished high school, I had visited every single one of them. After I went to college, went in the Army, and came back home, I continued to visit these various bar rooms, where there were some mighty good-looking girls, and a whole lot of them, From the French girls down at Head of Island to the Hungarian girls in Albany, to the Redneck girls around Springfield, and Holden. In visiting all those bar rooms, I ran into all kinds of characters, who later on when I started practicing law were some of my best customers.

In 1972, I ran for District Attorney against Leonard Yokum from Hammond. He and I were opposite on politics and, lucky for me, I didn't get elected. I found out the best feeling in the world. When I ran, elections were in early September and qualifying was about June. Without going into a lot of detail about it, I qualified the last day of the qualifying period and began my race. I didn't have much money, but I had a good many friends who for whatever reasons were mad at Leonard and I picked up a lot of support from them. I talked to Marshal Vic Anderson over at Hammond when I first decided to run and asked for his support. "Boy," he says, "you can't win." I said, "Well, I'm going to run anyway." He said, "Well, I'll tell you how I've been re-elected marshal for thirty years. My little district is Ponchatoula, Robert, Hammond, and the rest of the Seventh Ward of Tangipahoa Parish. The way I do it, at six o'clock in the morning I'm at Ponchatoula shaking hands with all the people who are getting ready to car pool to go down to work at Norco in the refineries. I will spend a little while there, maybe at one of the restaurants, talking to people. An hour later, I'm at Robert at the east side of Ponchatoula out in the country talking to dairy farmers at their dairy barns. An hour later, I go all the way back to Pumpkin Center, and visit strawberry farmers. An hour later, I'm back in Ponchatoula again, and then I go back to Hammond. After that I make another round west of Natalbany. Every day, I crisscross every place. I might not see but a few people each place, but every morning, I'm at a different place and three or four times a day, I'm at different places." Well, I decided I would use that same strategy. So, in a period of about three months, I put 18,000 miles on my car. And there were no interstates those days. I'd be up at the state line at Kentwood at daylight then drive 40 miles to Denham Springs and be there around 8:30 or 9:00 o'clock. Then I would switch over to Ponchatoula, and meet people there, and then go back to Independence, and then zig back towards French Settlement to meet people coming home from work. I did that every day for about three months, and people got to seeing me all over the place, and I got my name out. Lawyers couldn't advertise in these days and the best way to advertise was to run for office. I came within 750 votes of beating Mr. Leonard, but people chose to re-elect him.

The last day before the election, on Friday, I had been up since daylight driving all over the district. I came back by my office in Springfield around 2:30 or 3:00 o'clock in the afternoon and had two other places to be that evening. I just stopped by my office to check on whatever phone calls I had received, since we didn't have cell phones in those days. When I came in, there was a fellow waiting to see me. He was a ne'er-do-well, and I knew his word wasn't too good, but I wanted every vote I could get, so I told him to come on in, and I talked to him a minute. He says, "I'm out of work, and my wife's sick, and my babies need milk. Can you help me?" I reached in my pocket and I gave him a twenty-dollar bill. I told him, "Go get you some food for your kids and take care of your wife, and I appreciate you helping me." "Well, I'm going to be for you 100%," is what he said. I thanked him and made about three or four phone calls, then pulled out from my office right outside of Springfield and headed back towards Ponchatoula. When I got in town at Springfield, I had to pass Schenk's Bar on the right-hand side right by the river. And lo and behold, when I looked at the parking lot of the bar room, there was my friend's truck parked right in front. I wheeled on in and walked inside. There he was, sitting at the bar with a cold beer in his hand and the change from my twenty-dollar bill laying on the bar. About three other fellows were in the bar room, so I walked up to the bar and told the bartender, "Give everybody a drink," and I bought one for the fellow that had taken my money, as well as everybody else. I said, "I don't have time to drink with ya'll, because

155

I'm trying to get elected. I've got to go, and please, ya'll vote for me."
They all said yes, and I left. I got in some time around midnight, and the
election was the next morning. I was gone from before daylight until the
polls closed at 8 p.m., visiting almost every polling place.

I went into the election with my eyes open, and figured I just had a
shot, but by election day I was kind of pumped up and hoping to get in
the second primary. I knew if I could do that, I could win. Well, it didn't
work that way. I came back to my office and there were a lot of folks
there. The votes were being counted and we started getting the results
from the different courthouses. About 10:30 p.m. I knew I had been beat,
and everybody left, and that was it. I was exhausted. I hadn't gotten
more than three or four hours of sleep a night for three months, so I went
to bed and went to sleep. My office was right there in my house, as it is
today. About 8:30 the next day, Sunday morning, I heard somebody
knocking on my door. I got up, put on some clothes and pulled on my
boots, and went to the door, and who was standing there but the same
fellow that had took my twenty dollars and went up to that bar room and
drank it up the day before. I looked at him, and he says, "I'm so sorry we
didn't make it. We all voted for you. We did all we could do." And
before I could say thank you, he said, "By the way, you reckon you
could lend me another twenty dollars?" All of a sudden, it was just like
somebody had dumped a bucket of ice water right in my face. It hit me
like a brick. I realized that I didn't have to be nice anymore. And I did
the best I could to stick that cowboy boot right up his ass. I literally ran
him off of my property and told him don't never come back. I walked
back inside and felt like a million dollars. I didn't have to be nice any
more. I'll be nice to my friends, but I don't have to be nice to my
enemies.

Chapter 13. Joe Mitchell Trial

One of the first jury trials I ever tried was a murder case. I had known Joe Mitchell, since I was a boy. When I was working with my daddy cruising timber, driving a tractor, hooking tongs, and occasionally pulling a cross-cut saw to cut logs, I did it on a part time basis. I was 15 years old during summer vacation, because I had to go to school. Joe started working in the woods full time at age 14 or 15 and was one of the first persons I had ever seen using a power saw to cut trees down, into logs, and he did it because he had to. He was a small man, about 5'3 or 4, quite muscular, and tough as nails. I saw him many times in bar rooms around Springfield and the Killian and Maurepas area. We never had any kind of cross words and were always friends. After the election for District Attorney in 1972, he was in his late 20's, married with a kid or two. He had a friend named Cotton Bassemier, who operated a bar room for a time in Springfield. Cotton, also a friend of mine, was older, probably 40, and had many, many, friends and very few enemies. Cotton was a big man and had no problems at his bar room whatsoever from anybody starting any trouble there, because nobody wanted to mess with Cotton. One night, Cotton and Joe Mitchell were making the rounds in the bars in the Springfield area and wound up at Bill Gregoire's place. Bill's place started out to be a restaurant with a small bar, and after Bill sold out, it went through several hands, and got to be nothing but a bar room and pool hall. Its customers were the local people who flocked there on Friday and Saturday nights, as well as all day long on Sundays, to play pool, visit with their friends and their families, and drink as much as they wanted.

On this particular occasion, in addition to all the regulars who were local folks, there was a man from northern Tangipahoa Parish who, along with his wife and teenage son were at the bar. They had been staying at a fishing camp in the area along the Tickfaw or Blood River, when they went to the bar room. He was a large man, and during the course of the evening, he and Joe Mitchell and Cotton Bassemier got into a pool game. As you came in the front door of the bar room, there was a bar on the right-hand side, a jukebox, several tables, and a dancing area, in addition, it had an open door into the room where the pool table was located. The bar was crowded, Joe and Cotton and the guy from Tangipahoa Parish were in that back part of the building which was partially walled off, playing pool. An argument ensued, and during the course of the argument, a fight erupted, and during the fight, the fellow from Tangipahoa Parish got stabbed to death and Joe Mitchell ended up getting charged with murder.

I heard about it within the next day or two and kind of figured Joe would be getting in touch with me. I knew he didn't have much money, but in those days, I was taking on just about any case I could. I was surprised to learn that instead of hiring me, Joe hired Gordon Matheny from Tangipahoa Parish. Gordon Matheny, at that time, was the son-in-law of Vic Anderson, the Marshall of Hammond City Court, who was also a very good friend of Cotton Bassemier. Gordon had only been practicing law about a year or so. I had been in the business a couple of years longer, and I had been in several criminal trials. Judge Gordon Causey, a good friend of mine, was the judge. Gordon thought he could just make a deal, get the charges reduced to manslaughter, or negligent homicide, work out something so that Joe could plead, spend a couple of years in jail and be done with it. Well, the prosecutor had been in the business a long time, and he would have none of this plea bargaining. The lawyers went through the motions and had different court appearances before trial, and the case was set for trial on a Monday morning at 9 o'clock.

At the last pretrial conference, about two weeks before the trial, Judge Causey, had suggested to Gordon Matheny that maybe he ought to get somebody with a little more experience to help him with it. I got a phone call from Gordon asking me if I would help him try the case. Gordon was a good friend of mine, and I knew his family well, but had never actually tried a case with him. He was a good attorney, but he just didn't have any experience, and the judge saw that same thing. When Gordon asked for my assistance, I knew up front that Joe didn't have any money, but the way Gordon approached me with it was that the District Attorney had said when Judge Causey suggested putting my name in it, he didn't care who was in there, but Hobart Pardue wasn't going to be able to get in there and do anything on this kind of case. Well, that could have been true or not true or whoever said what, but it got back to me, and that whetted my appetite. Gordon had talked to me on Thursday, trial is on Monday. My normal feelings were, "Okay, if I'm going to get in it, we're going to continue this case, and I'm going to get ready to try it." Gordon told me he had already been through pretrial conferences and motions and everything else and the District Attorney was insisting on trying the case and there was not going to be any continuances. Well, in the meantime I had seen Joe in jail and he also asked me for help, so I told him I would help Gordon with the case. I told Gordon to meet me at 5 o'clock on Friday evening, the weekend before the trial, at my office in Springfield.

At 5 o'clock, Gordon drives up, dressed to the 9's, with a new suit and tie on, like he was going to some kind of bank meeting in Hammond. I had on a pair of jeans and just an open shirt and cowboy boots. I told Gordon, "Look, take your tie off and take your coat off, because we are going to a bar room. We are going to go find out what happened in this case. We are going to find out everything about it, and these people are not used to people coming in this kind of little country bar wearing a necktie." He got in my car and we drove down to the bar room.

When we went in, I knew everybody who was there, as well as the ones who came in later. In those days, you could buy a beer for a quarter, or drink whiskey for about fifty to sixty cents. I figured I'd invest about twenty or thirty dollars and I would get to the bottom of this case right quick. It worked like a charm. I went in and bought everybody a drink. I had a yellow pad and a pen in my hand. I introduced everybody to Gordon and told them we were going to be representing Joe Mitchell in this case where he was charged with killing that fellow from Tangipahoa Parish, and I needed to find out exactly how it happened and all about it. At least eight people in that bar room that Friday night had been there when the actual killing took place and were eyewitnesses to the whole thing. About three or four hours passed while we drank beer and talked, and I had the witnesses re-enact the whole killing.

I put Gordon Matheny behind the pool table and said. "Okay, Gordon is going to be Cotton Bassemier. I'm going to be Joe Mitchell."

159

I got another fellow and said, you're the fellow that got killed. I positioned each person where they had been sitting at the bar, or a table, or standing when the fight occurred in the pool hall and went through the whole fight. Joe was charged with killing the fellow with a knife during the fight. Cotton Bassemier wasn't charged at all, but he was right there in the melee. All the folks in there knew Joe. He was local. So, it didn't take a whole lot to have them all on my side in a minute. After going through the motions and making my notes I had the name of each person who actually was there, where they were standing, where they were sitting, what they saw during the fight, as it progressed until it was over with. By midnight, the crowd was still going strong. I asked the barmaid what time she was going to open up the next morning. Well, in those days, some of those bars never closed at all on weekends, but I knew that this one usually closed around 2 o'clock in the mornings and then opened back up around 10 or 11 o'clock on Saturday. She told me she normally would be back over there about 10:30 a.m. With the help of a twenty-dollar bill, I persuaded her to be open at 9.

In the meantime, before I had gone down there to visit the crowd and get my information, I had called my old friend, John D. Adams, who lived in town and had been a surveyor for over 40 years. He liked to sip his Jack Daniels whiskey several times a day and had taught me how to hunt wild turkey's. I told John I needed his help. So, at 9 o'clock on Saturday morning, John D. Adams and I were at that bar, went in and met the barmaid, and proceeded to spend about an hour taking measurements of everything in the bar. We measured the height of the bar, the width of the bar, the width of the doors, where the doors were located, where the tables were located, where the chairs were located, where the pool table was located, the height of the pool table, the width of the pool table, the length of the pool table, and the size and location of the windows. John D. Was making notes when we were doing these measurements, and on Tuesday morning, when the trial started, and I started picking jurors, John D. had provided me with a drawing to scale of everything in that bar room and made several copies for me. On one copy I had put the location and name of the witness I wanted to have, what they could see and what they couldn't see. I also put the location of the victim, his family, and the location of everybody in that bar room, by

160

name. When I picked the jury, I made certain that I had several people who weren't tee-totallers and had nothing against anybody who liked to drink beer and play pool. I also had two or three ringers that didn't really think much of the law trying to put people in jail when they got in a fight in a bar room, especially, when a big man comes after a little man, and the little man has to get the big man off of him. When we tried the case, I had as my witnesses the people who actually saw the fight that I had talked to on that Friday night and I had Mr. Adams, who qualified as an expert surveyor, to make an expert's opinion about the location of all of the furniture, fixtures, and the exact measurements of everything in that barroom. During the trial of the case, the District Attorney put on his evidence that Joe Mitchell had started the fight. Joe was standing on one side of the pool table, and the victim was on the other side of the pool table. They came at one another, and Joe Mitchell pulled a knife out of his pocket and stabbed the victim. The victim's teenage son, who was in the other part of the building, looking through the door into the pool room part, swore that he saw Joe reach in his pocket, pull out a knife, and stab his daddy. My witnesses said they did not see Joe Mitchell stab anybody. They did see the fight between the victim, Joe and Cotton, who all were fighting and fell to the floor. My position was that Joe Mitchell was an innocent bystander, Cotton Bassemier and the other guy got into a fight, Joe got knocked around, and Cotton did the cutting. None of my witnesses would actually say that Cotton cut the guy, but they surely all said that they didn't see Joe cut the guy. I had the drawings of the bar room and the pool table, with the measurements, and asked the dead man's son exactly what he saw. He swore he saw Joe Mitchell's hand go into his pocket and get that knife and bring it out. He was standing on the opposite side of the pool table. Joe Mitchell was across the room and on the other side of the pool table when this happened. In my closing arguments to the jury, I had Joe Mitchell come up before the jury in the middle of the courtroom where there was a table in front of the judge's desk and I told the jury to imagine that table was the pool table, and I gave Joe Mitchell a yardstick. Joe Mitchell stood there behind the table with the yardstick in his hand with one end on the floor. John D's drawing of the pool room had revealed the pool table was three feet high. When Joe Mitchell, being a short man, put his hand down by his

161

side, his hand was eight inches below the top of the pool table. The jury could see it would have been impossible for anybody on the other side of the pool table to have seen Joe Mitchell stick his hand in his pocket and pull out a knife. The pool table blocked the witness's view. I had irrefutable evidence of the height of the pool table, according to Mr. Adams testimony and the drawings. The three-foot yardstick showed that Joe's hand was a foot below the top of the table, and there was no way the young man could have seen Joe Mitchell pull a knife. The jury could not reach a verdict and the District Attorney demanded a new trial.

That put everything off for a year or so. I got some other evidence, filed a lot of other pleadings, and by the time the second trial was set to begin, the District Attorney had lost his enthusiasm. The victims had been told that Joe was probably going to walk completely free and the District Attorney offered me a deal for Joe to plead to attempted manslaughter and serve about a year. Joe had been in jail for several months right after the killing, so that, with good time, put him free in less than a year when I made the deal.

Chapter 14. Marshall Virgil Stafford

In the late 1960s, most of my criminal cases involved thefts, fights, and DWI's, but very few cases for narcotics violations.

Before I finished law school, I ran into a character named Frank McCarroll. I was in my early 20s, and old man Frank was in his 60s, and wore wire-rimmed glasses with one glass missing. He loved to play poker and would shut one eye or the other while looking at his cards, often commenting that he couldn't see very well. Actually, he could see perfectly, and the one glass had no magnification. He used them to deceive his fellow players. Mr. Frank was also one of the characters who dealt in politics, and anyone running for office could get his support for the right amount of money. He was from the fourth ward of Livingston Parish. and I was from the sixth ward, which were next to one another. During the campaign for an election that took place in early 1963, Mr. Frank asked me to drive him to meet some voters he controlled, so he could tell them who to vote for. We went to several houses, and he took me in to meet people who lived there. He didn't ask them to vote for his candidate, he just told them Mr. So-and-so is the man we are voting for. He and I would stop at barrooms and buy beer between visits to voters. Mr. Frank had several sons who became my friends, and all of his sons had brushes with the law. His son Ralph had several children that he didn't support, and he would be sentenced to six months in jail for non-support. After about three months, he would get out for good behavior, then he would not support them for another year or so until he was put back in jail for another six months. I usually was successful in putting off his return to jail for several months each time his former wife filed charges against him.

Ralph was an alcoholic and the smallest of the brothers, but that didn't stop him from getting into fights in barrooms almost every weekend. When he was in his 40s or early 50s, he lived with another fellow in Independence, Louisiana. They were best friends and got drunk together almost every night. One night, they got in a fight and Ralph shot his friend in the face but did not kill him. It was a senseless act, and Ralph was charged with aggravated battery. I represented Ralph and kept putting the trial off for several years. The man who Ralph shot felt

163

the justice system was not working and decided to take things into his own hands. He had gone through several operations, was terribly disfigured, and to him it seemed Ralph was getting away with it. One day, he got his shotgun, met Ralph in the middle of town, and shot and killed him.

On another occasion, one of Frank's son's and another young man had been charged with theft, and I had represented them and got the charges dropped. However, the Sheriff's office was convinced that the other young man was a thief. The warden of the jail, Virgil Stafford, who was also the former Marshall of Walker Louisiana, was determined to put my client in jail. Marshall Stafford was of medium height but weighted about 240 pounds, with a big belly. When I had run for district attorney a couple of years before this, I had asked for his support and he told me that he couldn't vote for me. He was for Leonard Yokum, the District Attorney from Hammond, in Tangipahoa Parish. I had told him that he ought to support me because I was from Livingston Parish. I did have a lot of support from the local black community, as I had always represented black clients in the past and had a very good relationship with those who knew me. But then, Marshall Stafford went to the black leaders in the Walker area, which was 30 miles from my home in Springfield, and told them I was a member of the Ku Klux Klan, an outright lie. I believe that one thing caused me to be defeated. After the election, Marshall Stafford went to work for Sheriff Odom Graves as Warden. I told him I would get even with him. He just laughed at me, knowing that he was no longer going to have to run for election, and I couldn't do anything about it.

About two years after the District Attorney's race, the young man I represented found a new girlfriend, who lived in Maurepas, with her boyfriend. They had a break up, and she moved to Holden with her new boyfriend near Frank McCarroll's home. When she moved, she brought a deep-freeze with her which she had purchased and kept the receipt for her payment, and they placed it on the back porch of their house. A few days later, the Sheriff's deputies came to their home, searching for stolen goods. Despite their protest, the deputies seized the deep freeze and took it to the jail, where they plugged it in and began using it. The next week, one of Frank's sons contacted me about it, and I told him she needed to file criminal charges against Marshall Stafford for possession of stolen property, which she did. The next week, I was at the courthouse when Marshall Stafford approached me in a hallway. He told me I was a no-good shyster lawyer, and I ought to be ashamed of myself for having those outlaws file criminal charges against him. He said that he had never been charged with any violation of the law in his 30+ years of service as a law enforcement officer. I looked him in the eye and told him that I been waiting for two years to pay him back for lying to the black community about me in the District Attorney's race. I confirmed that I had advised my clients to file the charges against him, and payback was hell. He told me to tell my clients to come get the deep-freeze. I told him that since the deputies picked it up, they needed to return it, and if the deputies didn't and the District Attorney dropped the charges against him anyway, I would sue him in civil court for conversion of the lady's deep-freeze and make sure I got the story in all the newspapers. The deep freeze was returned the next day.

Chapter 15. Jimmy Huntley Forrest

Before I was born in 1939 Mr. Huntley T Bailey was a long-time member of the Livingston Parish police jury and during the Great Depression of the 1930s was its president. Mr. Bailey lived next to the Springfield High School in a large wood house. I remember as a small boy he had large prickly pear cactus plant in his yard which had beautiful flowers in the spring. He had three daughters and a son. I remember my parents talking about the Bailey boy who got in trouble with the law had moved to Arkansas to escape punishment.

One of his daughters, Amy, married Jim Forrest and they resided on the Perrin Ferry Road near the Tickfaw River. They had several children, the oldest, Jimmy was named after his grandfather and was my age.

When we were in high school Jimmy and I fished in the Tickfaw and Blood rivers. We would launch a small boat after dark and paddle along the banks using our headlights to look for fish in the shallow water. I had a heavy metal gig to try to spear them. This was illegal but there was hardly any danger of getting caught. On the rare occasion that we heard a boat coming, that might be operated by the game warden, we would tie a trot line to the gig and drop it overboard with the other end of the line tied to the boat. After the other boat was past us we would then pull up the gig and resume fishing.

Our quarry was largemouth bass, but most of the fish we saw were small needle nose gar and bream. The gar were trash fish and were protected by heavy scales. When we tried to spear them the gig usually bounced off their bodies. So, we would try to approach one when it was facing the bank, then hit it near its tail with the gig which caused it to jump out of the water to the bank.

The bream were too small for the heavy gig. We could see dozens on their beds along the bank. Males, called bulls, would use their tails to dig small circular holes in the shallow river bottom along the bank where the females would deposit their eggs in the spring. The males would fertilize the eggs with roe and after they hatched would swim around the beds protecting their young from predators.

We concocted a scheme to catch the fish by using a short piece of stovepipe to drop over the fish, push it into the mud and reach down inside to catch the fish with our hands. We quickly learned that this wouldn't work very well since we only caught one or two fish. We knew we could catch dozens of fish with fly rods or cane poles using worms or crickets for bait, and that method was legal, so we gave up night fishing.

After finishing high school Jimmy joined the army, married a girl from up north, and after he was discharged they lived in a northern state. I did not see Jimmy again for more than 10 years when he returned to Springfield and got a job with the school board as a substitute teacher. I had been practicing law five or six years when he came to my office.

We talked for about an hour, reminiscing about our boyhood. Jimmy told me that his wife had died recently and that he planned to continue his education in Louisiana. He asked me questions about the type of cases I had handled and was particularly interested in my experiences as a criminal defense lawyer. I told him about how I won several murder trials and he asked me many questions about the competency of the sheriff's deputies who had investigated those cases. I didn't think anything about his motives and was surprised to receive a call from his sister a few days later saying he was in jail and needed to talk to me.

I went to Livingston and checked with the Sheriff's office to find out what his charges were. The detective who was handling the investigation was a close friend of mine. He told me that Jimmy had been arrested on charges of murdering his young brother-in-law. When I talked to Jimmy he insisted that he was completely innocent, and he wanted to hire me to represent him and his sister who was also under investigation.

The next day I received a call from a woman who had purchased a lot in a subdivision from my father where she built a small house. She had a son, whose name was Bezar. He was about 20 years old and was mildly retarded. She told me her son was in jail also charged with murder and she wanted to hire me to represent him.

I went to see Jimmy's sister at the jail and she told me that Jimmy had found a potential employer for her young husband who was several years younger than her and also mildly retarded. She had two small

167

children by a previous marriage and said her husband had wanted to adopt her children.

I investigated the case and discovered that Jimmy, his sister and her husband had recently gone to the office of one of my very good friends, Tom Kent Stewart who was an agent for Prudential Insurance Company. They told Tom Kent that the young husband was getting a job as a truck driver that would require him to drive all over the United States and they needed to buy a life insurance policy, so his wife and stepchildren would be protected in case he had an accident. They purchased a $50,000 policy with double indemnity in case of accidental death with the wife being named beneficiary.

On the night of the murder the Sheriff's office received a call from a motorist who had been driving in rural Livingston Parish near an intersection of two country roads that were surrounded by woods with no houses nearby. The motorist said that as he rounded a curve he saw a large dark-colored automobile that had been stopped ahead of him suddenly speed away. When he reached the place, he had first seen the car the body of the young man was in the roadway. Jimmy Huntley Forrest owned a large dark green late-model Pontiac.

Further investigation revealed that on the night of the murder Jimmy had picked up Bezar, the retarded man, drove to his sister and brother-in-law's house and told them he was taking him to meet the man who was going to give him the high-paying truck driving job. As the three of them approached the location of the murder site. Jimmy stopped the car and told the others everybody needed to get out and take a leak. The young man was standing at the side of the car when Jimmy opened the trunk from which Bezoar took a shotgun and shot the young man in the back of the head at point-blank range. Shortly thereafter the other car approached as Jimmy and Bezoar sped away.

When the detectives arrested Bezoar he quickly confessed and took them to a culvert in the subdivision where he and Jimmy's brother-in-law lived where the shotgun was found.

A couple of days later after I had determined the events surrounding the murder, I came back to the jail to talk to Jimmy. He continued to profess his innocence but told me that if I could get him bonded out all he wanted to do was get in his car and drive away. I told him that under

168

the circumstances I did not feel comfortable representing him for such a cold-blooded murder. He told me that if I represented him and his sister that they would pay me the entire amount of the hundred-thousand-dollar insurance policy which was the equivalent of $1 million today.

I believe that I could have won an acquittal for Jimmy Hunt and his sister. The codefendant, Bezar was probably incompetent and also had confessed when he was questioned by the deputies without having been provided a lawyer. I knew that the district attorney would probably have entered a plea bargain with me for Bezar. I would not have let him testify if I had taken his case and without that testimony, the circumstantial case against Jimmy Hunt and his sister would have melted away.

I told Jimmy Hunt that he didn't have enough money to hire me to save him on the charge and even if he did I would not take the case. I handled murder cases and other serious criminal cases when I knew my clients were probably guilty, but there was always other circumstances that came into play. I understood crimes of passion and tried cases where the original intent was robbery that ended in murder. In this case I felt Jimmy Hunt's meticulous planning to kill his young brother-in-law solely for money, and involving his much younger sister, as well as the retarded trigger man warranted the death penalty.

Jimmy Hunt was tried, convicted of first-degree murder and sentenced to death. His sister was convicted and sentenced to life in prison. Bezar pled guilty to manslaughter and was sentenced to 21 years in prison after testifying against Jimmy Hunt. While his case was on appeal, the United States Supreme Court declared the death penalty unconstitutional and he was resentenced to life in prison. About 30 years later he attempted to escape from Angola prison by concocting a scheme to arrange for his transfer to a local jail, but the plan was discovered, and he lives in Angola where he will probably die.

Years after the trial my friend Kearney Foster, who became chief of detectives of the Livingston Parish Sheriff's office, told me that he believed Jimmy Huntley Forest had killed his first wife in the other state where they lived but they could not find enough evidence to convict him. His sister contacted me after she had served more than 20 years in prison and I arranged for her early release.

169

Chapter 16. Judge Sam Rowe

When Sam qualified for judge, Joe Eddie Anzalone from Tangipahoa Parish qualified against him. That put me in a box because I had agreed to go along with the consensus of lawyers from Livingston Parish, but Joe Eddie had been a personal friend of mine since my campaign for district attorney, and he spent his money to help me. He went all out for me and helped me anyway he could, and I owed him a debt of gratitude. I went to see Sheriff Odom Graves and told him that I had to be with Joe Eddie and I knew Joe Eddie could not win. I knew that from the politics of the situation in Tangipahoa Parish as well as Livingston. Joe Eddie's mama was a Lard from Livingston parish and had lots of kinfolks in Livingston parish, but she had married an Italian from Independence. Joe Eddie's daddy was a hard-nosed hard-driving contractor and businessman. In those days there was a lot of discrimination between Blacks and Whites and still a lot of discrimination between Italians and Rednecks in Tangipahoa Parish. I knew in Tangipahoa Parish Joe Eddie would have trouble getting elected just in that parish alone, and in Livingston Parish which had very few Blacks, and lots of Rednecks, and almost no Italians, Joe Eddie was a lost goose. Odom knew it too.

I visited with Sam about his race and he told me don't worry about it. He knew just like I knew that he was going to win, and he and I were going to remain friends no matter what. He told me to go ahead and vote for Joe Eddie. Well I did that knowing Joe Eddie was going to get beat and sure enough Sam won a landslide victory. It was really easy in Livingston Parish to persuade the rednecks to vote against the dago from Tangipahoa Parish.

Sam always wanted to be a judge, he had not had as much experience as some of the older attorneys in the district but was eager to learn. After a couple of years serving as judge he got over what I call "judgeitus" and realized that he was not always right in his decisions and could be reversed by the Court of Appeals.

After he had been judge for a while he mellowed and generally tried to help people as much as he could and still be fair and follow the law. Courts in those days operated rather loosely and followed the rules set up by the local judges, and I had lots of cases in all three parishes of the district. Many times, I would have cases set in both Livingston and Tangipahoa parishes on the same days before different judges. This resulted in me going to one parish for a case and then to the second parish for another case. I usually had my secretary call the judge's office on those occasions to advise the judge that I would be late for one case or the other.

Sometimes, usually after carousing with my friends and clients the night before court, the next morning, I would forget to make the phone call. The judges and other attorneys knew that I was working very hard and subject to be late on occasion.

After Sam became judge he decided that everybody had to be in his court on time when he called the docket. Otherwise they would be subject to a fine. This rule had been in effect for many years but was mainly directed to the defendants in criminal court and the litigants in civil court. Sam decided the rule also would be directed to the attorneys.

This ruling was very popular with the litigants in civil cases, and defendants in criminal cases, who had to be at court on time, and sometimes sat for hours in the courtroom waiting for lawyers to appear. The lawyers, on the other hand, didn't like it at all. Many times, I would appear in court on a rule day when 20 or more cases were on the docket, and after the docket was called would have to wait for several hours for my cases to be argued.

I explained to Sam, that I checked with the Clerk of Court before court started and determined how many cases were on the docket and where my cases were positioned. If my cases were at or near the top of the list I would be in court when it opened. On the other hand, if my cases were far down the docket list I felt it would make more sense for me to go to another court, or work from my office making or returning telephone calls and seeing clients with urgent needs. I would tell my clients to be in court on time and answer when their names were called, but I would call the judge's office and ask my cases be passed until I arrived. I would not be wasting the court's time because the judge could be hearing other cases until I arrived. Sam insisted that all the lawyers had to be in his court on time, and while he might not impose a fine for tardiness he certainly would give a lecture, much to the enjoyment of the

171

audience in the courtroom, about how he was going to punish the unfortunate attorney when he or she finally arrived. I knew Sam very well, and I often appeared late in his courtroom. On those times my clients would meet me outside the courtroom and tell me what Sam had said he was going to do to me for being late, I would ask them how long before I arrived he had made the statements. If they told me it was only a few minutes I would go to the office of the Clerk of Court, Lucius Patterson, and visit with him as we drank coffee for 15 to 20 minutes and talked about Sam's actions. I told Lucius I needed to kill that much time, so Sam would cool down after lambasting me in my absence in his court. I then went in the courtroom and made my appearance, explaining to the judge that some urgent matter had arose requiring my presence. Sam would then instruct the minute clerk to delete from the record what he had said about me being late.

Sometime later, Sam arrived at his office before court, and had an impromptu visit from some of his old friends. They got to talking and he arrived some 20 minutes late for court. I and several other lawyers who he had criticized for not being on time were in the courtroom, and he read our minds about how it was okay for him to be late but not us. Sam was very well aware of the fact that only a lawyer could run for office against a judge, and he didn't want any future opposition. He then put on the court record that since he was late he was violating his own rule and he fined himself $50. Shortly after that Sam stopped his practice of imposing a fine on a lawyer for being a little late.

When Sam became judge, I had been trying cases for over 10 years and in almost every case that I had with different insurance companies, I settled them, except with Allstate Insurance Company. Allstate was created by the people that ran Sears, Roebuck and Company who used to sell dry goods from catalogs and later established chain stores. The slogan they used was "we are the good hands people, you're in good hands with Allstate." Well, the good hands people did business this way. If you got in a wreck with someone who was insured by Allstate, who was at fault, Allstate would lowball you and try to starve you out before offering any kind of settlement that was anywhere near fair. They would delay every case by asking for jury trials. Jury trials would automatically delay the case for at least a year. In non-jury trials by Judges, 5 or 6 trials could be handled in the time that it took for one jury trial. So, Allstate in every case I had against them, wouldn't settle, I had to sue, they asked for a jury trial and it would be put off and put off and put off.

Just before Sam took office we had a meeting and I said, "Sam I would like you to give me a special jury term, so I can try these cases that have been delayed by Allstate." He agreed to do that, and one of the first things he did when he became judge was to set pretrial conferences. He set a week when he had no other cases for jury trials for me. He asked me how many trials I could try a week. I told him I could try three. He said, "I don't believe that, usually it takes a week to try one jury trial." Usually, the first day you pick a jury, start the trial the second day and finish the third day. Then you only have two more days. You don't have time to pick another jury and do another one. "I told him I could do it." So, he set three jury trials with Allstate one after the other. We had one jury pool. So, when we picked a jury for the first one and we tried that case we could use the same jurors except for the ones that actually served on the next jury and so on. Allstate Insurance Company had been very very successful in defending its cases in New Orleans. New Orleans at that time as it is now had a majority of blacks. And the black jurors in Orleans Parish tended to give a lot of money from insurance companies to people who were injured. Allstate countered that by hiring as their number one trial attorney a beautiful young black girl who's was skin was the color of cream. She had very few characteristics of the Negro race. Just a beautiful young woman in her mid-30s who spoke perfect English and was very very smart. She would pick those black juries and relate to them. She would flirt with the Black male jurors and she knew exactly how to manipulate them to lowball the plaintiff's attorneys against Allstate. She was the Attorney they sent to Tangipahoa Parish to try the cases against me.

To get prepared for a jury trial, I did then, as I do now, get the jury list 30 days before the trial. I then went through the list to see if I knew anybody or recognized any family member that might be on the list. Then I went to every plaintiff's lawyer in Tangipahoa Parish and asked them to look at the jury list and tell me if there was anybody on the jury list that they might have represented or they might know that might be inclined to give an injured person money, or might not be inclined to

173

give any money. I had learned shortly after I began practicing, in a big case you never put any retired person who is also receiving social security on the jury. They will be sympathetic to the injured person, but if their income is only $5,000 a year and you're asking for $50,000 or $100,000, they would think that's way too much and only maybe give you $10,000.

Bankers and business people were usually very conservative unless you really knew who they were ahead of time. On the other hand, union people, Blacks, and working people were ideal. I never wanted to have a schoolteacher on the jury because they never gave much money to anybody. It's probably because they weren't well-paid for their jobs and they didn't think the people that were injured should get very much. Anyway, we picked the first jury. I was representing Ms. Erdey, a 61-year-old widow, who lived between Albany and Springfield. She worked as a clerk in one of the stores in Hammond. I had known her for many years prior to this accident. She was hit in the rear at a stop light in Hammond, Louisiana by an agent who worked for Allstate Insurance Company. He had an insurance policy with one hundred thousand-dollar limits. Ms. Erdey went to her local doctors for treatment of soft tissue injuries to her back. She had problems in the past which were aggravated by the accident. When she got hurt she was on the way to her job and received Worker's Compensation Benefits after the accident, so she had enough income to survive and carry on without working, while we were waiting more than a year to get to court. Her doctors told her due to her injuries should retire and when she reached the age of 62 she got her Social Security Pension from her late husband and did so.

Before the trial began, I checked the case law, and determined, based on prior decisions of the courts, that a fair settlement of this case would be about twelve to fifteen thousand dollars. I told the Allstate attorney that I would settle the case for $12,500.00, she offered me $2,500.00 which was typical of Allstate Insurance Company.

I knew we had a good case. To get ready to pick the jury, I received the jury list from the Clerk of Court. When I went through it I saw it was full of ringers. Now a ringer, in lawyer terminology, is a person who, when he is selected to be on a jury, will ring the bell for the plaintiff. In other words, they would give money to somebody that had been injured.

One of the ringers was a fellow who within the last five years had brought his girlfriend to my office and got me to handle her divorce. His name was on the jury list, as well as his wife. Another lady on the jury list had a grandson who had come to me on a minor criminal matter that I'd handled a year or two before. I had represented the brother of another person on the jury list, in a criminal case in the past and I knew several other people on the list. One of my best friends was Milton Cox, who was my banker. Milton had been a banker in Ponchatoula, Hammond, and in Springfield. He lived in Ponchatoula.

I had never represented Milton professionally but had known him socially for years and had represented many of our mutual friends.

When I started the selection process. My opening statement to the prospective jurors was this, "Have I ever represented any of you on this list as your attorney, or have I ever represented any friend or relative that you might have that would cause you to be prejudiced either for or against my client? In other words, can you be fair?" Well hell, everybody wants to be fair, and everybody answered no. That New Orleans woman lawyer for Allstate bought that hook line and sinker. When it came to those particular ringers, I never asked them the first question about money. Nothing about how much the case was worth and how much they might give or not give, I asked questions as to what kind of work they did and about their families. I already knew the answers to most of my questions, and I just asked them again if they could be fair. When I got to Milton I asked him what his profession was. He said that he was a banker and that's all that girl from New Orleans wanted to hear. She wanted a banker on that jury because she thought he would be conservative. I didn't ask Milton what bank he currently worked at, which was in Springfield, and was my bank. I asked him if he had been a banker in Hammond and Ponchatoula in Tangipahoa Parish where he lived, and he said yes, and that's all she heard. She didn't think to ask him where he was a banker right now. If she had asked that question he would have had to tell her Springfield, and she would have realized I was from Springfield. The next question would have been "Mr. Cox is Mr. Pardue a customer of your bank?" She could have knocked him off the jury just like that, but she never asked those questions. Judge Sam Rowe knew Milton Cox, but he didn't ask the questions either.

When the jury was selected. I got the grandma whose grandson I represented, the man with the girlfriend, and his wife, and the brother of the guy I had represented. Out of 12 jurors and I had four and I had Milton Cox. That was 5/12 of the jury. I wasn't worried about the other seven because I knew if I had two or three strong advocates on that jury, that would be enough. That was fine with me.

After putting on the witnesses, and the testimony of the doctors, Ms. Erdey testified that she had been working full time as a store clerk before the accident. She was on her feet most of the time stacking and loading heavy merchandise, and things that she couldn't do anymore. This was verified by her Doctor. I had an expert, who said she could probably have worked until she was 70 if she hadn't been injured so she was due 9 years of lost wages, she would have pain-and-suffering for the rest of her life. The lawyer from Allstate thought she was in good shape because she had a couple of black women on the jury, but I knew those black women were jealous of the high yellow black lawyer because she was such a good-looking thing. They weren't going do anything for her. I had excused any black men from the jury who might have been influenced by her.

When we finished the case, the judge gave instructions to the jury on how to answer the jury interrogatories and how to deliberate about the case. He told them if they had questions they could get the bailiff to come and he would give them the answers. He summed it up this way "When you walk out of here the case in your hands. Here is a set of instructions and jury verdict forms for you to sign. You will now go back in the jury room and choose a foreman of your group who will fill out this form. When you reach a verdict, let the bailiff know and he'll get me, and we will come back in the courtroom. Your foreman will bring your verdict form back to me." Now the normal thing would be for the judge to give that verdict form to the bailiff and the he would take the jury back to the jury room and hand it to them, where they would pick a foreman. Sam did not do it that way. Sam finished his speech about how it was all done and go into the back and pick yourself a foreman. Then he said "Mr. Cox, come here and take this verdict form" by doing this, the jury must have thought that the judge knew what he was talking about. He gave the verdict form to Mr. Cox, so the Judge wanted Milton

176

to be foreman. Of course, Milton was smarter than that and better educated, so he probably would have got to be foreman anyway. He told me later that when they got in the back room he had the verdict form and he told them the judge wants us to do this and I can go ahead and take care of this thing, has anybody got any objections, and nobody objected. That's how Milton got to be foreman of the jury. The jury was out for no more than an hour. Milton told me later that he suggested the figures on the jury verdict and the jury unanimously agreed. Where I'd offered to settle for $12,500 the jury gave me $65,000 which was the highest verdict for that type of injury in Tangipahoa Parish history. An award in that amount for soft tissue injury was just unheard of, and of course Allstate would appeal. I got a verdict for more than twice as much as could be expected.

Judge Sam Rowe proved to be my true friend. He knew, as I did, if the jury came in with that kind of verdict Allstate was gonna appeal it to the Court of Appeals, where some conservative judges on that Court would probably knock that verdict down to maybe $10,000. But Sam also knew if he reduced the verdict, the Court of Appeal would have a whole lot more trouble trying to reduce it further. After the jury came in, Sam immediately called a recess and got me and the other lawyer in his office. He told us that the jury's verdict was out of line and that he was going to dismiss the jury, and then he was going to address the jury's verdict. The attorney for Allstate thought she had her a big victory. I was little disappointed, but I knew what would happen in the Court of Appeal if Sam didn't reduce it. After the jury was gone Sam put on the record that he had heard the whole trial and he felt the jury's award had been excessive in the amount they gave my client and that he was going to reduce it down to $47,000, which was $20,000 more than I could've got at the Court of Appeals. Allstate appealed, and sure enough, when it went to the Court of Appeals it affirmed what Sam Rowe had done. Allstate had dragged out the case over 3 or 4 years and I got interest on the judgment from the date I filed suit. My client wound up with a total award of around $65,000, the amount the jury wanted to give me in the first place.

We finished the trial that we had started on Monday, late on Tuesday. On Wednesday morning I was back in court to pick another jury on another case against Allstate. We tried that case in one day and I got a jury award for about $20,000 about 10 o'clock that night. The next morning, I was back in court about 9 o'clock in the morning and on Friday we finished that case. I got another award that was much higher than Allstate had offered me. After that week of trial, the black female attorney never showed up in Tangipahoa Parish again. For years Allstate had used house counsel to defend its cases. It would not hire any local attorney from Tangipahoa or Livingston Parish to represent it even though there were many qualified defense firms who represented other insurance companies. When I beat Allstate on the first case, and it appealed, they discharged the girl who tried the case, and hired a different blue-ribbon defense firm from New Orleans to do the appeal. It didn't do them any good, because they couldn't change what Sam Rowe had done. After that, anytime I filed a lawsuit against Allstate Insurance Company it had a local lawyer on the other side. Sometimes it might be somebody from Baton Rouge or Covington, but it wasn't the same firm from New Orleans that they had been using to fight for the company.

Chapter 17. Justin Wilson

I first met Justin Wilson through Van Foster when we were members of the Bear Island Rod and Gun Club on Blind River. I had helped Van's brother Carew in his election for school board member from the sixth ward of Livingston Parish. I was still attending Southeastern Louisiana College in the early 1960's when Carew told me about an opening in the club membership and I purchased it for $300 from Boo Boo Piper, from Denham Springs who had grown too old to hunt the swamp. The club had an old barge with living quarters on it that was pulled on the bank of Blind River about a mile from Lake Maurepas.

Carew was a carpenter and we decided to level the barge and add porches and extend the wharfs. All labor was done by members and their hunting guests who used the camp. While we were working jacking up the barge, Van and Justin arrived In Van's boat.

Justin was a local celebrity who was employed as a safety engineer by large oil and chemical companies. He had recorded Cajun stories and written a cookbook on Cajun food. He lived between Walker and Port Vincent, Louisiana and had married a lady who was an heir to the company that made Pearl beer in Texas. I was very impressed to be able to meet him in person. He was not impressed with a brash twenty-year-old college student who was covered with mud and had a hammer in his hand.

During a break from work we sat down, and I got a Budweiser beer from an ice chest. Justin told me that I ought to be drinking Pearl beer. I told him that I didn't like the taste of it and Budweiser was better. From that day forward Justin never liked me.

Over the years Justin's fame grew and he made several recordings of his Cajun tales and jokes. Justin supported many politicians in South Louisiana but never was a candidate for election himself. In the election for District Attorney when I ran he was against me and in the next election between Joe Simpson and Duncan Kemp he backed the loser.

Duncan held a fundraiser at Sammy's restaurant in Hammond after he was elected District Attorney and invited Justin Wilson to be master of ceremonies at the dinner. Justin quickly agreed even though he had

179

been a strong supporter of Joe Simpson. A few days before the event I met with Sammy Graziano, the restaurant's owner who was a good friend of mine and concocted a plan to embarrass Justin.

I told Sammy I wanted him to prepare a special covered dish for Justin, consisting of a Cornish hen, to be presented to him after all the other guests had been served. The day before the event I shot a crow and carefully cut off its head, wings, and feet and delivered them to Sammy to place around the Cornish hen under the cover of the dish. I also gave Sammy one of my business cards to place on the platter.

When the dish was delivered Justin refused to uncover it and sat through the meal without eating. The crowd was mystified at this event, and after Justin made very few remarks and started to leave the head table with the still uncovered crow in front of his seat, I took the opportunity to remove the cover. The crowd roared with laughter when they realized I had sent Justin Wilson the ultimate message of his having to eat crow for his actions in changing sides after his candidate had been defeated. Justin never forgave me for that, either.

A few years later after his wife died he married a much younger woman. He was the star of a very popular TV cooking show where he prepared various dishes and told humorous Cajun stories. He purchased property on Coyell Bay near the Amite River and built a large home in French Settlement. To get to his house he built a driveway across a small swampy area near the river.

About the same time, I purchased some property on the Tickfaw River at the Rome's Ferry Bridge near Killian Louisiana from the heirs of Hazel Foster who had operated a small bar and boat landing at that location. I planned to expand the parking lot and build a new establishment. To do so I had to go through an extensive and expensive permitting process since the property was located in the coastal zone.

Livingston Parish officials had been promised future federal funds if the parish agreed to become part of the coastal zone which was South of Interstate 12. They readily agreed not realizing that any developers would have to receive permits not only from the US Corps of Engineers but also the Louisiana Department of environmental quality.

When these regulations went into effect, many developers contacted me about having Livingston Parish removed from the coastal zone, so they would only have one set of permits to obtain. I contacted parish officials who had no objection to the proposed change in law and also contacted representative Juba Diez about introducing the legislation.

When the public became aware of the proposed change in the law hearings were held by the legislature. A restaurant owner in French settlement whose property had been filled with dirt, from a canal dredged nearby, objected to the change since he believed new development would result in competition with his business. One of his best customers was his new neighbor Justin Wilson.

Before the hearings I went to the restaurant whose owner objected and discovered that he had placed old automobile tires and other debris in the canal next to his business without a permit. I also discovered that Justin Wilson had filled in the swamp to make a driveway to his new home without a permit from either the Corps of Engineers or the DEQ. I made pictures of both areas that had been illegally filled and brought them with me to the state capital for the hearings.

When the hearings began the chairman of the legislative committee made an introduction of Justin Wilson to the committee and audience praising him for his contributions to Louisiana and to protecting the environment. Justin made an impassioned statement about his concerns for protecting the scenic beauty of Louisiana from greedy developers who only wanted to make money. He didn't mention my name, but it was very clear that he was talking about me.

When my turn to testify came, I pointed out that the coastal zone was created to cover the southern parishes, most of whom already had extensive commercial development, and the consequences of the zoning had not been explained to Livingston Parish officials who now did not oppose the proposed legislation. I then presented a copy of the pictures I had taken of the restaurant owners and Justin Wilson's property to each member of the committee and pointed out that I didn't come around telling funny stories like Mr. Wilson did, but I had just proved him to be a hypocrite.

The committee chairman admonished me for personally attacking Justin Wilson and the committee took no action on the bill.

Chapter 18. Ed Layrisson

Ed Layrisson was a few years behind me at Ponchatoula High School where he played football after I graduated. I had no contact with him for several years until I had started practicing law, and I had no idea that he was interested in politics. Ed and his friend John Dahmer, classmates at Ponchatoula High School, purchased an old van which they painted with flowers, let their hair grow long, and wore beards. Many called them hippies during the age of Aquarius. John's father had been mayor of Ponchatoula in the late 1950s and was good friends with Ed's father. Ed went to college, graduated from Southeastern and got a job teaching school at Maurepas Louisiana.

In 1972 I ran for district attorney in Livingston, Tangipahoa and St. Helena parishes. Frank Edwards, who had recently been elected sheriff of Tangipahoa Parish supported Leonard Yokum, who was elected. Six years later Joe Simpson, Mr. Yokum's first assistant ran for District Attorney against Duncan Kemp, III, son of the late Duncan Kemp Jr, the former District Attorney, and a third candidate, Charlie Palmer from Amite. During the same election Gordon Anderson was elected Marshall of the seventh Ward of Tangipahoa Parish.

Joe Simpson, with the support of Sheriffs Odom Graves of Livingston Parish and Frank Edwards of Tangipahoa, ran first in the primary, a few votes ahead of Duncan Kemp, and the election appeared to be a tossup. Gordon, fresh from his victory in the Marshall's race, met with his father, brother Tom, and a few of his very close supporters to consider his possible candidacy for Sheriff the next year.

Frank had openly supported Joe Simpson in the first primary and contacted Gordon and his father, Mr. Vic, the former Marshall, to help in Joe's race. The Anderson's decided it would be in their best interest to support Duncan, given Gordon's interest in the upcoming Sheriff's race and turned Frank down. When Frank relayed this news to Odom, he withdrew his support for Joe, who decided to concede defeat to Duncan even though he had received the most votes in the first primary.

The night Joe conceded defeat, he met Calvin Fayard, Bob Morrison, and Jimmy Kuhn, attorneys from Livingston Parish who had supported him, at Schroler' s restaurant on the St. Helena and

Tangipahoa Parish line. Joe and his friends were drinking heavily when Lynn Singleton, a St. Helena attorney who supported Duncan arrived. An argument began when Art Macy, Duncan's law partner, who was in his 60s and used a walking cane joined the group. Joe who was much younger than Art Macy began to curse him, and Macy hit Joe with his walking cane.

Frank Edwards was considered vulnerable in his reelection bid. Marshall Vic Anderson from Hammond had served for more than 30 years and had often been considered a likely candidate for Sheriff, but never ran. After his last term in 1978, his son Gordon was elected Marshall. Frank's enemies encouraged Gordon to run for Sheriff in 1979 and Gordon did so.

Both candidates were well-financed and had fathers who had been elected to public office in law enforcement. Gordon and his father had hunted with me at my camp in Mississippi and I carried an honorary Marshall's badge from their office. Frank and I had made peace after he had attacked me in my run for district attorney, and we became very close personal friends. Frank and his sons had also hunted with me in Mississippi. I told both of them that I wasn't going to take sides in their fight, and while I would not openly support either, I would not oppose either one of them.

Ed Layrisson also entered the race. I did not have any idea that he was a serious candidate since he had no political organization. I figured some of Frank's friends may have encouraged him to run to split Gordon's support in South Tangipahoa. On the other hand, I figured that maybe some of Gordon's friends had got Ed in the race to run Frank into a second primary where he could be defeated by Gordon.

The election appeared to be developing into a tossup between the two with Frank as incumbent, drawing most of his support from the north part of the parish and Gordon drawing his from the South.

Gordon attacked Frank with the usual political ads and complained about jail conditions. Frank had recently attempted to pass a tax to build a new jail and upgrade equipment for the sheriff's department that failed.

Frank took out advertisements in the local newspapers using a format of a comic page cartoon entitled "The Anderson Fairytales", in which Gordon was portrayed as an unintelligent son of an old political

183

boss who had put his other son Tom on the payroll of the Marshall's office while he was going to college. Every week the political ads got more and more personal and people were wondering what the latest chapter of the Anderson Fairytales would reveal.

Meanwhile, Ed pursued a grassroots campaign without attacking either of the other candidates, simply saying he would make the better Sheriff. During the campaign someone told Ed that I was against him and he called me about it. I told him that I was completely neutral in the race and that I would do nothing to hurt his candidacy. I fully expected him to be eliminated in the first primary, and Frank and Gordon to be in the runoff.

When the votes were counted there was a second primary between Frank and Ed with Frank slightly in the lead and Gordon running last. After all the negative campaign ads, the majority of the people were looking for something positive and, in the runoff, supported the new man.

When a new Sheriff is elected in Louisiana the old Sheriff is responsible for any deficit in the funds for operating the office he is leaving. The campaign had been very bitter and the two would hardly speak to each other. Ed's half-brother William Cleveland, a lawyer from New Orleans, filed a suit to force Frank to make an accounting of the assets of the Sheriff's office that Frank had been selling as surplus equipment to cover the deficit. The case was assigned to Judge Brent Dufreche for hearing.

I had seen newspaper articles about Frank selling guns, police cars and other office equipment, but I had not talked Frank for several weeks when he stopped me in the lobby of the courthouse in Amite one morning. I had just finished court and he invited me to lunch. When I asked him how he was doing he told me "I need a lawyer." I asked him what was it about and he said he wanted me to represent him at a status conference with Judge Dufreche and Ed's lawyer at 1p.m. that afternoon. I told him that it was like he was giving me the last ticket on the Titanic. I had made peace with Frank after our political fight, but it took several years for our friendship to really develop. If I took his case, it would be damn near impossible for me to get friendly with Ed, who would certainly be in office for 4 years. He said, "You got to help me." I told him okay, but I sure didn't have much time to get ready.

We talked over lunch about the strategy I would use at the meeting and agreed that we should compromise with the best deal I could get short of costing him money out of his pocket. When we went to the judge's office, Ed and his lawyer met us at the door. The judge came to the door and told us to come in, but when Ed started to enter he told him to stay outside and I told Frank to do likewise. The judge and I were personal friends, and he, being from Ponchatoula had known Ed since he was a boy. He had known Frank's father who had been sheriff until 1952 and Frank since he started practicing law in the early 1960s. William Cleveland started to make a speech about Frank selling the assets of the Sheriff's office so that Ed would have no vehicles or weapons for his new deputies. Brent quickly stopped him and told him the case needed to be settled. He said that what Frank was doing was legal and that the state police and sheriff departments from other jurisdictions would assist in providing equipment and manpower until new equipment could be acquired. Cleveland started to object, and I told him that this outcome would benefit Ed more than Frank because Frank couldn't pass the tax for a new jail and equipment, but now Ed could get the people's support due to the emergency. The case was compromised and shortly thereafter Ed proposed a tax election for the Sheriff's office which was passed by a large margin.

This enabled him to build a very badly needed modern jail, purchase new patrol cars and other equipment, and ensure his reelection for many years. Frank on the other hand went to work for the state under the administration of Governor Edwin Edwards and reestablished his law practice.

Frank told me about his experience with people after the election. While he was Sheriff he said, every Christmas he would receive gifts of hams, turkeys' wine and liquor, as well as invitations to go on fishing trips and vacations with his political friends. Two years after his defeat he did not receive a single Christmas gift from them. We remained close friends and worked together on the Combustion class action lawsuit in Livingston Parish that lasted more than10 years until we finally made a settlement for more than 4000 clients.

185

When he took office, Ed made John Dahmer chief deputy and reorganized the Sheriff's office with more than 90% new deputies. I had a meeting with John shortly after he took office and he assured me that I would receive full cooperation from his deputies and jail personnel in my visits to my clients who were incarcerated, as well as access to their criminal records to the extent legally permitted. I couldn't ask for more, and this insured my future support for Ed and John.

Chapter19. Earl Jones and the Teamsters

I first met Earl Jones when I ran for District Attorney in 1972. Earl was born and raised on Pea Ridge Road near Albany. He was a couple years older than me, in his 30s and was an assistant business agent for the Teamsters union which was run by Edward Grady Parton from Baton Rouge. Baton Rouge and the surrounding area was undergoing a rapid period of growth, new subdivisions and industrial expansion of the plants along the Mississippi River required lots of concrete. There were two major concrete companies that provided concrete culverts, slabs for buildings and roads and driveways.

Along the Amite River in Livingston, St. Helena, East Baton Rouge and East Feliciana parishes there were mining operations that provided sand and gravel from pits. The operators of the gravel pits sold products to Heck Industries and Dunham Concrete Company in Baton Rouge. The raw materials were trucked to concrete plants and concrete products were trucked to the construction sites. The Teamsters union organized truck drivers that drove for those companies.

I read newspaper reports of the strikes called by the Teamsters against the companies to shut them down until they gave pay raises to the drivers. When the company's resisted the union, picket lines were put up at construction sites, and when nonunion truckers crossed those lines many fights broke out. Company trucks were sabotaged, and concrete pipes used for drainage ditches and parking lots were damaged at great cost to the businesses.

The concrete pipes were precast into 10 to 12-foot sections with a large lip on one end. When the pipes were brought to the job they were connected with heavy equipment by placing the small end of the pipe into the wide lips on the next piece of pipe and concreted together in the trenches or ditches where they were installed. During these labor strikes teamsters would go to the job's sites at night with sledgehammers and break the lips on the pipes which rendered them useless, since they could not be connected. This cost the company's thousands of dollars and they retaliated by placing armed guards at the construction sites to prevent the sabotage.

The union provided many benefits to the workers in the form of higher wages, hospitalization, insurance and pensions. The contracts with the companies required that all workers whether they were union members or not had money deducted from their payroll checks as union dues. These funds were paid directly to the union. Part of those dues were placed in pension funds from which loans were made for investments in projects for construction of new subdivisions and businesses.

There were lots of news reports of businessmen who could not get financing for their projects from the banks, that would go to the Teamsters for the financing. When these businesses could not pay their debts there were reports of violent threats against the debtors who in fear of their lives would pay the Teamsters before paying anyone else including state and local taxes.

There were congressional investigations in the 1960's, and Robert Kennedy, the United States Attorney General looked into the national Teamsters union whose president was Jimmy Hoffa. Ed Parton was an ally of Hoffa who ran the local Teamsters union in Baton Rouge. Earl Jones was one of his closest associates and was rumored to be involved in some of the damages the concrete plants.

One of toughest, most unscrupulous members of the Teamsters union was Tommy Craig. He lived in Baton Rouge and was one of Edward Parton's closest associates. He would go anywhere and do anything that Ed told him to. He was ruthless with his enemies and took advantage of his friends.

I first met him through my friend Charlie Abels, who was a state police trooper in the late 1960s and 1970s, Craig was a big man, about 6'5" tall and weighed about 245 pounds. He had shoulder length hair and often wore a beard. His hangouts were the roughest bar rooms in North Baton Rouge where he regularly participated in dice games using loaded dice and crooked card games with marked cards.

Charlie Abels became friends with Tommy when he invited Charlie to hunt turkeys on some of his relative's land near Liberty, Mississippi. Charlie and I made several turkey hunts with him, and he told me about some of his experiences.

He regularly put out corn and built blinds in the woods belonging to timber companies where he could illegally kill wild turkeys, and he had no scruples about killing hens as well as gobblers. He paid no attention to posted signs on property belonging to private owners and had no respect for the game wardens or game laws.

He told me about a dispute that he had with a wealthy cattle farmer who had refused to let him hunt on his land. Tommy said he drove out to the farm late in the afternoon the next day and shot the farmers registered bull and two registered cows in their bellies with a 22-caliber rifle. I asked him why he did that, and he told me the cattle would not die immediately from the small bullet wound to their stomach and there would be no way for the farmer to determine what killed his cattle.

Tommy bragged about controlling the activities of his associates in the bar rooms he frequented. He was the undisputed leader of the group and would fight anyone who disputed his authority. One night a couple of men from New Orleans came into a bar where Tommy and some of his friends were drinking. A dispute arose, and they got into a fight. Tommy beat the other man senseless then took out his knife and cut off the other man's long beard. A couple of days later Tommy was sitting alone at the unoccupied bar where the fight had occurred. He was talking to the barmaid when another man walked up behind him and shot him in the back of the head killing him instantly.

In addition to negotiating contracts with the companies, the union controlled the votes of its members and backed candidates for state and local offices. Local sheriffs, assessors, legislators and police jurors, as well as state wide office holders quietly sought this large block of votes and the money the union could provide to get them to the polls. When the union members got in trouble with the law or needed their driveways graded and graveled, or their assessments lowered, elected officials who had been helped by the union were happy to do the favors for the members who voted for them. Earl Jones was very effective in helping to get out the vote at election time and to see that his friends and members requests to politicians were granted.

Earl and his friends loved to hunt and fish and didn't pay much attention to the game laws. A group of them traveled to Colorado one fall to hunt mule deer and elk and set up camp in a national forest. The season on grouse was closed which made no difference to the Teamsters. One night after they had feasted on roasted grouse and illegal venison, they were gathered around the fire at their tent camp when they received a visit from game wardens who found grouse feathers on the ground. A big warden addressed them sarcastically as he would a child "what kind of bird has red feathers?" One of the big Teamsters looked him in the eye and said," A damn red bird." They were charged with hunting violations but returned home and never paid the fines.

I represented Earl and many of his friends over the years when they got in trouble with the law and needed my legal services. The investigations into the damages the Teamsters allegedly caused contractors using nonunion labor resulted in several federal indictments. When the feds could not make a case against Earl, he was charged with income tax evasion. A review of his tax returns revealed he had failed to report some income and I advised him to enter a plea which would save him from doing any jail time and only resulted in him being on probation for a short time.

On the day we went to court in Baton Rouge before Judge Frank Polazola, we were sitting in the courtroom when Lewis Unglesby, a Baton Rouge attorney, and his client, Barry Seal arrived. I had been friends with Lewis since he began practicing law a few years earlier and was familiar with the charges against Barry Seal.

There had been stories in the newspapers and on television About Seal smuggling cocaine into the United States from Columbia. He was caught by the drug enforcement agents in Miami, Florida as well as in Louisiana. Lewis managed to make a deal with the DEA in Florida for Seal to receive immunity from prosecution if he would install cameras inside his airplane and film high-ranking members of the Colombian drug cartel supplying thousands of pounds of cocaine to be shipped into the United States. Some of those pictures were shown by President Ronald Reagan on national television when he was speaking against the Colombian drug trade.

Seal was given immunity in the federal court in Florida, but in Louisiana the federal prosecutors refused to do so. They wanted Seal to be punished for bringing large amounts of cocaine into the state and urged Judge Polazola to give him a long prison sentence. Lewis argued

190

that he should receive probation since he had risked his life to obtain the pictures and other evidence against the Colombians which resulted in indictments against them. The judge refused to place Seal on probation and sent him to a halfway house in North Baton Rouge instead. Lewis objected strongly to this development, but the judge told him that Seal could be released each morning to go to work and return to the halfway house each night. Earl and I heard Lewis tell the judge, "You are giving him a death sentence, the Colombians will have him killed." News of the judge's decision was broadcast on television throughout the world. Within a few days several Colombian nationals shot and killed Barry Seal when he returned to the halfway house.

I became good friends with Earl and other members of the Teamsters and they did me favors. When I had my hunting camp in Mississippi one of the members who had organized the club was Bill Johnson, one of my teachers in high school. Bill found the property on Buffalo River, got members to put up money to buy it and we set up rules for the operation of the club.

The other members put trot lines in the river to catch catfish and they caught a few fish. I quickly figured out that the easy way to catch fish was with nets. The river was shallow enough to wade across in most places but had some holes several feet deep between sandbars. These deep holes would hold catfish that would move from one hole to another when the river rose a few feet after rains. I placed my hoop nets with the open-end downstream in the deep holes. When the river rose, the fish would move upstream, and many would go into my nets. I provided enough fish to feed all the members of the club and had more to take home. Bill Johnson's son, William was jealous of me catching so many fish and turned me in to the game warden for illegal fishing.

One of my best friends, Tom Kent Stewart and I were turkey hunting at the camp and returned from the woods late one afternoon to be greeted by the old game warden who told me I would have to go to the justice of the peace's house to answer the charges. Tom and I had our shotguns in the truck with us when we were stopped by the game warden outside my camp. I told the warden that he would have to wait until I went in the camp and cleaned up and left him fuming in the road in front of my camp. We went inside, had a leisurely drink, changed

191

clothes, came back to the game warden and told him we would follow him to see the judge.

The judge had his office at his home about ten miles away. I had never been there before. We drove down a narrow gravel road that wound through the hills to get there. The judge was an old uneducated black man who had recently been elected by the newly enfranchised majority black population of that ward in Wilkinson County, Mississippi. Bill Johnson knew the old black gentleman and contributed to his election. The game warden, a white man who had worked as a warden for many years, obviously showed his disdain for the old judge who knew nothing about game laws. Neither of them knew anything about the technicalities of navigable streams. I contended that the river was too shallow to navigate and did not fall under the fishing regulations prohibiting the use of hoop nets. The game warden who had picked up two of my nets thought I was going to pay a fine and that would be the end of it. Instead I told the judge I wanted a trial and we agreed to come back to the judge's house in about two weeks just before dark on a certain date.

Bill Johnson made a lot of remarks to the other club members about how if I was convicted I would be violating the club rules and he would kick me out of the club. Bill was a big bullying type of man who would fight at the drop of a hat and never fight fair. To get to the judge's house I would have to travel several miles through the woods on the narrow road that could easily be blocked. I figured correctly that Bill would probably have his boys who were younger than me, and some of his goons waylay me going to or coming from court. I, therefore, called on Earl Jones and his friends to give me an escort to the trial.

I met Earl and five more Teamsters in Baton Rouge about an hour before we had to be in Mississippi. I drove my car with a young Teamster sitting next to me in the passenger seat and Earl and Hubert Stilley, another Teamster member who was one of my best friends, in the backseat. Behind us was another car with four big Teamsters in it. When we arrived at the judge's house Bill Johnson, his son George and two other men were standing on the porch. I had a 38 revolver between the front seats my car. When we stopped I pulled the gun and started to place it in my boot. The Teamster sitting next to me stopped me and said "let me have that Mr. Pardue." I gave him the gun, and he placed it in one of his boots and put his gun in the other. All of the other teamsters were also armed.

As we walked to the front of the house one of the men with Bill Johnson was Peewee Gatlin, who had been a classmate of mine in high school and was now a member of the Teamsters union. All of the men with me knew Peewee and he knew all of them. Peewee stuck out his hand to shake hands with Earl and the others who ignored him and walked up the steps. The game warden who was talking to Bill Johnson looked at us with fear in his eyes. Bill Johnson demanded to know what the men who were with me were doing there and I told him they were my witnesses. It was a warm evening, and the old judge who was in his 60s, had a little office on the porch of his house. His old mother who was about 90 years old was inside and had a fire in the fireplace. I told the judge I wanted the witnesses sequestered and Bill Johnson's sons, Peewee Gatlin, and the other guy from Southwest Louisiana were told to go inside the house where the old woman was sitting by the fire. Four of the Teamsters stood on the front porch by the door and when Peewee and the rest of Bill's bunch wanted to open the door because of the heat inside, but they refused to let them come out. When we began the trial I took a tape recorder and turned it on and informed the judge, the game warden, and Bill Johnson that I was going to have a record of it. The game warden had not seen me fishing the nets and had acted strictly on what he had been told by Bill and his son. The game warden questioned Bill Johnson over my objections and the old judge knowing nothing of the law felt he had to rule for the game warden no matter what. I knew ahead of time that I was in a kangaroo court that I couldn't win but I made the most of it because the judge didn't know how to stop me from asking questions that had nothing to do with the game violation.

When Bill Johnson took the stand, I had the chance to cross-examine him. I asked him about all kinds of shady deals that he had pulled in the past. I asked him about him paying for a breast implant for one of his girlfriends to be performed by Dr. Randolph Howes in New Orleans. All of this was completely irrelevant, but I had Bill mad enough to do almost anything to me by the time we were through. He knew however, he was outnumbered and the people I had on my side were just

193

as bad as he was. He also knew they would do anything I told them to if he tried to mess with me. After the trial the judge found me guilty and I appealed his ruling. On the way back to Louisiana the Teamsters told me they wished I would have given them the okay because they wanted to beat the hell out of the whole bunch including the game warden and the old judge. I told them that if we had not been in Mississippi I would probably have okayed them dusting up Bill, Peewee and the rest but not a Mississippi Justice of the peace and game warden.

When I got home I called my friend Alonzo Sturgeon who was the Clerk of Court in Woodville Mississippi about my chances to reverse the ruling of the Justice of the Peace on appeal. I had met Alonzo shortly after I started hunting at the club and had given him catfish I had caught in my hoop nets, after his son and friends had hunted at my camp

Alonzo had been elected with the help of newly enfranchised Blacks who were first registered to vote after the passage of the federal voter's rights act, but he also had the support of most of the white voters. Later he was elected district attorney for Adams and Wilkinson County where he served many years.

He told me that since my fine was only $100, my making a fool of Bill was worth more than that; and I didn't need to stir up the game wardens and other locals with an appeal, even though I was probably right according to the law. After I cooled down, I realized that my friend had given me some excellent advice. I put my hoop nets back in the river and Bill and I called a truce in our dispute for a while.

Chapter 20. Joe Green Trial and the Deck of Cards

In the early 1980's I represented some members of the Green family from Holden Louisiana. I had met Joe Green who lived in Livingston Louisiana but didn't know him very well. One of his relatives contacted me about representing him after he had allegedly shot and gravely injured his former girlfriend.

The Sheriff had arrested Joe, charged him with aggravated battery, and incarcerated him in the parish jail. A local judge set his bond at $50,000. I agreed to represent Joe for a fee of $5000. When his relatives put up the money, the next day I went to see Judge Gordon Causey about reducing Joe's bond.

Joe's girlfriend had been shot in the head and remained unconscious at the Lady of the Lake Hospital. I told the judge that Joe was well known in Livingston Parish, a member of a large family, and was not a flight risk. I also told him I had talked to Sheriff Odom Graves and he had no opposition to reducing the bond. A bond of $50,000 in those days would be the equivalent of $160,000 today. A modest home could be built for about $20,000 at the time, and Joe's family could not afford to post the large bond. I also pointed out to the judge, that the victim was still alive after two or three days and might very well survive. The victim was not very well known, had no large family in Livingston Parish, and there would be no public outcry if the bond was reduced to $5,000. I did not confer with anyone in the District Attorney's Office about my efforts to secure the release of my client on a reduced bond, and when the judge asked me about the position of the district attorney I, simply replied "I don't know".

I knew that I had to move fast to get the bond reduced and have my client released from jail, because if the victim died and the charges were increased to murder, Joe could be held without bond until the trial. The judge reduced the bond to $5,000, and Joe's brother met me at the courthouse, signed the bond, and Joe was released by the sheriff. The next day the victim was taken off life support and the charges were increased to murder.

Joe followed my advice, and moved to a friend's house In French Settlement, where he avoided bar rooms and any and all controversies

195

while he was awaiting trial, and no one suggested that Joe should go back to jail. In the meantime, I filed several motions which delayed the trial for over a year until 1988 and gave me time to thoroughly investigate the events that occurred up to the time of the shooting.

I found out that Joe's girlfriend had been previously married and had a son about 10 or 11 years old who lived with his mother and Joe for more than a year before the incident. They lived in Joe's house in the town of Livingston located on the main highway from Livingston to Frost, and the boy attended the local school.

Joe worked every day, and his girlfriend had lots of time on her hands while her son was in school each day. I found out that she had a new boyfriend to occupy her time while Joe was working. Joe told me that he had no idea of her activities until after an argument, when she suddenly left the house with her son and moved in with her new boyfriend in Denham Springs, Louisiana and got married.

Joe began drinking heavily, grieving over the break up. He told me that after she left he had attempted to have a reconciliation with her, but she refused all of his advances. In fact, whenever she saw him she would mock him and go out of her way to punish him.

On the day of the incident that resulted in Joe's arrest his ex-girlfriend picked up her son at his new school in Denham Springs. She drove to Livingston with the boy to pick up one of his former schoolmates who was going to spend the weekend with them.

Instead of driving directly to the schoolmate's home, she went several blocks out of her way to pass by Joe's house, where he was sitting on his front porch drinking beer. When she saw Joe, she blew her horn to attract his attention and gave him the finger. She then proceeded to the home of the other little boy who was waiting for them.

When Joe saw her obscene gesture he became enraged, ran to his pickup truck that was parked in his front yard and proceeded to follow her car. At this time Joe's nephew, who lived next door, whom I had previously represented when he was charged with criminal offenses, saw what happened. He got in his truck and began to follow Joe and his former girlfriend.

The woman and her son proceeded to the driveway of the house where the other boy was waiting alone for them. When they turned into

196

the driveway and stopped the car the other boy came out of the house to go with them. As the boy approached, the woman and her son, who was sitting in the front passenger seat of the car, saw Joe Green's truck coming down the street towards them.

She told the other boy to run back in his house and call the law, put her car in reverse and backed out of the driveway. Unfortunately for her she backed across the street and into the ditch where she was stuck.

Joe got out of his truck and walked to the front of her car and began pounding on its hood. The woman shoved her son to the floor behind the dashboard. Joe came around to the passenger side of the car and pounded on its roof with a pistol in his hand. At this time the woman got out of her car. As she stood up, Joe's pistol went off. One bullet struck the roof of the car and struck her in the head. Joe went back to his truck, passed his nephew who had just drove up, and proceeded to French Settlement to a friend's house, where he was later arrested.

Joe's nephew also left the scene prior to the arrival of the Sheriff's deputies. One of the first deputies to arrive was Herman Wilkinson, a young deputy who worked as a radio dispatcher, who had never investigated a murder case. After an ambulance arrived and took the victim to the hospital, Herman had her car towed to the Sheriff's office where it was placed in storage. No law enforcement officer examined the car for several months while it remained there. When Herman finally opened the trunk of the car he found a small baseball bat in the trunk. No shell casings, or bullets, or other weapons were searched for or found at the scene or in the car. A battered broken revolver was found several miles from the scene on the road from Livingston to French Settlement. That pistol was tested by the state police and later by another firearms expert but was so badly damaged it could not be positively identified as the murder weapon.

Before the trial began I filed discovery motions requiring the state to produce autopsy records of the victim and test results of the pistol. A very good friend of mine, Eric Pitman, was the assistant district attorney assigned to prosecute the case. He was an experienced prosecutor but had never tried a murder case before. I realized that the state had a strong case of circumstantial evidence and the key to my success, would be to pick the right jury.

The list of potential jurors was made available to me through the clerk of courts office about 30 days before the trial. I made about a dozen copies of that list and gave them to Joe, his friends and relatives, and every lawyer in Livingston Parish that handled criminal defense cases, so they could tell me everything they knew about the potential jurors. I also contacted outlaws and their relatives who I had represented as well as politicians, bartenders, and ordinary citizens from all over Livingston Parish to get information on the background of every single potential juror from the list of 100.

By the time the case came to trial I had checked off every name on the list as being very favorable, favorable, open-minded, unfavorable, very unfavorable and simply unknown. I also made notes about who had given me information on each name.

In analyzing the information my research revealed different people had different opinions of the way a potential juror would vote to convict or acquit my client. I had to determine the probability of a juror voting in my client's favor. I also knew that Eric Pittman who was from Tangipahoa Parish, but had recently married my good friend V E "Son" Settoon's daughter, from Springfield, would talk to some of the Sheriff's deputies about the jurors.

Each potential juror's name had been drawn from a list of registered voters, and the Sheriff's deputies were required by law to serve them with a notice to appear at the trial. Many of the persons on the list sought to avoid jury duty and they contacted the judge's office prior to the trial date with their excuses. The judge's secretary would give this information to the judge and he would decide to excuse them or not. Every few days, as the trial approached, I would call the secretary to get the names of the persons who were excused and take them off my list. This saved me a great deal of time that I could devote to getting information on the rest of the potential jurors.

By the time the trial date arrived the list of 100 names had been cut in half and I knew the names of at least 15 people that I wanted or did not want on the jury. I would have to decide on who I would choose from the responses I received from my questions to the others at the trial.

In a jury trial I was allowed 12 challenges, as was the district attorney, and these could be for any reason. We were also allowed to use additional special challenges for cause, where a potential juror had already made up his mind or was closely related to the victim or the defendant for example. If either side chose to challenge a potential juror for cause, we would argue to the judge why we took our position on that juror. The judge would then decide if the juror was rejected or not. If the potential juror was rejected for cause, that challenge did not count against our 12 challenges.

When the trial began the judge had the Clerk of Court draw 14 names from the jury box and asked them general questions about their qualifications to serve as jurors. Eric and I then questioned them one by one. I began my questioning of the potential jurors in this manner. "Ladies and gentlemen, I want to thank you for your service in this matter. I know it may be difficult for you to be here in court for several days if you are selected to serve on this jury.

We as citizens of this great country are guaranteed by the Constitution of our right to trial by jury. This guarantees that no person can be deprived of their liberty by the accusations of law enforcement officials without having those accusations being proved before a judge and jury beyond a reasonable doubt.

In any case where you as a juror find that there is a reasonable doubt as to the guilt or innocence of my client the judge will instruct you that you must give the benefit of that doubt to my client and vote not guilty.

I will be asking you all some general questions about yourselves in an effort to select a jury to judge my client fairly. If they seem to infringe on your privacy, they are only for the purpose of my need to gain information that will help me make that determination."

I would then question each potential juror individually, asking for their name, address, marital status, number of children, and place of employment of each one and their spouse. I would also ask about their recreational preferences. Then I would ask if they, their friends, and members of their families had been victims of criminal activity. If they answered affirmatively I would question them closely about the circumstances. I would also question them if any of their acquaintances had been charged with criminal offenses, and if any had testified in criminal trials.

In most cases I knew the answers to these questions before I asked, due to my extensive background research. If I knew the answer would be favorable to my client I would not ask the question. If I knew or found out from the answer that the juror would be unfavorable to my client I would sometimes ask the question in order to obtain a challenge for cause.

If there was a potential juror on the list that I definitely wanted to reject, I made sure to reserve a challenge for that person, even though I had to accept someone I had doubts about whose name came up sooner on the list. This tactic became critical as my challenges were exhausted. We accepted several names from the first 14 who the judge instructed to remain seated and the others were excused. They were then sworn in as jurors and sent to the jury room. The judge then had the clerk of court call 14 more names and the process was repeated. It took us almost a full day to select the jury. Each juror was assigned a seat in the jury box, the first 12 being members and the last two being alternate jurors in case any original juror had to be excused during the trial due to an emergency. In that event the first alternate would fill the seat of the juror who could not continue the trial.

After the jury was selected the judge gave opening instructions as to how the trial would be conducted. Each side would have opening statements. Then the prosecution would put on its evidence followed by the defense. The prosecution was then allowed to present rebuttal testimony and evidence. The prosecution would then give its closing argument, followed by the defense and the prosecution's rebuttal.

The first witness called by the prosecutor was a deputy sheriff who testified he came to the scene of the shooting about the time the ambulance arrived, picked up the victim from the ground near the driver's side of her car and took her to the hospital.

He said he had talked to her young son and determined Joe Green was the prime suspect. The search for Joe ensued and he was located in French Settlement, Louisiana where he was arrested at a friend's house. When he was questioned he stated, "she shot at me", and refused to answer any other questions.

200

When Herman Wilkinson was called to testify by Eric Pittman, he answered his questions about coming to the crime scene and having the victim's car stored at the Sheriff's office. I considered Herman a good friend of mine, but I showed him no mercy in my cross-examination. He was a small man in his early 30s who had worked as a booking deputy and radio dispatcher at the jail but had never investigated a murder case and certainly but had not been elevated to the rank of detective.

I closely questioned him about what he had or had not done during his investigation of the crime scene. I asked him if he had examined car to see if it contained a gun he told me no. I asked him if he had examined the roadway or the ditch where the car had been stuck to determine if there was a gun located there. He again told me he did not. I asked him if he found anything in the car during his examination and he said he found a child's baseball bat in the trunk of the car. I asked him when he found the bat and he said it was several months after the car had been in storage at the Sheriff's office. I asked him where the victim's son was located when he arrived at the scene and he said the boy was sitting in the front passenger seat with the door locked.

The boy was called as a witness by Eric. Before he testified the judge instructed Eric and I be very careful not to upset him during our questioning. In response to Eric's questions the boy said he was in the front seat of the car when Joe approached the car and hit the hood with his fist. At that time his mother pushed him to the floor and he heard Joe strike the roof of the car. After that he heard shots and saw his mother fall. He said he got out of the car picked up his baseball bat from the back seat and beat the big man and made him leave.

I asked him where he got the baseball bat and where he put it after the big man left he said he found it on the backseat and put it back there. I asked him about his mother pushing him to the floor and he admitted that she had. I asked him how he could see Joe Green beating on the car if he was on the floor face down under the dashboard and he said he could see him.

The coroner of Livingston Parish was called and testified that the victim died of a gunshot wound to her head several days after being shot.

The other little boy testified that he came out of his house to the car when it drove up, and he saw Joe's truck approaching. The woman also saw the truck and told him to run inside and call the law as she started to back up. He ran inside, made the call, and stayed there until the police arrived. He did not see or hear anything until the shots rang out.

The prosecution called the deputy who had arrested Joe at his friend's house and I closely questioned him about his interview with Joe. He said he put Joe in handcuffs in his car and drove to the jail in Livingston. On the ride he asked Joe what happened, and Joe's only response was "she shot at me". When they got to the jail a detective attempted to question Joe, who when given his Miranda rights refused to answer any questions.

Before the trial I had filed motions to have the prosecution give me all its information on the testing of the pistol that was found on the road. The results were inconclusive as to whether it was the weapon used in the shooting. I hired an expert to examine the gun, but he could not absolutely say the gun was not used in the shooting.

After the prosecutor questioned its expert about the gun I cross-examined him. He admitted that the gun was so badly damaged he could not properly test fire it to determine it was the weapon used to shoot the woman.

My main purpose in retaining my expert was to have him rebut the prosecution's expert if he said the gun was used in the killing. After the testimony of the other expert I decided that I didn't need my expert to testify and take the risk that he might say something that would help the prosecution.

During a recess early in the trial, Eric and I talked to the judge in his chambers about the number of additional witnesses we might call and how long we expected the testimony would take. Eric told us he planned to call Herman Wilkinson, at least one more deputy, the coroner, and the two boys. I said I would probably call Joe, my expert, and several character witnesses.

Based on our early conversation with the judge, Eric assumed that he would have the opportunity to cross-examine Joe and my witnesses as well as call back the woman's son and other witnesses to rebut Joe's testimony. What he didn't know was that I had planned from the beginning on not having Joe testify. My casual conversation with Eric and the judge was an elaborate trick to help me win.

When Eric rested his case in the early afternoon it was my turn to call my first witness. I stood up and shocked the entire courtroom when I stated the defense rests. This meant that I would call no witnesses or introduce any evidence but would try to convince the jury in my closing argument by picking apart the prosecution witness's testimony and evidence to gain an acquittal for my client.

I had talked to Joe about this strategy beforehand and he agreed with me that this was our best chance to win. The judge recessed court early to allow us to prepare for our closing arguments the next morning.

Before the trial began, I thought about a movie I had recently seen starring Edward G Robinson and Paul Newman, called The Cincinnati Kid. In the movie a poker game of five card stud was won with a royal diamond flush. On my way home, when got to Joe Erdey's OK Bar between Albany and Springfield I stopped for a drink.

I had played poker many times in the past at that bar with Joe and his father, and knew he was an expert gambler. There were no customers at the bar when I arrived in the early afternoon and talked to Joe about my case. I told him my plan and asked him if he could stack a deck of cards so that a certain result would occur in the game. He assured me he could, and he got an old deck to practice with. Joe placed the cards in order, so I could deal two hands and obtain the result I wanted. I then purchased a brand-new deck of cards that was still sealed in cellophane, very carefully opened the cellophane, and had Joe stack the new deck as we had planned. He then put the cards back in the box and replaced the cellophane covering.

The next morning Eric made his closing statement giving a summary of the testimony and evidence he had produced in his effort to persuade the jury to find Joe Green guilty of murder and have him imprisoned for the rest of his life.

When I stood up I looked around the courtroom. Every seat was taken and there were many more people standing on the sides and back of the room. I began my remarks by thanking the jurors for their time and their attention to the testimony of witnesses. I reminded them of the questions I had asked, and they had answered at the time they were selected, about reasonable doubt and the burden of proof being on the prosecution. I went through the testimony of Herman Wilkinson. When I asked him about searching for a second pistol at the scene of the crime, his response had been "no there was no other pistol and there was no need to search for one". When I asked him why he had not opened the trunk of the car to examine its contents for several months he had no explanation.

At the time of the trial a very popular television program starring Andy Griffith as a small-town sheriff had been playing for several years. A small squeaky talking actor, Don Knotts had played the character of a bumbling, dim witted deputy named Barney Fife, who got his job because he was the Sheriffs cousin. I told the jury about the TV program that almost all had watched and referred to Herman Wilkinson as Barney Fife.

I also told the jury about the findings of the prosecution's expert who examined the pistol and could not prove that it was used to kill the woman, much less by Joe Green. I told the jury about the woman's small 10-year old boy testifying how he beat Joe, who weighed over 240 pounds, with his baseball bat and ran him off, and how he said he could see Joe when he was lying face down on the floorboards of the car under the dash in front of the front seat. I reminded them of that and how the second boy said he heard two (2) shots, one of which could have came from the woman's gun, or from Joe's nephew's gun. Every time I pointed out inconsistencies of the Sheriffs investigation I told the jury this was enough to cause a reasonable doubt in their minds about Joe's guilt or innocence and they had promised me that they would give the benefit of that doubt to Joe and vote not guilty.

Finally, I told the jury that I would prove reasonable doubt in this case by a demonstration that they could see. I walked to the jury box, pulled the deck of cards out of my pocket, made an exaggerated effort to tear the apparently sealed cellophane cover off the deck, removed the cards from the brand-new box and appeared to shuffle them.

I reminded them that they had all told me that they had played five card stud poker when I had questioned them before they were secluded as jurors. I told them that I would demonstrate the issues in the case with the cards.

I dealt two cards face down on the rail of the jury box in front of the jury. I told them the first card was the state's hand and the second card was Joe Green's. I then turned the king of clubs up on the state's hand and the ten of diamonds on Joe's. I told them the state claimed Joe's girlfriend had been shot. Joe admitted that and called the bet. I then turned the seven of spades on the states hand and the Jack of diamonds on Joe's. I told them the second card of the state represented its claim the woman had died. Joe admitted that and called the bet. I next turned the seven of hearts on the states hand and the Queen of diamonds on Joe's. I told them that the pair of sevens represented the claim that Joe had been charged with murder. Joe admitted that and called the bet. I next turned the five of hearts on the states hand and the King of diamonds on Joe's hand. I told them that the state with its pair of sevens was betting that Joe Green was guilty of murder and he called the bet and raised the ante with his life, based on reasonable doubt.

I told the jury there were several possible explanations for what happened the day the woman was shot, according to the evidence put on by the prosecution, any of which would raise reasonable doubt as to Joe's guilt or innocence.

First, there was no question that the woman was the aggressor when she deliberately drove out of her way to go by Joe's house and taunted him with her obscene gestures, which she knew would infuriate him.

Second, when Joe arrived and pounded on the roof of her car, with the gun in his hand he had no intent to harm her, only frighten her. When he hit the car's roof the gun went off accidentally, the bullet hit the roof and ricocheted into the woman's head.

Third, she could have pulled her gun as she got out of the car and shot at Joe first, and he returned fire in self-defense. Her gun could've fallen in the nearby ditch or the floorboards of her car which was never searched by the bumbling Barney Fife type deputy sheriff, Herman Wilkinson. Fourth, the fatal shot which killed the woman could have been fired by Joe's nephew, who had a criminal background but was never questioned by the deputies as to why he was at the scene or what he saw or did.

I reminded the jury again that they had promised me they would give Joe the benefit of the doubt and that any of the examples I presented were reasonable explanations that caused doubt about the prosecution's case.

I then returned to the cards on the rail of the jury box I placed my finger on the state's down card and asked them if anyone had a reasonable doubt that it was the ace of diamonds. I let that sink in a few moments, then flipped the hole card for the state and revealed it to be the deuce of spades. I then turned Joe's down card up and showed them the ace of diamonds.

I told the jury that Joe Green knew the prosecution had not proved him guilty beyond a reasonable doubt, and there was no need for him to put on any more evidence. I asked them to please keep their promise to me that they would give Joe the benefit of that doubt and vote not guilty. The jury was out about 20 minutes and came back with a unanimous verdict of not guilty.

EPILOGUE

The Rules of Court and the Bar Association prohibit attorneys from discussing any aspect of a pending case with perspective jurors before they are selected and during the trial.

When investigating prospective jurors' backgrounds, I have always told people who gave me information about them never to talk to them about an upcoming trial, or during recesses until the trial is completely finished. To do otherwise could subject a person to a charge of jury tampering. However, if a juror is not asked to tell about any relationship he or she may have had with a party in a trial, they are not compelled to reveal it.

Several weeks after Joe Greene was acquitted I received a call from one of the jurors. She was an attractive young woman in her late 20s who had a minor legal problem. I had never seen her before the trial and she was one of the last jurors we picked. I had serious doubts about whether I could persuade her to vote in Joe's favor.

I knew nothing about her background, and no one who I questioned about her was able to give me any information. During the vodire questions she stated she had attended college in Mississippi where she and her family lived before she moved to Denham Springs about two years before, and got a job working in a library in Baton Rouge Louisiana.

She and her family had never been victims of crime, nor had she any friends or relatives that had ever been charged with any type of criminal activity. I remembered telling Joe that I didn't feel too good about selecting her, but I had run out of challenges when her name was called and had no choice but to accept her on the jury.

After the jury was selected the judge instructed them that they could not make notes about the testimony given by witnesses. During the first day of testimony by a deputy sheriff I noticed her making notes on a scrap of paper and brought it to the attention of the judge and Eric Pittman.

The judge called a recess, sent the jury to the jury room, and called me and Eric to the bench to discuss this possible infraction of the rules. She was brought into the judge's office by a deputy and asked about what she was writing. She explained that she was making a list of some errands she needed to run after she got home. Neither Eric nor I asked for her removal, I certainly did not want the alternate juror, who I was afraid might vote against Joe, to take her place, and the judge told her not to write anything for the remainder of the trial.

When I received her phone call I asked her what day she was off from work, so she could come to my office and not lose any pay. The day she told me she didn't have to work was a day I had to be in court in Livingston for a short hearing, so I asked her to meet me at the courthouse. She was there when I arrived, and I told her to go have a seat in the courtroom while I went to the front to represent my client.

I checked the docket and found I was going to have to wait about a half-hour before my case was called and my hearing shouldn't last more than 20 or 30 minutes. I came back to where she was sitting and sat with her while waiting for my clients' name to be called. As we sat there I noticed Eric Pitman in the front of the courtroom looking at me and the young lady. When I saw that I slid closer to her and put my arm on the bench around her shoulder and whispered in her ear that I was going to play a trick on my friend Eric. She smiled and moved closer to me as Eric studied us closely.

After my case was finished, I walked back to her seat, took her by the arm, and walked her out of the courtroom where Eric was standing and said to him." Eric, you should remember Ms. Smith who served on Joe Greens jury." She put out her hand to him and said, "Nice to see you again Mr. Pittman". Eric glared at me as we walked away, and I made sure he overheard me telling her "let's go have lunch".

I believe that to this day, 30 years later Eric Pittman thinks that I got my girlfriend on that jury.

Chapter 21. Billy Cannon

I first met Billy Cannon when we were both enrolled at LSU in the fall of 1956. I stayed in one dormitory while he, as a football player stayed in a different dormitory. At that time all male students were required to take military training through the ROTC program and Billy and I were both enrolled in the Air Force ROTC. Our training consisted of marching, learning how to take care of our uniforms, cleaning rifles and studying rules and regulations of military service.

I only saw Billy on one occasion at the beginning of our training in the fall during football season and thought it strange that he would be able to skip those classes. Billy became the star of the LSU football team and won the Heisman Trophy in 1958. He later played professional football for the Houston Oilers before his career was cut short due to an injury. Billy continued his education following undergraduate studies and became a dentist.

I next met him many years later when Shorty Rogers, a lifelong friend and client of mine, Frank Edwards, the former Sheriff of Tangipahoa Parish, and his sons Sheriff Daniel Edwards and then Representative John Bel Edwards, who later was elected Governor of Louisiana, traveled to the Louisiana State penitentiary at Angola, Louisiana. During our tour of the prison we went to the dentist office where I was reintroduced to Billy by Shorty Rogers, his close personal friend.

Soon after that meeting Shorty contacted me about a fundraiser he was planning for the Johnny Robinson boys' home in Monroe, Louisiana. Shorty owned a restaurant and motel in Hammond, Louisiana and Billy contacted him soliciting help for the boy's home.

Billy and Johnny Robinson had been teammates on the 1958 National Champion Football Team at LSU. Johnny, like Billy had played pro football after college and later took some disadvantaged boys into his home. He kept expanding the project until he was housing more than 20 boys who had been referred to him by law enforcement officers and other social workers. The state of Louisiana offered partial funding for the project until Governor Bobby Jindal was elected, and the funding ended.

Johnny's health was deteriorating, and he was unable to maintain the program on his own. Within a couple of years, the enrollment and dropped to 10 or 12 boys and he told Billy that he would probably have to end the program. Billy told Shorty about Johnny's predicament, and Shorty suggested they have a fundraiser at his restaurant with Billy and Johnny in attendance to meet potential donors.

In the discussion about the fundraising Billy explained to Shorty that they had no funds to cover costs, and that all funds that were raised would have to go for the boys. Shorty told him that he owned the restaurant, the meeting room, and the food that would be provided, and that he had a bar and lounge in the same building and he could make his expenses back by selling drinks. Billy told him that any monies raised from tickets for meals and drinks purchased by those attending would have to be given for the boys. Shortly agreed to this requirement and started promoting the fundraiser. He contacted me, and I readily agreed to purchase some tickets and encourage other friends of mine to attend.

At the initial meeting Billy had encouraged several of his teammates from the 1958 National Championship Team to attend and meet with their fans. Shorty provided the steak dinner and drinks and more than $10,000 was raised for the boys.

One of the attendees, from Covington Louisiana offered to help organize another fundraiser in his area, which also turned into a great success. One of those attendees, a former player from Lafayette, Louisiana, who was now a successful physician decided to sponsor a fundraiser in his hometown. Billy, Johnny, and other members of the team encouraged more of their former teammates to attend that function, and over $50,000 was raised. Later one of the attendees of the Lafayette fundraiser, a successful businessman from Houston Texas sponsored a fundraiser in that city and provided a jet airplane to transport all of the surviving 1958 players to that event, where over $100,000 was raised.

Johnny's boys' home has helped hundreds of young men who once were in trouble with the law and had no friends or families to assist them become successful members of society.

Billy told me the story of one boy about 10 years old who had no family, rebelled against all authority at his school, was expelled, and arrested by the police. One of the police officers contacted Johnny to see

210

if he could do anything to help the child. The school had strict rules, requiring attendance and maintaining grades in the classrooms, and good behavior at all times.

The boy refused to study, to do his chores, and follow instructions of the teachers and supervisors. He only wanted to ride the bicycle that was provided for him. After several weeks Johnny told Billy he didn't know what else to do with the boy. Billy came to visit and couldn't reason with him to change his behavior.

There was a large oak tree on the campus and Billy got a long rope and tied it to an upper limb of the tree. He tied the other end of the rope to the bicycle and hoisted it to the treetop. He told the boy that he would have to follow all the rules, eat his meals, study every day to bring up and maintain his grades, to get the bike back. The boy quickly agreed, figuring that he would have the bike back in a few days and then could revert back to his former behavior. Billy told him there was another condition that would have to be met for him to get the bike back. Every day the boy followed instructions the bike would be lowered from its position in the treetop exactly 1 foot which was measured every day.

After about two months of following the rules he had agreed to and watching the bike being lowered at the rate of 1 foot per day the boy was finally able to touch the wheel of the bicycle with his hand while standing underneath it. At that point he excitedly told Johnny he had completed his probation and wanted to ride the bicycle. Johnny told him that the deal was he could ride the bicycle when it touched the ground and not before. Three or four days later the bicycle was lowered at the 1 foot per day rate and he was allowed to use it again. The young man's grades had improved, his attitude had changed, and he eventually completed the school, but he and the other boys who observed his punishment never forgot that backsliding into their former behavior would result in a resumption of the loss of privileges.

Billy told me that many times over the years he has met many men who graduated from Johnny's boys' school who thanked him for the opportunity they had received to make a good life for themselves and their families. He also told me that when he talked to Shorty about the successes of the school, after the fundraisers, Shorty said he was rolling aces and eights since he had helped them start the project.

At the time Shorty put on the fundraisers for the boys home he had a young black lady named Annette who worked in his restaurant as a cook and waitress. She volunteered her services and later established her own restaurant in Hammond Louisiana named Annette's Country Kitchen, which has become very successful. I feel this might be another unforeseen result of Shorty's generosity as well as Annette's hard work.

Chapter 22. John Ratcliff

John was born and raised on Miller Road in Killian, Livingston Parish Louisiana on September 19, 1946, one of 8 of children of Clarence Ratcliff. His family was very active in politics, some of his uncles and cousins had served as school board members, police jury members, and mayors of Killian and Springfield. One of his cousins Barney Dewey Ratcliff had served as mayor of Springfield, police jury member and later Livingston Parish President.

John recently told me about some of his experiences as a young man.

"I left Springfield school in the 11th grade and went to work painting microwave towers. We traveled around the United States from east to west painting AT&T towers. Most of the towers were 275 feet to 335 feet tall. Most people don't do well at that height. We didn't have money to buy ropes and boosting chairs to hang down the side of the towers, so the first year we would walk the beams and hold on with one hand and paint with the other. Later we made enough money to buy ropes to do the job safer.

Uncle Sam got itself into the Vietnam conflict. They didn't call it a war at first because it would last long enough for President Johnson's company, Brown and Root, who his wife had an interest in, could get filthy rich building bridges, roads, airports and so forth.

I got called to duty. Well, I didn't think Uncle Sam needed me, so I sent the letter back and said I was in school. About a year past, and I got another letter to be in New Orleans on a certain date. I was 19 years old.

I found out that the draft board man in Livingston Parish and my dad were enemies from years back. I was told that my dad, Clarence Radcliff, had took his two girlfriends away from him and he tried to whip him over it. Dad gave him a country boy whipping instead,

All the years went by and the draft board man didn't forget the whipping. My dad went to the draft board to try to get me out because he needed me to help on the farm and the raising of my seven brothers and sisters. The draft board man told my dad "what's wrong with you, have you got leukemia or something?" Well, Dad jumped over the railing in front of his desk and told him he would whip his ass one more time.

213

The secretary, Ms. Mary Webb grabbed Dad and told him not to get in trouble but let her handle it. She knew the draft board man was trying to get me in the war to get back at him for the ass whipping. I got another notice to go to New Orleans, so I saw a doctor who gave me a letter saying I had a bad back. When I got there, I showed the man the letter and they sent me to a doctor downtown to check me out.

The doctor told me to cross my legs and he was going to check my reflexes. He hit me in the knee with a rubber hammer and my foot almost kicked him in the mouth. He told me" you are in the damn Army. I told him no Doc I'm not in the damn Army because the damn bus has already left. Ms. Webb got me in the Army reserve.

That's when things got down to business because the Army was the only place that totally took my freedom. My first day in the Army they gave me a damn number and told me I needed to remember it because I no longer had a name.

I thought they were kidding with me until they started calling out numbers and I forgot mine. Each time they called a number a soldier would run and get in formation. I had to watch each time to see if anyone ran, and if not, that might be my damn number. Well finally after about 100 soldiers ran they called a number, and no one ran. I waited for a minute and when they called that number again I finally said that must be my damn number and I ran out to formation. The drill Sergeant hollered at me "Don't you know your damn number?" I hollered back "I know my damn name, but I don't know that damn number." By that time every damn soldier in the company knew me.

Shortly after that while getting my uniforms I was in a long line chewing gum which I always did back home. A black Corporal asked me if I was chewing gum and I told him yes. He told me to swallow it, so I did what he said, choked on the gum and had to cough it back up. That made me mad as hell and like my dad I dove over the counter and went to work on his ass. They pulled me off of him and he told me to get in the back of the line. I told him I was going to the front of the line and if he thought he was man enough, to come get me and put me in the back of the line. The other soldiers behind the counter started laughing at him and told him it was about time he got his ass kicked because he had been picking on the recruits a lot.

214

First day in the field, I was in trouble again. The drill sergeant told us to write home and tell our mamas to sell the shit house, because our asses belonged to him. Out of 100 men I was only one that thought it was funny. The drill sergeants' nose was touching mine and he was screaming at me at the top of his voice. At that moment I knew my ass was out of my control and in theirs. The next morning, I got woke up by a giant of a man who was black and big, and I knew I was not going to be able to whip his ass, that's for sure, so I got up and done what I was told.

As time went by I began to notice that every man there was for the same reason, and that was to be trained. I got into several more disagreements with drill sergeants, but they all understood my smart country boy attitude, and I was there because I had to be, not because I wanted to be. As time went on I began to notice all the men were the same, that the black men were going to have my back and I was going to have theirs. From then on, we were just soldiers, and 50 years later I still feel the same, every man is created equal."

The community where John grew up was lily white and there was a great deal of prejudice against Blacks. John had attended segregated schools before joining the Army, but after serving with black soldiers and officers his personal views moderated.

After he was discharged, he remained in the Army Reserves for several years. This required him to go to reserve meetings and serve on active duty for 30 days every year. When he was called to active duty in his last year as a reservist his longtime girlfriend left him, and when he returned home he figured he was done with the federal government for life. His story continues

"When my foot hit the ground after the plane ride from Fort Sill Oklahoma, I was out of the Army. That was a good day, no more girlfriend, I had a new Dodge 440 Magnum with 375 hp that was fast. I was free at last to do what I wanted. I joined the union as a crane operator, making good money at last, then damn I got hit again with another lick. I got a letter from the federal court for four and a half months of jury duty, so away I go to the federal court building and report to Judge E Gordon West.

I still had a neat haircut, appeared to be a bright young man, needless to say pretty handsome at that, and I knew I was going to be doing this jury duty often. I got picked as the number one member of the jury by the prosecutor.

A young black man stole a welfare check and had two underage boys sign the check and they split the money. Court went on most of the day and the boy was guilty as hell. The young man got up and said just because I'm poor they going to make an example of me. The other boy's family had money and hired a lawyer. Judge E Gordon West was down on that lawyer to shut him up, but I heard loud and clear about being poor since I had been raised very poor myself. I figured these boys would never do this again and when the old white jury foreman said let's vote guilty and go home I was the only one to vote not guilty. My strength and military training was coming out again.

I was an ex-military policeman, probably at the top of my game and headed to a better life but not forgetting my past. They underestimated me and had a problem because I had to outsmart the feds, get out of this shit, and back to my new job as equipment operator before the crap got me fired because union people were hard on you in those days.

I told the black jurors to get with me and help the boy out and some of them did. I then pulled another card. I told them that the two young boys that signed the check would go free anyway, but they would be tried in juvenile court. That will scare the hell out of them if we let this boy walk.

I told the other jurors they better get us some rooms because we're going to be here a long time. I said let's scare the boys here and send them home, so they won't get in anymore trouble. A guilty verdict on this young man will send the underage boys scot-free to get in more trouble. I also told them to pick another foreman because the one y'all got is going to have you all spend several days in a motel as a hung jury. As more time passed Judge West sent a bailiff to inquire if they needed further instructions in order to reach a unanimous verdict. The foreman of the jury sent a note to the judge stating they could not agree, and the judge told them to continue their deliberations. We took another vote and it was 11 to 1 not guilty with the foreman being the only holdout.

At this point I told them that they might as well get ready to sleep in that motel because the foreman wasn't going to change his mind. With things going my way, I told the foreman he would be to blame for making the rest of us spend the night in a motel instead of going home, and several of the other jurors agreed with me and also told the foreman. After that another vote was taken, and this time the we voted unanimous not guilty.

When we went back into the courtroom and the verdict was read, old Judge West almost broke his gavel showing he didn't like the results."

After more than 35 years John Ratliff has never been called for jury duty in federal court again.

BOOK 4 HUNTING AND FISHING 1950'S THROUGH 1990'S

Chapter 1. Hunting and Fishing – Early Years

Chapter 2. 1950 - 1971 Fishing and Deer Hunting – Southeast Louisiana

Chapter 3. 1971 Grand River

Chapter 4. 1951 - 1967 Duck Hunting – The Beginning

Chapter 5. 1967 - 1971 Concordia Parish 3 Rivers Deer Hunts

Chapter 6. 1970'S Turkey Hunting – The Beginning

Chapter 7. Leonard Jerry Kinchen

Chapter 8. 1973 Tensas Parish Deer Hunt with Charlie Abels

Chapter 9. 1973 – Slim Hughes - Alligator Hunt

Chapter 20. Trip to Mexico to Hunt Ocellated Turkey

Chapter 21. Ecuador Duck Hunt

Chapter 22. 1993 Western Hunt

Chapter 1. Hunting and Fishing Early Years

During those years when I was in high school and shortly thereafter, my hunting consisted of squirrels and rabbits. Once in a while I shot some doves. The only deer hunting was done in the swamps and that was done, if you knew somebody that had some dogs and had a boat and had a camp. The hunters would go down the river, wade back into the swamps maybe a mile stringing a line of hunters approximately a hundred yards apart, then another hunter would bring the dogs from different location and drive the dogs through the swamp towards the line of men with the guns. When the dogs jumped a deer, it would run towards the line of hunters and if it came across that line near a hunter, maybe, with a big maybe, somebody would shoot the deer. If you killed a deer, then you had to bring it out of the swamp, and the only way to get it was to wade in there and wade back out. Young men were always welcome because they were always needed to take the last or next to the last stands far back in the swamp. If anybody killed a deer between where you were on that last stand and the river, when you came back out, you had to help pull that deer through the mud back to the river bank. I did that from the time was I was in high school until the time I was in college and then I learned about hunting deer in the highlands of North Louisiana where we didn't have the swamp to contend with. Later on, I would still hunt, rather than with dogs.

My duck hunting experience was similar. When I was deer hunting in the swamp, as a teenager, we would go into the swamp at daylight and maybe sit there several hours on that deer stand waiting for the dogs to bring a deer by us. We used buckshot and a shotgun, so we wouldn't shoot anything but deer. When I was sitting in that swamp without any activity, the ducks would come in by the hundreds and feed on the Tupelo Gum balls and duckweed in the swamp. The swamp around Lake Maurepas was unique in its habitat. The huge virgin cypress trees had all been cut in the early 1900's and there was some second growth cypress and Tupelo gum which was not valuable enough to cut at the time they cut the big cypress. The fruit of the Tupelo gum were called gumballs, the size of a small pecan or acorn. In the fall of the year they would drop in the water and the ducks, as they migrated South, would come into this area around Lake Maurepas and feed on those Tupelo balls as well as on the duckweed that was all over the water. In the swamp itself, the water was usually about a foot and a half to two-foot-deep and the bottom was hard. It was muddy but not real soft like you find in the marsh where you might step out of a boat and go to your waist. The only time you got into soft mud and deep water was right behind the lakeshore and right behind the river bank. If you went from the river back into the swamp, you walked down a bayou bank and by the time the bayou ended in the swamp, you could step out anywhere and walk-in knee-deep water, but as you approached the river, right behind the riverbank, you may go to your waist getting through a narrow strip. The same thing held true right behind the lakeshore, the lakeshore had a beach which was high and dry, maybe one hundred yards across and right behind that, going back towards the swamp, you'd hit a real deep area approximately fifty to one hundred yards wide and then behind that, it would get shallower again with the hard bottom and that was where you found the ducks.

While sitting on those deer stands, I observed mallard ducks and listened to the way they called. I quickly realized that the sound of the drake ducks was different than the quack, quack, quack of a hen. This call would attract new ducks coming in more than the hen's call would. There were no commercially made calls that sounded specifically like a drake, but with a lot of practice, I learned to call with a regular duck call and make the sound of the drake. My method of hunting ducks in those days was not sitting in a blind and calling them in, using a dog to retrieve. Instead we would go in before daylight in the morning, get back in the swamp, with four or five mem or boys spread out about seventy-five to one hundred yards apart and start walking through the swamp abreast. When we saw ducks in front of us, we would try to creep up on them through the cypress boughs and tupelo gum trees and get close enough that when we jumped them up, we could shoot some. If I was creeping up on the ducks and I jumped some and started shooting, ducks would start flying all around. My friends to my right and my left would start to call and entice some of the ducks that jumped up to come back around by them and they would get some shots. I would immediately start to call after I shot and some of the ducks that had jumped up further away, or that my other friends had shot at would come back by me and I'd get some shots. When we would pick up our ducks, we didn't have any kind of packs or any way to carry them, so we carried trot lines with us. We would make a loop in the trot line, put the duck's heads in the loops and string the ducks behind us and tie the trot line to our belts. As we moved out through the swamp, we might have five or more ducks floating in the water behind us on that trot line. That way, we didn't have the weight to carry and the floating ducks were easier to bring with us. It wasn't unusual for several of us to enter the swamp, in the early 1960's and kill thirty ducks in a day. We would come back out, about one or two o'clock in the afternoon and then we would have all those ducks to pick. It certainly wasn't all legal, but you did not want to shoot too many because you couldn't carry them out. The other thing about it was that the mallard ducks would always, come in huge numbers a few days after the season ended and they stayed for another two months after that. The season always ended on January 1st and the ducks got here January 2nd, 3rd or 4th. It never made sense to me why the Wildlife and Fisheries Department set the seasons that way. They had opened the hunting season in early November and the only kind of ducks at that time were wood docks until about January when the mallards got here.

The main reason that we could slip up on those ducks in the swamp, at that time of the year, we picked days that the weather was calm and there was a lot of fog in the swamp. We could creep on those ducks a whole lot easier in that fog than you could on a crispy clear day when there was no fog and there was a lot of wind. Just like the deer hunting in North Louisiana, I later learned more about duck hunting and I changed my whole method and moved from the swamp to other areas.

Many years later, with the use of air boats, I went back to the swamp and had some pretty good hunts in the same areas where I used to wade through the swamp.

I can't remember when I went on my first dove hunt. I guess it must've been in the late 1950s. We didn't have a lot of birds to shoot and couldn't afford many shotgun shells. My friends and I, all teenagers, would go to a hayfield that had recently been harvested and shoot at doves coming to pick up grass seed. They were hard to hit and if we each killed five or six we had a big day.

Once when I was dating my wife Loretta we went to her grandpas' field with some of her cousins to shoot birds. I had an old 12gauge Winchester automatic that my uncle Earl Moore had given me that really kicked when it was fired.

Loretta was shooting a 20gauge double barrel shotgun but was having difficulty hitting the doves. I told her she could use my shotgun but did not mention how much the gun kicked. She only weighed about 95 pounds and when she shot at a passing dove, the recoil from the gun knocked her flat on her back. I don't recall if she hit that dove, but she sure did give me hell for giving her that gun to shoot.

I lived next door to my uncles Roy and Eugene Coats who had a flooded pasture between their houses. In the wintertime Jack Snipe congregated there to feed on earthworms. In the afternoon after school I often put on my boots and waded across that pasture flushing the birds and trying to hit them as they darted erratically. Those birds were the most difficult to hit that I ever hunted. I didn't kill a lot of them, but my shooting skill greatly improved when I later hunted doves.

The next time I got a chance to hunt birds was in the late 1960s after I finished law school and was invited on a trip to West Texas by one of my classmates, Lynn Singleton. He and a group of his friends had a Winnebago and were driving to the Davis Mountains near Marfa Texas to hunt mule deer.

I had never hunted mule deer before but eagerly accepted the invitation. Lynn told me that I needed to bring a shotgun as well as my rifles, so we could shoot some quail and white winged doves in the afternoons after the deer hunt. In those days there were no interstate highways and it took about two days to drive from my home to West Texas.

Instead of wasting four days in travel time I decided to fly out to El Paso, where I rented a station wagon and purchased a mattress to sleep on in the back of it since the camper was full. I had brought my sleeping bag and pillow, two rifles, my Winchester 7 mm Remington Magnum and Loretta's 308, which was lighter to carry but had a shorter range than the Magnum.

224

Each morning before daylight we would drive from the campsite to the mountains and climb towards the summit where we could observe the movements of the deer. The mountains were about three or four thousand feet tall and covered with short sagebrush and cactus. I was not used to the altitude nor was I in very good physical shape to climb those mountains.

The first morning I took my Remington Magnum and did not reach the top of the mountain I was on until well after daylight when almost all the deer had bedded down. The second morning I took the lighter 308 rifle and left a little earlier, but still hadn't reached the summit when it began to get light. I sat down and waited for the light to get stronger and heard a deer walking in the rocks behind me but never could see it.

As the sky brightened I heard a clicking noise on the next ridge and realized it was the sound of deer fighting with their antlers. I didn't have a pair of binoculars with me, so I used my rifle scope to locate the deer which were about 500 yards away. They were two of the biggest bucks I have ever seen.

I had sighted in the rifle at 200 yards before the hunt, but these deer were about twice that far away. I aimed at the largest mule deer, but when I shot the bullet fell so short that the deer never stopped fighting. I shot three more times and the deer looked around but never moved. I reloaded the gun and raised the scope completely over the back of the largest buck and squeezed the trigger. The bullet struck at the deer's feet and they quickly disappeared. After that I took my Winchester rifle which had longer-range with me every day but never saw another deer big enough to shoot.

After hunting deer each morning Lynn and I took our shotguns and drove around the desert roads to water tanks that the ranchers had built for cattle to use. The tanks would overflow and wildlife, especially blue scaled quail, gambels quail, white wing doves, and jackrabbits would congregate near them. As we approached the birds would run or fly making difficult targets for our shotguns. The most unusual trophy I took that trip was a roadrunner. I had never seen one before and when he ran across the road I thought he was a big gambels quail and turned him a flip before I realized what I'd shot.

I brought him home as well as a couple of the other species of quail and had it mounted in a glass top coffee table in my office with a large cane break rattlesnake that I killed in Mississippi, where roadrunners do not exist.

Chapter 2. 1950 - 1971 Fishing and Deer Hunting
Southeast Louisiana

After I came home from the Army and entered southeastern college I had a lot of time to fish. Some people used methods to catch bass that were completely illegal. The headlights used for hunting and fishing in the 1940's and early 1950s were not electric lights using batteries but were lights powered by burning carbide that were strapped to your head like an electric headlight. The banks of the rivers in South Louisiana are often shallow where panfish make their nests, and predator fish such as gar and bass come out of the depths to feed. As you quietly moved your boat along the bank one fisherman in the front with the light would shine it into the water while the other fishermen would paddle the boat. The one in the front would use a four-prong barbed gig attached to a 6-foot wooden handle to try to impale the large bass. If he was successful, he would pin the fish against the bottom of the shallow water. Then reach down with his hands, catch the fish in its mouth and bring it aboard.

This activity was illegal, but as a matter fact, it has been used to catch fish since the first settlers came to Louisiana. Not very many fish were caught this way so there was not a large threat to the fish population. To young boys in the boat, in the darkness, the thrill of the hunt for the fish was amplified by the knowledge that although very very remote, there was always a chance a game warden would come down the river and you might get caught. We planned for such an eventuality by tying a line from the gig's handle to a brick which was then tied to the boat. If we heard a game warden's boat coming, we would throw the gig overboard, and quickly retrieve it after he passed, I learned this trick by listening to old hunters and fishermen who shot squirrels in late August when the season didn't open until October and caught fish any way they could to feed their families.

One of my cousins, John Halbert, who was a few years older than me, purchased a boat and went bass fishing at night. He never invited me to go with him, but he did show me some large bass that he had caught. When I looked at the bass, I did not see any marks where they had been impaled with a three or four-pronged gig, but only one wound was located near the fishes' head. When I asked him how he caught the fish, he said he had taken his 22 rifle and shot the fish. He did this by sticking the barrel of the gun under the water and pulling the trigger. Many times, the concussion of the shot would kill the fish and the bullet would not even hit it.

I didn't feel that this was giving the fish any kind of sporting chance. I figured if you got caught shooting fish, you would likely go to jail, which was an experience that I was not ready to have. If you got caught gigging fish the old-fashioned way you probably would only have to pay a fine.

Blue Gill Caught in Natalbany River

When I went fishing on Amite River I would launch my boat at Carthridge Landing which is about 5 miles from where the river empties into Lake Maurepas and there are several oilfield canals that have been dredged from the river back into the swamp. At the end of the canals the water was shallow where bream would build their beds, and we would fish for them with fly rods. The technique I used was to slowly drive my boat to the bream beds, cut off the motor, and catch four or five before the rest of the fish would stop biting due to the water being stirred up by the ones I caught. I would then crank up the motor and run to another bream bed and repeat the process. Once you knew the location of the bream beds you could go from one to the other and not waste your time fishing along stretches of the bank without catching many fish.

At the mouth of the river a large washout had occurred where the lake waters which are very shallow had washed into the deeper water of the river. This area was full of stumps and cypress trees growing in the water along the lake shore. A narrow channel, in places only a few feet wide, connected the river with the lake. If you got out of the channel you would run into the shallow bottom and likely hit a log or stump. The lower limbs of cypress trees were only a few feet from the water and many had Spanish moss hanging from the limbs into the water. If you arrived at the lake at daylight, the water was usually slick as glass and you could see the activity of fish catching insects on the surface.

I would ease my boat out of the channel and would cast my fly around the trees where the moss was hanging in the water. Usually there were many fish right below the surface of the water which was less than 2 feet deep. My fly rod was about 10 feet long and I would use the tip of the rod to shake the hanging moss that was covered with mosquitoes in the still air. When the mosquitoes were disturbed they would begin to fly, and many would light on the surface of water. Mosquito hawks would fly around to catch the mosquitoes and sometimes a fish would jump out of the water to catch the flying insects while smaller fish would catch the mosquitoes on the surface. I used a small popping bug that resembled a mosquito hawk and threw it near the hanging moss were the insects were swarming. Every throw resulted in a fish striking my lure, and I would set the hook and catch it or snatch the bait from its mouth and miss it. The missed fish did not discourage me because all I had to do was to throw the bait back and catch another.

On the other side of the river at the washout the wave action from the lake had eroded the bank along the swamp which was covered with cypress and tupelo trees completely surrounded by shallow water. The trees were close together and you could not maneuver a boat among them to get to the fish, who were in beds behind them. I wore tennis shoes when I went fishing and I would drive my boat as far into the trees as I could then get out and wade in the shallow water and catch fish on my fly rod in the pockets around the trees.

About that same time, I was introduced to Blind River. Elliott Foster, his brother's Van, who was State Policeman, Carew, who was a carpenter and School Board member, Mike Erdey, and several other older men from all over the parish had banded together and bought an old barge. They pulled it up on the bank of Blind River and constructed a camp on the river. Mike and Elliott weren't interested in hunting and fishing, but they did like to go down there to gamble and get away from everything and spend a few days on the river. They had trot lines across the river, where all you had to do was bait up, and you could catch all the catfish you could eat. If you were inclined to fish for bream or white perch the rivers were full of fish, and it was a good place to play cards if you wanted too. I had heard about the place, but I'd never been there.

One night, when I was about twenty years old, I was at the OK Bar. Mike and another group of men announced they were going to go to the Blind River camp for a couple of days, and they invited me to go with them. I readily agreed and drove to my house which was only three or four miles away, got another set of clothes and followed them to Black Lake at Bear Island where they met some other people. We all loaded up in a couple of boats and started off. We traveled through a narrow channel in the swamp between Black Lake and Chen Blanc Bayou to get to Blind River. It was a very clear night; the weather was warm and the stars in Orion's Belt were as bright as I had ever seen them in my life. The boat driver used a headlight as he wound around horseshoe bends and through little narrow cuts to get from Black Lake to Blind River and it was just fascinating to ride through the darkness to get to the camp. It contained a twenty-five-gallon butane tank that the men would bring back and forth, so they could have gas lights and gas to cook with. There were many bunks in one part of the camp, a big kitchen and dining area in another, a skinning rack in the back for skinning deer and cleaning fish, and a wharf and porch in the front. You could walk out on the wharf or run the trot line to the other side of the river to catch fish. Then you would come in the back of the camp, clean your fish, bring them inside and cook them. They were some of the best tasting fish in the world. Soon after that an older member wanted to sell his interest in the camp and I quickly purchased it for three hundred dollars.

That old camp had lots of memories for me. It's the first place I really learned how to hunt ducks in the lake swamp. In the fall of the year, the wood ducks would roost in the swamp across the river and every morning at daylight small flocks of birds would fly into the swamp behind the camp to feed. You could stand on the wharf and see them as they made their squealing calls. They were flying very high, out of shotgun range, until they got right in front of the camp close to the riverbank then they would dive down low towards the swamp. If you were good, and lucky, you could once in a while kill a duck as it flew across right in front of you.

When we went deer hunting, we would start out after eating breakfast in the morning around seven o'clock and then string a stand line back in the swamp. This means we would get a group of men and wade along the bayou bank behind the camp and into the swamp for about a mile in a straight line, leaving men about one hundred and fifty yards apart. After we got a couple of hundred yards away from the river, the water was about a foot deep and the swamp had a hard bottom. Then a driver would take a boat and a load of dogs and drive back up the river to Bayou Chen Blanc which ran north to south from Black Lake to Blind River which ran from east and west. The driver would go to Chen Blanc and unload his dogs on that bayou and then start driving the dogs towards the stand line. Which was between Chen Blanc and Lake Maurepas. Any deer the dogs would pick up in the swamp and start the chase would have to cross our stand line and somebody would get a shot at a deer. At least that was the theory. If the dogs got after the deer very hard sometimes they would turn north and go completely around the stand line or they would turn south, swim the river, or they would get by

232

us and go to the east to Lake Maurepas and swim out in the lake to escape the dogs. There was always at least one boat left in the lake with an old man or two in it that watched the river and lake so if a deer was driven into the water, they could run the boat up and kill the deer that way. I imagine there were more deer killed in the river and in the lake then they were on the bank.

One morning, Elliott Foster was at the camp. He was short, and fat, and really didn't do any hunting at all in the swamp or even on high ground, but he would sit in a boat with his shotgun and ride around the area to shoot a deer if it swam in the river. On this particular morning my friend Jerry Foster, Van Foster's son, had come to the camp with us. Jerry had been in an automobile accident several years before when he was about twenty-one or twenty-two years old. His legs were paralyzed, and he used a wheel chair. He had been in the Air Force and qualified as a disabled veteran and drew a good pension. He owned a boat and a car that he could drive with his hands. He and I were very good friends and we would often fish together. When I started law school, I lived in Kenner near New Orleans and Jerry lived in Metairie, where we visited every day. Ed Barnum, another young man from Springfield, and I, got up early and decided we were gonna shoot some wood ducks that flew across the river. So, we were out on the wharf just at daylight when the ducks were flying and shot a couple. The wharf was built like a "T". The deck came out from the camp into the river and then teed off. It also had a walkway around the side of the camp that led to an outhouse over the bayou. While Ed and I were out on the front of the wharf, I noticed Elliott come out of the camp and walk around to use the outhouse. I told Ed, "watch this show" I gave Elliott enough time to shut the door of the outhouse and take his seat. It was cold that morning, and I eased around on the wharf and I shot in the water underneath the outhouse. The shot causes the water to splash up and freeze Elliott's ass. He let out a roar and came storming out cussing at whoever did that to him. Ed and I both ran inside the camp before he got outside the outhouse. So, he didn't know who did it. But he did know who did it. We proclaimed our innocence and said it was Jerry Ray or somebody else, but it couldn't be us. I've never saw Elliott Foster so mad before or since, but he was

233

always one that would play jokes on people, and we played this one on him.

During that same trip he had bought a brand-new pair of hip boots. Hip boots in those days and I guess still today are either ankle grip boots or otherwise. If you were going to be in the swamp, you need ankle grip boots which fit tight around your ankles so when you stepped in the mud, the boots won't stick so bad. If you had the type of boots that are loose around your ankles, when you walked through the mud, your feet could come out of the boots that were stuck in the mud. The problem with ankle grip boots, was they were very hard to get on, you have to pull and pull and pull to get them on your feet and once you get them on your foot. You had to lace the inside of the boot up to make it tight around the calf of your leg, so it won't pull off when you're walking through the swamp. Elliott being short, and fat struggled to get his new boots on every morning for something like twenty to thirty minutes.

One morning, Jerry Ray decided he would play a trick on Elliot. While Elliot was in the bunk area, or maybe still in bed, Jerry went in the kitchen and got a raw egg and wheeled his wheel chair by Elliot's boots and put that raw egg in one of the boots. Elliott started to put his boots on that morning and as he struggled and struggled and struggled he couldn't feel that egg in the bottom of that boot because it was tight before his foot got to where the egg was. After all of the struggle, he finally got his foot all the way down in the boot and pulled hard and as his foot went down to the bottom of the boot, his heel hit the egg and crushed the egg. He cussed for a while. Everybody in the camp was roaring with laughter. We told Elliott, we would help him take his boot off and clean it for him, but he said "hell no" he was going to wear the boot with the egg in it, which he did all day long.

I also fished on Blind River for bream and catfish and largemouth bass. We had trot lines across the river near our camp about a mile from the lake. The river had no current most of the time and was controlled by the tide from the Gulf of Mexico which was some 40 miles to the east. During my senior year in law school I invited my friend Jud Downs from Shreveport to spend a weekend from school and go fishing with me. We got up at daylight, put our rods and reels and bait in the boat and drove about 15 miles to the Black Lake Club at Bear Island and launched our boat. We fished in Black lake about an hour without getting a bite then proceeded through Bayou Chen Blanche to Blind River stopping to fish along the way. We still couldn't catch any fish and Jud opened a can of sardines and crackers for lunch. I told him I was going to wait until we got to our camp and cook some fish. He told me we didn't have any fish to cook and it didn't look like we were going to be catching any.

We proceeded down the river to the camp, docked our boat and went inside. I told him I was going to get some bait for the trot line that crossed the river in front of the camp. He asked me what kind of bait I was going to use, and I told him P and G soap. He looked at me like I was crazy and told me he never heard of anything like that. I got a bar of the white soap and cut it into quarter inch squares. We then got in the boat, started pulling ourselves across the river with the trot line, and I started putting the pieces of soap on the hooks that were attached to the main line by 18-inch drop lines about 6 feet apart. Before we got to the middle of the river I could feel fish pulling the line behind us that I had just baited. When we got the entire line baited, which was about 300 yards long, we cranked up the motor and returned across the river where we started. We then started to run the line back across the river. There was a 2-pound catfish on the third hook. I took it off, put it in the bottom of the boat, and rebated the hook with more soap. By the time we got across the river we had eight or 10 fish in the boat and I could feel more pulling on the line behind us. We pulled the boat back across the river and picked up a few more fish. We then went back to the camp where I put a large frying pan with some grease in it on the fire to get hot and started cleaning catfish. We dipped the fish in cornmeal and put them in the hot grease to fry. Some of them were still moving when they hit the grease. In the meantime, Jud had peeled and cut up potatoes for french fries. I gorged on fresh fish and teased him about being full of canned sardines.

At the time we were catching the fish the tide was running out towards the lake. After we finished eating we went back to the line and caught more fish which we took to the camp and cleaned. We went back to the line a third time and halfway across after putting all the fish in the boat I noticed the tide had stopped running and we never caught another fish.

Every weekend when I was going to law school I came home, and many times went fishing somewhere in the area. When I was 20 years old and too young to vote I helped Carew Foster get elected to the school board in the sixth ward of Livingston Parish. Carew was a carpenter and a strong union man who worked on large construction jobs in the New Orleans area and he loved to fish. We spent many days together on Lake Maurepas, North and South pass between that lake and Lake Pontchartrain fishing for croaker, speckled trout and catfish. We used my little 7 ½ hp Scott Atwater motor on a flat boat to run down south pass to its mouth in Lake Pontchartrain. The pass was 30 or 40 feet deep but at the lake the water got shallow to about 5 or 6 feet. When the tide is running out, bait fish will be concentrated near the bottom, at the point the water begins to get shallow.

We each had a rod and reel with a bell type sinker on the end of the line and attached two drop lines above the sinker that were about 12 inches long. We attached catfish hooks to the short lines and baited with worms. We anchored our boat at the edge of the bank and cast our baits into the fast-flowing water toward the middle of the pass and let the bait sink to the bottom. The current would carry the bait to a point where the water began to get shallow that contained a huge school of catfish that weighing from 1 to 3 pounds. As soon as the bait reached that location we immediately hooked two catfish each. Sometimes we caught almost 100 before the tide turned and the fish stopped biting.

This kind of fishing was seasonal, the catfish run was in the early spring, the bream were on their beds in April and May, and the speckled trout, redfish and croaker were caught in the summer and fall.

When I first started to practice law after I quit working for the Louisiana Department of Revenue in 1968, Richard Nixon was elected president, and by 1969 my income dropped about 30%. My clients were working people, credit got tight, and the economy slowed down with many people out of work.

My philosophy has always been: Out of any disadvantage you can find an advantage. In this case I had more time to hunt and fish.

In Springfield two of my older friends, Tucker Richardson who was retired, and Son Settoon, whose wife Ruth Ella sometime drove his school bus, also had more time to fish. They mainly fished for bass in the oilfield canals near Bayou Pigeon and Lake Verret, but they also fished with fly rods for bream during early spring in the same area.

The bream bite began a couple of weeks earlier in that area than in the Springfield area and when I saw them bringing home ice chests full of fish they told me they would show me where they caught them.

A few days later my wife, Loretta and I took our boat, a small flat with a 10 hp outboard and followed Tucker and Son for the 1½ hour drive to Napoleonville and launched our boats in Lake Verett. We crossed the shallow lake and entered a bayou that was lined with tupelo trees whose leaves had just started to emerge. The trees were infested with small caterpillars who were falling in the water. Every time a worm fell in the water a fish would strike it. The worms were black and white, and we used a small popping bug with a white body and black feathers with a number 10 size hook for our bait. I would paddle near the trees where the worms were falling, and we would quickly catch eight or 10 fish before the activity of the fighting fish frightened the others away. I would then paddle to the next tree where more worms were falling.

In several places along the bayou, oil companies had dredged canals in the swamp and marsh to drill for oil. At the end of the canals the companies had dredged a larger area to place their wells. When the well stopped flowing, it was shut down. The bream would then make their beds along the banks in that area, where they were not disturbed by wave action from passing boats. Bass congregated in these dead-end canals to feed on the small bream and other bait fish.

Within a couple of weeks, the caterpillars had stripped the leaves from the tupelo trees, and the fish moved to other areas to make their beds. After the early bream fishing stopped at Lake Verret, the tupelo trees in the Springfield area were putting out new leaves and the cycle began again on Natalbany, Tickfaw, Amite and Blood River.

237

About this same time Van Foster, who was a state policeman, hunted deer with dogs. I made my first deer hunts in the Blind River swamp with him. Van, with his connections to other state troopers, was invited to hunt in Iberville Parish in the Bayou Pigeon area. A group of troopers leased a campsite across from Grand River Landing in the Atchafalaya basin and built a hunting camp. The troopers got permission from large landowners to run dogs near the camp and also to still hunt deer along the pipeline right of ways in other areas.

The terrain was completely different from the lake swamp where I had been hunting that required hip boots or tennis shoes to wade in the swamps. At Grand River the land was mostly dry except in the late winter and early spring when the Mississippi River rose and flooded parts of the spillway. The oil pipelines outside the spillway were protected from flooding by the levees and the land was covered with hardwood timber.

Carew's son, Kearney, was several years younger than I when he started hunting with his uncle Van and his grandfather Bryant Smith. He told me how his grandfather would sit on the edge of a pipeline with his rifle near a deer crossing and wait for a deer to walk into the pipeline where he could get a shot. I talked to Van and he told me I could hunt on the pipelines, but the rules of the trooper's club limited their guests at the clubhouse to members and their families.

Without having a place to stay in the hunting area my friend Andy Berthelot and I decided to improvise. Andy had a pickup truck with a camper shell on the back that he used carry his tools to work. I bought a small mattress that would fit in the bed of the truck and a one burner butane stove to cook on. We put food in a cooler, took one pot, a frying pan, paper plates, knives, forks, paper towels, our guns and went hunting. We slept in sleeping bags in the back of the truck parked at the intersection of a pipeline crossing the road and cooked on the tailgate. In the morning we drove to whichever pipeline we decided to hunt on then walked about a mile down the pipeline to a deer crossing, set a folding chair at the edge, and waited for deer to cross shortly after daylight or just before dark. I never killed a deer on those hunts, but I shot at and missed one of the largest bucks I ever saw.

I had only used a shotgun loaded with buckshot or a 30/30 rifle when I hunted in the swamps where we ran dogs and no shot was longer than 50 or 60 yards. On the pipeline shooting could be four or five times that distance. On this particular afternoon I had been visiting Van at his camp and told him I wanted to go try to kill a deer on a pipeline. He was not going to hunt that afternoon but volunteered to drop me off at the pipeline and let me use his 308 rifle. The road we traveled on the way to the pipeline had been built by dredging a canal along its side and using the dirt for the base of the road which was then covered with clamshells.

I told Van that I needed to shoot the gun before I started my hunt. He told me that he had sighted it in at 100 yards and it was dead on. As we rode along the road I saw a nutria on the opposite bank of the canal about 80 yards away. We stopped, and I got out of the truck and shot the nutria in the head. I never questioned Van about shooting his gun at longer distances.

Van dropped me off at the pipeline and I walked down it. About 200 yards from the road I crossed a deer trail then went another 200 yards and crossed a second and continued to a third deer trail where I stopped. I then decided to set up my chair about 40 yards from the crossing. About an hour before dark I heard a shot in the woods further down the pipeline and then saw a Jeep coming in my direction along the pipeline from the place I heard the shot. About 400 yards from me the hunters in the jeep got out and went into the woods. A little while later I saw them pulling a deer to the pipeline and loading it in their Jeep. They then returned the way they had come. The noise they made in retrieving their deer caused all the other animals in the vicinity to stay in the woods rather than try to cross the open pipeline. The deer crossings had several inches of water in them, and the deer would tend to walk along those low areas which provided them more cover than the open woods. Just before dark when things had quieted down, I heard a deer walking in the water towards me, but it either saw me or got my scent as it approached the edge of the pipeline, for it turned and walked away before I saw it. I realized I had set up too close to the crossing but there was nothing I could do about it at the time. I looked to my left and saw several deer crossing about 200 yards from me, but none had any antlers.

239

I looked to my right and about 400 yards from me at the first crossing I had passed on my way to my stand and saw a doe walk out in the pipeline. At the edge of the pipeline behind her I saw a huge deer. He then stepped out in the pipeline and stopped broadside to me and even at that distance I could see his antlers with my naked eyes.

I was using the 308 caliber rifle I had borrowed from Van and I knew it was an extremely long shot with that small rifle, but I had no other choice so I decided I would try. When I shot at the deer, it did not move so I shot again. The deer stood there looking my way. The third shot I aimed completely above the deer and as I squeezed the trigger I dropped the scope and saw the splash of my bullet in the water at the deer's feet and it ran away. The next day I told Carew about my experience and he told me I needed to get a rifle that would be effective at 500 yards, especially if I ever wanted to hunt mule deer, elk or sheep in the mountains. I purchased a Winchester 7 mm Remington Magnum and have used it for 50 years, taking a moose, caribou, mule deer, elk, pronghorn antelope, numerous white-tailed deer and all four species of North American Bighorn Sheep. I took the Dall Sheep in Yukon, Canada, the Stone Sheep in British Columbia, Canada, the Rocky Mountain Bighorn in Colorado and the Desert Bighorn in Loreto, Baja California, Mexico.

Desert Bighorn Baja California, Mexico

Desert Sheep Habitat
Baja California, Mexico

Chapter 3. 1979 Grand River

In the early 1970s the Mississippi River rose to historic heights. The gauge at Red River landing was more than 50 feet. For the first time in history the Morganza spillway was opened, flooding the Atchafalaya Basin. As a result, the state police camp, located inside the levy on the bank of Grand River took in 6 feet of water, and when the waters receded there was over a foot of mud on the floor.

The state troopers, who built the camp only a couple of years before were devastated. Van Foster contacted me and asked if I would be interested in buying the camp since they did not want to repair it. I told Bobby Moore about the offer and we went to Grand River Landing, crossed the river and surveyed the damage. Bobby was an experienced carpenter who loved to hunt deer with dogs.

I made a deal with Van for Bobby and I to purchase the camp for $5,000. Bobby rounded up a group of his hunting buddies who did construction work and began cleaning out the mud and ripping out interior walls and flooring. By the end of the summer following the flood we had made the camp livable and scrounged up used beds and furniture, stoves and refrigerators and a deep-freeze. We also built a dog pen next to the camp.

Bobby had a pack of Walker dogs, one of whom had just delivered a half-dozen pups that spring. He suggested that I build a dog pen at my house to raise the pups and I readily agreed. I had purchased a 20-foot boat with a 50 hp motor to fish on the lakes and we used that boat to ferry lumber and supplies across Grand River to rebuild the camp. I had installed a siren on my boat when I first purchased it. When not in use the boat was parked next to my dog pen. As the pups grew I decided to teach them to come when I blew the siren, and to do so every day before I fed them I would blow the siren and then give them food. By the time they were grown I could take them to the river and put them in the woods to chase deer. When the dogs jumped a deer, they would often chase it for miles and I would follow them along the river and bayous and oilfield canals in my boat. After the chase I would go to the area I last heard them barking and engage the siren and the dogs would return to the boat.

The area we hunted was almost completely surrounded by water. In the early morning we would take a half-dozen or more men from the camp and go up Grand River a couple of miles in my boat. I would then lead them through the woods from the riverbank approximately a mile to the swamp, leaving men approximately 150 yards apart to create the stand line. I would always take the last stand in the swamp.

The swamps at Grand River were different from the lake swamp where I used to hunt at Blind River. In the lake swamp there was no high land except right along the lake shore. At grand River the silt from the annual flooding of the Mississippi River created low ridges in the swamp. These ridges were used by deer as bedding areas.

When I would bring hunters to their stands, I would always place a few on the ridges where the deer often traveled to escape the dogs. After the hunters had taken their stands Bobby would take a pack of dogs to a location on the river or canal about a mile from the other hunters and drive the dogs towards the others. When the dogs jumped a deer they usually chased it towards the line of hunters who would get a shot if the deer crossed near them.

After the dogs crossed the stand line, one of our group who had stayed in the boat traveled up the river to get ahead of the dogs and tried to call them back. If he was successful he would load the dogs in the boat, go back to the place they were first released, and together with a couple of fresh dogs would drive the same area again.

This tactic often resulted in someone killing a large buck which during the first chase had split off from the does and circled back behind the dogs to one of the ridges. On some occasions a hunter would get a shot at a deer that was slipping across the stand line before the dogs were turned loose. As the hunters walked through the woods to their stands the deer could hear and smell them and would move away to avoid the activity. Often the deer would then circle back and cross the line where other hunters stood.

On several mornings, when I was driving dogs I would jump a deer near the edge of the swamp who would run a couple of hundred yards toward the stand line then turn into the swamp and lose the dogs in the deep water. He would then return to one of the ridges where he was first jumped. The dogs, after they lost the deer, would travel through the woods jump another and chase it through the stand line.

I decided to see if I couldn't figure out how to kill the deer that got away from the dogs. To do so I had Bobby drop me off from the boat between the place he was going to drive the dogs and the stand line. I walked from the river back to the swamp and crossed to the second ridge where I stopped with my 12gauge Remington Magnum shotgun loaded with three shells containing number one buck shot.

When the dogs jumped the deer, the main pack followed some toward the stand line, but a couple dogs followed the buck deer who turned left into the swamp. The sound of the dogs was deafening as they approached me with the deer within their sight.

I was standing on the edge of a small bayou when the deer, and eight-point buck, came running directly towards me. I shot, and the deer fell about 40 or 50 yards from me. It immediately jumped up and I shot again. He stumbled, and I could see his hind leg was broken and, in my excitement, I shot the third time and the deer disappeared. In seconds the hounds were all around me and ran away in full cry and suddenly stopped barking as it began to rain.

I had never killed a buck before, and in my excitement, I made every mistake that an inexperienced hunter could make. I don't remember how I crossed the bayou to the ridge where I shot the deer, but suddenly I was on my hands and knees looking for blood as the rain washed it away. I then began walking back and forth in the area where the deer had disappeared, and the dogs had stopped barking. But I could find nothing, and the more I searched the more confused I became. I finally came back to the river, met the other hunters and went back to the camp. Later that day I searched the area again and could not find the deer. I had to go to court next day, so I left the other hunters at the camp. Two days later one of them found my buck. The meat was spoiled but they saved the cape and antlers for me.

Over the years since then I have found many deer that I and other hunters have shot that disappeared. To do so I wait after the shot for at least 15 to 20 minutes before approaching the place I last saw the deer. I next hang a hunter's orange vest from a tree or put a stick in the ground to hang it on at that location. From the orange vest I then take 150 steps in the direction the deer was going the last time I saw it, at the same time looking on both sides of my trail. At 150 yards I turn right and step 10 to 15 steps, then return to the vest looking on both sides of me. I next walk another 150 steps about 15 to 20 steps away from my previous trail checking the ground for the deer or any sign of blood. I continue searching until I have made a 360° circle around the place I last saw the deer. Often this takes more than an hour. Sometimes I extend the number of steps to 250 depending on the terrain. If I have not found any blood or the deer after making this kind of search I know the animal has survived. Had I known how to use this technique at the time, I would have found the first good buck deer that I killed.

After we purchased the camp On Grand River we spent many days during late spring and summer repairing and refurbishing it after the 1973 flood of the Mississippi River. The area around the camp was a hunting and fishing paradise. It consisted of lakes, bayous, canals and main and sub channels of the Atchafalaya river that was created by the confluence of the Red and Mississippi rivers. On the east side of the Atchafalaya Basin, Grand River flowed south along the side of the levee.

When the river went down in the summer and fall, the water cleared, and we used bass boats to navigate the small ditches between the lakes and the Bayou where, we caught bream, bass, crappie and catfish. Bobby made some wooden slat traps which were 2 feet x 2feet x 6 feet with a funnel at one end and an opening with a slatted door on top. After they were made we put heavy weights inside them and sunk them in the water for several days until the wooden slats soaked up enough water that they would sit on the bottom of the river rather than float to the surface. When the traps were ready we attached a line and a float to each and baited them with rotten cheese which we obtained from dairy farmers. The opening of the funnel was so small that only small catfish could enter them, and no large fish like carp, buffalo, gaspagoo and gar fish could get in to the bait.

We ran the traps every day or two and sometimes they were packed with small catfish until no more could enter them. These catfish were undersized and could not be sold on the market, but the 10 to 12-inch fish when fried whole were some of the sweetest, most tender that I ever ate.

246

We caught bream with fly rods and artificial bait as well as with worms and crickets. We caught white perch and Bass with artificial baits as well as minnows and small river shrimp. We built a small wharf at the front of the camp and swam in the river near the edge of the bank. When we were swimming we could feel the tiny river shrimp picking at our skin in the shallow water. This sensation fascinated the children as they played in the water.

The camp had several bedrooms, a large kitchen, dining, and living room with a pool table, card table, and television. We had separate ice chests in the room that always contained beer and soft drinks. The tables were covered with packages of potato chips, cookies and candy for the kids.

One afternoon when my 10-year-old daughter, Beth was watching television, Bobby and I saw her go to an ice chest, reach inside, pick up a can, open it without looking, and take a large swallow. She immediately spit it out with a surprised look on her face and loud exclamation. Then she looked at the can and saw it contained Schiltz beer as we roared with laughter.

During that same summer and early fall I began to take my pack of dogs to the camp to train them to hunt deer. The dogs had a natural instinct to run the deer who lived in the woods along the river and the swamps. I would take the boat with the dogs a short distance from the camp, turn them loose and soon they would jump a deer. Sometimes they would run it for miles before they stopped. I would follow the sound of the dogs along the river until the deer would finally swim the river or a bayou and lose the dogs. I then would go as close to the dogs as I could with the boat, turn on the siren and call them back.

One day my wife and I took the dogs to the camp, and the only person there was Jerry Addison, an old friend and client of mine who I had represented when he got hurt working on a ship. Jerry couldn't walk very far due to his injuries, but he loved to fish. We arrived at the camp about midday and after lunch Jerry went fishing in the Grand River Flats, a small lake with lots of cypress trees growing in the shallow water. The flats could only be reached by running up the canal along the levee to a small ditch that led into the lake.

After Jerry left I took the dogs behind the camp and jumped a deer. The dogs chased the deer up the river and soon were out of hearing. I had recently purchased a new bass boat with two gas tanks. When one tank ran low on gas, usually I was able to slow down and change the hose to the second tank while the motor was still running. Loretta and I got in the boat and ran up Grand River to follow the dogs and I heard them far away from the river. We turned around, came back past camp and went a couple of miles to a bayou that ran parallel to upper Grand River. The Bayou eventually connected to a pipeline canal that ran back to the river not far from the camp. An earthen dam had been built there prohibiting access to the river to prevent erosion. We found the dogs on the canal bank, loaded them in the boat and started back to camp. Shortly after we entered the Bayou from the canal the first tank of fuel ran dry. I changed the tanks but not before the motor stopped running.

I had purchased the boat only a few days before we came to the camp and was not familiar with the Mercury motor that powered it. When I tried to start the motor, it got flooded and before I could get it running the battery went dead. I had a trolling motor used for fishing and started back down the Bayou using it. It was very slow going, and before we got back to Grand River its battery stopped. I tried paddling the boat but could get almost nowhere against the tide. It was getting dark and the early September air was getting cooler, so I tied the boat to the bank. We had not brought any jackets and as the light failed swarms of mosquitoes covered us as we lay in the bottom of the boat. Luckily, we had lots of mosquito repellent that stopped them from biting us. The sound of their buzzing was very loud, and the insects clouded the air around the boat as the sun set. After dark the night got colder, and we huddled together with five young dogs that helped keep us warm. When daylight came so did the clouds of mosquitoes, but fresh bug repellant did the job.

After the sun came up I got into the water and waded along the bank pulling the boat. When the bayou made a turn, I would have to cross to the other side to continue pulling the boat in the shallow water along the bank. To do so I had to swim across the Bayou pushing the boat ahead of me. It was very slow going and I had only covered about a mile when we heard a boat coming.

One of the most wonderful sights I ever saw was Jerry Addison coming with his boat to rescue us. He told us that when he came in from fishing, he had no idea which way we had gone and went the other way up Grand River looking for us. Not being successful, he returned to the camp late at night, got up at daylight and traveled the other way to eventually find us.

Jerry had an extra battery in his boat and being more familiar with Mercury motors he quickly got my motor running. When we got home the next day I sold that boat and motor at a loss and bought one that I knew how to run.

Chapter 4. 1951 - 1967 Duck Hunting - the Beginning

I always liked to hunt ducks. Some of the most successful hunts I made in many places across the United States, Canada, Mexico, Argentina, and Ecuador are related here.

The first duck I ever killed was when I was about 12 years old. Reverend P. W. Sibley, The Methodist preacher, in Springfield Louisiana, where I grew up, had a large family and liked to hunt, which supplemented the food on his family's table. Brother Sibley took me hunting with him one morning in the swamp surrounding Lake Maurepas, between the Tickfaw and Amite rivers.

My uncle Ernest Coats, owned property on the lower Rome Road that extended through pine and hardwood timberland into the swamp. I had hunted squirrels on his property on the high ground adjoining the swamp in the past, but never ventured through the tall palmettos into the swamp.

The preacher picked me up and hour before daylight and we drove about 15 miles to our hunting site. We got out of his car and walked through the dark woods towards the swamp. I had no hip boots and wore khakis and tennis shoes as we waded into the water. As we went deeper into the swamp we heard hundreds of wild ducks calling in front of us. The swamp was a mixture of tupelo gum trees, cypress breaks, and water covered with algae and water lilies. As we moved forward, the noise of the roosting ducks increased to a roar in the fading darkness of early dawn. I had never heard anything like that before. As the morning light increased ducks started to fly. We could hear the squeal of the wood duck, quack of the mallard hens and the hissing call of the drakes.

The preacher told me that I should stay in a grove of tupelos, while he waded into deeper water where most of the ducks were. I had no duck call and wouldn't have known how to use one if I had. As the sky brightened ducks began to fly and I heard the preacher's shotgun go off. Instantly the sky was black with ducks. I had a .410gauge single barrel shotgun and I missed every duck that I shot at as they flew by me. Nobody had told me that when you shot at a flying duck, you had to aim in front of it in order to bring it down. The ducks continued flying around me and suddenly a hen wood duck flew right in front of me.

250

Amazingly, it lit on a limb of a tupelo gum that had a large growth on it, about the size of a football, which provided a landing place for the duck. When it stopped flying, I managed to hit it with a full load of shot from my gun. Within a few minutes the ducks had left their roosting area, which we had invaded, and the sun was rapidly rising in the sky. The preacher waded back to my location with several ducks that he killed, and we began our return through the shallow water into the palmetto's then through the oak trees at the swamp's edge into the pine, white oak, and hickory woods to our car.

A few years after that the timber company which owned the property built wooden plank runs through the swamp to harvest timber. As a teenager, my cousins and I would walk down those abandoned plank runs to get deeper into the swamp to hunt ducks. This mainly resulted in very little success since we had no duck calls, no decoys, and no dogs. In fact, I only hunted wood ducks at their roosts when they came in right at dark, and rarely killed more than one or two ducks on a hunt.

In the early part of the hunting season most of the ducks were wood ducks. And wood duck hunting only lasted a few minutes, right at daylight or right at dark, when they returned to the roost. At the hunting camp on Blind River the wood ducks would fly across the river in the early mornings, and we would shoot them from the wharf in front of the camp before we went deer hunting. We couldn't shoot ducks back in the swamp because, shooting at the ducks would spook the deer and mess up the deer hunt.

As the season progressed, more and more mallard ducks would migrate into our area, but each year the season for ducks usually closed right after New Year's Day. Invariably, by the middle of January there were hundreds of thousands of mallards in the swamps, but the season was closed.

In January1965, some of my younger friends and I decided that we would take a chance and try to go into the swamp a few weeks after hunting season closed and try to kill some ducks. Kearney Foster, Dickey Abels, and I launched our boat at the Black Lake Club, a bar room at the end of the road in Bear Island one afternoon in mid-January, during the middle of the week. We figured, there would be few people

251

on the river and lake, and hopefully no game wardens. We traveled through Black Lake, Bayou Chen Blanche, and Blind River to our camp where we spent the night. Early next morning, we loaded our boat with shotguns and shells and proceeded down Blind River to the lake. It was very very foggy that morning, and we traveled along the lake shore in a northeasterly direction for a couple of miles until we rounded Big Cypress point. We continued to hug the shore and then put in to the beach. The beach was covered with hardwood trees and was several feet above the water in the lake and the water in the swamp behind it.

After we crossed the beach and entered the swamp, the water was covered with water hyacinths for about 50 yards, and in many places was waist deep. For that reason, we did not wear hip boots because they would have filled with water. Instead we wore tennis shoes and even though our feet were freezing, the water was not as cold as the air. After we passed the lilies, the water became shallow with a hard bottom that made it easy for us to walk through. We could hear thousands of ducks calling in front and to the sides of us, so we spread out about hundred yards apart and began to approach the ducks. We could see them swimming in the water in front of us and we used the cypress and tupelo trees, as well as some low bushes, to hide us as we crept closer. When we got in range the ducks would fly up and we would shoot which caused many more to fly. We then started calling, and some would circle around and come to one or the other of us. When they got in range we would shoot some more. We soon had more ducks than we could carry, and we were deep in the swamp.

We had planned for this outcome by bringing some trot lines that we used to string hooks across the river to catch catfish. We made loops in the trot lines which we tied to our belts and inserted the duck's heads in the loops. The ducks would float in the water as we pulled them on our lines until we reached the beach. We then carried them across the beach to our boat and that took a couple of trips.

We figured that it wouldn't be prudent for us to go back to the Black Lake Club with all those ducks, so we decided to cross the lake which was not very rough and most of the fog had lifted. We ran to the mouth of Tickfaw River and up Natalbany River to Springfield where the Abels family had a private landing. When we arrived there, late in the afternoon, one of us stayed with the ducks and the boat while the other two walked about a mile to Dicky Abels' house where we called our wives to come meet us and help us clean the ducks. When they arrived, we got in a truck, went back to the boat and got our guns, gear, and ducks. We returned to Dicky's, built a big fire and put a big pot of water on to boil to dip the ducks in so the feathers could be easily removed. It took us several hours to completely clean the ducks and when we counted them, we had almost 100.

Many years later I hunted in that swamp from an air boat, but we followed the law on seasons to hunt and limits to take. Now there are very very few mallard ducks migrating to the swamp since most are short stopped in northern states and salt water intrusion from oil field canals and hurricanes has killed most of the cypress and tupelo trees.

The first teal hunt I made occurred while I was working as an attorney for the Louisiana Department of Revenue in 1967. My job included traveling all over the state to file legal documents and appear in court to collect past due taxes. I got to know and made friends with office supervisors in Shreveport, Lake Charles, and New Orleans, as well as in Baton Rouge where my office was located in the legal division.

These local revenue employees would often receive invitations to visit peach orchards when the peaches ripened in North Louisiana, citrus groves in the Mississippi River Delta, strawberry markets in Southeast Louisiana and boat landings along the coast where shrimp and oysters could be purchased at wholesale prices. These invitations were also extended to any of the employees from Baton Rouge whose duties required them to travel to the local offices.

In September 1967 the owner of a large car dealership in Lake Charles contacted the manager of the Lake Charles office of the revenue department and invited him and some of his fellow employees to hunt teal in the marshes south of the intercostal waterway in Cameron Parish where he had a duck hunting lease on several hundred acres.

The Louisiana Department of Wildlife and Fisheries was conducting an experimental early-season hunt for teal that September, which lasted 14 days. This enabled hunters to have the opportunity to hunt blue winged Teal, which were the earliest migrating ducks each year. Most of

253

the teal would only be in Louisiana a few weeks and then would migrate across the Gulf to Mexico and Central America as far south as Ecuador where they remained until after the regular hunting season closed each January. The rest of the ducks migrated into Louisiana after most of the blue winged teal had left, when the regular-season was opened from mid-November through early January.

When he received the invitation to the hunting camp the Lake Charles manager called his superiors in Baton Rouge and invited them as well as other managers from different areas of the state to come to Lake Charles for the hunt. I received an invitation to join the group, and took Herman Stuart, a student at LSU who worked part-time in my office with me. We drove from Baton Rouge to Lake Charles in the morning and hunted that Saturday afternoon and Sunday morning.

I had never hunted teal before and asked some older duck hunters about what size shotgun shells to use and to explain to me any tricks they knew that would help me be successful on the hunt. They told me that teal were very small ducks that flew very fast and erratically. They suggested using 7 ½ size shot and leading the duck 18 inches to 2 feet when I shot.

The season opened in mid-September about 14 days after the opening of the dove season Labor Day weekend. I hunted doves every year in the fields near my home, using high-powered number nine shot in my 12gauge. I had a few boxes of those shotgun shells left over from my Dove hunts, so I decided to bring them as well as some 7 ½ size shotgun shells.

Our group left the car dealership in the early afternoon on a bus ride to the intercostal waterway. We were then ferried across to a waiting Marsh buggy which pulled us in a large rubber-tired wagon about a mile to the camp. We unloaded our gear, got our guns, put on mosquito repellent, got back in the wagon and were taken to our blinds. Herman and I were dropped off at the first blind which was located in the middle of a shallow estuary that was less than knee-deep with a hard bottom. The decoys had been set out by the hunting guides the day before. One side of the estuary bordered the marsh; the other side was a narrow strip of land a few feet higher that was covered with small Live Oak trees and Palmetto, called a Chenier.

The weather was hot, and I wore a light khaki shirt, khaki pants, and tennis shoes to wade in the water. There were no camo clothes in those days. When we arrived at the blind, there was no breeze blowing and the decoys had no movement whatsoever. We sat in the blind and I noticed the estuary along whose bank the other hunters had gone made a sharp left turn a couple of hundred yards away. As the sun began to set, a few ducks started moving in the distance but only one or two came by our blind. The ones that did saw the motionless decoys and flared away out of range, and we never fired a shot. As the evening got later I saw flocks of ducks flying across the estuary from left to right at the place the estuary turned where there was no blind. We heard only a few shots coming from the other hunters.

About dark we were picked up and taken back to the camp where a delicious meal had been prepared, and beer, wine and liquors were provided. I did not see any Jack Daniels black label whiskey there, so I produced my own bottle that I had brought for just such an eventuality. After the meal and drinks, we were provided cots to sleep on and awoke to the smell of coffee brewing and bacon and eggs frying well before daylight. After our meal we got back in the wagon for our trip to the blinds.

When we didn't get to shoot any ducks the first day I asked our host if Herman and I could hunt somewhere else, but he told me they had no more vacant blinds and we would have to hunt in the same place. I figured since he didn't know me or Herman, both for us being first time guests and the youngest hunters there, the best blinds were being assigned to his old friends.

When the marsh buggy pulling the wagon got to the blind I told Herman that I was going to go down the estuary and hunt the area where I had seen the ducks flying the evening before. He decided to go back to the blind where he could sit on a chair out of the water. I told the driver of the marsh buggy that I would show him where to drop me off. When we got to the bend in the estuary I had him stop and leave me.

It was just starting to get light as I waded across the estuary to the side of the marsh. The water was only a few inches deep and I looked for some high grass to hide in. The grass in that location was about 2 ½ feet tall. When I was standing the ducks could see me and flared away as they passed. My feet and lower pants were already wet from the warm water, so I decided to sit down in the grass which made a perfect natural blind despite me having a wet ass.

In the breaking dawn I heard the whistling wings of ducks flying a few feet over my head as they crossed the estuary, and when the sky brightened I saw flock after flock of teal flying toward the place I was sitting. The birds were so close I decided to use the number nine shotgun shells which had many more shots than the 7 1/2's. They also spread a much larger pattern from my 12gauge improved cylinder Remington shotgun. I began shooting and quickly started knocking down ducks, sometimes killing two with one shot. The limit for ducks was four, but the guide told us that our entire group of eight hunters could kill 32 ducks. I heard the sound of the other hunters shooting but not very many individual shots, so I decided to kill extra ducks to make up for the others. After I killed 22 ducks I decided that I better stop because the other seven hunters should certainly have killed at least 10 ducks. I put 12 ducks in my backpack and put 10 more in the grass next to where I sat and waited for the marsh buggy.

As I sat by the estuary I noticed some ripples made by a large fish swimming in the shallow water. As it approached me part of its back was out of the water, and when it got in front of me I realized it was a bull redfish that must've weighed over 30 pounds. I had no fishing rod or other way to catch it so when it got about 15 feet from me I shot it with the number nine's, hoping to stun it so I could catch it with my hands. At the sound of the shot the fish exploded out of the water, and quickly swam away. My shot pattern covered the entire fish, but all the pellets bounced off its heavy scales and merely scared the hell out of it.

I waded back across the estuary to the dune buggy trail along the oak trees, and while waiting for my ride I saw hundreds of colorful songbirds in the trees, resting from their migration before they began their flight across the Gulf of Mexico to their wintering grounds in Central America.

When the dune buggy and wagon with the other hunters approached I brought my backpack full of ducks to the wagon and asked the guide how many ducks the other hunters had killed. He told me that they only had a few so I asked him how many more would it take to fill out everyone's limit. He told me including my own we needed 27 birds, then told him wait a minute and waded back across the estuary to retrieve the rest of my ducks, which gave us five less than the total allowed. I could've killed far more than the overall limit if I had not stopped shooting while the birds were still flying that morning. The other hunters were pleased that I had killed enough ducks, so everyone would have some to bring home, but I also knew they were jealous of my skill and my luck.

Chapter 5. 1967 - 1971 Concordia Parish 3 Rivers Deer Hunts

The first time I ever hunted up around 3 Rivers, which is next to Roccourci Island, I was working with the Department of Revenue over in Baton Rouge about 1965 or 1967. I had worked for the Revenue Department while I was in law school from 1964 until 1966. In the summer I'd work in Baton Rouge, attend LSU Law School each morning and work at the legal division of the Department of Revenue in the afternoon. In the winter, I'd go to law school in New Orleans and work down there. One summer when I came up to Baton Rouge I met a young fellow named Herman Stuart. Herman was a lot taller than I was. I am about 6' tall and Herman was 6'3" or 6'4." His daddy, who had adopted him, was the Chief Deputy Sheriff for Rapides Parish. Being the son of the Chief Deputy for Rapides Parish and the son-in-law of State Senator Sammy Downs had got him a job through political connection and he showed up in the legal department. We called him a gopher, go where ever needed, do whatever needed to be done, run errands and that kind of thing. He was attending LSU at the time, but he wasn't very interested in getting a degree. I don't think he ever finished. Anyhow, he and I got to talking about deer hunting, duck hunting and fishing. He told me that they had a lease on a piece of property that they called The Willows located near the intersection of the Mississippi River, Red River, and Old River. The US Corps of Engineers had built a spillway and a canal there that cut between the Mississippi River and the Red River to take care of flooding.

That was my cup of tea. I got with him and we went up there that summer to fish in a small oxbow lake they called Sugar Mill Chute, which was an old channel of one of those rivers. In the fall we went deer hunting. The camp was primitive. The floor was dirt, and the beds were cots, but they were up graded cots, they were made of metal instead of the old fold up army type cots like I used to sleep in when I was in the army a few years before all that. The whole camp was built out of tin, the roof, the sides, and even the door, and like I said, it had a dirt floor. The heater was a masterpiece, a work of art. It was made from a 55-gallon drum with legs made of iron rods that somebody had welded to the bottom of it so it would be up off the ground. They had cut a hole in the side of it and attached a stove pipe to go up from the drum through the top of the roof, so the smoke would go on outside, most of the smoke anyway. A door had been cut into the end of the drum to let you put the wood in it to burn. When it got cold, and I'm telling you it got cold up there, if you stood next to that drum, you would be cooking on the front side of you when facing the drum and your ass was freezing cold like it was frozen. You turned around to warm your ass up and it would burn you but the front of you would be froze again. Anyway, when we went from Baton Rouge to that camp, the old Deputy Sheriff, Herman's daddy, used to come from Alexandria and he ran things. He was a gruff old son of a bitch, he had been Chief Deputy Sheriff for Rapides Parish for probably 30 or 40 years and he always brought him a prisoner from up there at the sheriff's office to come down there to cook, cut the wood, and or do whatever he told him to. If I remember correctly he was a skinny little black guy, maybe 22 or 23 years old. The old Deputy didn't call him by his name, he only called him the "N" word. He had to wash dishes, he had to peel potatoes, and he had to do whatever the old Chief Deputy told him to do. Of course, his job of cleaning the camp wasn't too bad because all he had to do was to take a broom and sweep up where somebody threw up on the dirt floor. He didn't have to mop anything because there wasn't nothing to mop, and it sure beat sitting in a jail cell all day long. Anyhow, they ran deer with dogs and took us out and put us in a stand line and it seemed like, for me anyway, the dogs always ran the deer somewhere else. We made that trip several times that winter, and I never fired a shot.

Along the side of the big canal where the lease was, there were soybean fields. The camp was right in the middle of the soybean field surrounded by 300 or 400 yards of woods. There were other pockets of woods in the middle of those soybean fields where it was too wet to farm which was good habitat for the deer. One morning, we got up to go deer hunting. As we loaded up in 2 or 3 trucks it was real cold, probably down around 8 or 10 degrees. We traveled from our camp about 4 or 5 miles through the soybean field up to the tract of land we called The Willows, the place we did our deer hunting. The Willows track had formally been a Cypress swamp. When the Corps of Engineers dug that canal, they started to dig it with huge drag lines and bulldozers, but they also used pumps to pump the mud out of that canal into the cypress and hardwood swamps along its length. The mud and sediment that came out of the Mississippi River filled in all this area between the bank of that canal, to an area that was cleared off and made into soybean fields. The swamp area that they filled was raised more than 15 feet with mud from that canal and extended inland from the Mississippi River to the Red River. It must have been 300 yards wide and several miles long when they pumped the mud in there. Years before all the big virgin cypress timber had been cut and logged, but when they cut that virgin cypress, all hollow trees were left standing. Nothing was cut that wouldn't make lumber. So, there were a lot of huge hollow cypress trees that were still alive when they dug that canal. The 15 feet of mud that was pumped around those trees killed them. When I got there around 1967, or 1968 some were still standing, but many had fallen. Those huge hollow cypress trees, that were 10 to 15 feet in diameter, were laying on the ground where they fell after breaking off at ground level. If you went to the stump, you could look down 15 feet to the bottom of it. We lost a lot of dogs during the hunting season when the dogs would come through there chasing deer and fall down in the holes in those old cypress where they would starve to death and die. The bones of many other animals could also be seen in the holes. Well, the cypress didn't regrow in that area, but willow trees, dewberry, and blackberry briars were everywhere. The dewberry and blackberry briars were the best food in the world for deer, so those willow areas, became prime habitat for deer, providing them food and cover for their bedding areas.

On that freezing morning, we were driving along in our little convoy of Jeeps, Broncos, and 4-wheel drive trucks, with several hunters in each vehicle. We traveled across a soybean field that had been flooded a few inches deep from rain water. At 10 degrees all the water was frozen and as we looked out across those fields and we saw thousands of geese and ducks feeding. We stopped to look at them and one of the guys in the back of one of those trucks decided he was going to shoot one of those geese. Of course, all of them were about150 yards away, and he decided he'd shoot one with a 30-06. When he shot that goose, luckily, or unluckily for the goose, he killed it. He did not hit it square in the middle because if he had, the hollow point bullet would have blown it completely to pieces. He hit it up in the head and neck area and that was a big whoop de doo. Somebody went out there and picked up that goose and brought it back to show us. A goose that big should have weighed at least 10 or 11 pounds, but I doubt if that one weighed 1 pound because it was starving to death, after the long migration it wasn't anything but skin and bones.

We did kill some good deer in that area and we hunted there for a while. The next year the Department of Wildlife and Fisheries bought The Willow tract which contained about 1100 acres. It had belonged to Mobil Oil Company before the state bought it and turned it into a Wildlife and Fisheries Management Area. The first year it was purchased in 1969, it had to be surveyed, and while they were doing that, we just kept on hunting on it. Nobody told us not to, so we hunted for that year. The next year, 1970 they got it surveyed, but they didn't get around to posting it, or regulate hunting as they did later. So, we continued to hunt on it. Of course, it had lots of deer, and lots of game.

I was from Livingston Parish, where you might hunt in the swamp for 4 or 5 years before you even saw a deer, and if you did it was probably going to be a doe or a spike buck. Concordia Parish was a paradise to us, so as the word went out, and more people from Livingston Parish went up there to hunt, more outlaws came. At this particular junction, the people that I had first hunted with, old man Stuart, Herman Stuart, all the people who had the leases originally had gone. We didn't have the camp back where we used to have it, so we did our own thing, Bobby Moore bought an old army surplus tent, a big tent, that probably 20 men could sleep in, and we put the tent up and got us a little trailer and we made a camp in The Willows. We built a dog pen for our dogs and hunted deer almost every day of hunting season.

Before hunting season one year, I invited a couple of New Orleans lawyers I had graduated with at Loyola to bring some of their friends hunting with us. They were all union members from the carpenters union who were their clients down in New Orleans. They all came up to our camp. We had about 15 men and we all went hunting that day. It was a day that you could hunt either sex deer. We killed about 15 deer and out

261

of the 15 deer that were killed, half of them were bucks, but half of the bucks we killed were still spike bucks. When we killed all those deer, we skinned them out, butchered them and laid the meat on tarpaulins on the ground to divide the meat. Well the New Orleans guys brought their coolers over to put the meat in, and they went though there picking up all the hind quarters, the back straps and the best part of the meat and putting in their coolers. The rest of us went there to get our meat and there wasn't anything, but neck roasts, ribs and legs left. Well, quickly the Livingston Parish hunters took over, dumped all the meat back out of the New Orleans guys coolers and made a more equitable division where the Livingston Parish people got the prime cuts and the New Orleans people got the bones.

A short time later I took my son, who was 6 or 7 years old, another friend of mine, Robert Threeton, from Springfield who worked offshore for Shell Oil Company and his son that was a couple years older and we went up and made a hunt. We left early one morning and drove up and met the group that was there to make a hunt for the kids and the other hunters. When we got to the camp we discovered that the night before, the people that were already there, our friends from Livingston Parish, had decided to get some extra meat after dark. They had killed several does which they brought back to the camp and hung them around in the woods behind the camp and butchered them.

When we heard about the game violation we went ahead and made the morning hunt but did not kill any illegal deer. My son and I, and my friend and his son left the group after the hunt and got in my car to come back home, about 11:00 a.m. As we came out from the camp to the gate, which was located at the river and the main road, a game warden met us and checked us out for licenses and game. We had nothing to declare and had done nothing illegal, so we came home. We later found out that the game wardens were informed by the local people who heard shooting the night before. They went down to the camp, searched the woods, and found the illegal deer. All the Livingston Parish hunters, except for Bobby Moore and one other who escaped capture, were taken to jail in Concordia Parish and their guns were confiscated.

A couple of days later I got a call from Bobby who told me what had happened and asked me if I could get their guns back. I knew Frank

Delaughter, the chief deputy of Concordia Parish and I asked him if I needed to file a formal request with the Sheriff's office to get the guns released. He told me that if I came to his office to pick them up he would give them to me.

A few days later I drove up to Ferriday and went by the courthouse. Frank told me to go downstairs to the Sheriff's storage room and tell the deputy on duty he said to give me the guns. When the deputy opened the cabinet where the guns were stored he asked me which ones I wanted. I did not have a list of guns that were seized, but I did recognize Bobby Moore's 12gauge Belgian Browning shotgun, which was very valuable. The deputy gave me all the guns and I brought them back to Livingston Parish.

A few days later Sheriff Taft Faust from Livingston called me and told me that he had heard from Sheriff Noah Cross in Concordia Parish. He said one of the game wardens had told the judge about Bobby Moore's Belgian Browning shotgun, and the judge wanted it returned immediately. I didn't want to get crossways with the old judge who I knew wanted that shotgun for himself, so I had Bobby bring me the gun back and I delivered it to the Sheriff's Office. Bobby didn't want to lose his gun, but I told him the old judge had the keys to the jail, and if he didn't want to be locked up for a long time he had to follow my advice.

Later I made arrangements for Bobby and a couple others to enter a no contest plea and they were sentenced to six months in jail and had to pay a fine. Through Frank, Bobby was made a trustee and spent about two months fishing and visiting his wife at her motel every day, but he had to sleep in the jail every night.

Chapter 6. 1970's Turkey Hunting - The Beginning

I first started hunting wild turkeys in the late 1960s with John D Adams, a surveyor from Livingston Louisiana who was 20 years older than I. John D had hunted turkeys all his life and was a master of the sport. His favorite turkey call was one he made himself from the wing bone of a hen turkey and the leg bone of a gobbler. To make this call the turkey bones had to be cleaned of all marrow, and the small bone from the hen turkeys wing was inserted into the leg bone of the gobbler.

John D. Adams and Hobart Pardue

John D. and I would drive to the woods where he knew from experience turkeys ranged. We would slowly drive along logging roads and gravel roads of the timber companies or national forest property a day or so after a rain and look for turkey tracks in the ditches. He showed me how to look for the large, gobbler tracks and also to look for the turkey turd from the gobbler which is much larger than the hens. We usually made the scouting trips in the afternoon. When we located fresh sign, we would return to the area late in the evening to try to roost the turkey.

Turkeys will fly up into the trees to roost as soon as it starts to get dark, so they can make sure that no predator can catch them. If you are standing in the woods in an area where turkeys roost, sometimes you can hear the sound of a large gobbler flying up into the tree limbs. During the mating season in early spring gobblers will often gobble once or twice just before dark. If this happened, we would then try to slip to within 100 yards or so of the bird to determine his location, so we could hunt him in the morning.

I learned to locate the roosting turkey and if I was close would not move until after dark, so I would not frighten the bird as I returned to my truck. If the turkey was disturbed from his roost he would fly several hundred yards to another roosting tree, which could be in any direction from the first. Often, a turkey that has seen something that was unusual before dark will not gobble the next morning.

Wild turkeys often roost along creek banks and bottoms of ridges, or a short distance into a swamp. They do this, so they can hear anything walking through the water in the swamp or creek that might approach them. The area I hunted in the southeastern states had large populations barred owls who also mated in early spring. The owls were very vocal just before dark and just before daylight. I learned the different calls of the owls and could mimic them with my voice.

Many times, late in the evening when I did not know exactly where turkeys were roosting I would give the call of an owl, and a turkey would gobble in answer. I would then move towards the turkey and if he was a long way off would stop every hundred yards or so and call again. Many times, I continued to do this until I reached the turkey.

Since I was a boy I read magazine articles about turkey hunting and all of them stated that it was unethical to kill a turkey off a limb where he roosted. I will agree that it is wrong to roost a turkey then go back the next morning when it is black dark, creep up on the tree and when daylight comes see him against the sky and shoot him.

One of the most disappointing feelings I have had is to be in competition with another turkey hunter who does this. More than once I have driven miles from my house or camp to a remote place in the woods, walked a mile from my truck, counting my steps, to return to the place I had roosted a turkey the night before. After setting up well before daylight, I would hear another vehicle coming in my direction which would then stop. When the turkey began to gobble on the roost, while the surrounding woods were still dark, the other hunter would creep under the turkey. I would hear the shot and the sound of the turkey when it struck the ground.

On the other hand, I do not know of a more challenging hunting experience than to owl for a turkey in the late afternoon, make him gobble a mile away from you through the woods, then hurry to approach him within shooting distance before dark. To do this requires calling skills as well as stalking skills when one misstep would scare the bird.

In the early 1970s I hunted turkeys in the Homochitto national forest in Southwest Mississippi. My friends, Lynwood Stilley, Charlie Abels, and Tom Kent Stewart would ride with me from our homes in Springfield and Albany Louisiana up Highway 43 through St. Helena parish to the Mississippi state line. We would continue north through Gillsburg, Mississippi, which was only a crossroads, until we reached Liberty, Mississippi then Northwest into the Homochitto National Forest.

It took us more than an hour and a half to drive from our home to the woods. We would drive a vehicle several miles into the national forest on the gravel roads maintained by the United States Forest Service and stop on top of a high hill to wait for a turkey to gobble at daylight. As the dawn began to break, the first sound we heard were birds chirping. We watched the stars fade as the sky began to brighten and sometimes heard a turkey gobble in the distance. We would then try to course him and if he was a long way off we would get back in our vehicle and drive as much as a mile towards him before we stopped, listen again for his gobble, then hurry towards him.

266

In those days we had no camouflage clothing, much less camouflage boots and caps. I usually wore khaki pants and dark brown shirts to try to blend in with the dead leaves on the ground. When I was discharged from the U.S. Army in November 1958, I brought a heavy field jacket home with me. I used it as a hunting jacket for more than 10 years. In the late 1960s, when I was hunting in the Grand River area, the State of Louisiana and many other states required hunters to wear vests containing 400 inches of blaze orange material when deer hunting. I realized this regulation would save many lives but did not like the idea of wearing a large solid bright colored vest the deer could plainly see, even if they were color blind. To remedy this situation I took a vest, cut it into irregular strips and had my wife sew the strips to my jacket, breaking the solid pattern.

A couple of years later I received a call one night from my friend Tom Kent Stewart who had just returned from Gillsburg, Mississippi where he had roosted a turkey. He told me to meet him at his house at 3:15 a.m. the next morning and he would take me with him to try to kill my first turkey.

We traveled to the hunting area in his Ford bronco and proceeded into the woods toward the place he had heard the turkey gobbling the evening before. He told me that when he heard the turkey he had approached to within 200 yards of it, made a single soft yelp of a hen turkey with his call, and the turkey immediately gobbled back.

We got out of the Bronco about 400 yards from where the turkey was perched in a tree just as dawn was breaking. We had not covered more than a few steps when we heard the turkey gobble. We hurried forward to try to get closer and set up a blind in the open woods near the place Tom Kent had made his call the evening before. Before we could get there the turkey flew to the ground, gobbling as he started moving towards the location where Tom had called.

We did not have time to build a blind or even make a call as the turkey approached in front of us from our left moving to our right. Tom told me to sit down behind a large oak tree and not move because the turkey would certainly see any movement of the hunter's orange on my jacket and would run away. I did as I was told and watched the turkey walking across the woods in front of me until he got within 40 steps, still

267

looking in the direction that he had heard the hen call. I waited until he stepped behind a tree and raised my gun. When he made his next step where I could clearly see him I shot striking him in the head. At the impact of the shot the turkey began to flop on the ground.

When I hunted deer, I was taught that if you shot a deer and knocked it down and it started to get up you should shoot again to make sure you killed it. Nobody had ever told me that one shot was enough to kill a turkey if it was hit in the head or the neck. When I shot that turkey, I was so excited every time it flopped I thought it was going to get up and run or fly away, so I shot the flopping bird two more times.

Since then I have heard turkeys gobble when they heard a single gunshot from another hunter in the area and been able to call that turkey to my location. When I shot those three times right at daylight, it scared every turkey within miles and no one heard anymore gobbling that morning.

The next turkey season I wore short boots that I had purchased from the catalog of L.L. Bean hunting goods store in Portland Maine. These boots had dark brown rubber bottoms and lighter brown leather tops. The sole of the boot was made of light-yellow colored rubber and it was called The Maine hunting shoe. This type of footgear could not be purchased in local stores. I found my boots to be much lighter and more comfortable than the knee-high black rubber boots that we wore when we hunted rabbits and squirrels in the fall.

On one of the first turkeys hunts I made after buying the new boots, I had roosted a turkey near a creek bottom deep in the national forest. I was no more than 100 yards from the turkey when he flew into the tree that night. I waited till black dark to move away from him back to my truck. I counted my steps through the woods until I reached the path I had used on my way to the turkey then counted my steps along that path until I reached the national forest road. I then broke a green pine branch and put it in the road where the path began. I then walked back to my truck and drove home getting there about 11 p.m.

At 3:30 a.m. I was up and ready to drive back to the turkey woods. I drove through the dark on the national forest road until I reached the pine branch that I had put there the night before. I parked my truck on the side of the road and began walking down the path in the starlight counting my steps towards the turkey. When I reached the correct number of steps from the road, I turned into the woods counting my steps until I was less than 100 yards from the sleeping bird.

I sat down with my back to a large tree about halfway down the ridge facing the other ridge where the turkey was roosting at about the same elevation. I was still new to turkey hunting and had not gathered any blind material on my way to the place I sat, and there were no small bushes near the large trees for me to place around me before the sky got bright.

As the stars faded, the small birds began chirping and I heard a barred owl call in the distance. At the sound of the owl, the turkey gobbled right across the ridge from me. As the sun began to rise the turkey gobbled over and over at the sound of owls calling and large woodpeckers hammering dead limbs.

There were no turkey decoys at that time, and in fact when hen turkey decoys were first made, some states outlawed their sale and use. I was sitting in the open woods as the sun came up and I made a small yelp on my box call. At the sound the turkey immediately gobbled. I was sitting with my legs stretched out in front of me facing the turkey and every time I called he would gobble back trying to make the hen come to him. I expected him to fly down towards me at any minute, but he would not move off the limb. The longer I sat without moving the more my legs began to cramp. After more than an hour my left leg was hurting so bad I could hardly stand it, and I decided to move my foot about three or 4 inches. As soon as I did so, the turkey, who was looking directly at my location, waiting for the hen to appear saw the slight movement of the yellow bottom of my shoe and immediately flew away. He never gobbled again that morning and I returned home empty-handed but a little wiser.

I never wore yellow soled boots again when I was turkey hunting and is soon as it became available I purchased some gray camouflage netting 50 feet long and 4 feet tall. I always carried it in the bag of my turkey vest to make a blind that would cover my feet and legs, so I could move them without being seen.

Chaney Phillips Trophy Decoy Kill

Michael Smith Caseyville, Mississippi

    I purchased the first turkey decoy I ever saw advertised in a sporting goods catalog from Missouri. I believe it was the first decoy used in Louisiana and Mississippi. The decoy was made of heavy Styrofoam molded in the form of a hen turkey with a heavy 2-foot-long steel bar connected to the body that you would stick into the ground. The decoy weighed about 15 pounds and was carried in a burlap sack with a drawstring. It was deadly if you had the opportunity to set it up before daylight near a roosting turkey, make your blind nearby, and call him to you.

Even with the decoy things would often go wrong on a turkey hunt. I had told a very good friend of mine, Judge Kenny Fogg from Denham Spring, La, about turkey hunting shortly after he was elected in 1982, and he asked me to take him on a hunt. I had joined a hunting club in Northern Livingston Parish near the St. Helena Parish line that leased several hundred acres from a timber company. The property was crisscrossed with logging roads and contained many turkeys. The membership also contained several turkey hunters who competed with each other for the birds.

For several days before the turkey season opened my friend Tom Kent Stewart and I scouted the area for turkeys. Tom Kent had purchased the first pop up turkey blind I ever saw. He would set it up along a logging road where turkeys often strutted in the mornings after they had flown down from the trees. The gobblers would spread their tails and strut in the openings to attract hens who could see them from long distances, when they came to the roads, then approached them. Tom hoped to call one to him where he sat in his blind.

The afternoon before turkey season opened I roosted a gobbler in a stretch of woods between two logging roads that contained large oak trees in a swampy area. After Dark I walked out of the woods to my truck and met Tom Kent in his truck. We took his truck and parked it at the end of a logging road on one side of the woods where the turkey was roosted to keep any other hunter away the next morning. I then dropped Tom Kent off at his house and told him I would pick him up with Judge Fogg in the morning. The next morning after picking up Tom Kent we met the judge at the gate to the lease long before daylight. On the way to the place where I had roosted the turkey, we dropped Tom Kent and his blind on a woods road and I parked my truck closer to the turkey we were hunting. The judge followed me through the woods to the place where the turkey was located. I built a blind with the camouflage netting

272

around a large oak tree and set the decoy about 25 steps in front of us. We were sitting on the ground with our backs to the tree with the blind material stretched in front of us about 4 feet high.

Opening day of turkey season was in late March that year and the oak trees had not budded out with new leaves. The area where we sat was covered with very shallow puddles of water and we were facing East towards the brightening sky.

When the songbirds began to chirp I made an owl call and the turkey gobbled right in front of us. The sky got brighter, and when the turkey gobbled again we saw him strutting on a limb about 80 yards away from us. I made a soft wine with my slate call and he gobbled again facing us and the decoy. He continued to gobble as the sun rose over the horizon and I heard a hen walking through the water behind us headed towards the gobbler. Both the judge and I had camouflage face masks, gloves and caps on. As the hen turkey started to walk past on my right about 10 feet from the blind the light from the sun struck the judge's gold rimmed glasses. The hen let out a startled squawk and ran away. The gobbler who had been rocking back and forth on the limb getting ready to fly down suddenly straightened up and quit gobbling.

We had been sitting there for almost an hour when this happened. I whispered to the judge that it would be 30 minutes to an hour before the turkey flew down. After about an hour the turkey, who had been watching the decoy all this time, suddenly flew down from the lamb. He flew directly at us and lit about 15 feet away between us and the decoy. I told the judge to shoot him and he stuck the barrel of his shotgun through the blind material and shot and missed the turkey. I had leaned my gun against a tree where we sat when we first arrived. When the judge missed I grabbed my gun and brought it down across the top of the blind to shoot as the turkey turned to run away. Just as I was aiming at the turkey's head the judge jumped up with his gun still sticking through blind material. This caused the blind material to rise up and I shot over the turkey. The judge shot twice more at the flying bird and never cut a feather.

Meanwhile Tom Kent had been sitting in his blind in the road and had not seen a turkey. Tom was a heavy smoker and after an hour or so decided to smoke a cigarette. As he smoked he discovered the window

273

in his brand-new cloth blind was not wide enough for him to shoot through. He looked in his pocket for his knife to make the window larger in the new blind. When he couldn't find his knife, he decided to burn the hole wider with his cigarette lighter. Unbeknownst to him the fabric was highly flammable and the entire blind caught fire. He managed to escape unhurt but was the butt of our jokes for years thereafter.

In the early 1970s, I became a charter member of the foundation for North American wild sheep.

In 1973 I became a charter member of the National Wild Turkey Federation. I met with other interested turkey hunters from Livingston, St. Helena, and Tangipahoa Parishes to establish a local chapter of that organization. When I contacted the national chapter about fund raising to help restore the wild turkey population, I was told that we could put on fund-raising banquets and that the national organization would furnish some pictures, a shotgun, and a few other items for sale or as raffle prizes at the banquets.

We would print and sell tickets, provide the food and facilities for the meeting and whatever funds we raised would be sent to the national organization with the exception of about 10%. I asked the national organization what about funding projects in Louisiana and especially in our three-parish area to restore the wild turkey population. They informed me that they would select the projects and the money would be spent as they saw fit.

I called the meeting of our group and we decided that we would form the Tri Parish Wild Turkey chapter and do our own fundraising for our own projects. For more than 25 years we have done exactly that. When we first started raising money we made donations to the state wildlife and fisheries department for the purpose of purchasing Cannon nets to trap wild turkeys to be tested by biologist's and then released in areas where the wild turkeys had become extinct. Our members also volunteered to participate in locating and trapping and transporting the wild turkeys we captured.

We solicited door prizes and donations of shotguns and other sporting equipment as well as hunting and fishing trips to sell or raffle to raise money for our projects.

Over the years we have consistently sold, raffled, or given away 20 or 30 guns each year at our banquets, including drawings for young hunters to win guns. We have conducted turkey calling contests and established a Hall of Fame for members of our organization who had contributed to the hunting and conservation of wild turkeys.

The population of wild turkeys has increased tremendously in Louisiana since our club was founded and now there are few local projects that are needed. Now each year we solicit donations of cash to be used as scholarships for the children and grandchildren of members who are attending colleges and universities in Louisiana. These scholarships range from $500-$1000 each and currently between five and 10 scholarships are awarded each year.

The winners of the scholarships are selected by a random drawing of names submitted by members with the requirement that the student must be enrolled in a local college or university, must maintain passing grades and the funds are not delivered to the student until after his enrollment for the current semester to ensure that only active students benefit from this program. I proposed the scholarship program many years ago. Our system of selecting the winners of these scholarships was debated over a period of two years before being adopted. Colleges and universities welcomed donations but told us that they would make the selections of the students who would receive the benefits. We refused to be dictated to by the colleges and came up with our own method to select the winners of these awards which guaranteed impartiality and the funds would be used only by our members children or grandchildren who were attending college.

Chapter 7. Leonard Jerry Kinchen

Leonard Jerry Kinchen was one of the best turkey hunters I've ever met. Before I started turkey hunting with John D Adams in the late 1960s Leonard Jerry was killing 5 to 10 turkeys every spring in Southeast Louisiana and Southwest Mississippi. This was an amazing feat because turkeys in most of the area were very rare, having been killed out many years before. In fact, when I first started, some years I only heard one or two turkeys gobble during the entire spring turkey season and I never got a shot.

When we would meet, Leonard Jerry would tell elaborate tales about where, when, and how he killed so many turkeys. Most of these tales proved untrue. If he killed a gobbler in St. Helena Parish, he would say he killed it in Mississippi but never ever tell you exactly where. Often after he killed a gobbler he would tell another hunter that he heard the turkey gobbling at that location a few days later. The hunter would then go where Leonard Jerry said he heard the turkey and waste two or three mornings trying to hear that dead turkey. He also told tall tales about his other hunting experiences, claiming he called a turkey and killed it in the national forest when he actually killed it illegally while trespassing in a local farmers pasture.

He was a very shrewd businessman who bought and sold real estate and timber like his father, Mr. Leonard M Kinchen had done before him. But there was a vast difference. Mr. Leonard could be depended upon to do what he said he would do. Leonard Jerry often told you one thing, then did the opposite.

Over the years I began calling him Lying Jerry Kinchen at our annual Tri Parish Wild Turkey Banquets. Many times, I have told him to his face he was the only white man I ever knew that would climb up in a thorn tree to tell a lie when he could stay on the ground and tell the truth. We remained good friends however and went on hunting trips together in many different locations from Hudson's Bay to Mexico. He played tricks on me and I played tricks on him much to the amusement of our regular hunting companions Chaney Phillips and Charlie Abels.

On one of our trips to Canada a large group of us went into a restaurant for dinner. I went to the restroom before the waiter took our order and told my companions to order me a rare steak. When I returned to the table we had a drink while waiting for our food. I casually asked Leonard Jerry if he had made sure that the waiter understood I wanted my steak cooked rare. He assured me he had and resumed his conversation with the other hunters.

When the waiter arrived with our food, I thought it strange that all the others were served before me, and the waiter had returned to the kitchen. After the rest of them had started to eat, the waiter returned and placed my steak in front of me. You can imagine the look on my face when I started to cut the meat, which was not only cold, but still frozen.

The crowd roared with laughter at me when I demanded an explanation from the waiter, why my steak was uncooked. Before he could answer, Leonard Jerry told me, "You said you wanted it very rare, now eat it." I tried to save face, as best I could by telling the waiter to take it back and thaw it out. When he returned the steak was no longer frozen, and for the first, and last time in my life I ate a raw steak, while enduring derisive comments, jeers, and laughter from Leonard Jerry and my other companions.

To add insult to injury he had told the waiter to bring me the bill for the whole group after we finished eating. I would not give him the opportunity of labeling me a cheapskate, and begrudgingly payed the entire bill, with a generous tip to the waiter.

In the early 1970s we joined the National Wild Turkey Federation and I made up my mind to be the first turkey hunter from Louisiana who killed one of each of the six species of wild turkeys in North America.

On one of my trips to Mexico hunting wild turkeys, Charlie Abels and his wife Kathy, Chaney Phillips and his wife, Linda and Loretta and I flew to South Texas near the Mexican border to meet a guide who was supposed to have Gould turkeys on a ranch about hundred miles south of the border.

We arrived shortly after noon, crossed the border, and were taken to a small airstrip with a dirt runway. A four-passenger plane was being fueled by the pilot, who was pouring gasoline through a flour sack from a gas can into the airplanes tank. When I asked him what he was doing he said the gasoline came from Mexico and he wanted to make sure it was clean enough that we wouldn't have any trouble on our flight to the ranch because there was no search and rescue flights available if we crashed. Charlie, Cheney, and I told our wives to get in the plane and fly to the ranch with the pilot and then he could come back and pick us up. Loretta, Linda, and Kathy told us that we were sending them first to make sure the plane would fly before we took a chance on the trip. We didn't disagree with them, because they wouldn't believe us anyway. So, we drank beer for a couple of hours until the pilot returned for us.

This Mexican ranch consisted of about 5000 acres and was very similar to the hill country in Texas. The ranch house was built of stone and was very comfortable. A generator provided electricity, we had butane and a young Mexican man was there to cook for us. We had an excellent dinner and beer, wine, and liquor that we had brought with us.

Before daylight the next morning the guide took us to areas where turkeys were roosting, dropping off one hunter at each place turkeys had been observed. I heard a turkey gobble just at daylight about a half-mile away but being unfamiliar with the terrain I was not able to get close to him until he had already flown down and got with his hens. He then started moving along the rim of a canyon that was between me and him and I could not entice the turkey to come to me. My companions were also unsuccessful the first morning, so that afternoon we decided to hunt in another location several miles from the ranch house.

We rode in a pickup truck that was fueled by butane. A large tank was placed right behind the cab which held enough fuel for several hundred miles travel since there were no filling stations in the semidesert area. The bed of the pickup truck had a metal frame around it that we could hold onto while we stood or sat on a bench behind the cab. This provided an ideal shooting platform for hunters using the truck during the quail season in the fall.

Water wells had been drilled in the hills, and waterlines brought the water from windmills at the well sites to large tanks which overflowed, providing water for vegetation for the cattle as well as wildlife.

Large numbers of scaled quail and desert gamble's quail congregated around the water tanks which were also used by deer, jack rabbits, wild turkeys and predators. As the truck approached the water tanks, quail would run away from it providing targets that were more difficult to hit than if the birds would fly. We were told that during the quail season, hunters had the opportunity to kill dozens of these quail if they were quick enough to shoot before they ran into patches of cactus to escape.

That afternoon our quarry was turkeys, not quail, and each of us was dropped off near a water tank approximately a mile from each other. Not long after the truck disappeared I found a place to hide alongside the road not far from the water tank and begin to call with a loud yelp. Immediately a gobbler answered several hundred yards away. I then heard another gobbler further away from the first who was located on the other side of a canyon. The second turkey continued to gobble as he moved through the Mesquite covered plateau near the canyon. I called several more times and every time he would answer as he moved in large circles through brush with his hens but would come no closer.

Suddenly I saw movement at the edge of the road in the opposite direction from the gobbling turkey and a second bird stepped into the open about 35 steps from me. When I shot the turkey in the head he began to flop on the ground, and the other turkey gobbled to the sound of the shot. I picked up my turkey and on close examination determined he was a cross between a Rio Grande and a Gould turkey.

I hung the turkey in a mesquite bush and crossed the canyon to try for the other turkey that was still gobbling. When I reached the top of the plateau, I saw it was covered with mesquite brush which was full of thorns, interspersed with openings and cactus. I sat down at the edge of an opening and began to call the turkey. He immediately gobbled his answer and began to move away from me. I knew he had hens with him and he wouldn't leave them to come looking for a new one, so I decided to try to circle around him.

The brush was so thick, and had so many thorns, I couldn't go through it and had to move through the openings to try to get a shot. I spent over two hours trying to get close enough to shoot the turkey, but every time I moved, or made a call, the turkey would change directions. As it got later in the afternoon I followed the turkey in large circles without ever seeing him.

In the meantime, Charlie Abels had seen and heard no turkeys near the water tank where he was hunting but had been listening to my turkey continually gobbling as he moved around. Finally, he decided that if I couldn't kill the turkey, he would come down the canyon to where I was hunting, kill the bird, and tell everybody he had to kill him for me.

The canyon was a couple of hundred yards wide and had tall pine trees growing in its bottom along the dry creek bed. These were the only trees in the area where the turkeys could safely roost at night. The turkeys did not have to fly up from the ground on the bottom of the canyon into the pine trees, they just walked to the edge of the canyon and sailed over to light on a limb near the top of the tree. The next morning, they could sail back to the top the plateau with very little effort.

The turkey, still gobbling, moved towards the edge of the canyon as the sun began to set. I quickly moved parallel to him to the canyons edge and watched him sail over and light in a large tree. There was no cover along the edge of the canyon between me and the turkey, who was about 80 yards away. I knew if I moved he would see me and fly further across the canyon.

I was using a 10gauge Ithaca shotgun that I bought at the beginning of turkey season and had killed a turkey with it at 65 steps a few weeks before. I didn't think I could kill a turkey who was as far away from me as this one was, but I knew this was my only chance. As I put the bead of my shotgun over the top of the turkey's head and squeezed the trigger, I had no idea that Charlie Abels was standing under the tree where the turkey had lit.

Charlie had come down the bottom of the canyon where the turkey could not see him, and as luck would have it the turkey flew into the tree right over his head. He had aimed his gun, and his finger was on the trigger when I shot, and the turkey fell at his feet. When I got to the bird Charlie was still cussing about me outdoing him again.

I had already killed Eastern turkeys in Louisiana and Mississippi. In 1983 I killed a Rio Grande turkey in Texas, and a Merriman turkey in New Mexico. I Killed an Ocellated turkey in the Mexican jungle in 1985 and hunted unsuccessfully for a Gould turkey in northern Mexico with Chaney and Charlie and our wives in 1987. The guide on that hunt told

280

us he had another area in the high mountains southwest of El Paso that had many Gould turkeys, so I booked a hunt for four hunters about two weeks later, and invited Leonard Jerry to come with us.

I kept my hunting gear packed and ready during turkey season every year as did my companions, so we were ready to go out to El Paso, Texas on short notice. We flew out of New Orleans early one morning and met our guide in the afternoon. He had a pickup truck, so we rented a small automobile to follow him to the hunting area.

The guide told us that we would try to get off early the next morning after we obtained our hunting licenses, gun permits, and certain necessities, such as a few cases of beer, some Jack Daniels whiskey for me and Charlie, and some Scotch for Chaney. I don't think Leonard Jerry had ever been to Mexico before, so we decided to introduce him to the carnal opportunities of boy's town. He maintained that he was a deacon back home and was not interested in any pleasure seeking. We knew of his reputation for not telling the truth, so when we left him and sought dark-haired, dark eyed, brown breasted bed threshers, ourselves, there was little doubt in our minds whether he back slid or not.

The next morning after a two hour wait to get the final approval of our gun permits we started Southwest with Leonard Jerry riding with the guide and the rest of us following in the car with me driving.

A few miles out of town we had to stop for an inspection of our guns and ammunition by the federales who had never seen a 10-gauge shotgun or it's 3 and ½ inch shells before. I gave them one of my 10gauge shotgun shells and they passed us through without delay.

A couple of hours down the road we stopped at a very good restaurant for lunch and everyone except Leonard Jerry and the guide began drinking margaritas. During the rest of the ride Charlie, Chaney, and I drank beer. After we passed through the town of Nueva Casa Grande, Charlie began driving up the narrow mountain road and I tried to take a nap. I was unsuccessful on the rough winding road, and when we reached the ranch house shortly before dark I told the others I would finish my nap while they tried to roost some turkeys.

There were two Mexican cowboys at the ranch house who were going to guide some of us on our turkey hunts the next morning. Their monthly wages were about five dollars each, and neither could speak English and I knew almost no Spanish.

After Charlie, Chaney, Leonard Jerry, and the guide left the house, I offered the cowboys some beer. It was hard for me to communicate with them, but I used the few words of Spanish at my command to express my interest in killing a turkey. The conversation went something like this.

Me, pointing my finger at my chest said, "Hombre, mañana, Mucho Grande' turkey" the Cowboys who understood the part about I, tomorrow, very big, stared at me with blank looks on their faces, not recognizing the English word "turkey"

I tried again, "Hombre, mañana, Mucho Grande', gobble, gobble, gobble." Smiles broke out on the Cowboys faces, "Si`, Si`, Signor "they said.

I then took a $20 bill from my pocket, tore it in half and gave one half to the cowboys. I put the other half the bill in my shirt pocket and patting the pocket with my hand I said "mañana, Mucho, Mucho, Mucho, Grande' gobble, gobble, gobble," "Si`, Si`, Si`, Signor." they replied. I gave them several more beers while they cooked supper before the rest of my companions returned with no news of hearing turkeys gobbling on the roost.

The next morning Charlie and Chaney went in one direction with the guide and Leonard Jerry and I went in the opposite direction with the cowboys. After riding through the darkness for 15 or 20 minutes they stopped the truck and I got out, but one of the cowboys took me by the arm, saying " No, No, Signor". He pointed to Leonard Jerry and then toward a trail leading from the road. Leonard Jerry started down the trail and the Cowboys and I got back in the truck. We then drove another 15 minutes or so and parked in a bottom between two small hills.

It was still dark where we parked the truck, but the sky was beginning to get bright behind the hill on the left. The Cowboys led me about halfway up the hill on my right when I heard a turkey gobble behind me on top of the other hill. I immediately turned around and ran down to the bottom and started climbing the other hill.

We were hunting at an elevation of about 5000 feet and I found it difficult to breathe. As I slowly made my climb toward the top of the hill, I saw the cowboys following me with their white straw hats on their heads. I immediately stopped them and motioned them to go back to the truck, so the turkeys would not see them.

By this time the first rays of the sun were beginning to reach the top of the hill, and I was still in the shadow. I could now hear two gobblers on top, one directly in front of me and another a couple of hundred yards to my right. As I approached the top of the hill the turkey in front of me started moving away to my left, gobbling every few minutes. When I reached the top, out of breath, both turkeys had stopped gobbling.

I figured both turkeys now had hens with them which would make it much more difficult to call them. Since I was between the two gobblers I thought if I could make them think a hen was coming towards one, the other would try to reach her before she got to the first one.

I used my mouth call to make a hen's fly down cackle. I then ran about 100 yards, as fast as I could down a cattle trail toward the turkey I first heard, that was now moving away. I then stopped, sat down under a mesquite tree, where I could watch the trail in both directions and made a low whine and cluck with my slate call.

A few minutes later I heard what I thought were horses running down the trail towards me from the direction I had just come from. Suddenly two of the biggest turkeys I had ever seen appeared about 30 steps from me. I shot the biggest and as he began to flop on the ground I shot the second one.

Shortly after, the Cowboys arrived and carried my turkeys back to the truck. When we got there, I pulled the other half of the $20 bill from my pocket and gave it to them. I knew those cowboys knew where every flock of turkeys that lived on the ranch were located, and that $20 bill enabled me to have the opportunity to take the number one Gould's turkey in the world.

All of my companions killed turkeys on the hunt, and like me eventually got the world slam, but I never let Lying Jerry forget I bested him with a $20 bill and a few beers. Chaney Phillips, on the other hand, still accuses me of paying the cowboys to put out a pile of corn to attract them.

A year or so later Leonard Jerry and I went to Orlando Florida to hunt the Osceola species of wild turkeys. These turkeys have darker

283

feathers than the eastern variety which we hunted in Louisiana and Mississippi. Where the range of two species of turkeys overlap such as Eastern and Rio Grande, Rio Grande and Merriman, and Eastern and Osceola they will interbreed with some having different characteristics in the same flock. In Southeast Louisiana I have often taken turkeys that seemed identical to the Osceola species which are locally known as moss head turkeys. The national wild Turkey Federation, which keeps the records of trophy gobblers killed by its members, only recognizes Osceola turkeys that are killed south of Orlando Florida as being pure bloodied.

Our guide, Jim Conley who lived in the area we hunted, took us to the property and we hunted on our own. I had killed a turkey in the same area a year before but wanted a bigger one. The first morning Leonard Jerry killed a large gobbler, but I never heard anything.

The habitat was much like that in Southeast Louisiana in Livingston and St. Tammany parishes, mixed pine and hardwood on Sandy savannas interspersed with shallow areas of Cypress swamps surrounded by Palmetto and larger palm trees. The turkeys, like the ones at home, roosted in cypress trees in the swamps and fed on crawfish as well as other insects and vegetation. The other wildlife species were also similar to those I saw at home, with a few notable differences. In the early morning I often saw Sandhill cranes feeding with their young in the open pastures where turkeys also fed. I saw a very rare blue runner snake one morning that was at least 5 ½ feet long. It looked exactly like the black runners I saw in Louisiana except for its color. I also found the tracks of a Florida panther in the Sandy ground. They were exactly like the tracks of a cougar I saw in the snow on a mountain in Idaho many years before on an elk hunt.

In addition to the wildlife, I ran across signs of human activity. I had often observed poachers in Livingston Parish Louisiana and Southwest Mississippi. While scouting for turkey sign near the border of the area I was hunting, I came upon an unusual amount of scratching in the leaves and dirt made by turkeys. I had seen this type of sign in the woods at home where hunters would put corn on the ground to attract turkeys. A more careful examination of the ground revealed cracked corn, and I soon found a blind made of pine branches with a bucket inside for a seat.

I decided to play an elaborate trick on the poacher. First, I shot my gun and put the empty shell on the ground next to the bucket in the blind. I then took one of my business cards from my pocket and wrote a note which said: "thank you for the setup, he weighed 21 pounds, had an 11-inch beard, and one and a quarter inch spur." I then placed three breast feathers that I carried in a pocket of my turkey hunting vest and the card on the ground next to the shotgun shell. I figured that message would bother that fella for the whole hunting season and make him mad every time he thought about it.

The next day Leonard Jerry and I hunted together, and he called a large turkey in for me that now graces my trophy room wall.

Neuvo Casas Grandes, Mexico – Gould's Turkey Hunt – Leonard Jerry Kinchen, Charlie Abels, Hobart Pardue - # 1 Gould's Turkey in the World

Chapter 8. 1973 Tensas Parish Deer Hunt with Charlie Abels

Charlie Abels was one of my best friends. We had hardly seen each other after we finished high school, he was a little younger than me, but we really got close after I finished law school. Charlie was a state trooper, his daddy, "Bubbie", had been elected Assessor of Livingston Parish when he was about 21 years old. Charlie's grandfather was a Justice of the Peace, and members of his family were some of the founders of Springfield. One of his ancestors was Springfield's last Mayor in the late 1890s.

Springfield went into decline for many years until the early 1950s. The town was reincorporated, and Charlie's uncle Harold was elected mayor when he was 22 or 23 years old. Charlie's daddy was injured in automobile accident and lost his leg before he was first elected. He got a lot of sympathy votes because of his condition and made a career of being Assessor in Livingston Parish for over 40 years. Charlie disappointed his daddy terribly because he had no mercy whatsoever on arresting drunk drivers in the area in the mid-1960s. It hurt his politics to have his son arresting so many voters who always voted for Bubbie.

Charlie married Otis Ratcliff's oldest daughter Diane, and they had two children. Charlie loved to hunt wild turkeys and I loved to hunt wild turkeys, and deer, and ducks, and all the rest.

Otis had a lease on some property in Tensas Parish, south of Tallulah, right on the Mississippi River. Dawes Easterly, from Denham Springs, had a plantation in Tensas Parish where he took all of his friends to hunt deer and it was truly a hunter's paradise. I never got invited when I was a boy because my daddy was not that close to the Easterly's and really didn't deal with the politics that much. But the Easterly's from Denham Springs and Watson were powerhouses in the politics of the west side of Livingston Parish. Otis Ratcliff was elected Police Juror in the 10th Ward in Killian when he was 21 years old. In fact, he ran against his father-in-law who had been a police jury member for many years and beat the old man. He was brilliant, a big man, who would fight at the drop of a hat.

When he was first elected to the Police Jury, Earl Long was elected Governor. Otis became very close to him and got a job as a boiler inspector for the State of Louisiana. In 1952 Robert Kennan was elected governor on the Anti Long ticket. He passed a law that prohibited dual office holding so Police Jurors could not work for the State. In Livingston Parish Otis's enemies moved to have him removed from either his State job or he would have to resign from the Police Jury. He chose to keep his State job, which allowed him to travel all over the State where he could help many people politically and have a good expense account. When he resigned as Police Juror, at the special election to succeed him, his wife Lois, ran for Otis's seat, and she was elected overwhelmingly. This was Charlie Abels' mother-in-law and father-in-law.

Otis then went into the creosote business. He had connections with a lot of people that owned timberland, and some of the timber companies. They would sell his company their piling and timbers to build bulkheads and wharfs and decks, in the coastal parishes where oil wells were being drilled. Otis formed a company in Natalbany, Louisiana next to a sawmill with Judge Warren Comish, and his neighbor, Mr. M. C. "Bilbo" Kemp. They called it R and K Creosote Company. The creosote plant in those days was not regulated as to waste disposal and so forth. Otis made the right kind of deal with the mill to buy all of the timber he needed to make creosote timbers and decking. With his company and his many political connections, he sold his products to oil companies all over South Louisiana and the Gulf of Mexico.

In the beginning, the venture was a risky one, and old Judge Comish decided he didn't want to stay in the business, so he got out, as did "Bilbo" Kemp. This left Otis as sole proprietor of R and K Creosote, and he really went to work. He entertained oil company executives by taking them to his deer hunting camps across Louisiana. He also took them duck hunting and fishing in the marshes and coastal waters. He developed a near monopoly on selling his products to oil companies, and he made a lot of money. He had some of the finest deer stands in Louisiana. They were built along the Mississippi River on property he leased from Dawes Easterly, and his guests killed some very big deer there. Charlie only got to go hunting up there a few times, because Otis didn't want him killing the deer that his rich guests and business associates hunted.

While Otis was off on trips, Charlie would sometimes slip up to North Louisiana and make a hunt on Otis's lease. In 1973 Charlie and I took our wives to supper one Saturday night in Hammond, Louisiana. While we were in the restaurant we decided that we would go hunting in North Louisiana the next morning. It was about 9:30 p.m. when we got back to my house. Charlie still had to drive about 20 miles to Killian where he and Diane lived to get his gun and hunting gear. The late hours didn't bother us a bit, he told me he'd be back to my place about 11 o'clock and we would drive up to Tensas Parish and make the deer hunt the next morning. We knew it would take us more than 4 hours to get there, and we figured we would arrive just before daylight. Well, Charlie came back and got in my car with me and we pulled out about11:00 p.m. Before we left Springfield, we stopped at Frank Brent McCarroll's barroom. It was raring and roaring about 11:30 at night, packed with people drinking and gambling. We told everybody that we were going to North Louisiana to kill a big deer the next morning and they all laughed at us. We got some beer and some whiskey and started on our trip. I had a brand-new automobile, the biggest Ford that was made with the biggest engine. The engine in that car was the same size engine that Charlie drove in the state police cars.

We drove from Springfield to Jackson Mississippi and then on over to Tallulah, Louisiana, and then down the levee to the hunting lease and got to the camp about an hour before daylight. Otis had converted two Volkswagen cars into hunting buggies by taking the tops off of and fixing the windshield, so they could be laid down, so you could shoot out of them. Both were four-wheel-drive and had special tires on them to get you through the muddy areas. It was cold that morning and we weren't really thinking right, so I pulled my car down the levee to the camp and parked there. We got in a Volkswagen, drove up to the top of the levee and drove on it about a mile down the river. I had never been there before and had to rely strictly on Charlie to find the stands in the woods. After we left the levee going toward the river, Charlie said it didn't matter we would find them. We soon got to a large ditch where we had to stop the Volkswagen. We walked across a footbridge then

289

followed a trail through the woods to a point where there was a rope hanging from a tree. This told Charlie where the first stand was, and he led me through the woods about 100 yards to the stand. It was an open stand about 16 feet high without a roof on it and had a bench to sit on. It was made of pipes and timbers and had lots of room. I had never been in one that comfortable before. Charlie walked on back to the trail to his deer stand. As it started to just break a little bit of light, I listened to the sounds of the coming dawn and I heard an animal moving in the oak leaves, coming from behind me, in the darkness.

The Mississippi River at that location was out in front of me, to the East of the levee, which was behind me. Between the levee and the Mississippi River there was a barrow pit which had been dug to obtain the dirt to build the levees. That pit was filled with water. The noise of the animal coming through the leaves behind me got closer and then I heard it splash into the water of the pit. When it came out of the water on the other side closer to me and I heard noise in the leaves again.

It was just breaking dawn when that deer came right out in front of me. I could only see the shape of the deer, it was just a dark shadow and I couldn't see any antlers in the darkness. My rifle had a scope on it that was attached directly to the barrel of my gun. I lowered the rifle down, and I could see the deer but when I raised my rifle, I could not find it in my scope. The deer came right out in front of me and walked directly under my stand. I could see its white antlers in the early light, but I couldn't get a shot because I still couldn't find the deer in the scope. That deer must've wanted to commit suicide, because then it turned and walked about 40 yards away from me, stopped and it turned sideways. I was cussing myself for not having a see-through sight under the scope of the rifle where I could shoot the deer with open sites. Finally, I saw the white antlers in my scope, and I knew it was now or never. I lowered the scope to what I thought was the shoulder of the deer and squeezed the trigger. The deer then bounded out of sight. I'd been deer hunting several years, and I knew better than to get out of the stand and go after that deer right away because that would cause it to run off further, where I couldn't find it. I stayed in the stand for what seemed like hours waiting for it to get light enough for me to go look for blood. Finally, it got light enough, and I came down the stand and went over to where I had shot. I looked around, but it was still too dark on the ground to find any blood. There was nothing to do but just wait. After a while the darkness faded, and it got bright enough for me to find a large puddle of blood right where I had shot, and I started following the signs of the blood trail. Within 100 yards I found the deer laying there dead, a beautiful eight-point buck. At that time, it was the largest deer I had ever killed.

When I found the deer, I let out a whoop and Charlie came through the woods to me. We got the deer by the antlers and drug it several hundred yards back to the hunting buggy. We loaded it in the buggy, but we discovered that we had pulled the vehicle right to the edge of the ditch in the darkness, and the transmission of the buggy would not allow us to back up. Luckily, we found a come-along in it just for that purpose, so we hooked the come-along to a tree and winched the buggy back around until we got it where we could pull the vehicle around and start out. We got in the vehicle and were back to the levee in about 30 minutes. We then drove along the levee to the camp. By this time, it was probably 7:30 in the morning. Had I not killed the deer, we would've been hunting till 10:30 or 11:00 a.m., before we came out of the woods. Luckily, we had been successful really quick. We loaded the deer in the trunk of my brand-new car which did not have a license plate. In fact, I just got the car the day before and had less than 500 miles on it when we started our trip.

In those days when you bought a new car, the dealer recommended that you break it in by driving it no more than 55 to 60 miles an hour until you traveled at least 250 miles. Mine and Charlie's plan was to break the car in our trip to North Louisiana which was more than 250 miles round-trip. Well when we started to go back up the levee, there was frost all over the ground and that brand-new car had slick tires for highway use only. We could get no traction to go up the levee and there we were. The hunting buggy wasn't powerful enough to pull the car up the levy and there were no houses for miles. We had decided to take the hunting buggy and go to find another camp somewhere and get some help, when we heard a tractor coming down the levee, operated by an employee of one of the neighboring farms. We flagged the driver down and asked if he would pull the car up to the top of the levee which he graciously did, and we pulled out and headed back towards Tallulah. On the way we stopped by the Easterly camp, and showed off the deer, grabbed a bite to eat, and filled up one coffee bottle for the ride home.

When we started out I was driving. We got on the interstate at Tallulah and I was cruising about 70 miles an hour. At that time the speed limit was 55 miles an hour because of the oil shortage. Between Jackson and Vicksburg, a State Trooper stopped me for speeding, and he gave me a ticket. Charlie and I had put some Kahlúa in our coffee bottles and we were drinking Kahlúa and coffee on the road. Luckily, I hadn't had too much to drink, and had sobered up from the night before. The trooper questioned me about drinking anything when he gave me the ticket and I showed him the coffee bottle and told him I was only drinking coffee. We drove on into Jackson and turned south on I- 55. When we stopped at a filling station to get some gas, as the attendant came out and put gas in my car and I went inside to pay the bill with a credit card. The manager said he needed the license number for the car. Well, I had no license on the car and he didn't want to take my credit card, so I paid cash for the gas. I came back out to the car and the attendant, who was expecting a tip, looked at me very thoroughly and asked if I was going to give him a tip. I told him to get his ass out of the way. Charlie told me to get in and he would drive. Neither one of us was thinking about the speed trap that existed in Brookhaven. Anytime you were going to Brookhaven, Mississippi in those days there was always a trooper right there running radar. If you got a ticket, he would take you to the Justice of the Peace and you'd have to pay the fine right there. When we passed Brookhaven Charlie was running probably 75 to 80 miles an hour and sure enough that trooper pulled out and got after us. I thought Charlie was gonna stop, but he said the trooper couldn't catch us. He told me he drove the same car as mine, but the bar lights on top of the car would not let it run as fast as the one we were in without lights on top. I told Charlie he was crazy as he pushed the gas petal to the floor and the blue lights were getting further and further behind us. Charlie was right, he was out running the trooper. I looked over at the speedometer and it was over beyond 120. So here we are coming south down Interstate Highway 55 on Sunday morning at120 miles an hour with a trooper behind us. When we got to McComb, Mississippi the trooper had radioed ahead and there was another trooper coming out going north trying to get to a crossover where he could help the first trooper. That trooper doubled back across the interstate and got behind us also, so now we had 2 State Troopers behind us, with sirens going and lights flashing. Charlie just kept running a little bit faster and the troopers just got further and further behind. I said, "now what in the hell are you gonna do Charlie?" He said, "we want to get across the state line then and they will be there in my territory." I said, "What if they start shooting," he said he didn't think they would shoot at us and luckily, he was right. When we crossed the Louisiana line, the troopers didn't even try to follow us any further.

When we got back to Springfield we went back by Frank Brent McCarroll's barroom. By this time, it was about noon and we walked inside and got a beer. The same bunch that was in there the night before had left and came back. They told us "ya'll must have not been hunting at all." I told them to come outside and look what we got. We paraded the deer around and did a lot of talking and showing off. We then brought the deer back to my garage and cleaned and butchered it. I sent some deer meat to Otis Ratcliff, who cursed his son-in-law for taking me up there and killing a deer he wanted one of his customers to kill.

Chapter 9. 1973 - Slim Hughes - Alligator Hunting

One summer during the early 1970's, the State of Louisiana held its first alligator hunting season in September. I decided that I wanted to kill a big alligator, and have it mounted to place it in the trophy room that I was planning on building. I didn't have a trophy room then, but I certainly intended to construct one. I wanted to put different kind of trophies that I intended to hunt in different parts of North, Central and South America if I had the opportunity. I had a bass boat that I used for fly fishing for bream in the Tickfaw, Natalbany, Blood, and Amite River areas of southeast Louisiana at this time. I also used the boat to fish for speckled trout and red fish in the marshes south of New Orleans.

When the first alligator hunting season opened there was no provision for alligator hunts as such. A regular hunting license was all you needed, but to kill alligator's, you would need a trapping license and a permit. A certain number of tags were allocated to different trappers in each area of the swamp.

My friend, Bubbie Abels, who was the assessor in Livingston Parish managed to make sure that he and his friends and relatives had hunting rights from the big companies that owned the swamps surrounding Lake Maurepas in Livingston Parish. One of Bubbie's brothers was Harold Abels, who as a young man in the 1950's, was mayor of the town of Springfield. Harold was a little older than me, and we were very close friends. Harold had one of the first air boats that I ever saw in Livingston Parish. Where I had gone in the swamps hunting ducks in the 50's and early 60's, I along with my friends, used regular boats to go down the rivers to the lake and then wade in the swamp back to the places we hunted ducks. In the early 1970's, Harold's air boat allowed him to go through the swamps without any of the wading and he had a hunting lease to trap mink and otter and other fur bearing animals in that area, as well as to hunt alligators when it became legal to do so.

Harold told me that he had a lot of the big alligators on his lease, and I knew that to be true because nobody had hunted those alligators for more than ten years. Since they were an endangered species, the illegal taking of the animals was almost completely prohibited because you could not legally sell the hides. Harold had permits to take about 10

294

or 12 alligators during that first season and I told him that I would like to kill one of the big gators and have it mounted. We struck a deal that would allow me to kill a big gator, and I would pay him the same amount that he would receive if he had killed the alligator, skinned it and sold it the skin. This was going to accomplish my goal of having a big gator and it was a good deal for Harold because I was going to pay him the price of the hide, but he didn't have to skin it.

At that time, I had a black man that everybody called "Slim", that worked for me. Slim, a WWII army vet who had served in Europe and North Africa, was a man who knew almost every black person in Livingston and Tangipahoa Parish. Slim was very intelligent, and we became very close friends. I first discovered Slim when I represented a man who had been in an automobile accident, and Slim was a witness.

The insurance adjuster had found him since he was not listed on the police report. At the trial I questioned him closely about how much the insurance company was paying him to come up there to court and testify. Slim, being smart but not schooled properly by the insurance adjuster, admitted that the insurance company was going to pay him his expenses for missing work to come to court. This was all legal and happened all the time, but I knew Slim didn't work at any regular job. He did some work in the woods and he did some handyman work from place to place, but I got it out of him that, he could have done the same job that he was being paid for missing, the day before and didn't do it, and would probably go to work the next day and do the job he was getting paid to miss. That certainly didn't go over very good with the Judge, who didn't really like insurance companies that much anyway. I got an award for my client.

Shortly thereafter, Slim came to see me, bringing a couple of his friends who had been in a car wreck. I was surprised to see Slim come in and I didn't know the people he had with him. After they came into my office and we talked about their accident, I asked Slim why he brought me the new clients when he had been on the other side before, I told him that I appreciated him bring his friends to see me and I would do what I could for them and try to get them some money. He said, "That's the reason I'm here Mr. Hobart." He said, "I seen you operate in court and I figure you was a pretty good lawyer and if me or my friends need a lawyer, I'm gonna come see you." That was the beginning of a long friendship.

When I decided to go kill that alligator, I made arrangements with Harold to meet him at a canal that led off of Tickfaw River into the swamp where he had his lease, about daylight on opening day of the alligator season. Harold had put his lines out the day before. The way he did it then is the way they do it now. He had a long line with a big hook and he, instead of using chickens like the alligator hunters do now, just killed a white crane and used it for bait. He then hooked that bird and dropped the line over a limb so that the bird was about a foot or so above the water. This was done that way because if you hooked the bait and put it in the water, turtles would pull all the meat off of the hook and the alligators would not get hooked. By suspending the bait above the water, a foot or so, an alligator could swim up, grab the bird that was bait, pull it into the water and then swallow it along with the hook and then swim off. An alligator's mouth is almost solid bone, and no hook is going to catch it by hooking him in the mouth. The only way you're going to catch that gator, he's got to swallow the hook, so it gets hooked in his gut and he can't pull it loose or get away from it.

Slim and I took my boat to meet Harold in his air boat at the mouth of the canal. I changed over into the air boat with my rifle and we headed down the canal into the swamp where Harold had set out the gator lines. Slim stayed in my boat at the river. We shortly came to a place where an alligator had been hooked on a line. The water lilies and other vegetation in the canal were all torn up and piles of mud were on the bank. Harold told me, "well, we got one here and he's a big one". We came to the line that was tied to the tree and Harold began to pull on the line. As he pulled the line towards the boat, the gator, feeling the pressure of the line swam to the surface. There wasn't any fighting about it, he already had been trying to get loose and couldn't. He had torn up the whole area by rolling and trying to get the hook out of his gut but it had not worked. He just came to the surface and quietly swam towards us as Harold pulled the line in closer to the boat. When the gator got within about ten feet of the boat I shot him right in the top of the head. Later on, I found out that most alligator hunters, carried a 22 pistol to dispatch the alligators. With the smaller gators, Harold would pull them up close to the boat where he could reach over with a hatchet and cut them right through the top of the head. After I shot the gator it thrashed about a little bit but soon died and we pulled it out to the bank.

We left that one and went further into the swamp where we harvested 5 more that morning. The two biggest were each about 12 feet long and the others were 6 -9 feet long. Harold had made a big pay day for that trip. We came back to my boat with the gators in the air boat. My boat was built in such a way that it had seats in the front and back but along one side was a compartment covered by carpet that held guns and fishing rods which could be used as an additional seat for fisherman or hunters. We got that big gator in my boat and stretched him out on top of the compartment at the side of the boat. I then told Slim to sit on the gator so I could take his picture. His eyes rolled, but he sat on the top of the gator with the gators head facing towards me for the picture. I then told Slim to catch this gator by the snout and pull it so its mouth would come open. Slim didn't like that idea at all even though the gator was dead. Alligators are amphibians, and like turtles and frogs, after they are dead, there may be muscle contractions that can go on for several hours. When cleaning alligator snapping turtles, I have seen the heart of a turtle, which beats very slowly continue to beat for many minutes after the turtle had been killed. When cleaning bull frogs I have seen their legs twitch and move after I removed the skin and put them in a hot skillet, to be cooked.

When Slim reached over and pulled that alligator's mouth open, the gator's tail and back legs began to move. Slim thought the gator was still alive and jumped overboard to try to escape. I have a picture of Slim, sitting on the big alligator with its mouth open and his expression shows that he was mighty worried about what that gator might or might not do. It was taken just before the gator made its move, and Slim went overboard.

Slim often accompanied me to my hunting camp in Leslie, Mississippi to help set out hoop nets and make repairs. One fall I took Slim with me to help build a duck blind. I had a small 14-foot boat that I used for fishing and for duck hunting. Slim and I left the camp which was on a high bluff near the flood plain of the Buffalo River early one morning and drove down the hill in my truck to get some material to

297

build a duck blind. We took some machetes to a patch of switch cane and we cut enough to completely fill the boat. We loaded the switch cane in the boat in the back of the truck and we drove to a pothole where I intended to build the blind. When we reached the water's edge, Slim and I got out of the truck, unloaded the boat and sat it in the water. The water at that point was maybe 3 inches deep. I had a pair of hip boots on and Slim had on a pair of brogans, which were just heavy leather shoes. When we put the boat into the water, I told Slim to get in the back of the boat, so he would not have to get his feet wet. I had my hip boots and I walked around to the front of the boat and climbed on top of the switch cane. Slim was sitting in the boat on top of the canes with a paddle and I told him to shove off. He tried to push the boat with a paddle but Slim, who weighed about 260 pounds sitting in the back of the boat, and I weighing about 220 pounds in the front, caused the boat to sink in the mud and it wouldn't float. I got out of the front of the boat and told Slim to push with the paddle and I grabbed the rope and started to pull the boat. We got the boat floating with Slim in the boat and me with the rope across my shoulder. As I pulled the boat out into the pond the water got about knee deep and Slim, riding on top of the cane filled boat started laughing. I looked back at him and said what in the hell is the matter with you? He continued whooping and hollering and laughing his head off. I said" You stupid son of a bitch, what in the hell is the matter with you, what are you laughing at? "He said" Mr. Hobart, "I's the only black man in Mississippi that's got him a big time, high class, rich white lawyer pulling him around in a boat." I had to laugh at that myself. I pulled him the rest of the way out where we built the blind and afterwards pulled him back to shore.

Slim Hughes, Tickfaw River, Louisiana

Lake Maurepas Swamp
12 Foot Alligator

Chapter 10. 1973 - 1978 Mexico Fishing and Hunting

My first trip to Mexico was about 1973. I had talked to Charlie Abels about going with me. He had been down there when he was a kid with his daddy and momma on vacation. It was all going to be a big adventure, and I had been reading about the fishing in Lake Guerrero for bass. Guerroro is a manmade lake about 100 miles south of the border town of Brownsville, Texas. I had seen some articles in some magazines like Field and Stream and Outdoor Life describing the bass fishing where you could go down there and catch 40 or 50 bass in a morning. Most weighed about 2 pounds but every once in a while, you'd catch some real big ones. I had done very little bass fishing in the local rivers except with a hogging pole. Hogging for bass when I was a boy was done with a 10' heavy cane pole with a heavy piece of trot line tied to its butt, the line was wrapped around the pole, all the way out to its end and then extended past the tip out about 2'.

In those days there were no electric trolling motors, but if you had a small motor, say about 2 or 3 horsepower, that would be ideal for hogging. Of course, we didn't have a motor, so I had to have somebody paddle the boat along the bank while I fished on the front end of the boat using the hogging pole. Then I would paddle, and my companion would fish. The bait we used on the hogging pole was a lucky 13 which is a big bass bait with three treble hooks with a red head and white body. The ideal time for hogging would be right at daylight in the morning or just before dark at night. To do this kind of fishing you would get in the front of the boat and have your partner in the back doing the paddling along the bank. I took that hogging pole and jerked the bait back and forth across the top of the water, just beating the water and letting the tip of the pole go into the water and make as much racket as I could. Anybody looking at me doing this would figure I had lost my damn mind, because it appeared all I was doing was splashing in the water, knocking the bait around, and scaring the hell out of every fish in the river. That would be the normal thing to expect, but somehow that big bait popping back and forth in the water right around the edge of the bank, especially when bass were bedded up, would infuriate the bass that were guarding their nests. The fish must have been thinking that whatever it was popping in the water, making all that racket was some type of predator trying to get their eggs or small hatchlings in the beds. The bass guarding its nest wasn't necessarily trying to get the bait to eat it, he was going to hit it to run it off. The bait had 3 sets of treble hooks on it. One at the front, one at the middle, and in another the back. If that bass hit the bait any kind way one or more of those hooks was going to snag him. Well, you can imagine what you would do with a 5-pound bass on the end of a pole that only had a 2-foot line on it. The bass immediately would jump out of the water and start shaking his head and lots of times would sling the bait off. The way to get the bass, to catch him, was not to lift it out of the water, but immediately take the pole and push the tip with the bait down deep underwater. That created additional friction so the bass, trying to get away, would be fighting the water and the pole as it moved back and forth on that short line as it tried to spit out the hook. The trick was to put the pole deep in the water but not deep enough to hit the bottom. You would then move the pole back around the boat into deeper water until at least 8 or 9 feet of the pole was in the water. Then you merely moved hand over hand from the butt right down the pole to its tip, and then lifted the fish into the boat. This is a particularly deadly kind of way to catch bass, and in many states, it was illegal because you caught fish right on the spawning beds.

Anyway, I had rods and reels I had bought for speckled trout fishing and I figured I could use them for bass fishing. This trip to Mexico interested me because there were so many bass that you could catch. I had talked to one of my friends, Paul Fredrickson, a lawyer from Baton Rouge who the been to Guerrero the year before. He reported that he and one of his friends had caught hundreds of bass on a 3-day trip. He generously let me have some of the baits that he used. I purchased some others of the same kind and talked to Charlie Abels and Charles Bender, who was Chief Deputy for Sheriff Frank Edwards of Tangipahoa Parish, about the trip. Both said they wanted to go, even though neither one of them were bass fishermen. We made our decision in early spring, Charlie just for the adventure of it, and Bender so he could buy him a cat eye ring at one of the markets that they had right across the border. I didn't know what a cat eye ring was, or the significance of it but the ring has a beautiful stone that is kind of a brownish color with a light yellowish slit in the middle, looking just like the pupil of a cat's eye.

I had talked to Bobby Moore about Mexico before we made this trip. He had been down there a couple times but never went fishing, only visiting the whorehouses at boy's town. All this was fascinating to me. I couldn't speak any Spanish, but everybody told me that a lot of people there spoke English and we could get along fine. Having never been there before, I carefully planned the trip. We decided that we would fly to Brownsville Texas, cross the border into Matamoros Mexico and drive the hundred miles or so south to Victoria and go out to the lake to fish.

Our plan was to rent a station wagon in Brownsville, load all our gear and drive down for our trip. Everybody I talked to that had been down there before, as well as the articles I read about Mexico warned not to drink the water because it could give you Montezuma's revenge, consisting of diarrhea, nausea, and terrible stomach cramps. We decided to adequately prepare ourselves for this possibility, so I purchased a booklet that was advertised as a guide to that particular part of Mexico. It was like an enlarged comic book with illustrations and a map showing the route to take. It told about every town or village that we would pass through from the Mexican border to the city of Victoria and beyond to the fishing Lake. The interesting thing about that little book was that it gave you travel tips such as, there were no policeman on patrol for speed on the highways and they are not generally modern or paved. Most were gravel even though they were main thoroughfares from one city to the next. The book warned that they were people on donkeys, and cattle, goats, pigs, and other animals that roamed at large. You had to be careful you didn't run over something. There were no red lights at all between the two cities even though we traveled through several small towns. There were very few road signs to warn you of anything ahead of you. This little travel book gave detailed instructions about the size of the village, the distance between them, and if there was food, drink, gasoline or repair shops available. There were no motels. If you had to stop to sleep, you slept in your car. We decided that the only thing we would drink while we were down there was beer, wine or whiskey that were mixed with canned drinks without ice, so we could absolutely avoid

303

water. We also prepared ourselves for any other unforeseen problems when we got to Brownsville. Before we crossed the border, we went by a drugstore which in those days also served as a supermarket of kinds, and bought some canned ham, crackers, cookies, and soft drinks. There we met a clerk who was a very nice old lady. We explained to her, we were going to Mexico on this big trip to fish for bass and had never been there before. We were the only customers in the store, and she showed us the location of whatever we wanted to buy. When I told her, I wanted to get a tube of blue ointment, she said "what," and I said, "blue ointment" and I guess she didn't quite understand what I meant. Finally, I told her in plain English "it is an ointment that kills crab lice" "oh," she exclaimed, with a disapproving look on her face. Then I said, "we don't have any crab lice but in case we get any we want to make sure we get some blue ointment, so we can kill them and not have any discomfort." She gave me a shocked look and a frown of disapproval, because she immediately figured out that the only place we could find any crab lice would probably be at boy's town. Anyway, we got the crab lice medicine, put it in our duffle, and started out. Charlie had told us about visiting Mexico with his parents when he was just a pre-teenage boy. After they crossed the border, there were a lot of little kids that would run alongside the car and try to get them to go to certain liquor stores, to buy cigarettes, whiskey, beer and other goods at discounted prices. The prices were very low. A bottle of Jack Daniels whiskey that sold for $10.00 in the states could be purchased there for about $3.00. Beer was about ten cents a can and bottles of Kahlua and tequila could be bought for less than a dollar a piece. After we crossed the border into the town of Matamoros, there were dozens of young boys, running up to our car and speaking fairly good English. They told us to come to certain stores to buy whiskey or cigarettes or beer. One boy about 13 or 14 years old spoke very good English so we got him in the car with us and he gave us directions to the store that he was trying to promote. The owners of the stores gave those kids a few pesos if they brought rich gringos to their premises to buy supplies. We bought whiskey, beer, cigarettes, and other goods and added them to coolers full of ice that we had purchased in the United States and headed south.

We had started drinking Bloody Mary's when we got on the airplane about 7 o'clock that morning in New Orleans for our flight, changed planes in Houston, and then went on down to Brownsville, where we arrived before noon. We had continued to partake of Bloody Mary's on the plane and when we got to Brownsville we started drinking beer and continued on our ride. When we got into Mexico. Bender and I told Charlie Abels that he couldn't drink anymore because he was the designated driver, although he already had a little buzz on. Bender and I continue to partake, and Charlie reluctantly agreed to the deal. He was a state trooper at the time and an excellent driver. I sat on the front seat next to Charlie with the teenage boy and Charlie Bender sitting behind us in the backseat. We told the young boy we needed to have his services to show us through the city of Matamoros till we got outside the town and show us the way to Victoria. By the time we got out of town, with the aid of a few pesos, we had convinced the kid to come with us fishing. He had never been fishing in his life, and he was all enthused about it. We didn't even think about the need to contact his parents or anything like that. We stopped somewhere, and he made a phone call to somebody to let them know he was going. A few miles out of town we came to a check station that was operated by federal police.

All along the Mexican border they had these check stations where anyone coming into the country had to stop and produce their papers and get a three-day, five day, or one month pass to stay in the country. I had read up on all of this in the tour guide and was quite familiar with what we needed to get across the border and go through the check station. I also knew from talking to Bobby Moore and Paul Fredrickson that the best way to make it very easy to get through a check station in Mexico was to have some extra pesos in your pocket. The exchange rate for pesos at that time was about 12 to a dollar. A 5-peso bill placed in the hands of the guy, giving you your permit to get through would make everything go very quickly. People who didn't know this, and didn't pay those extra pesos, sometimes were held up for hours.

After clearing the check station, we got back on the road. The road soon turned from paved to gravel and our map and guidebook advised that while there was no regular speed limits, for safety's sake we shouldn't drive more than about 45 miles an hour. The road was straight, and the land was flat and there was almost no traffic. Charlie Abel's said the hell with what the guidebook said, and we barreled down the highway at about 70 miles per hour on the gravel road. Bender and I didn't really give a damn, our beer was cold, tasted good, and we had our driver. In those days there were grain fields from the outskirts of Matamoros down towards San Fernando which at that time was a large village, about halfway between Matamoros and Victoria. About 20 miles south of the city of Matamoros all grain fields disappeared and there was nothing but mesquite trees and cactus on both sides of the road. As we got further south towards San Fernando there were some small hills in the area we were traveling through.

I later found out that this was the best habitat in the world for white wing doves. Millions of birds nested in the mesquite trees and fed in the adjacent grain fields. When we passed through very small villages, we saw people living in primitive one room houses, the floors were dirt, and the walls were made of sticks with cracks in between them. The roofs were made of straw, and there was no plumbing in them, or windows that could be closed. Many of them had no doors. The people were very poor. Each little village had donkeys and goats and chickens in the people's yards. The main industry in each village seemed to be a garage where travelers coming through could get tires fixed and buy fuel. It was not pumped from tanks like a regular filling station, but poured out of 55-gallon drums into small containers and then poured into automobiles. The guide book was right about one thing, it said to make sure you filled up the tank completely when you left out of Matamoros, because the next regular filling station would be in San Fernando, and more than 100 miles south there would be another one in Victoria. These big filling stations were run by the Mexican government.

We got to Victoria late in the afternoon and drove into the middle of the city. Our little Mexican guide talked to people on the street and got directions to a hotel. It was located right in the middle of the town, a three-story building that appeared very comfortable and it was probably 25 or 30 years old. The clerk at the hotel seem very glad to see us and spoke pretty good English. We told him that we wanted a room for the night and the next day we were going fishing. We had all our gear in the station wagon and he got a bell boy to take all our baggage and gear, put it on a dolly and wheeled it into the elevator, we got on the elevator. and started to go up to our room and I told the clerk we wanted to see some senoritas. He says no, no, no, no senoritas in room. I said we want to get some senoritas, he says no it is not allowed here police will not allow that. I said, "okay take us back downstairs." We immediately turned the elevator back down, went back to our car, loaded up all our gear and went to find another hotel to stay in. The second hotel was an elegant type hotel, with a restaurant on the premises. It had ornate tile floors, stone walls and was a very impressive place. It was very old and had very few people staying in it. We went to the clerk in that hotel and I told him we wanted to stay in his hotel, we were going fishing the next day, but we wanted to have some senoritas visit us. He said no problem, so we went to our rooms with all our gear and then went downstairs to get some food. I had read in the guidebook that one of the best foods to get in that town, or anywhere in Mexico, would be soup. They would always feed you soup with your meal, and it was usually very spicy and very good, so I told Charlie Abels and Bender that the we need to try the soup. Well, we also ordered steak and potatoes and chips and salsa and such. Our soup came out first. It was served in a small bowl and as we noted in the guidebook, it was delicious. We all noticed when we were eating the soup that there was pieces of what we thought were bone in the soup. We didn't think anything about it because we knew to make soup at home, you had to cut the meat cut off the bone. It made no difference if a piece of bone was in your soup, you just ate the meat off the bone and went on about your business. Well imagine my surprise when I got to the bottom of the bowl and there was no bone in it. What I had felt clicking against my spoon in the bottom of the bowl when I was eating soup was clam shells. When they made the soup, they opened the clams and just threw clamshells and all in the Soup pot.

The steak came out next, it was one of the toughest, stringiest steaks that I ever ate in my life. In those days, just about the only way to eat beef in Mexico was ground meat in fajitas, but the best fajitas were made with chicken rather than with any type of beef. The reason for it was that the beef cattle down there weren't on feed lots and fed grain like they are in the states. At that time cattle were ranging in the brush and had nothing but the grass to eat and that didn't make the meat tender.

307

Well that night after supper Bender and I went back to the room to take a nap because we had been drinking all day long. Charlie Abels had started drinking beer again when we got to the hotel and he and the little Mexican boy went out to see if they could find some senoritas. I was sound asleep in one bedroom, Charlie Bender was in the adjoining room, when Charlie Abels came up and knocked on the door. I got up and put my pants on, and Charlie Abels says, "I got senoritas, but they won't let them in the hotel." I put on my shoes, bounded down the stairs and went to the desk clerk, who was a different one than the one than we had talked to in the beginning. He said no senoritas, no senoritas, so I reached in my pocket and pulled out three 1-dollar bills which was equivalent to about 20 in Mexican money. When I laid them down in front of him I said "1 senorita, 2 senorita, 3 senoritas" he said "si senor." Charlie ran out and found the girls and the little the Mexican and came on up to our rooms. The party went on for a while with Charlie Abels and I in one room and Bender and his girl in another room. All of a sudden, we heard a screech and the front door of Bender's room slam, we jumped up to see what was going on and observed the young girl going out the door, leaving Bender in his room by himself. When we asked him what the hell happened, and he said when she saw how big he was she took off. We never let him live that down.

The next morning, we got up and headed to the lake. It was a beautiful, clear day when we got out to the lake about an hour and a half after daylight, which was really late when you are starting off on a fishing trip. The reason we were so late was, we didn't know how to get there to start with, and we had to get special directions to find the landing where we could rent a boat. We found two boats and two guides and got them to take us out fishing. The lake was new, having been a dammed off and filled about three or four years before. When these new lakes have been built in places like the one at Toledo Bend on the Sabine River between Texas and Louisiana, the fishing was fabulous for the first few years. The bass population exploded because they had few if any natural predators. It proved to be just as Paul Fredrickson told me, on almost every cast you either caught a bass, or one hit your bait and you missed it. We quickly caught 50 or 60 bass. All of them were fairly small, weighing about 2 pounds but the action was fast and furious. The only problem with Lake Guerrero was the wind. It is a large lake, very close to the Gulf of Mexico. Prevailing winds in that area generally run from East to West and the wind over the open gulf can be pretty strong. When the wind comes ashore there are only low hills between the lake and the gulf, and there's not any timber or anything to break the wind, which can quickly increase over the open lake and cause very dangerous waves. Paul Fredrickson had warned me about this, and I had also read about it in the articles on fishing Guerrero. When conditions for high winds are prevalent, you cannot go fishing at all. If you do fish, you can only fish in a few sheltered bays where creeks had flowed before the lake was flooded.

The first morning we were able to get out in the lake and fish around the flooded timber. We caught lots of fish then returned to the place where we had met our guides. We had the Mexicans clean our fish and the restaurant at the landing cooked them for us. But the meal was disappointing. While the fish were just caught and normally would have been very tasty, the Mexicans did not have their grease hot the way we fry fish and potatoes at home, and they didn't have corn flour or cornmeal to put on the fish to form a crust. They just took the fish filets and kind of stewed them, completely different from what we were used to.

That afternoon we decided to go back out and fish some more but we couldn't get in the lake because the wind had come up, and as luck would have it the wind advisory reported that the winds would be blowing for the next couple of days, so it really wouldn't be worth our while to come back and try to go fishing the next day. We went back to our hotel for another rendezvous that night, and then decided, since we couldn't fish, we would cut our trip and head back to Matamoros the next morning.

When we got to Matamoros we decided to stay for a day in the border town. I had read about the markets, but Charlie Bender had been in Matamoros before and he knew more about them. It was a fascinating experience for me just to go through solid blocks of many many many little booths and shops in the marketplace where you could buy anything from spices and seasoning to jewelry to wood carvings to clothing, hats, boots, and just about anything. We spent hours in that market looking at all the different goods and haggling with vendors over prices. No matter what the price was listed on the signs where the goods were sold, the prices were subject to negotiation. If they wanted 10 pesos you offered them 2 and they would immediately come down to nine, and somewhere between five and seven you could make a deal. Charlie Bender, Charlie Abels and I all bought cat eye rings, and other items for souvenirs to bring back with us. The markets were right next to large hotels that had restaurants and lounges attached that catered to the tourist trade. It was interesting to sit in a very comfortable bar with huge overstuffed leather chairs and sofas and be served cold drinks of tequila and Kahlua and margarita's or any other drinks you wanted, and observe the tourist's and Mexican's trying to buy and sell market goods to each other.

The rest of the trip was uneventful, and we came back across the border, loaded our gear on an airplane and returned to Louisiana.

After that first trip to Mexico, I was fascinated with the place and went back several times. I had talked to a lawyer from Denham Springs named Jerry Bunch who I guess, was 2 or 3 years older than me and had been down to Mexico several times hunting white wing doves. I had read about the white wing shooting down there and how there was no limit and the birds were there by the millions. The farmers welcomed hunters because by killing the doves, that meant more grain for the people, and I had never been on that type of dove hunt in my life. I had shot doves around my home in Springfield for years but that was done by 7 or 8 people meeting on a September afternoon when dove season was open. We would stand around a pasture which had goat weed that attracted the birds to feed, and sometimes had been planted with rye grass. This also attracted the birds when the seed was still on the ground, but that was considered hunting over bait which was illegal. A real good dove hunt at home might result in you killing 8 or 10 doves.

The tales that Jerry Bunch told me of killing 50 to 100 doves in an afternoon really got my attention. Jerry had the name of a very wealthy Mexican who owned several ranches in Mexico as well as banks, and other businesses, and also had business interests in the United States. The man spoke excellent English and he set up dove hunts at his ranch right outside of San Fernando, a village about 75 miles south of the border. I first went down there in the mid-seventies. Through Jerry, I had

310

got in touch with the banker, arranged for the hunt to be conducted on certain days, and negotiated the price to pay him for outfitting the trip. I got a group of about a dozen people that wanted to go with me to shoot doves.

Jerry Bunch told me that they could handle 30 or 40 hunters on this ranch. They had the accommodations, sleeping quarters, good food, and the birds would be there. They had trucks to take you to the fields, bird boys to pick up the birds and later pick and clean them and all the facilities of a fine hotel to stay there. I contacted several of my friends who included a group of lawyers, of course my friend Charlie Abels, who hunted with me all over North America during his lifetime, Calvin Fayard, Charlie's cousin, who was an attorney from Springfield and later had an office in Denham Springs, Jimmy Durbin who was an attorney in Denham Springs, who later became Mayor of Denham Springs, Otis Ratcliff, who had been a police juror from Killian, Louisiana and later was Mayor of Killian, who loved to hunt birds, mainly ducks and doves, and who was also a successful businessman operating a creosote plant. Several of Otis's friends and customers, Percy Lee, Principal of Maurepas High School, a very close friend of Otis and mine, Hubert Stilley from Albany, a couple of Otis's employees, Judge Buddy Causey and 2 or 3 others from Livingston Parish who all wanted to experience a Mexican dove hunt.

It worked out to be one of the best trips I ever made. We flew to Brownsville, Texas, and as usual, we started drinking Blood Mary's at the airport before we got on the plane in New Orleans. We got to Brownsville in the afternoon and contacted our guide who made arrangements to pick us up the next day and escort us across the border with all our guns and gear and we had absolutely no problems what so ever getting through customs and getting through the checkpoints which could be very very difficult in Mexico without the right gun permits.

We rode down to the ranch and passed through the grain fields that I'd seen a few years before when I came down fishing, but I noticed that the thorn trees and mesquite brush, that had covered the land after we left the grain fields were being cleared to make more fields. I'd never before seen a clearing operation like that. At home bulldozers used their blades to push trees and brush to build roads and clear land for

311

development and I was quite familiar with all of this, but here there were 2 of the largest bulldozers that I'd ever seen. They were side by side and in between them a huge chain connected the 2, and when I say huge, I'm talking about the size of the links on the chain. Each link was probably 10 feet long and 4 feet tall and would probably weigh several hundred pounds. The chain had 3 links which stretched about 30 feet between the two dozers. Those dozers would go side by side pulling the chain through that mesquite brush and cactus, uprooting the trees which were then pushed into piles where they could be burned. After the trees were taken out, other dozers and farm equipment would go in, till the ground and turn it into farm land where grain could be planted. This was an ongoing thing after we left the border heading south. A few years before, on our fishing trip we ran into trees about 20 or 30 miles south of the border. This time we were probably 40 miles south of the border when we ran into trees again.

When we got close to San Fernando, we were passing through the mesquite trees along the side of the road and our guide told me that this was where his ranch began. I asked him about how far and he said, "well it goes so many miles down the road and then it goes back so many miles towards the Gulf of Mexico and along the Gulf of Mexico back so many miles and comes back into a square." Shortly after we passed the edge of his land we noticed a car parked on the side of the road over near the trees, the guide said something to his driver in Spanish, which I didn't understand, and we continued to travel on down the road. He was quite excited about that car being there and I asked him about it and he said "well, that's an agitator, some communist who came in here to try to stir up the people." We soon turned off the main highway and drove back into his ranch.

The ranch house was a three-story stucco type building, very elegant, all tile floors, stucco walls inside and out with porches around it and a place where you could go to the roof and sit in the evenings or at night and look out over the whole area. The ranch had Charolais cattle in the pastures and had huge grain fields just a few hundred yards from the ranch house itself. Thorn trees and mesquite bordered the fields, with drainage ditches and canals used to irrigate the farm. When we got to the ranch we were greeted by a Chinese cook. I had told the owner when we met him that we could stop and get some canned ham and other food and he said "no, we have a gourmet cook and we will feed you."

I brought some Jack Daniels whiskey, but he had beer, wine, tequila, and just about anything else you wanted to drink there. When we got there, the owner went outside while we were unloading our gear. He sent one of his employees to go down to an out building and as we stood at the front of the ranch building, a two-and-a-half-ton army truck loaded with about 20 soldiers with rifles drove up in the yard right in front of us. The owner went out and talked to the commander of the soldiers and they drove away followed by a truck loaded with several of the owner's employees.

I asked him about what the soldiers were doing there, and he told me the story of his ranch. He said that before the revolution, which I think was in the 1920's, the ranch was owned by a wealthy man who supported the current government. The present owners father opposed the government and backed the revolutionaries. After the revolution a new government was formed, and the President of Mexico and the owner of the ranch fled to Spain. The new president of Mexico gave the ranch to the present owner's father together with 2 other ranches in other parts of Mexico. His father was also granted some banking concessions and became very very wealthy. At that time there was very little farming. On the ranch there was a couple of villages and those villagers worked for the ranch. The owner continued to employ those villagers to drive the tractors and do all the farming on the big ranch. The fields were literally miles long and miles wide. They used much heavy equipment to plant and harvest the grain.

There was a lot of unrest in the early 70's in Mexico where some people were trying to promote land reform, so the peasants could own some land, and a lot of big ranches like his were being broken up and divided among many of the people. This particular owner of the ranch had a very close relationship with the President of Mexico and when people came to his area to talk about taking his land, he got the government to send him a company of soldiers to live on his place and to protect it. About an hour or two after the soldiers had left, they drove back, and the owner went out to talk to their commanding officer. When he came back in the ranch house, I asked him what they found. He reached in his pocket and pulled out a little 32 caliber silver colored pistol and said, "my soldiers brought this pistol back" and before I could say anything else he said, "the owner will never need it again." It was obvious to me the soldiers took care of the guy with the pistol who was coming in there to stir up the local population against the ranch owner.

After a delicious gourmet meal and a few after dinner drinks we went to bed and were awakened shortly after daylight and fed a large breakfast. After that we got our guns and cases of ammunition loaded into some trucks and were taken to a large grain field bordering mesquite scrub where the doves roosted and had their nests.

We were spaced out in the middle of the field along the turn rows. Each truck had ice chests full of cold beer, soft drinks, fruit juice, snacks and sandwiches for the hunters. Each hunter had a bird boy who would sit near the hunter and as the hunters shot birds down the boy would go out, pick them up and bring them back to the hunter's location. We had a rivalry between us as to who could shoot the most birds. I was pretty good at wing shooting and was always among the top ones killing birds. Otis Ratcliff was very good at wing shooting also and he and I had a continual contest over who would kill the most, but he never played fair. When I competed with him I didn't play fair either.

One of the dozen bird boys was wearing a large white hat that morning, and with the help of a couple of pesos Otis persuaded the Mexican in charge of our hunt to make sure that boy was dropped off with me to pick up my birds. As the birds began to fly from the trees into the grain fields in large flocks I stood in front of my bird boy and began to shoot. After a few shots I realized that the birds were flaring away from me just as they got in range, and I was missing a lot of shots that I should've made. When the next flock of birds approached I watched them and the bird boy with his white sombrero and realized the birds were turning away when they saw that white hat. I took his white hat away from him and covered it with some brush. Then I began to kill more birds, but Otis had got a large head start on me and I lost the bet. As the morning progressed the truck that had brought us to the field brought us more shotgun shells, drinks and snacks. By noon we had killed hundreds of birds which were given to the farm workers families. We then went back to the camp for lunch and a siesta, after which we

314

returned to the fields to shoot more birds. After three days my hands were blistered and bleeding from the shooting and my shoulder was swollen and bruised so that I could hardly hold the gun and shoot.

It was incredible hunting, we killed literally thousands of birds. It was feast time for the local people because the birds we killed, except for the very few we ate, were given to the local population and this was some of the only meat that they had during the year. The trip had another side show. That afternoon I told the owner that we would like to get some girls brought out to the ranch. He readily agreed, and we loaded up in a couple of vehicles and headed to Matamoros to boy's town with the owner. I don't think he ever fooled around those places, but he knew who owned them, and he may have owned some of those bars himself. In the normal situations they would not let any of the girls leave the premises, they had to live there where they worked. In this case he made a deal with the owners of the bar and they put five girls in the vehicles to come back with us to the ranch, where they stayed for the couple of days that we were there. They were all given good food and whatever they wanted to drink, and all made lots of money. When we got ready to leave, they were taken to the highway to catch a bus back to Matamoros.

Otis Ratcliff was always a joker, he liked to pull tricks on people and of course I did too, and in our group, there was always someone to pull tricks on. Percy Lee was kind of known as a ladies man back home, and he picked out probably the prettiest girl of the group and made the announcement that this was going to be his Mexican wife, the fact that Percy had a wife at home didn't make any difference, but this was his Mexican wife and he didn't want anyone else fooling with her. The girls were placed in a room that was connected to the large sleeping quarters where the rest of us slept and they had four or five beds in that room. The rooms had no doors between them, they were wide open. There was no air conditioning or anything, the adobe type walls kept it cool in the daytime in the summer and warm in the winter, but the walls didn't go all the way to the ceiling. They came up about 6 and a half foot high and then there was a 2- or 3-foot space between the top of the wall and the ceiling between the sleeping areas and the hallway outside it. Percy and his Mexican wife were engaging in some activities in the bed next to that wall after the hunt. Otis walked over to the doorway of the room and

315

looked in and saw where Percy was and what he was doing, he came back and got me and we went and found a bucket which we filled with ice water and ice and came around the opposite side of the wall where Percy's bed was located. I brought a chair which I placed next to the bedroom's outside wall near Percy's bed. and Otis, who had the ice bucket, got up in the chair and dumped the bucket of ice water across the top of the opening between the two walls on top of Percy and the girl. Percy knew who did it, but he didn't see who did it and nobody would admit it or there would have been a fight. He was some kind of steamed about it, being interrupted so rudely from his activities with a bucket of ice water on him. The party after the hunt went on, the girls were happy to change partners, and everybody had a big time.

We hunted for doves down there for 2 more days before being taken back to Brownsville where we stayed in an American hotel on the American side of the border and caught our plane the next morning back to New Orleans.

When I went back to that same ranch a year or two later, things had changed somewhat. The owner had been affected by the land reform and a portion of his property had been confiscated by the government and given to some of the poor people. He was well compensated for the price of the land they took but he was very upset with the government for taking his land, and he was not at the ranch when we went down there. The other accommodations were about the same and the doves were still there. What I noticed was the big dozers had probably moved another 8 or 10 miles south clearing more land. As the brush was cleared, the dove population began to fall because there was less nesting areas for the doves. The last time I went through that country, about the year 2008 or 2009, I organized a group to go on a fishing trip to a fresh water lake south of Victoria closer to the gulf than Guerroro. That lake was much smaller than Guerroro and we didn't have the problems with wind. By the time that we made that trip, the highways were all paved, most of them 4 lane almost like interstate highways here in the states, and the trees were all gone. It was just a vast area of farms for 80 miles from Matamoros to San Fernando. San Fernando blossomed and increased in size from a town of maybe 3,000 or 4,000 to a town of, at least 50,000.

The bass fishing trip that I set up was with a tour group out of Monroe, Louisiana that chartered buses all over the United States and especially had charters for fishing in this particular lake which was a trophy bass lake. The rules were that you could take and keep one bass if it weighed more than 6 pounds. Many of those bass that were caught, would weigh 12 to 15 pounds but you could only keep one and release the others. They suggested, which really made sense, that if you caught one of those big bass it would be released also. Then a mold could be made by your taxidermist for a replica exactly the same size as the bass you caught that could be put on your wall.

There were no particular limits on small bass. You could catch and release as many as you wanted. Each day our party of about 10 or 12 fishermen, would catch and keep enough small bass to have fish fry's almost every day.

The fishing lodge was made like a motel with rooms for the fisherman, a large kitchen and dining area, where card games were held each night. The fisherman would be taken out early in the morning, brought back around noon, have a siesta and go back in the afternoon to fish again. Meals were breakfast, lunch and a large meal at night. Drinks, other than marguerites that were made in the outside bar were brought by the fishermen and the marguerites would be furnished by the owners.

The owners provided the transportation, the lodge and the guides. I set up the 3-day trip which originated in Hammond, Louisiana. The bus picked us up in Hammond around 5 o'clock in the afternoon. We purchased a meal to take with us and got on the bus. We had our drinks, started a card game as we traveled. The bus was setup in such a way that it had bunk like sleeping compartments in the center, and also large couches around the back of the bus, which also had a tv set where video's or movies could be played. We had 2 bus drivers that took turns driving while each other slept, so the bus drove nonstop until we arrived in West Texas. Around daylight in the morning, we stopped and went into an all-night diner and had a meal. We then got back on the bus and rode down to Matamoros, crossed the border there and preceded on down to the lodge.

We arrived at the lake shortly after noon, and as we arrived another group of fishermen who had fished that morning and had a lunch, were ready to get on the bus and come back to Louisiana. As the bus pulled out, we brought all of our gear into the rooms, which had just been cleaned by the staff, and got us something to eat and drink. We got in boats with our guides and went fishing, then came back to the lodge for supper. The next morning, we went fishing again, and except for meals and siestas, we fished for 2 more days. We got all of our gear out of the room about the time the next bus arrived with another group of fishermen. It ran like clockwork for the season during the early spring, from January through April. The food and accommodations were wonderful, there were lots of fish and you could catch some real trophy fish. On the way back, we stopped at the point where we had got our breakfast, on the way down. We arrived at about 6 or 7 o'clock at night, had a large meal, got back on the bus and were back in Hammond, Louisiana just about daylight the next morning. All of us had a good night's sleep on the ride home. It was just a good trip.

I went to that fishing lodge twice, but then all the dope dealing and fights between gangs to control the dope trade in Mexico made it just too dangerous to go back. There were reports of busses, such as the one we traveled on being stopped on the highway by gangs of outlaws, people being robbed and in some cases being killed. I have never gone back to Mexico since, for either the hunting or the fishing.

In between the hunting and fishing trips in Northeastern Mexico though, I did make a couple of trips to Northwestern Mexico.

In the early 1980's I organized a group of friends to go hunt doves and catch bass at Lake Obregon. Our group from Livingston and Tangipahoa Parish, flew from New Orleans to Tucson Arizona and got on a Mexican Airline airplane to fly to Obregon, which is a very large city near a manmade lake. The area around Lake Obregon was semi desert, with the lake waters providing irrigation very much like the part of Mexico where I had hunted and fished South of Matamoros. It had large grain fields, irrigation canals for the water and nesting areas for tens of thousands of doves. The lake had been stocked with lots of bass. It was more like Lake Guerrero than the small lake that we fished in for bass south of Brownsville. There were more doves to hunt than any place I've ever hunted before or since.

I made one terrible mistake when I set up that hunt. I always used a Remington shotgun with interchangeable barrels on my hunts. I used modified and improved cylinder choke barrels for hunting doves. If I was hunting turkey's, I'd use my full choke, if I was hunting duck's, I'd either use full or modified chokes with 3-inch shells.

When I first started deer hunting in North Louisiana, I would use that shotgun with buckshot and a full choke barrel to hunt deer. It was a heavy gun, but it was very accurate and if I was shooting doves with Number 9 shot with an open choke barrel, I could kill doves when they were close with incredibly accuracy. The reason for that is that the pattern was very large, and when doves are dipping and diving as they come by you, if you know anything about shooting doves and lead them properly, that large pattern would catch them while a smaller pattern of shot from a full choke barrel will often cause you to miss.

Well, before we went down to Obregon, I talked to the outfitter, and he told me that we didn't need to bring our guns, that they had shotguns that we could use. This would eliminate the problem of going through the process of bringing guns across the border and getting the gun permits, which was a lot of red tape and could delay your border crossing. He told me that the guns we would be using would be pump guns with modified or open chokes which was fine, with me.

When we flew to Obregon, some of the people on that trip were Otis Ratcliff, Lucius Patterson, the Clerk of Court for Livingston Parish, the Sheriff of Livingston Parish, Odom Graves, Judge Sam Rowe from the 21st Judicial District Court, his father-in-law Bumbo Alford, the former Legislator from St. Helena Parish, Carmen Moore, the Clerk of Court from Tangipahoa Parish, Peck Edwards, a lawyer from Ponchatoula, and my friends Charlie Abels, and Shorty Rogers from Hammond.

Odom, The Sheriff of Livingston, had a van that he used to transport prisoners, and he provided a driver to take us to the airport. We all met at my house and got in the van. Carmen Moore had made a bucket full of Bloody Mary's for everybody to have a drink on the ride. When we got to the airport, we naturally had another Bloody Mary in the lounge and probably another one on the plane. Everybody was feeling

319

pretty good by the time we hit Houston where we had to stop and get on another plane to fly to Tucson.

When we got on the airplane, I was sitting next to Lucius and I told him, "you know when we take off and the pilots going to really rev up the engines and it's going to get on up there." Lucius, who was middle aged, had never flew before and was very nervous. When the pilot revved up the engines, I could see his hands gripping the sides of the seat and his knuckles were white. His lips were clinched, and he was really worried. When the plane got up I told Lucius, "Now everything's alright except the wings are going to start flapping." He said, "How in the hell can a wing start flapping on something this big?" It was a huge plane. Well, sure enough as soon as we got up a ways I said "Look at those wings" and the wings were moving. I thought he was going to jump out of his seat. Anyway, by the time we got to Houston and took off again, Lucius was like an old hand at flying.

When we got to the airport in Houston to change planes we had to go up an elevator to get to a different concourse. The whole group of 8 or 10 of us were all together and we were talking about hunting, and fishing, and this big trip we are on, and there were a couple of very distinguished looking gentlemen in suits and ties on the elevator when we got on it. We crowded on up against these two fellows and they didn't like the idea of being crowded. One of them made some kind of a remark about country people. Otis Ratcliff was standing next to him, and I though Otis was going to hit him. Otis just crowded him a little bit further and then let out one of the stinkiest farts you ever smelled. Those two guys reached over and hit the button to stop at the next floor and both of them immediately got off the elevator. The damn thing smelled bad enough, the rest of us should have gotten off too. But we rode the rest of the way up.

We arrived in Tucson, changed planes there to a Mexican Airline and went on down to Obregon. On that leg of the trip, the pilots allowed some of us to go to the cockpit of the airplane where we could watch its progress over the Mexican desert from altitudes of a few hundred feet. It was a once in a lifetime experience which will never be duplicated in a post 9-1-11 world. Our guides met us at the airport and took us to a motel. We were picked up every morning and taken out to the places

320

where we would hunt or go fishing. Some members of the group, like Carmen Moore, would rather catch bass than shoot doves. He, Judge Sam Rowe, and a couple more went to the lake and caught some bass. Each one of them caught 7 or 8 bass that weighed more than 5 pounds, and many smaller ones. The rest of us went out to the fields to shoot doves. It was hot when we got out there to start with, probably 80 degrees, and it got hotter as the morning progressed, I was sitting right next to an irrigation canal that wasn't deep enough to swim in, with only a couple feet of water going through it. It was lined with concrete, so it wasn't just something you could easily wade across. The doves were flying from mesquite and thorn trees on one side of the canal to open fields right out in front of me. When they started flying they never stopped. It was just a steady flock, after flock, after flock. At home, lots of times when you're dove hunting you see 1 or 2 birds come by you or sometimes 3 or 4. Here every flock would have anywhere from 7 or 8 to 15 or 20 birds in it, and just one right after another.

We were each given 8 boxes of shotgun shells, 25 to a box. The Mexicans put them in a big 5-gallon bucket and gave me another bucket to sit on. I had on a T shirt because it was so hot, and that little 12-gauge pump gun which was very light. I had shot pump guns before, but not very often. I didn't realize that when you shoot a pump gun or any gun that is light, the recoil can be much worse than a heavy gun. With the doves steadily coming over me, the gun barrel got so hot, I had to put it down. I couldn't touch it, or it would burn my hand. The flocks of doves would come within 15 or 20 yards from me and I would shoot 3 shots every time they passed. Lots of times I was knocking down 2 or 3 birds with 1 shot. I discovered after I had shot almost all my 200 shells, that my finger was bleeding. I was shooting and ejecting shells from the pump gun so fast that I actually cut my finger and didn't realize it. I also burnt my hands from the damn barrel getting so hot.

While I shot those 200 shells, my bird boy had been picking up birds all along and it still took him probably 15 or 20 minutes to pick up the rest of my birds when I stopped shooting. I know I knocked down at least 4 or 5 that sailed across the canal where he could not retrieve them. As he picked up the birds, he put them in the 5-gallon shell bucket. When he got through, I dumped the bucket and counted those birds. I

321

had 185 birds out of 200 shots. I've never shot that well before or since. The main reason I shot that well was that the birds were very low and very close, and the gun had an open choke.

Well, the next day I went fishing and I didn't catch many bass, but the ones I caught were 5 pounds or better, and it was a good trip. The following day I went out to shoot again in the same area. What I had not noticed, but realized it very quickly, my shoulder was not just black and blue from the pounding of that recoil. It was black and blue and yellow and green, terribly bruised. It hurt me just to hold the gun against my shoulder. I shot only a few birds that morning. The only way I could shoot would be to raise the gun and hold it very tight against my shoulder and squeeze off, then the recoil would not slam my sore shoulder. My shoulder stayed sore for 4 or 5 days after I came back, but we got the doves and we had the trip.

Odom Graves was Sheriff of Livingston Parish for many years but did not hunt. He never hunted deer and he never hunted rabbits and he never hunted birds, he didn't hunt period. He liked to meet with people and liked to go on trips and all that but he just didn't hunt. Bumbo Alford was probably in his 70's when we made this trip and he didn't hunt either, I don't think Odom even went fishing but he and Bumbo went down to the town everyday while the rest of us were off hunting or fishing. They saw the sights, visited around, talked, and passed the time. After the hunts, we would all get together and have our meals and drinks. It was really just a wonderful trip. Odom told me that one day during the time that he and Bumbo were walking around the town sightseeing, they were sitting on a bench watching people walk by. Odom said he thought that none of them could speak English since they all were speaking Spanish. He and Bumbo were speaking English so he just didn't figure that these people that were walking by could understand what he was saying. A real distinguished looking middle-aged woman walking down the street approached them. She was very well dressed and as she walked by him, Odom, who always wanted to joke and wise crack, punched Bumbo in the side, and said "watch this." When the woman got to them Odom said, "Would you like to come visit me at my motel?" thinking that she didn't understand what he said. She turned around and looked down her nose at him and said, "absolutely not." Odom, for once in his life was speechless, and he could not come back with any other comment.

The last day in Obregon, I violated one of my cardinal rules, you don't drink the water when you are in Mexico. I wasn't thinking about ice and apparently the ameba that causes the dysentery and all the problems is alive even after the water is frozen and it can get you. I saw a snowball stand where a little Mexican guy was selling snowballs. One of the flavors of the snowballs he was selling was mango. I'd never eaten mango syrup that was put on a snowball, and I decided that I would try one. It tasted so good I ate the whole snowball, then another one. The next day when we got back to Tucson, it hit me. I was sick at my stomach and had dysentery for 2 days after I got home.

Lake Obregon Mexico – Percy Lee, Bennie Sandifer, Carmon Moore, Judge Sam Rowe and Hobart Pardue

Obregon Mexico - Dove Hunt and Bass Fishing, Bumbo Alford, Lucius Patterson, Odom Graves, Hobart Pardue, Otis Ratcliff, Carmon Moore and Peck Edwards

There Were No Limits – Lake Guerrero
Charlie Abels, Charles Bender
and Hobart Pardue

Chapter 11. 1974 Yukon Hunt

In 1973, I decided to go on a hunting trip up in Canada to try to kill a grizzly bear. Charlie Abels, Hubert Stilley, and I had talked about this off and on for two or three years. On the only hunt I had made in the mountains prior to that, Charlie Abels, Calvin Fayard, Bobby Moore, Jerry Addison, and I went out to Idaho on an elk hunt. It was a crazy type of thing, I didn't know anything about outfitters, or hunting elk, or climbing mountains. In fact, none of us did.

I talked to a travel agent in Hammond, who's main experience was sending people to places like New York City, Los Angeles, or somewhere in the Bahamas, and told him I wanted to go elk hunting. He had never gone elk hunting himself but, he told me that he had a deal. And a deal it was. We flew out to Idaho got on some horses and rode to the top of a mountain where a tent camp had been set up. Every day the guides would ride us around and look for game through binoculars and a spotting scope. After 3 days we had seen only 7 elk on another mountain miles away. We never did anything about killing any. The closest we got to an animal was to see tracks of a cougar in the fresh snow, and a porcupine eating bark in a small spruce tree. Finally, Bobby, Jerry, and I left Calvin and Charlie on the mountain with most of the guides. We told them we'd met them in Las Vegas, left the mountain, and came back to civilization.

As luck would have it, the day after we left, Charlie killed a bull elk and they met us later in Vegas where we were waiting for them. I had never been to Las Vegas before. After a couple of very boring days watching other people lose their money, we came on back home.

I had read about the bear hunts in Alaska and Northern Canada, and finally was making enough money to afford a trip. I always wanted to go somewhere and kill a grizzly bear, that was my big deal, and Hubert felt the same way. Charlie, of course, was always ready for anything and wanted to come for the ride. Hubert had actually killed a black bear in Idaho two or three years before, but the grizzly was the challenge we wanted. It was a dangerous thing, because often when you hunt a grizzly, the bear, who has no fear of humans, could be hunting you.

327

When I talked to Calvin about it he said he'd like to go, but he had recently been appointed Assistant District Attorney and couldn't get away. Calvin knew a young lawyer named Jim Thompson, who practiced in Baton Rouge, who had recently returned from a hunt up in Canada who could tell us all about the type of hunt we wanted to make. We decided to talk to him before we spend all that money and booked the hunt. We got in touch with Jim, and he invited us over to his home where he showed us pictures of the hunt he made the year before. He had hunted with a fellow named Vick Hotte, up in the Yukon Providence of Canada. It was a mixed bag hunt where you hunted bear, Dall sheep, caribou, and moose. He told us, he had three or four problems with the hunt, but they weren't the fault of the guides, the outfitter, the accommodations, nor was there any lack of game. The pictures revealed all that, and he had killed a grizzly bear, a moose, a caribou, and a snow-white Dall sheep.

The problems he reported were, number one: the only kind of whiskey you could buy up in that part of Canada was rye whiskey or Scotch whiskey. He didn't like either one and neither did I. Number two: every day you are going to get on a horse and ride all day, either going to the place where you'll be setting up your hunting camp, or after you get there, you ride several miles each morning, climb the mountain, and then you have to ride back to camp in the afternoon. This will cause you to be saddle sore like you've never been in your life, because you ain't no cowboy. Number three: you are going to have to sleep on the ground. I had done that before, but not like he described. He said that the ground was rocky, and you were going to be lying down on the side of a mountain. There weren't any level spots. Fourth: when you go up there, the outfitter is going to pack your food in wooden boxes that are strapped on pack horses. Some of it is prepared by the cook at the base camp who makes cakes and pies for desserts. When you are in a spike camp, and sleeping in a tent on the ground, and you and your guides are hunting. You don't have time for cooking much except for canned goods and meat you bring with you or what you kill. So, if you have a sweet tooth like me, there ain't gonna be no desserts, not after the first day or two. Fifth: you are 3 or 4 thousand miles from home, and several hundred miles from the nearest town which might be nothing but a crossroads. When it gets dark, the only music you're gonna hear are the wolves howling somewhere in the distance. The silence of those big woods, mountains and tundra in the wilderness is profound. There is no entertainment when the sun goes down.

Well, we were all for it. We were young and in our prime time of life. I got in touch with Vick Hotte and sent him several thousand dollars for a down payment on our hunts. We were to pay the balance when we got there. He told me to either bring cash or travelers checks. He didn't want a check from somebody in South Louisiana, who was going back to South Louisiana after he got through hunting and might stop payment on a check. We had no problem with that and made the necessary arrangements for traveler's checks.

Our hunt was scheduled to begin the next year in mid-September. In July, before we left we started to get ourselves in shape. I always had a sweet tooth and loved good desserts, jambalaya, red beans and rice, hot biscuits or pancakes with cane syrup for breakfast and all the good food in South Louisiana, as a consequence, in 1974, I was 35 years old, starting to get a beer belly and all three of us were woefully over weight, and out of shape. We were all very active, but not ready for climbing mountains. I studied on that and remembered my experience in climbing those mountains in Idaho. I knew I had to get my legs in shape. I started by running laps around my house and arranged for Charlie and Hubert to bring some horses over to my pasture. I already had a horse or two that my son rode, and I told them I was going to get on that damn horse every day and ride to get my ass in shape. They agreed to join me, but Hubert actually came and rode a horse two different days in the two weeks before we left. Charlie came and rode horses probably five or six times in that two weeks. I made damn sure I rode every day at least for a couple of hours, just to get used to it again. Hell, I had grown up on horses and it wasn't no big thing about that, but when you haven't rode a horse for several years, you are going to get saddle sore if you get on one and ride 10 or 12 hours every day for 2 or 3 days just to get where you want to go hunting.

The other thing I figured out, was to do something about the lack of Jack Daniels whiskey. I did a little research and found there was very little Jack Daniels whiskey up in Whitehorse, Canada, and it cost about twice as much as it did here in Louisiana. The problem seemed insurmountable, so we decided to do the next best thing. I had drank Scotch before with my daddy when I was a teenager, but never really cared a lot about it. The Scotch I drank was always with water, so I told my friends what we needed to do was acquire a taste for Scotch. For about a month before we left, that's all we drank, no margaritas, no vodka and orange juice, no whisky and 7 up or whisky and coke. Just Scotch and water. After a few days we got used to it and enjoyed it very much.

Jim Thompson had told us was that there was water everywhere in those mountains. Springs bubbled up and there were muskeg bogs with clear water every few hundred yards. Creeks ran down the mountains everywhere. The outfitter had recommended that everybody bring a canteen which we could fill with water from any creek we crossed, and not dismount our horse if you got thirsty.

In those days we used 8 track cassette tapes which were the latest way to listen to music. My car had a tape player in the dash and I'd listen to Hank Williams, Loretta Lynn, Charley Pride, Willie Nelson, George Jones, and all the country singers when I traveled on my way back and forth to court or anywhere else in my car. As a consequence, I had bought a number of 8 track tapes. In fact, I had an 8 track tape carrier, like a little suitcase with all my favorite songs in it. I checked the latest technology on tape players and bought one that ran on flashlight batteries as well as plugged in to the wall, if you happened to be at a motel somewhere. I figured the four batteries in the player would run it for about three or four hours. We figured we would be out there hunting for fourteen days, so we did the math and bought about 60 flashlight batteries to run our tape player. Hubert insisted on bringing along a Jimmy Rogers tape and Charlie joined us for the ride.

When we got to the Yukon, our outfitter met us in Whitehorse and took us to a motel where we spent the night. Early the next morning, he picked us up and told us we were going to get some last-minute supplies. I told him I had to get some things also. We went to the only supermarket/hardware store in Whitehorse, which was a small town, except it had an airport and some motels. It also had several bars and some restaurants. We went to the supermarket/hardware store where I bought about 40- or 50-dollars' worth of candy. I figured I'd get enough candy so everyone of us would have at least two or three candy bars every day that we would be out there on that mountain. That would take care of any sweet tooth after we finished supper. I walked around that store and I found a 20-gallon plastic water cooler which I purchased. Vick Hotte told me that I must be losing my mind, because there was water everywhere and I didn't need it, but I bought it anyway. Then I told him to take us to the liquor store. Well he understood that. We bought a couple of cases of beer, a couple bottles of Schnapps and I bought 25 fifths of Something Special brand Scotch. It was about the same quality as Chivas Regal which we had drank back in Louisiana where we trained ourselves to get used to the taste of Scotch. Since they didn't have any Chivas we got Something Special. We took that Scotch back to the hotel where we were staying and proceeded to fill up our water cooler with 20 gallons of Scotch whiskey. Instead of bringing one canteen per person for water, we had brought two canteens per person, one for whiskey and one for water.

The next morning, we got ready to fly out from the lake at Whitehorse to the base camp which was on Lake Aishihik. It was a 565 square mile lake with an average depth of 98 feet with 95 miles of shore line at an elevation of 2999 feet. It was more than a hundred miles from Whitehorse. The small float plane only held four people, and with Vick Hotte and the pilot, there was only room for two, so Charlie and Hubert went out there first. I figured that they were going to go up there and try to corrupt the guides to get the best for themselves, but there wasn't anything I could do about it. I drew the short straw and had to sit back and wait until the plane came back for me. A couple hours later the plane came back, we loaded it up with the rest of the gear and I flew out to our base camp. I had never traveled through the mountains at that time of the year before. It was September, and the scenery was spectacular. It was so different from home in Louisiana, the quaking aspens were just turning gold among the evergreens. As we flew across the mountains and the valleys, I could see the colors of the trees below and the snow-white tops of the mountains. It was one of the most impressive sights I'd ever seen.

As I talk about this, I am looking though a set of photographs which include pictures of Hubert, Charlie and I on our horses in Louisiana, pictures of Whitehorse Canada, the city where we stayed, and pictures of Hubert and I emptying those bottles of Scotch whiskey into our water cooler. I also have pictures of them boarding the airplane and pictures of the red and white float plane taking off to fly out to the place where we would hunt. The pictures I'm looking at now also show the terrain from the air, which is dotted with lakes and streams with all the colorful foliage of the changing leaves on the trees.

We arrived at the base camp, which was a permanent tent camp on the edge of the lake. Charlie and Hubert had interviewed all the native Indian guides and got the two oldest ones, Billy Sam and Joe Horseman. They had been recommended by Vick Hotte as being the best for their personal guides. That left the other guide, a much younger guy named Billy Hank Joe to be my guide. When I arrived, it was midafternoon, and Hubert had decided he was going to take a nap, Charlie and I were raring to go, so one of Vick's friends, who was visiting the camp, volunteered to take Charlie and I fishing on the lake that afternoon. The weather had changed from bright and sunny to overcast and kind of foggy. We were furnished rods, and reels, and bait, so we put on our rain gear and got in the boat with the guide to try to catch some lake trout. I had caught lots of fish in South Louisiana, largemouth bass, red fish and speckled trout mainly, and had read about lake trout, although I had never seen any. We started fishing and the fish were really biting. I caught one lake trout that weighed more than twenty-five pounds, the guide said it was one of the biggest that had been caught in the lake that season, although I think some really got up to forty pounds or more. I decided that I would get the guide to freeze that fish, so I could get it mounted. The fish was beautiful, colored like a rainbow with reddish yellow fins and dark spots on its brown body. It was much brighter than the regular rainbow trout that I've later caught in some of the western rivers. We had fish for supper that night and my big trophy was wrapped and put in Vick Hotte's big deep freeze.

The next morning was clear and cool, with the temperature in the thirties, when we geared up, got all the horses loaded, and started out on our trek. We had clothing to cover any type of weather that we might run into, as well as rain gear and warm gloves. The way we did it was to wear layers, Tee shirt and shorts then a pair of long handles, then a flannel shirt, and blue jeans, then a goose down sleeveless vest and a heavy down coat with a hood on top with a wool cap if it was cold enough. On warm days, I wore a white 10X beaver Stetson hat. That first morning we just tied our heavy coats behind the saddle with our rain gear and mounted our horses.

I had turkey hunted a lot in Louisiana and Mississippi before making this trip, and in those days, there was no camouflage gear. I mainly wore khaki shirts and pants to try to blend in with the leaves. When I was hunting turkey's, I wore a tee shirt or a long handle undershirt. All of them were white, and if I forgot to button the collar of my khaki shirt tight around my neck, and the turkey I was calling saw the little triangular white spot below my neck, the hunt was over. The slightest movement of that white spot would cause the turkey to spook and you could not get a shot on him. Consequently, I had my wife, Loretta, dye my long handle and tee shirts brown. And that was the long handles that I was wearing on this trip.

We rode for about four hours along the lake shore and stopped and ate some sandwiches. Our only drinks were water, some of the best tasting, clearest water in the world that you could dip out of the lake or dip out of the streams. We rode another three or four hours, to the end of the lake, about ten or twelve miles, more or less, all on flat land, and made camp. The next morning, we pulled out again and started into the mountains and rode for another fifteen to twenty miles. On this part of the trip, the scenery was outstanding, every time we went around a corner of a ridge, we'd always stop, get off the horses and take the binoculars to glass the hillsides to see if we saw any game. We didn't see any sheep for the first three days, but we saw a few caribou in the distant mountains and of course no bear or moose. Towards the late afternoons after we had been riding for several hours, we would break out our canteens and start sipping on our Scotch whiskey, chasing it with water from the other canteen so we didn't have to dismount during the last couple of hours of the ride. We knew we wouldn't be hunting any later than that, so it wasn't any adverse deal about drinking whiskey while we were hunting. We had a few more drinks after we made camp and ate supper at night while we listened to the music of the battery powered tape player.

After three days of riding and stopping and glassing different areas where we thought we might see sheep, we saw some late that afternoon, miles away on another mountain. It had warmed up considerably during that day's ride and by noon it was probably 70 degrees in the bright sunlight. I was sweating pretty heavily, and we started drinking our whiskey a little bit earlier. This caused us all to sweat a little bit more, and of course, we had not had a bath for three days. As we rode along, I started shedding clothes. I first got rid of the vest, then the flannel shirt, then the long handle shirt and got down to my tee shirt. After a couple more drinks of Scotch and water, we all decided that we were going to take a bath when we got to the next place we stopped. The Indians said there was a creek running by the place where our camp was going to be, and we could clean up there.

Those Indians didn't talk very much, they would answer you if you talked to them, but they didn't offer any conversation, except for a grunt or a yes or a no or something like that. It didn't bother us any, cause we had our own conversations, as we rode down through a valley towards the creek where we were going to camp. It was probably 3:30 in the afternoon, with the sun bearing down on us when we rode around a corner of the trail. All of a sudden, the mountain on the west side of us blocked the sun. It was still bright, and you could see very good, but the temperature dropped something like twenty degrees in the shade. Well, we had drank enough whiskey so it didn't bother us and we decided that we were going to take a bath anyway. When we got to the camp site, the Indians started to put the tents up and unload all the gear and we got ready to wash up. I found a cup and mixed myself a drink of whiskey and water and undressed. In the meantime, Charlie and Hubert had already gotten out of their clothes. When I got over to the bank, they were in the creek with only their head and shoulders out of the dark fast flowing water. Well, I wasn't feeling any pain from my Scotch whiskey, so I decided I would go jump in. I made a running start and luckily, I did not dive. I just ran out and jumped up in the air to make a cannonball flop into the water. When I hit the water, I realized that those idiots had been on their knees and the water was only about two-foot-deep rather than the four or five foot deep that I expected. I lacerated my ass when I hit the water and struck a sharp rock a few inches below the surface. Well a little bit more whiskey and a little bit of ointment on my ass took care of that problem. As we started to get out of the creek I heard our movie camera going and saw the Indians were taking pictures of us in that ice water. We filmed that whole trip, but I regret to say that after more than 40 years that film deteriorated and I lost it, but, I still have some pictures that I am reviewing as I tell this story.

Before we left home we bought some air mattresses made of plastic to protect us from the rocky soil and the rough ground we would be sleeping on. On the day before we got to the place where we took the bath, I woke up flat on rocky ground. The air mattress had been punctured by a sharp rock and was ruined. I think Charlie and Hubert's air mattresses might have lasted them one more day than mine did. The Indians told us not to worry, they would take care of it and they fixed our beds. They did this in an ingenious way. They cut the tips of evergreen limbs from trees in the area, got huge bundles of them and laid them on the floor of the tent probably two-foot-thick and covered them up with a tarpaulin. It was like laying down on a mattress and was very comfortable. For the rest of the trip, that's the way we slept at night.

The next morning, we started to go toward the place we saw the sheep feeding on the other mountain, but to get to them we had to cross a river. We rode to a place where the river had forked off into two or three channels. The water was running very swift and the water was coal black. What I didn't realize until I got to that point was the reason the water looked black. Actually, the sand on the river bed was black, the water was clear, but you couldn't see the bottom because of the dark colored sand. My Indian guide elected to try to make a crossing on a moose trail that led into the water. The river at this point was probably 30 yards wide but we didn't know if it was two feet deep or ten feet deep. The Indian rode out into the water about ten yards and the water was coming up to his stirrups, so he turned around and came back. He said he did not think we could cross there. I told him that I had come 4,000 miles to try to kill a sheep and I wasn't by God gonna let that little bit of water stop me. I got off my horse and took all my clothes off, including my boots. I wrapped all my clothes and boots in a tarpaulin,

335

gave all my clothes and stuff to my guide and I started across on my horse. I had fully expected that when we got deep enough for the horse to have to swim, I was going to slide off the side of the saddle and hold onto the horses' tail and let him pull me on across that creek. Imagine my surprise when I discovered that the water never got to the saddle. It got just about to the horses' belly and I raised my feet up and didn't even get my feet wet. Once I got across the creek, the rest followed me. I told them that they were a bunch of pansy asses who were scared of a little water, and they made comments about me wanting to act like Lady Godiva.

I got dressed again and we started up the mountain where we had seen several sheep in the distance the evening before. When we got on top those sheep had disappeared. All the time we were riding, we were always in single file with one horse following the other. We never had to run any of the horses for any reason. A slow trot was about as fast as they were used to going.

We got to the top of the mountain, which was not really that high, maybe 4,000 feet. It had no vegetation on top except some lichens and grass and a sheep trail along the crest which was relatively flat. There was one guide out in front of us, and as he came around a curve, he quickly stopped, jumped off his horse and made us get off. We eased up to the crest of the hill where we could see and there was a beautiful white ram laying on a ledge across a little valley about 400 yards ahead of us. We glassed all around and determined that there was only one ram there, so the guides told us that we would draw straws to see who would hunt that ram and the other two guides and hunters would go down the mountain and make a spike camp. They told us we would sleep out under the stars without any cover, and then go back to base camp the next day. I got lucky and drew the short straw and Charlie and Hubert and their two guides started down the mountain.

My guide and I got back on our horses and started riding towards the sheep. When we came around the corner, he had disappeared. The guide started beating his horse and got him into a gallop and my horse was following the same way, as we came down in the little valley across from the ledge that the sheep had been on. We started up the ledge, got off the horses, and ran up that slope, but the guide, instead of having me going straight, indicated to me that we had to go off to our left around the side of the mountain. This was fine with me because the sheep could not see us, and we weren't climbing any higher, but were running top speed around the side of that mountain.

I had got myself in pretty good shape by the time this happened, we had been hunting for four or five days at 4000 feet above sea level. I still couldn't breathe as good as I wanted to but was doing better the more I got used to it. When we rounded the corner, I looked out over an open area where the mountain had a big curve in it. The sheep had already gone around that curve and was on the other side of a cliff about 400 yards away. He was standing there with his front feet up on a rock looking at us. I was puffing and blowing, and could hardly breathe, and the Indian said shoot him. I said, "he's too damn far, I can't kill him that far," There was a little breeze blowing from behind us and it was going straight to the sheep, who could smell us. The Indian said, "Shoot him anyway, cause he's gonna run off and we can't get any closer." I didn't have time to sit down, take a rest or anything just had to stand there. I ran the scope up to 9 power, put the sheep in the scope and raised the scope up above the sheep's back to where I couldn't even see the sheep and squeezed off a shot. It was the luckiest shot I ever made in my life. That sheep dropped immediately right in his tracks. The Indian told me to go back and get the horses and he ran around the edge of the mountain to get to the sheep. I came back, got the horses, led them over to where the sheep lay and was astounded to see the sheep had only one horn, the other one was broken off. The Indian told me don't worry, we will kill you another one.

I had no earthly idea that Dall sheep's horns sometimes would be broken like that. The horn wasn't broomed back from fighting or hitting rocks or anything. It was actually a deformation which on one side was probably a foot or so long and the other side was a perfect 39 and ½ inch horn. We immediately started to butcher the sheep and the Indian said we were going to get another so don't worry about the cape and the horns and such. We are just going to take the meat, so he gutted the sheep and cut the hind quarters and front quarters off and the ribs and tied them to my saddle and to his saddle. I told him that I was going to bring those horns back, so I got his hatchet and hacked the horns off.

337

Later after I got through with that hunt, I realized I had ruined a very very very rare trophy because since that time, I have seen only two or three sheep mounted with one horn like the one I killed. Anyway, when I tied the sheep horns to my saddle horn, I didn't tie them very well and we started down the mountain. The sun had gone down but there was a full moon and it was as bright as day. We started off that mountain top where it was absolutely treeless, no brush, no nothing and as we started down, what began as just a spring became a trickle and then a creek that got bigger as we went down. As we got lower the willow scrub got higher and by the time we got halfway down the mountain, the willows were over our head. My guide was ahead of me and I was following on foot, both leading the horses when he asked me where was my gun. I said that it was in my saddle scabbard on my saddle, He said "You better get it" I said "Why" he said "We got fresh meat, they got grizzly bear here. Have your gun and put a round in the rifle and if the grizzly comes, you're going to have to kill him". That woke me up, I came down that mountain with the rifle at port arms.

Shortly after that, we saw the campfire that Charlie and Hubert and the guides had made for us and when we got to that fire those guys took that meat and immediately put some seasoning on it and started cooking the ribs. It was not anything like Tony Chachere's like we have in South Louisiana, mainly it was salt and pepper, but I can say that was about the best tasting meat I had ever eaten in my life up to that time. Of course, after you have been on a mountain for five or six days and have had nothing, but sandwiches made of sliced caribou, and no fresh meat at all, just canned stuff, fresh meat of any kind is going to be good.

We drank a bunch of Scotch whiskey at that camp. The guides had made the fire eight or nine feet long, and as the fire burned down, we all laid down around the fire. Problem was, as the fire burned down the ones of us who were farthest from the fire got colder and colder and the guides who were ones close to the fire stayed warm. I had all my clothes on and my down jacket with a hood on it. The hood had wolverine fur around the face of it which would not freeze, and I had zipped it up to where only my nose and part of my face was sticking out. I was sleeping pretty good and wasn't cold or anything, using my saddle as a pillow and a saddle blanket as a mattress to lay on top of the rocks.

338

Hubert Stilley woke up very cold and he saw that the fire had burned down so he put a bunch of wood on the fire and built it up. Very quickly the Indians that had been laying close to the fire got too hot and had to move back, and Hubert got close where he could stay warm until the fire died down again. I had my head on the saddle and my coat zipped up over my face and Hubert didn't realize that I was still in the coat. He thought that I had laid that coat on that saddle for a pillow and he was going to use my coat to cover up with, so when he reached over to pull my coat from under my head, I was still in it and I woke up. The only thing that went through my mind was that we had fresh meat and a grizzly bear had got a hold of me. I let out a whoop that scared Hubert half to death as well as the guides and Charlie. Then I realized what was really going on and there wasn't any bear in the camp.

The next morning, I looked for my horns, but they had fallen somewhere between the top of the mountain and our camp. I told the guide that we ought to go back and find them, but the guide said no, by that time now a wolf or grizzly bear or some kind of varmint would have already destroyed them. He said it wasn't worth fooling with cause we could get another sheep later which we did, but I've always regretted not having that sheep. As I sit and talk about it I'm looking at the pictures of us filling up canteens from the whiskey jug, Hubert Stilley having a drink of Scotch whiskey, me and Charlie Abels sitting on the wooden packs that you put the gear in, pictures of the lake, pictures of an old cabin that's almost falling down, pictures of us crossing that river, pictures showing my beard starting to grow, and right here is the picture I was looking for, the picture of that ram that I killed with that incredible shot.

After I killed that big one horn ram, we filled our bellies full of fresh grilled sheep meat. After sleeping on the ground that night, we got up early the next morning and came on back down the mountain, crossed the river where I had led the group the day before and got to the regular camp where we had left all our gear. The guides decided that we needed to pull up and go to another territory which was about two days ride away to try to find more sheep because we hadn't seen any other big rams in the area we were hunting.

The next day as we started out, Hubert started complaining about having indigestion and being sick. As we rode for several hours he continued to complain his legs hurt, his stomach hurt, and he was ready to go home. By the time it got dark we had traveled probably ten or twelve miles from the camp where we were staying the night before and set up camp, we got some sleep and then got up to move the next day. That morning Hubert insisted that he had to go home so his guide left the group and had to ride about fifty miles to an outpost where they could get a message to send a helicopter in to get Hubert. Charlie and I proceeded in another direction to the new sheep grounds where we would be hunting with my guide Bill Hank Joe. Billy Sam, Charlie's guide stayed at the camp with Hubert, who later told us that by the time the helicopter got to him he was feeling better and really would have rather stayed and hunted, but since he sent for the helicopter, he had to pay for it. It cost him several hundred dollars, so he decided to just go on home. Charlie and I had a long discussion over the next few days about Hubert and what really was the matter with him. We speculated on him having everything from crab lice to sore knees to just plain being out of shape as the reasons for him going home early. Hubert claimed it was from eating fresh meat, but it didn't bother anybody else except Hubert. If anything, he filled that big belly up maybe a little more than the rest of us. So, we continued our journey looking for a sheep for Charlie and another one for me.

As we rode along I had my binoculars around my neck and a movie camera in one of the saddle bags and of course one canteen full of Scotch whiskey and water in the other. Our rifles were in their cases on the saddles. We had the horses we were riding and two or three pack horses carrying our gear followed. We crossed over a range of low mountains and came out along a ridge which bordered a small creek where water was flowing down below us on our left side. A couple hundred yards down the ridge in front of us another small creek flowing from our right joined the bigger valley and the first creek. As we came around the corner, the guide was first, Charlie was second and I was third when suddenly the guide stopped and jumped off his horse and told Charlie to jump down and get ready to shoot. I looked, and two huge caribou were coming down the valley from the right-hand side toward the junction of the two creeks. There was no timber in this area, just willow brush and open land, and of course jagged rocks and tundra and muskeg. Those caribou were the biggest I had seen up to that time, with huge antlers, so Charlie jumped off the horse and got his rifle out of the scabbard. I grabbed the movie camera with my right hand and was going to take pictures while I was sitting on the horse with the reins across the saddle horn and my binoculars in my left hand. Just then Charlie shot, and when that rifle went off all the horses went crazy. My horse started bucking up to where Charlie and the Indian stood. Their horses were spooking away when Charlie shot again, and that time my horse really went crazy. I had a heck of a rodeo, I couldn't get my hands on the reins because both were full, binoculars in one hand and the camera in the other. Finally, I had to let the binoculars go and they went to the ground, and luckily weren't damaged. When I got my hand on the reins, it was all I could do to stay on the bucking horse and hang on to the movie camera. My horse bucked me all the way from the side of the ridge, right down the edge of a cliff, to the flat ground where the two creeks came together. Charlie and the guide had already ran down where the huge caribou that Charlie had shot was laying. I managed to stay on my horse and get control of him, although how I did it I don't know. If the horse had jumped two or three feet to the left, instead of staying on the little trail as he bucked me down that hill, we could have gone over that cliff and that would have been the end of me and the horse. When I got down to where the caribou was, the other horses were nowhere to be seen. They had all spooked off and ran away.

The Indian took my horse, left me and Charlie with the caribou and went to catch the other horses that had disappeared. We sat there for a while and low and behold here came another huge caribou down that same valley coming right towards me and Charlie. I didn't even think about really looking and trying to grade how big that caribou was, he was huge, and he had big horns, but he had no brow points, no shovels on his horns right above his nose. Those caribou horns are formed in the same way as brow tines on white tail or mule deer are, they come out right above the animal's skull. On deer they are pointed, but on mature caribou bulls the tines will often flatten out like the palm of your hand, kind of like a moose's antler and those protrusions are called shovels.

341

The caribou use them during the winter when the snow is deep to move it away from the leaves, grasses and vegetation that they eat so they can survive. Most bulls have one shovel, but rarely we saw one with two. The one I shot didn't have any shovels which made him far less of a trophy than Charlie's which had two, double shovels.

During the entire time we had been sheep hunting we had seen only a few caribou at a long distance and hadn't really looked at them close. Well, I killed mine and he killed his, and we both were proud of them, but when the Indian got back he told me not to worry about it, that we would find me another one later. We proceeded to set up camp a few hundred yards away from where we killed the animals and the Indian began to cape out Charlie's caribou while Charlie and I took the horns off them. After we got the hide off I looked at those back straps on the one that Charlie had killed and proceeded to start taking out a back strap to cut up for steaks. The Indian asked me what I was doing, and I told him this was going to be my supper. The Indian told me that they would not be any good. I told him he didn't know what he was talking about and just went ahead and did it anyway. I butchered out the back strap and we carried it, along with the horns and cape of Charlie's caribou several hundred yards away to where we set up camp.

I prepared three steaks to grill on the fire, but the Indian told me not to cook his. I seasoned the beautiful looking meat and placed it on our grill as the Indian opened a can of corned beef. As I watched the steaks sizzle on the grill my mouth was watering, but when I placed it on my tin plate and sliced into it the aroma almost made me sick. It smelled exactly like a piece of pork from a boar hog I had tried to eat many years before. I did try to take one bite, but the meat was so tough I couldn't chew it. After the Indian finished laughing at me he cooked some of our sheep meat for Charlie and I for supper and explained that the caribou were in full rut and were not fit to eat at that time of the year.

The next day we rode down the valley and did some glassing of the mountains on each side of the river and spotted a very good ram up top on the right-hand side. We also saw some sheep several miles away in another valley on the left but could not tell if they were rams or not due to the distance. We then came back to our camp and Charlie and I went to a ridge where we could overlook the pile of bones and meat from the caribou we killed. We sat there till dark hoping a grizzly bear would come along where we could safely shoot him. We knew we had to be at least a hundred and fifty yards away from that meat because if the grizzly smells you and comes after you, he can cover that ground very, very, quickly, and it could develop into a very, very, dangerous situation.

We didn't see any grizzly, all we saw was a coyote that spooked as soon as we went up to the gut pile. By the next morning, the Indian, Billy Sam, who had stayed with Hubert until the helicopter came for him, had followed our trail to our camp. The next day we decided that my guide, Billy Hank Joe, and I would go down the valley and Charlie and Billy Sam would ride up the right-hand side to where the big sheep were on top of the mountain. Billy Hank and I rode on down the valley to the next valley intersecting the one we were in to try to find me a sheep to hunt. Before we split up, Billy Sam and Billy Hank Joe, the two guides, had an argument on how Charlie was going to kill the sheep that we had seen the day before. The problem was, we were in the valley and the sheep was on top of the mountain. Billy Sam pulled rank on Bill Hank Joe and told him that he had been hunting there longer than he had and he knew how to hunt them, so Charlie and Billy Sam left their horses at the bottom of the valley and started climbing up that mountain. They went up one of the steepest areas that we climbed during that whole trip. Billy Hank and I rode on down the valley and when we got about a half a mile to a mile further down, we came around a curve where we could look back and watch Charlie and Billy Sam climbing the mountain with our binoculars. They looked like two monkeys going up the mountain Billy Sam, who was a lot older, probably in his fifties or early sixties was just running up and down that mountain back and forth between Charlie and the top in an effort to encourage him to go higher. Charlie, who was probably about 30 years old, was almost crawling, trying to get up the steep part of that mountain. Billy Hank was just laughing at what a damn fool Billy Sam was for taking Charlie up that way. He pointed out to me that all they had to do was ride their horses in another direction around the mountain, pick their way up on an area that the horses could climb, and ride the horses almost to the very top. Once they got on top, they could then hunt back down to the sheep. They didn't do it that way, they climbed all the way on foot, and they went up,

343

up, up. Charley later told me that when they got up to the top, he was so worn out and out of breath, that he could hardly see, and they got right on top of the sheep before they saw them.

The sheep were behind a ridge when they were climbing and when they got to the top they were within a hundred yards of them. The sheep saw them before Charlie could even sit down or make a stand to try to shoot, and the sheep started running away, Charlie shot at a large ram, but missed. When he shot, the sheep went over to the next mountain. We were about a mile away when we heard the shot, but of course could not see what was going on. A little later we could see the sheep as white dots climbing up on the next mountain and we knew Charlie had missed.

Billy Hank and I continued riding on down the valley, stopping, and glassing until we spied three more rams on the left-hand side that looked promising. We got closer, probably five or six hundred yards away, and with my big spotting scope looked them over good and saw one that was really outstanding. We then got on the horses and came right on back to camp where we met Charlie crying in his Scotch and water in his disappointment over missing the big ram. I ragged his ass, much to the delight of my guide, Billy Hank Joe, for letting his guide, Billy Sam, who I called a "company man" make him climb that mountain when he could have rode his horse all the way to the top. The next morning, we decided that Charlie, Billy Hank, and I would leave very early and go after the sheep we had found, which was my turn to hunt. Billy Sam stayed and broke camp, packed and loaded the horses and came to meet us at the convergence of the two creeks where we had found the sheep I was going to hunt. Charlie, Billy Hank and I rode down the valley a ways, but unlike Charlie and Billy Sam, we rode our horses up the opposite mountain from where Charlie had hunted. We took our time and after several hours, of mainly riding, but sometimes getting off and leading the horses, we got close to the top where we could creep up and try to spot our quarry. Billy Hank soon spied them down below us bedded down in a small valley. We left out horses and crawled up to the top, then decided we needed to get a little bit closer, so I could get a shot at the big ram down below me. We crawled about forty yards down the ridge, then moved to the top and looked down where the sheep had been, but they had already started to move coming straight up the valley

344

towards us. I quickly got a round in my rifle, sat down and waited for the ram to move out where I could get a clear shot at him. I was very excited. Since I had killed that first ram with one shot more than 400 yards away, I felt this was going to be duck soup because the shot was only going to be 125 or 130 yards. Imagine my surprise when the ram appeared about 70 yards away. It startled me so much I squeezed off too fast. The sheep started to run but the only place he could go was uphill where I could clearly see him, running broadside and quartering away from me. I quickly pumped another round in my bolt action rifle and shot three more times. Charlie, who was standing next to me counted my shots, so he could kill the ram when I ran out of bullets. On my last shot, the sheep collapsed. I didn't realize It at the time, but later I found that I had hit that sheep all four times. Once through his horn, once near his hoof and two shots in the body, one being fatal. As I look at the picture today, I remember the feeling I had of finally getting that tremendous trophy.

My old white Stetson that I had bought brand new for this trip was grey with smoke and ashes from the campfires. I had added an eagle feather to the hat that I had found near an eagle's nest on top of one of the mountains. The eagles feather was more than three feet long and it was a distinct trophy itself. It was legal to get eagle feathers in Canada, but you could not import them to the United States and are illegal to possess in the United States now even though the bird that the feather came from never had any human being close to it or harmed it in any way. After I killed my ram, Charlie and Billy Sam decided that they would hunt on up the valley the next day in the direction the ram Charlie had shot at the day before had gone. Billy Hank and I would break camp, take part of the horses, the sheep and the meat and go back to the base camp which was about a day's ride away. While the guides were caping out my ram, cleaning its skull, and butchering the meat, and in general, getting ready to pull out the next day, I had my long spotting scope set up and would occasionally look around the mountains where we were located. I could see herds of caribou moving around on a mountain approximately four or five miles away. It was the same mountain that Charlie had been on when he shot at and missed his sheep. I looked very closely and saw there were two huge bulls in that herd of maybe forty or

345

fifty caribou. They were in a full rut and those big herd bulls were circling those cows and fighting off the younger bulls that were around them. My guide said that they were big enough for me to go shoot one. We were not going to worry about that small one I killed earlier so Charlie and I went up the mountain on our horses with Billy Hank to try to get close to the caribou. Billy Sam, in the meantime, went in another direction to find Charlie another sheep. We rode for three or four miles over treeless mountains that were not sharp snow-covered peaks but were more rounded and covered with grass and muskeg, which were boggy places where springs of water just came out of the ground on top of the mountains. We got within several hundred yards of the caribou which were just milling around in circles with the herd bulls kind of herding the calves and cows together. Then we left our horses and began a stalk to get closer. When we got within two hundred yards of the caribou, we saw the two big bulls were almost identical in size and we had a long discussion on which one I should try to kill. Charlie had already killed a big one and wasn't going to shoot anything, so it was all up to me. Finally, I got a clear shot at one of those bulls. I couldn't shoot many times because the animals were moving among each other and I didn't want to shoot at the bull and maybe kill a calf or cow. With that 7mm Remington magnum I shot, it would be easy for a bullet to go through one animal and hit another and maybe even kill two at one shot. At least that's what I thought until I realized a few minutes later that they weren't so easy to kill. I shot that bull and he immediately stumbled but he didn't fall, and I shot him again and he still didn't fall. I shot that bull six times, hitting him almost every shot, and he would not fall. The other caribou stampeded away, and the wounded bull followed them at a much slower speed. The Indian ran back and got a horse for me and I jumped on the horse and the Indian and I rode after the wounded caribou. We finally got close enough and I got off the horse again and made a shot which knocked him down. I figured that this was finally it, but when I got within fifteen yards of that caribou, it still wasn't dead. It looked straight at me, and that was the first time I ever saw any animal or person look at me with such an intense hate, that I knew if the animal could get to me, he would kill me right there. The animal was broken down, at least one leg was broken, probably two, and he could not get all the way up, but he tried. I immediately put the coup de gras on him and put him out of his misery. That was one of the biggest caribou I had ever seen before or since and I finally had my last trophy for that Yukon hunt.

We cut off the horns and caped out the animal and Charlie and I cut the caribou's testicles off, to mail back to Charlie's cousin and my friend, Calvin Fayard at the District Attorney's Office in Livingston, Louisiana.

The next morning, Charlie and his Indian went one-way hunting sheep, Billy Hank and I went back down to the base camp by the lake where we had started from, and I got the first good hot bath, that I had in 17 days. The food was wonderful, Vick Hotte's wife was at that camp and she cooked pies and cakes and all kind of wonderful food on a wood stove. The camp was warm, and I still had enough whiskey to last me another couple of days. Charlie had actually taken two canteens full of whiskey with him on his way and I took what was left in the jug that was left there with me. When we split up I told Charlie I would wait for him until he got to the camp, but the plane was supposed to come in and get us in a couple of days, so he had about two days to get back to me. He and his guide killed a good ram the next day and were about one day behind us when we got to camp. Of course, didn't have any idea where he was when we came into camp.

For two days, Billy and I fished on the lake and didn't catch anything. We also rode up and down the lake looking for moose and didn't see any. As we were riding down the lake to fish, we saw a lot of smoke from a fire on the lake shore, where an old Indian was smoking fish. He had caught some of those big lake trout and had them drying over a rack where he built a fire with a lot of smoke to preserve the fish. We came on back to camp and I was ready to get away from there, I'd been out in those boon docks for 17 or 18 days and that was enough. When Billy Hank and I were fishing Vic Hotte's wife washed my clothes that I had worn for two weeks in a pot of water. When we returned to camp, my long handle underwear were laid out on my cot with my gear. Ms. Hotte told me that she had never seen such dirty underwear before and she washed them twice before she discovered that I had my wife dye them to use to hunt turkeys with.

347

I had my trophies and was ready to go home, so Vick got on the radio and called a plane to come and get me. The next day about noon, the plane came in and the pilot told us that he could only stay for about thirty minutes because the weather was building up in the mountains. We were about to be socked in, and we couldn't fly out if we didn't go on and get going. I wanted to wait for Charlie, but I didn't know where he was, so we took on off, and as we flew away from that camp, Charlie and his Indian topped the ridge and saw us flying away. Of course, I didn't know that at the time, and Charlie missed that ride by just a short time.

Billy Hank Joe and I got back down to Whitehorse where I mailed the caribou testicles to Calvin at the courthouse without telling him what they were. He later told me that when they arrived they were ripe, and he had a prisoner open the package which made him sick to his stomach. I waited for Charlie another day and a half and finally decided the hell with it. I made an airplane reservation to fly on back to Vancouver and down to Los Angeles, then make connections back to New Orleans. Charlie got to Whitehorse a day or two after I did and flew down to Edmonton Alberta, then down through Minnesota, to Chicago and back to New Orleans. When I crossed the border into the United States at Customs in Vancouver, I had my guns and all my gear and that eagle feather. Before I got to customs, I put the eagle feather in my hat. I just left there and wore the hat across the border, and nobody asked me any questions. After I got home, I replaced it with a wild turkey feather in that hat, which I wear on a very few special occasions.

Yukon Hunt - Getting Our Butts in Shape for 10 Mile Daily Rides

Necessary Supplies, Scotch Whiskey

Daily Canteen Fill-Up

Yukon Hunt

Yukon Hunt Starting Out

Yukon Hunt – Hobart Pardue's Dall Sheep

Yukon Hunt Charlie Abels Dall Sheep

Yukon Hunt – Hobart Pardue's Caribou

Alberta, Canada

Alberta, Canada

Alberta, Canada, Canadian Rockies

Chapter 12. Johnson Plantation Hunting Club - The Beginning

Bill Johnson, who had organized the hunting club I joined with Judge Brent Dufreche and Otis Ratcliff, near Woodville Mississippi, had taught school at Ponchatoula High School during the time I attended. In 1958 Bill Dodd began his campaign for the Louisiana superintendent of education. Bill Johnson took a leave of absence from his job and worked full-time as Dodd's personal assistant and campaign manager. When Dodd was elected he appointed Bill Assistant Secretary of Education.

Bill supervised programs that furnished food for the lunchrooms over the state and made contracts for storage of food that was received from the United States Department of Agriculture to provide the lunches. He also managed Dodd's re-election campaign.

During this time Bill Johnson got to be a member of a large hunting club in North Louisiana called Winter Quarters. The name was derived from General Ulysses S. Grant's army camp on the Mississippi River prior to the siege of Vicksburg Mississippi during the Civil War. Most of the members, with the exception of Bill, were millionaires who used the property to entertain guests. Bill quickly learned from them how to operate a large-scale hunting club, but soon tried to make changes which resulted in the other members buying him out. He then started looking for property that he could develop as a hunting club and make a lot of money at it. He had little money himself but was a master promoter who knew many people who loved to hunt and had no place that produced trophy white tailed deer like Southwest Mississippi.

When he heard about the failed soybean operation on what was then called Smithland Plantation, he met an agent for the owner on a Saturday morning to inspect the property. He then made a deal to purchase property on credit for $250,000 and gave him a bad check for $2500 as a down payment. He knew he had until Monday to make a deposit to cover the check, and met with his banker Milton Cox on Sunday morning and convinced him to honor the check. He then had 30 days to raise $25,000 cash to close the deal. To do so, he found members to invest in his new project.

360

The property consisted of a mixture of wooded hills, bottomland hardwood and soybean fields along the Buffalo River a few miles from where it flowed into Lake Mary. Part of the property had been channelized and levied when it was cleared for planting soybeans. In the early 1970s, shortly after the farming operation had been expanded by the previous owners, a series of floods occurred on the Mississippi and Buffalo rivers resulting in levee breaks. The Buffalo cut new channels through part of the soybean fields which reverted to small willow trees and tall grass. This was ideal habitat for deer to bed in next to the remaining soybean fields. When the beans were planted in the spring the rate of predation next to the willows would approach 80% of young plants. Faced with this loss the company owners of the property decided to sell. Some of the first members he solicited were Judge Brent Dufreche, Dr. Merlin Allen and Jackie Vaughan from Ponchatoula, Otis Ratcliff who operated a creosote plant in Natalbany, Louisiana, Johnny Johnson who operated an offshore supply company from Morgan City, Louisiana, as well as several of his former students who worked in refineries or other small businesses.

Each member was required to put up about $2500 and sign a promissory note for the purchase of the property which totaled more than $250,000. Annual dues were assessed for construction of deer stands, purchase of seed and fertilize for food plots, and payments on the mortgage. Rules were made by Bill that set limits on the number of deer each member could take and penalties for violations. Bill made sure that he and his sons retained 51% ownership of the club property and his son George would have the farming rights to raise soybeans for sale.

The wealthier members had no problem with this arrangement, since they understood the soybean farm attracted the deer that would make the entire project successful. Other members, who were struggling to make the payments were jealous of Johnson's son making money on the soybean operation and having the opportunity to kill more than a dozen deer each year with their 51% quota.

After the first year of operation Bill caught one of the member's son hunting deer at night before the season and immediately expelled him from the club. Others discovered after they had killed two bucks and filled their quota in the first days of the season they could not hunt again that year.

I heard about this growing controversy from Milton Cox, a close personal friend of mine as well as a close friend of Bill Johnson. Milton, who was a banker for both of us, also told me about the huge deer the members of Bills club were taking.

I had been hunting In Concordia parish for several years when the state purchased our hunting territory to create Three Rivers Wildlife Management Area and was looking for new place to hunt. About this time a new sporting goods store opened in Ponchatoula and a huge black bear standing mount was placed on display by the owner's nephew who had taken the animal on a hunt in Canada. The bear was so big the taxidermist had to use a grizzly frame to mount it on. I talked to the young man who killed the bear and he told me it would have been number one in the world for that species but had been disqualified because he shot it in the head fracturing its skull. He had been on his first bear hunt and his guide had failed to tell him that a trophy bear must not be shot in the head, because the bears skull must be measured to determine its score to place it in the Boone and Crockett records.

The young man had been a construction worker who loved to hunt and had paid Bill Johnson about $3,500 to become a member of the club. Bill did not explain to him that most of his money went for dues to operate the club and pay the indebtedness. For him to obtain a permanent interest in the club he would have to continue to make payments until the property was paid for. He came to see me about selling his interest in the club since he was planning to go to Alaska to work on the pipeline to transport oil from the North slope fields to the port of Valdez on the Pacific Ocean.

I paid him several thousand dollars for his interest, but when he refused to sign legal title to me we wound up in a lawsuit where I obtained a judgment against him. He figured he would never have to return my money since he had moved to Alaska and had no property in Louisiana. I then had the sheriff seize the bear to satisfy the judgment.

I had no desire to display the bear in the trophy room I planned to build, since I did not kill it, but intended to donate it to Southeastern University as a nature exhibit. The owners of the sporting goods store

362

and the young man who had killed the bear opposed the seizure. The case was tried in the local court and Judge Burrell Carter ruled in my favor. The other side appealed the decision to the Louisiana First Circuit Court of Appeal which reversed Judge Carter.

During the several years the case was tied up in court Sheriff Frank Edwards had custody of the mounted bear. He placed it in his private office just inside and to the right of the entrance door facing the Sheriff's desk. When people would come in to see Frank they would not notice the bear standing on his hind legs with his front legs spread behind them. After conversing with the Sheriff, they would turn to leave and suddenly see the huge bear towering above them. Frank later told me that some were so scared they almost wet their pants.

Bill had been very active in politics both in state and local elections and strongly supported Ed Layrisson in his run for Sheriff. That fall, after the election, Bill invited Ed and his boys to come deer hunting at our club. Ed Layrisson and John Dahmer, Ed's new Chief Deputy, considered him their favorite teacher when they attended Ponchatoula High School. Each member had his own personal camp and could invite several guests to hunt each day.

The second morning Sheriff Ed Layrisson shot the largest buck he had ever killed, but after the hunt he and the other hunters could not find it in the high grass and willow scrubs next to a soybean field.

When they returned to my camp Ed wanted me to go help him find his deer. I invited him and his boys to join my hunters and I for breakfast and then we would go look for the deer. After a leisurely meal I took about eight or 10 men in my truck and went to the location where Ed had last seen the deer.

Ed told me that he had walked all around the area where the deer disappeared and found no blood. Ed was the only hunter who brought his gun with him when we searched for the deer.

I hung a hunters orange vest in a Willow tree at the location Ed had pointed out and got all the men to line up about 30 feet apart then started all of them walking parallel to each other for 200 steps in one direction. When we found nothing I got all of them in the lineup again and walked 200 steps back in the direction we had came from near the vest. We then lined up again in the opposite direction from the vest where we ha/

363

started to walk another 200 steps. After about 40 steps a small three point buck jumped up from the grass and Ed shot and killed it.

I got all over Ed's ass about him shooting a small buck in the first place and then killing it because it was a violation of our rules to shoot any buck smaller than an eight point. Ed insisted that the first buck he shot was a eight or ten point and not the small buck that he killed. I crawled his ass some more for shooting the little deer at all.

We then lined up again and after walking about another hundred yards we found the big buck that he had first shot. We brought both deer back to my camp were we hung in the skinning rack and I later butchered them. Ed took the large buck to a taxidermist shop and had it mounted. I took the small buck to another taxidermist and had it mounted.

I had my taxidermist place a plaque on the mount which read "This is not an eight point buck, this is not a doe. This is a mistake made by Sheriff Ed Layrisson on his first deer hunt at this club." I hung that little three point deer near the doorway of my camp so everyone who came inside could see it. When my guests arrived I pointed at it and told them not to make the same kind of mistake the High Sheriff made.

At Bill's camp the guests were entertained by his sons and most of the food was cooked by the guests and the boys. His camp was sparsely furnished and had previously been used by the company that owned and farmed the land as lodging for the farm workers.

I made a schedule for the whole hunting season for my guests to make two-day hunts. My camp on the other hand was much more comfortable, and while I welcomed assistance from my guests, if they volunteered, I provided food, drinks, hunting equipment as needed, and my personal attendance. Each night before the hunt, the other members and I would have a private meeting to draw the stands the hunters would use the next day. We often would exchange stands between ourselves to accommodate special guests. The next morning the guests were taken by truck to each stand well before daylight and were picked up, together with any deer they killed after the hunt to return to camp.

I built a skinning rack off my back porch which overlooked a food plot in a creek bottom where deer could be observed from the camp. The skinning rack was large enough to hang several deer and was used by most of the members of the club, who with their guests, would watch me clean the deer. If a hunter killed his first deer in my camp, he was introduced into an initiation in which he was bloodied with the blood from the deer. At other camps this often consisted of an old hunter putting some blood on his hands and marking the first-time hunters face with lines of blood across his forehead and cheeks.

My initiation, especially with young boys and girls as well as with pompous politicians and business associates, was much more elaborate. Even in freezing weather I would require the hunter to take off his jacket and shirt while I extracted a length of intestine from the gut tub, cut the deer's stomach open, and empty the contents in a bucket with the blood from the deer. I would then turn the stomach of the animal inside out to make a cap and place it on the hunter's head and hang intestines around his neck. This was all done with many comments from me as well as the other hunters who had crowded around the skinning rack to observe the initiation. The smell of the blood and offal sometimes would cause the initiate to vomit when I poured the bucket over his or her head while the spectators cheered and took pictures. As soon as it was over I would return the skullcap and necktie to the gut bucket and using the ice-cold water from the nozzle of the hose wash the blood and offal from the hunter's face and hair and send him or her inside the camp to take a hot shower. This process became widely known as a "Woodville Blooding."

After the animals were cleaned, I would have someone take the gut bucket to the dump, and I would hose down the concrete floor of the skinning rack where the deer would hang overnight or longer if the weather was cold. If the weather was warm the deer were hung in a cooler on my back porch.

Supper usually consisted of huge amounts of fried deer back strap, potatoes, turtle or deer sauce picante, catfish courtbouillon, with rice, freshly picked mustard greens and turnips from the food plot, cornbread and sugar cane syrup, bread pudding, cakes and ice cream. I did most of the cooking myself during the afternoon while the guests were hunting. I was assisted by my wife, Loretta on weekends and holidays when she and my teenage son, DeVan, were at the camp.

I woke up my hunters about 5 AM each morning so they would be on the stand at least 30 minutes before daylight. Each stand was made of plywood with a roof and walls and shooting windows at least 12 feet off the ground. Each member had a truck to transport hunters, and whichever member was going to actually hunt would drop off all the rest of the hunters and take the last stand. After the hunt he would pick up the hunters and return them to the various camps. On mornings that I did not hunt, when I had deer hanging on the scanning rack, I would go out back after the hunters left and begin butchering the deer that had been hanging from previous hunts. I had all the tools that I needed and had learned how to butcher from my uncle Grafton Coats when I was a boy. I had a large wooden table with a ceramic top I used to cut the meat. I would quickly quarter the animals and using various meat hooks hang the quarters separately, so I could debone and cut them into portions for my guests.

I used my meat saw to cut up the ribs and the bones, and my knives to cut chops from the loins and back straps. I had a separate table that I used to wrap the meat in freezer paper from rolls on a dispenser. After I finished cutting and wrapping I labeled each package and placed them in the deep freeze for each guest to be able to bring home some venison.

When I was butchering the deer, I made certain cuts of meat that I used to play tricks on some of my friends. The best and tenderest cut of meat is the inner loin, next is the back strap, and then the hindquarters which are cut into boneless roasts. The least desirable is the neck, which is full of small bones with very tough meat that takes many hours to cook. Second least desirable are the ribs which usually contain heavy chunks of fat which is inedible. The neck roast, when wrapped in freezer paper is indistinguishable from a boneless hind quarter roast. The ribs, when properly wrapped and frozen are indistinguishable from packages of back strap or tenderloins.

I had a chest type deep-freeze on the porch next to my skinning rack where I would place the packages of meat, which I had labeled so my guests could bring frozen packages home with them. In one corner of my deep freeze I placed a container in which I would put neck roasts, labeled as hindquarters, and ribs, labeled as back straps.

If I had a particularly pompous or otherwise disagreeable guest, or sometimes a very good friend who played tricks on me, I would pack their ice chest with meat to take home with them. As I would do so, I would comment to them that the fine hindquarter roast and back straps should be cooked a certain way. Often, they would tell me they were going to have a special dinner for their friends with the deer meat I provided them, never knowing at the time that I had placed the mislabeled neck roast and ribs in their coolers.

In the early dawn and late afternoon, I would watch deer moving and feeding in the food plot below the camp, where I never allowed any hunting. For guests who brought non-hunting wives, or children. It was a special treat sit on the back porch in warmer weather or inside the warm kitchen and dining room when it was cold and watch the deer.

Johnny McGary and Judge Kenneth Fogg
At Johnson Plantation

Joey Fontenot, DeVan Pardue
and Hobart Pardue at Johnson Plantation

Chaney and Linda Carol Phillips
Buffalo River Catfish

Virgil Sandifer Best Deer Killed on Johnson
Plantation 1973 – 1995

Hubert Stilley's Best Buck

Tangipahoa Parish Sheriff Ed Layrisson

Hobart Pardue and Deputy Norman Rivers with
His 8 Point and Sheriff Layrisson's 3 Point

Judge Fred Blanche and Hobart Pardue at Johnson Plantation

Chapter 13. 1975 - 1985 - Paradise Lost Hunting and Fishing Johnson Plantation

I learned a lot about deer hunting, duck hunting, and fishing during the dozen years I belonged to the hunting club at Leslie Mississippi on the Buffalo River.

My first year there, the deer stands, and food plots had only been in place two seasons. The rules of the club allowed you to hunt with a bow and arrow anywhere on the club during the October and early November archery season, before the gun season opened around Thanksgiving. After that hunters were required to hunt from established deer stands that were located around the soybean fields, in the hills, or in the woods across Buffalo River. The deer would bed down in the woods during the day and come into the soybean fields and food plots to feed at night. They had many trails crossing the shallow river and loess hills from their bedding area to the fields.

Before the season opened that year, I scouted those trails through willow trees next to the river and built a couple of primitive stands out of a few boards nailed to trees overlooking the deer trails along the riverbank. The normal width of the river was from 20 to 40 yards, but in the back of the property a levee broke a couple of years before we purchased it, and the river cut new channels 10 to 20 feet wide. These narrow channels created many small islands covered with willow brush that were perfect habitat for deer to bed in.

I hunted with my bow in the early mornings and late afternoons from my stand in the trees and saw many deer including one very large eight-point buck but could never get a shot at him. When the gun season opened after Thanksgiving, each member of the club would draw lots to determine which stands we would hunt the next day. A few days after the season opened I drew number 15, a box stand located at the edge of the soybean field and the willows. That afternoon I walked across the field, but instead of climbing in the box stand I followed a deer trail through the willows to my primitive stand and climbed up in the tree with my rifle.

376

After about an hour I started to see deer moving through the woods around me preparing to enter the field to feed. From my perch I could see the deer trail where it crossed a small channel of the river to a small island then another channel to the bank where I was located. About 30 minutes before dark I saw two doe deer coming towards me on the trail followed by the huge buck I had seen during the archery season but had been too far away for me to shoot. This time I had my rifle and when he reached the island about 60 yards away I shot him. He jumped straight up then disappeared in the brush on the island.

I remained in my tree for 15 minutes as it began to get dark. Time crawled, but I remembered how I had lost the first good buck I had killed at Grand River a couple of years before. At that time, I immediately began searching for the deer which was mortally wounded, but it kept moving when it heard me coming and we didn't find it until two days later.

This time I didn't disturb the deer which traveled less than 100 yards from where it was shot and was dead when I crossed the waist deep river channel to the island and found it. I left the deer, which weighed over 200 pounds, where it fell and returned back to the box stand where I met some of the other hunters to return to the camp. I was very excited about killing that big deer, but I did not tell any of the hunters from the other camps how big he was. When they asked me, I told them I'd shot a spike which had ran a long distance through the woods, and I would get some of my guests from my camp to return with me and retrieve it.

I knew that I had violated the rules by hunting outside of the established box stand and the deer was more than 250 yards from it. The deer was too large to drag to a place where it could be loaded in my truck. When we got to my camp I told Bobby Moore about killing the big deer and that I was going to get Otis Ratcliff, another club member who owned a six-wheel hustler vehicle to take us back to the river where the deer lay.

When we reached stand number 15 Otis stopped the vehicle. I got a large light and told him to follow me through the woods to the deer. I walked along the deer trail in front of the hustler until we reached the riverbank. Otis who thought I had shot a spike told me that this was too much trouble for one spike deer and we ought to go back to the camp.

Bobby and I told him to stay in the vehicle and we would cross the river to the island and retrieve the deer. After we got to the deer the two of us could hardly move it. After about 15 minutes we managed to get it into the water and floated it down the river to the place Otis was waiting for us in the hustler.

The Hustler had two seats with only enough room for four people. There was no way to fit the deer in the vehicle and have room for the three of us to ride. We managed to tie the deer's horns to the rear of the vehicle and pulled it about a mile back to the camp. By the time we got to the camp, much of the deer's hair had rubbed off its shoulder from the gravel on the road. When we hung the deer at the skinning rack I decided to field dress it rather than remove its hide. It turned very cold that night and the next day we loaded the deer on top of my Thunderbird automobile and I brought it home.

The next morning, which was Monday, I got in my car with the frozen deer on its roof and drove to the courthouses at Amite and Livingston to show the judges and other officials my trophy. I then went by the local newspaper offices and had them take pictures which they published. It was many years before I killed other deer that large on Smithland.

We had a total of 2400 acres that we were purchasing on the Buffalo River for our hunting club. It took me several years to explore it, and every year along the river it changed. Not only did the Buffalo River flood several times each year from local rainfall, the Mississippi River during its annual spring rise pushed several feet of back water over the bean fields and willow covered former bean fields between the wooded ridges bordering the Buffalo's banks.

When the Mississippi River's floodwaters receded, Foster Lake, potholes, beaver ponds, and deep holes in the Buffalo River were restocked with fish and turtles. As the muddy water cleared in the spring and summer bass and pan fish as well as catfish could be caught on rod and reel. Beaver built new dams creating new potholes which attracted ducks in the fall.

In early September each year we prepared food plots near our deer stands by disking ground and planting wheat and rye grass for the deer to feed on in the winter. Often, we would see the signs of the deer hooking small trees to remove velvet off their antlers in early October. We looked for the larger trees with their bark skinned up, which would indicate a large buck was using the area.

The deer hunting season with firearms each year usually opened the weekend before Thanksgiving then closed the first Monday after Thanksgiving for about 10 days until it opened again from mid-December until mid-January. During the time deer hunting was closed I hunted ducks along the Buffalo River that flowed through our property. I didn't have a retriever the first couple of years I hunted there nor, did I have a blind. I walked along the banks of new cut channels the water had made where the levy had broken and jumped Mallard ducks feeding in the shallow water. I lost many ducks that I knocked down in the swiftly flowing current of the shallow river, so I purchased a Chesapeake Bay Retriever pup which I trained.

One morning as I explored a section of the river not far from the place I had killed the big eight point buck the previous year, I found some large willow trees that had been scraped by a deer. I checked further and determined the deer was bedding down on an island covered with tall grass and a few medium-sized willow trees. The next day I returned with a small ax to build a primitive stand in a willow tree.

It was midmorning when I waded across the shallow channel to the island and followed a deer trail to a small willow tree that had many limbs on it. The ground was marshy and covered with tall grass that reached my waist. I placed my rifle on the ground and began climbing the tree to cut some of the thick limbs that obscured my view. As I began hacking on the tree limbs a huge 10-point buck jumped from his bed about 40 feet away from me and bounded away through the tall grass.

I knew there was no way I could kill the deer that day, therefore I resumed removing limbs from the tree, so I could easily shoot my rifle. My perch was about 10 feet from the ground, and my feet were placed on limbs on opposite sides of the trunk as I faced the tree. I next took a short piece of rope, ran it through my belt loops behind my back and tied the rope in front of me around the tree. This allowed me to stand on the tree limbs at my feet and have my hands free to shoot on either side of the tree trunk while being secured by the rope.

379

I waited several days before I returned to my stand. It was a freezing cold day with intermittent rain and sleet. I had on heavy clothing and camouflage rain gear which kept me warm and dry. I saw no deer and after several hours I decided to climb down and return to the camp. When I started to untie my rope, I realized the rain had turned to ice and my rope had frozen to the tree. Luckily, I had a sharp knife with me, otherwise I might have spent a miserable night in that tree.

A few afternoons later I got a ride with Otis Ratcliff and another hunter in his hustler to go hunting near the river. I had them drop me off about a quarter-mile from the stand I had built in the tree. The weather had turned somewhat warmer and the sun was shining. I arrived at my stand about 3:30 PM and began climbing the tree with my rifle slung on my right shoulder.

When I reached the height where I placed my feet on the limbs, I was holding the tree trunk in my left hand. I started to hang the rifle by its strap on the stub of a limb with my right hand when the buck jumped up and ran quartering to my left through an opening in the trees. The grass was so tall that all I could see was the deer's head and antlers, and I brought the rifle down to rest it on my left forearm and squeezed off a shot. The deer immediately disappeared as I chambered another round in my rifle.

I was so excited I was actually trembling, trying to see the fallen deer about 70 or 80 feet away in the high grass. There was no movement and my imagination went wild. I knew I shouldn't get down from the tree and approach the deer for at least 20 to 30 minutes to give it time to bleed down, but I kept thinking it was probably crawling off and escaping. Time seemed to stand still, I kept looking at my watch as the minutes slowly crept by, and finally after 15 minutes I could take it no more and climbed down from my tree.

I was wearing hip boots and when I stepped on the marshy ground I sunk several inches in the mud. The grass around me reached my neck as I walked toward the place I had last seen the deer. I thought I was moving directly to the place the deer had fallen but suddenly it jumped up and ran away to my left. All I could see as it ran were its antlers above the tall grass, and I emptied my rifle shooting above the grass toward the staggering, mortally wounded deer, which again disappeared.

As I reloaded my rifle I realized that I had been shooting at the deer's antlers instead of its body which was hidden by the marsh grass. I cursed myself for being a fool and approaching the wounded animal too soon, but I immediately moved to the spot I thought I had last seen the deer, a few yards away. When I got there, I saw no sign of blood or any indication the deer had passed that way, and I began to panic.

I told myself to calm down and get smart. I took my hunters orange vest off and hung it on a willow bush where I stood and begin to count 50 steps as I walked in a straight line in the direction I thought the deer had taken. When I found nothing, I moved 20 steps to my right and walked back to the vest. I then moved 20 more steps to my right and began to walk out another 50 yards. At that point I found a heavy blood trail going in a completely different direction from where I thought the deer had run. I had never seen so much blood on the light-colored marsh grass before, and a few yards later I found the deer.

On closer examination I realized my first shot had struck the deer through the lungs, and during the first 15 minutes after I shot its lungs had started to fill with blood. When he jumped up as I approached, blood spurted out the bullet holes onto the white grass on each side of his body, every time his feet hit the ground.

The deer was a huge 10 point buck whose antlers curved around the front of his head almost touching each other at the tips of the longest tines. I took a shortcut across the marsh to the dirt road where Otis and the other hunters stands were located. When they met me at dark Otis and I took the hustler and retrieved the deer, which weighed over 200 pounds.

A couple of years later I met my friend Alonzo Sturgeon who had recently been elected District Attorney for Adams and Wilkinson counties. He had previously been to my camp to visit but had never hunted with me. He told me that he had a friend named Frank Carlton, who was District Attorney in Greenwood Mississippi who loved to hunt. I told him to invite his friend to come to my camp during the deer season. We picked a date for a two-day hunt, and Frank and his young assistant, Boo Hollowell, arrived in mid-December. My only other guest at the time was my friend Charlie Abels, a Louisiana state trooper from Springfield. Charlie took the other guests in my pickup truck to their stands that afternoon. I took my three-wheel Honda motorcycle in another direction across Buffalo River to scout out a place for them to hunt the next day.

It had rained the day before and The Buffalo River had a slight rise in its water level. I wanted to make sure that we could safely cross the river before daylight the next morning. When I arrived at the river it was too deep for me to drive the three-wheeler across, so I left it and crossed the river in a small boat. I was the only hunter on that side of the river, so I followed the dirt road about a mile past several stands and food plots to the border of our property. I was glad I was wearing my hip boots since the rising water from the river had begun to cover parts of the road.

I reached the last box stand on the border of our property overlooking scrub willows where a soybean field had once been located and climbed into the stand to see what I could see. I had been sitting in the stand for about an hour when I noticed the backwater from the flooding river had started to cover the trail I had used. I had seen no deer, so I decided to return up the trail to higher ground and take a stand there. The deer stands were about 250 yards apart, and as I approached the third stand from the one where I had been sitting I heard a couple of hounds began barking several hundred yards behind me. I realized that if I had stayed at the first stand I climbed I could have seen the deer the dogs were chasing. It was too late for me to go back so I hurried to the next stand in front of me and climbed up in it listening to the dogs. Shortly after, they stopped barking, and I figured the deer had gone in the water, so the dogs would lose their trail.

About 20 minutes later I saw movement in the Willows near me and a huge, cow horn spike walked into an opening. I knew from its size it was an old deer whose antlers were decreasing due to its age, and it probably would not survive another year. I had just about decided to take it out of the herd, when I saw other movement behind the first deer and two other large bucks walked into the opening behind the first one. As I raised my rifle to shoot the largest buck, a fourth deer stepped into the opening. It was a huge 10 point with long curving tines that almost touched at the tip, like the one I had killed two years before in the high grass bedding area about a half-mile away. I quickly swung my rifle to the largest buck, and at the sound of my shot he disappeared. The cow horn spike didn't move, but before I could shoot him he also vanished with the other bucks. I waited a while for the deer to bleed down then climbed out of the stand and soon found him about 100 yards away in the willow brush. I knew I'd need some help to bring the deer back to the camp, and it was getting dark, and I looked around to mark the place it lay so I could find it when I returned.

The deer was too big for me to pull it very far. Fortunately, it was lying a few steps from the edge of a food plot which extended across from another deer stand on a different branch of the road. I tied my hunter's orange vest to a willow on the edge of the food plot then begin the mile-long walk back to my boat at the river crossing. As I rode my bike back towards the camp it began to rain, and I knew the river would be rising. When I reached the camp, my companions had already broken out a bottle of my Jack Daniels and welcomed me with a drink. I told them that we had to go back across the river and get my deer before the water got any higher. I exchanged my rifle for a flask of Jack Daniels and we got on two bikes for our trip to retrieve the deer. To keep from having to drag the deer by hand over a mile, I devised a plan to ride the bikes about a mile across the soybean field and through the willows to a different river crossing where another small boat was located. Boo rode behind me on my new bike and Charlie followed us on another to the boat which was in a shallow channel. Frank, who was older, remained at the camp. We decided that the easiest way for us to get the deer would be to pull the boat up the narrow channel a couple of hundred yards to the food plot.

As I pulled the boat through the water my companions followed me on the adjoining trail. When we reached the food plot we left the boat and walked about 150 yards to the place where my hunter's orange vest hung. I then led the way through the trees to the deer. The rain increased as we struggled to pull the deer to the place where we loaded it into the boat. All three of us had to get in the water and push and pull the heavy loaded boat across logs and sandbars to the place we had left the bikes. We then got the deer out of the boat and tied his antlers to the back of my bike, so I could pull it through the woods and across the bean field to the camp. Charlie and Boo followed me on the other older bike.

Most of the way back to the camp I had to ride standing up and leaning forward on my bike to keep it from rising up and turning over due to the weight of the heavy deer I was dragging. About halfway across the bean field I realized Charlie and Boo were no longer closely following me. When I stopped I saw their bike was running around in circles. I walked back to them and we discovered something had broken in the steering mechanism. I left them with the broken bike and pulled the deer the rest of the way to the skinning rack behind my camp, then returned to the bean field with a rope to pull Charlie on the disabled bike while Boo rode behind me. When we arrived, we hung my deer which weighed 208 pounds on the skinning rack, washed the mud off the deer with a water hose and skinned and gutted it.

After a hot shower, a hot meal, and more Jack Daniels I felt like a million dollars, even though I had probably burned off at least 5 pounds since I first left the camp that afternoon. The next morning it was still raining, and we canceled the hunt. After breakfast I butchered the deer. We then got in my truck and rode back to the river which had risen several feet. If we hadn't retrieved the deer the night before there would've been no way for us to get back to the place I had shot it due to the flood. I gave Boo and Frank half of the deer meat to take home with them along with a coyote Boo had killed the first afternoon.

In late 1979 or maybe early 1980 Billy Abels who owned The Land the Sports sporting goods store in Hammond Louisiana, his son, and Carmon Moore the Clerk of Court for Tangipahoa Parish came to my hunting camp near Woodville Mississippi to hunt ducks. Part of our property was in the hills and the rest in the bottom lands that were subject to flooding when the Mississippi River was high, and the rains caused the Buffalo to overflow its banks. The Buffalo River divided into many channels on our property, some were no more than three or 4 feet across as the water flowed through a marshy area.

My camp was at the end of the road 5 miles from the blacktop at Leslie, Mississippi. Earlier that year I bought several dozen decoys from Billy's store and invited him to come hunting when the ducks arrived. I had two Chesapeake Bay retriever's, Dusty and Brandy, and a six-wheel hustler vehicle that we used to travel from the camp to the hunting area. The night before our hunt the temperature fell to about 8° and all the potholes and surrounding swamps and marshes froze solid. The only open water for miles was in the swiftly flowing river channels.

We left the camp long before daylight and crossed the soybean fields to the marshy hunting area with our decoys, dogs, and guns. When we reached a large pothole that was one of my best hunting locations I left Billy and Carmon and one dog. The pothole was frozen solid with ice almost an inch thick. I told them that we would have to break the ice with our boots in the shallow water to set up the decoys. We all four broke up the ice and threw out the decoys in the darkness. Then Billy's son and I walked several hundred yards across the frozen ground and found some open water in the small river channels flowing through the marsh. We placed our decoys in and alongside the flowing water and found some low willow bushes to stand in which gave us some cover.

We were dressed in camouflage coats, waders, caps and gloves. I wore a camouflage mask and the others used camouflage face paint to keep the ducks from seeing their faces. As daylight came we began to see a few ducks moving and we got a few shots as they passed over us.

Because of the frozen conditions thousands of ducks were concentrated along the Mississippi River and on Lake Mary, an old Mississippi River channel about four or 5 miles away. As the morning progressed the ducks left their roosting area on the lake and headed towards the flooded soybean fields to feed.

The ice prevented them from getting to their usual feeding areas that morning. When they saw the decoys in the pothole they were flying very high in large's flocks. Billy's son and I watched the ducks began to circle and drop down to the frozen pothole were Billy and Carmon were hunting. The birds reminded me of a tornado as they circled down to the surface. The decoys that we put out in that pothole had frozen in the ice and there was no open water for the ducks to land in. They did not realize this, however, until they reached the surface, and many slid across the ice when they landed. Billy and Carmon shot until their gun barrels got hot.

At the same time dozens of ducks saw our decoys and began dropping in even though we were standing in the low brush nearby. I guess the ducks thought we were broken trunks of trees with our camouflage garments. The limit for ducks that year was based on points and each hunter could amass 100 points. Some ducks like hen mallards were 25-point ducks while green heads and teal were 10 points. We concentrated on shooting only green heads and at the end of the morning had almost 40 ducks.

I had worn a backpack to carry the ducks, and also had straps to put the duck's heads in to carry across my shoulders. The other hunters also had back straps. I had purchased packs for my dogs and each one carried 4 to 6 ducks as we returned to the camp.

On the walk back from the hunting area while I was loaded down with ducks, Billy's son and I crossed a beaver dam across one of the main channels of the Buffalo. When I reached the middle of the dam, an eight-point buck tried to cross the same way and stopped about 20 feet from me. As I reached in my pocket to try to find a buckshot shell the deer just stood there. I didn't have any buckshot and finally he turned and disappeared.

When we got back we discovered the ice storm had knocked down the power lines and we could not use the mechanical duck plucker to clean our birds. We spent most of the afternoon picking and cleaning ducks.

That evening I fired up my charcoal water smoker and we feasted on smoked duck, turnips, sweet potatoes, and cornbread washed down with Merlot wine and later Jack Daniels Black Label whiskey. I cooked extra ducks on the smoker and the next day we had a smoked duck and andouille sausage gumbo.

Everybody who came to my camp never lost any weight no matter how much exercise they got in the woods and on the Buffalo River. We caught small blue catfish and 20 to 50-pound flathead catfish, as well as 40 pound and larger loggerhead turtles in hoop nets in the river, killed deer and wild hogs in the bottom lands and hills which I cleaned and butchered for my guests. I usually woke my guests about an hour before daylight to the very loud music of Doug Kershaw's "Louisiana Man". I would pound on the bedroom doors and announce "did you come to hunt or come to sleep? Get up and come get your coffee." Anyone who wanted to could have toast or doughnuts. We would go to the deer stands or the duck blinds before light and return to the camp around 9:30 or 10 AM. Breakfast would be served shortly thereafter and would consist of sausages, bacon, ham, eggs, grits, and hot biscuits butter and jelly or sugar cane syrup with coffee and Kahlua` and milk.

Buffalo River Bounty, Leslie, Mississippi

Art Macy at Johnson Hunting Club
One Shot, One Duck

Mississippi Duck Hunt – Lucius Patterson, Hobart Pardue, Gordon Anderson, and Harold Picou

North Carolina Judges Lacy Thornburg and Jud Downs

Odessa Coats Womack and Keith Baker
Johnson Plantation, Mississippi

Hobart Pardue – Buffalo River, Mississippi

Chapter 14. 1975 - 1980's Herb Plauche`, Mallards in Mississippi, Doves in Mexico, Sea Ducks in Coastal Maine

I first met Dr. Herb Plauche`, an Orthopedic Surgeon, in the late 1960 's when one of my clients who had been injured in an automobile accident was treated by him and I took his deposition.

Several of my clients recommended him highly. When the first man was sent to the moon in 1969, I watched the moon landing on TV for hours. I had a recliner chair where I was sitting and after several hours I started to get out of the chair without raising the back of it. When I started to get up I felt a sharp pain in my back. I went to bed and when I awoke the next morning I literally could not get out of bed. I had to turn over on my stomach push myself up with my arms and could hardly walk.

I had requested some medical reports from Dr. Plauche` and had received his bill for several hundred dollars a few days before. I called his office and asked for an appointment to see him. His nurse told me that it would be several days before I could get an appointment. I was in severe pain, so I called my cousin Sonny Womack to drive me to Baton Rouge to Dr. Plauche`s office. When we arrived, I had a check in my hand for payment of office bills for my clients in the amount of several hundred dollars. I could hardly walk to the nurse's desk due to the pain I was in and told her I had to see the doctor. She told me there was no way to see him without an appointment. I made out the check to the doctor but did not sign it gave it to the nurse and told her to tell him that if he wanted to get me to sign the check he would have to see me. The doctor who was about my age, came to the waiting room, took one look at me and said, "you're really hurting aren't you?" I told him I had to have some relief. He checked me out and sent me to the hospital where I stayed for five days, receiving traction treatment. During that time, I got to know him, and we later became best friends.

Herb loved to hunt ducks, he had been born and raised in Morganza Louisiana and his father like my mother was a pharmacist. In 1975 I had joined the Johnson plantation hunting club in Leslie Mississippi on the Buffalo River mainly for deer hunting, but in late December and early

393

January the river would flood our soybean fields and there were literally thousands of ducks on our property.

My hunting club camp was located on a bluff overlooking the bottom lands of the Buffalo and Mississippi rivers where the soybean fields were located. I invited Herb in January 1978 to bring his four brothers and come duck hunting with me. To get to my place you had to drive from Baton Rouge to Woodville Mississippi, then leave the main highway and drive 15 miles to the end of a gravel lane to reach the camp. The drive for the last 10 miles was through wooded hills with no duck habitat whatsoever. When my guests arrived, we unloaded their gear at the camp and got in my pickup truck. I drove them down to the soybean fields where we would later hunt. As we came down the hill you could see the flooded fields in the distance in front of us and as we approached the birds started to get up. The doctor exclaimed "look at the blackbirds" I told him those were not blackbirds, they are mallard ducks. He had never seen that many ducks in one location before. During the three-day hunt we had a rare snowfall and we took white sheets off the beds to wrap up in to camouflage ourselves in the flooded snow-covered fields. We killed limits of ducks every day for the best duck hunting trip the doctor and his brothers had ever made.

I later taught the doctor how to hunt wild turkeys and we went on hunting trips from Hudson's Bay Canada, to Mexico and Argentina.

A couple of years after Dr. Plauche` had come to my hunting camp to hunt ducks I organized a dove hunt south of Matamoros Mexico. A group of about 15 of my friends flew with me to Brownsville Texas where we crossed the border and drove to a hunting lodge located about 100 miles to the south. We shot doves in the mornings, took a siesta through the noontime, and shot more doves in the afternoon. The second day we decided we would visit boy's town, a red-light district on the outskirts of Matamoros. It consisted of a group of strip clubs and bars decorated with Christmas tree lights. The strip clubs were filled with tables and chairs where many girls sat waiting for their turn to dance on the open-air stage. Between dances the girls would approach the customers and solicit drinks. Rooms were available around the dance area for private meetings. Our group sat at a large table drinking beer and watching the dancers perform. Some of our members visited girls in the private rooms.

I knew that Herb had a birthday coming up soon because his wife had invited me and my wife to attend a surprise birthday party for him shortly after we returned from our hunting trip. Before we left home I had seen stories in the newspapers and on television about movie actress Grace Kelly, who had married the Prince of Monaco. She had a beautiful teenaged daughter, Princess Stephanie, who eloped with a European Playboy.

As we sat at a large table in the bar, a beautiful new dancer came to the stage and began removing her clothes as she danced. She looked exactly like the photographs we had seen of Stephanie. When I saw her, I went to the club manager and arranged for her to come dance on our table. She removed her G String as she danced down the table to Herb's chair and jumped in his lap. My friends and I began to sing Happy Birthday to Herb and told him she was his present. Herb was temporarily speechless, with a look of astonishment on his face as we roared with laughter and told him we would pay for her tip. He stood up, removing the girl from his lap and indignantly advised us "why eat hamburger here when you have steak at home". One of the other members of our group took her by the hand, thanked Herb profusely and disappeared with her in her room.

When we returned home Herb's wife, Virginia, called to remind me of the surprise birthday party to be held at Juban's restaurant a couple of days later. When my wife and I arrived, I was surprised to see that all the couples were not seated next to each other and my wife and I did not know some of the attendees who were seated near us. When Virginia introduced me to the other guests she told them that Herb and I had just returned from Mexico on an alleged dove hunt, but we must have been in boys' town because neither of us were sunburned. Everyone at the party began to laugh, and I asked her "What Is This Boys Town? I don't have any idea what you are talking about." She just rolled her eyes at me, and everybody at the party figured I was lying.

A few days later when I saw Herb I told him that I felt if he was going to be accused of something he didn't do he might as well have done it, and reminded him of his comment "why eat a hamburger when you had steak at home."

Many years ago, when I was actively collecting various species of wild ducks for my trophy room I read an article in the publication "The Bird Hunting Report" about a hunt for sea ducks in coastal Maine. I had several mounts of different kind of ducks I had killed in Louisiana and Mississippi but had never shot a sea duck. The article featured the guide service, Coastal Maine Outfitters, in Newport, Maine, and told of the various species that were available. These included Eiders, three types of Scoters, Surf, Black, and White Wing, Old Squaws, as well as Goldeneye, Black Mallard, Buffelhead, and American and Red Breasted Merganser's.

I had never been to Maine but had read about the high tides in the Bay of Fundy which daily exceeded 10 feet and sometimes much more. The hunting report article was very positive about the services rendered by the outfitter, the accommodations, the amount of ducks, and the various species available. I called my friends and hunting companions John Dahmer and Dr. Herbert Plauche` and booked a hunt in late December for six hunters which also included John, his wife Carol, my wife Loretta, Herb and his brother Tommy.

Before we met our outfitter and his girlfriend they sent us a sample menu of the food they planned to prepare for us during our three-day hunt. We chose lobsters, roasted duck, and ribeye steaks for our dinners. A large breakfast was provided each morning, featuring pancakes with maple syrup, ham, eggs, milk, juice, and coffee. We were also provided sandwiches and thermoses of lobster bisque to take with us on the hunts. When we arrived, our guide told us that we would be hunting according to the tides rather than early mornings and late afternoons as was the case for hunting ducks in other regions.

The sea duck hunts were conducted in the open waters of the Atlantic Ocean from small rocky islands scattered in Penobscot Bay. The ducks primarily fed on clams attached to the rocky sea floor, which opened and closed according to the tide. When the tide was high the clams would open, and the ducks would dive 50 feet or more to the bottom to pick the meat of the clam from the open shell. When the tide turned and began to fall the clams would close and the birds would fly to the lee side of the islands to rest out of the wind.

Our guides put out dozens of decoys in the calm water behind the island where we were taken to hunt. Two hunters were left at each island and told to walk through the large rocks and sit near the water's edge. Each of us wore insulated underwear and hip boots as well as heavy jackets with hoods, face masks, and heavy gloves to protect us from the icy wind. The guides, who had brought us to the islands in two large boats then went to other islands where large rafts of ducks were resting out of the wind. When the boats approached the ducks began to fly and some flocks spied our decoys and came into range of our shotguns. We killed scoters, old squaws, and Eiders, which were picked up by the guides in the boat.

As we were waiting for flocks of ducks to approach us, we watched the water rising among the rocks on the island, and every 20 minutes or so we had to move to higher levels to avoid it. After the guides picked us all up from the islands and we started back to the landing we came upon a boat containing fishermen who were diving for scallops in wetsuits. We pulled alongside the boat and purchased a gallon of freshly shucked scallops. Herb, Tommy, John and I began to eat some raw, the same way we ate oysters at home. We had no cocktail sauce, but the scallops had the briny taste of saltwater and were delicious. When we reached the shore, I walked along a small beach while the guides were loading the boats, and picked up dozens of scallop shells, clamshells, and the shells of sea urchin. When we returned home I gave them to my taxidermist to put them, together with sand, on the floor of the glass covered end tables containing the mounts of my sea ducks, which I placed in my trophy room.

The place where we launched the boats was used by lobster fishermen who had lobster traps together with their distinguished wooden buoys stacked in piles near the landing. Each fishermen's buoys were painted different colors, so they could be readily identified in the ocean. I located one of the fishermen and purchased a couple of his old buoys to hang on the walls of my bar in my trophy room.

The next morning the offshore wind had increased making it dangerous for us to return to the islands where we had been hunting in the open bay. Instead the guides took us to a freshwater lake near Newport to hunt for Goldeneye, Black Mallard's, and Buffelhead. It was well below freezing that morning and the wind blowing across the lake created whitecaps. As the large boats we were riding in bounced across the waves sheets of water sprayed from the bow, and immediately froze, covering our heavy coats with ice.

We hunted in a sheltered cove where I killed Buffellheads, a Goldeneye, Merganser's and Mallards. My wife Loretta killed a beautiful Black Mallard Drake. After another day of duck hunting we decided to rent a car and drive from Newport to Freeport Maine and visit the LL Bean store, which was only an hour and a half away. I had purchased hunting clothing and boots through the catalog published by that company and had seen pictures of its main store.

That was the first time I saw mounts of some of the different kinds of ducks and birds that I had never hunted before, as well as the latest types of hunting clothing and other gear on display. After making some purchases we returned to Newport where we went to a lobster tank which was located in a saltwater estuary. It had a fence extending from the bank out into the water about 50 yards then running parallel to the shore about 100 yards then running back to the bank. The fence ran from the surface of the water to the estuaries floor and contained hundreds of live lobsters that had been purchased from the lobster fishermen. We purchased several dozen lobsters which were packed in boxes with seaweed that we brought back home with us.

Loretta and Hobart Pardue, Carole and John
Dahmer, and Dr. Herbert K. and Tommy
Plauche` Coastal Maine

Hobart Pardue
Sea Ducks, Eider, Scoters, Coastal Maine

Chapter 15. 1975 -1980 Foundation of North American Wild Sheep - Hunting Alaska

After I killed my first wild Dall Sheep up in Yukon Canada, I received a letter from a group of sheep hunters from Minnesota inviting me to join a newly formed organization for the conservation of wild sheep. It was patterned after Ducks Unlimited, which was founded to improve habitat for wild ducks and geese and preserve and promote the species. It also promoted good ethics for hunters. There were only 15 or 20 members contemplating the formation of this organization and they invited me to come to a meeting in St. Paul Minnesota in late January the year after I killed my Dall ram. Loretta and I made arrangements for us to fly up to Minneapolis/St. Paul and join this organization.

I became a charter member for the Foundation of North American Wild Sheep. The purpose was primarily to raise funds for habitat, research, fight diseases that the wild sheep were subject to catch from intermingling with domestic sheep on some of their ranges and to set up regulations for registering the sheep that were taken by hunters from all over the world. The four species of wild sheep in North America are the Dall, the Stone, the Rocky Mount Big Horn, and the Desert Big Horn Sheep.

At the annual conventions of his organization outfitters, artists, taxidermists, gun manufacturers and sporting good distributors set up booths for visiting members and attendees to select places to hunt, and equipment that is needed for hunters. It was a wonderful opportunity for me to get to know other sheep hunters and outfitters. That was when I decided I was going to make it one of my goals in life to take a grand slam of rams, one of each of the four species of North American Wild sheep. At the time I doubt if there were 30 people in the whole world who had accomplished this. Certainly no one from Louisiana ever had, when I set out on my quest and joined the organization. The conventions were held each year and awards were given for those hunters who had killed the largest Rams the previous hunting season and also for those who achieved the Holy Grail of Sheep Hunting, killing all four of the Rams.

The second year the convention was held in Memphis Tennessee. It was an interesting group, 90% of those who were members were wealthy. The cost of the hunts in those days, in the early 1970s, ranged from about $6000 up to around $15,000 a hunt. I met world-famous outfitters, gun dealers, artists, sculptors, and taxidermists at these different conventions as well as authors of hunting books and books on guns. At each of the conventions we raised money for the promotion of wild sheep. We had raffles, and drawings for hunts, guns, trophy animal mounts, and other sporting equipment. We also had auctions for special hunts throughout the Rocky Mountains. Some of the special hunts took place in states like Colorado, Montana, Wyoming and other Western states, as well as the Western Canadian Provinces, and Alaska. These hunts were only available at high prices. In those days many trophy hunts were simply unavailable most of the time. First you had to apply for a drawing to get a hunting license, and while 30 or 40 people would apply, only one or two were issued. So, it was difficult to get permits to hunt in many cases.

When I went to the convention in Memphis an outfitter from Alaska named Keith Johnson donated a hunt for Dall sheep. I bought a ticket for the raffle even though I'd already killed a Dall sheep in the Yukon. Keith had his own territory in Alaska with a cabin, and two airplanes he used to transport hunters back in the bush to hunt. As luck would have it I won that draw, and we had the opportunity to talk about the upcoming hunt. I made a deal with him to pay him extra to allow me to hunt moose and bring DeVan, my son, who was about 12 or 13 years old at the time, to hunt the Dall sheep as well as caribou.

An interesting thing happened at the Sheep Convention that year. The committee in charge had booked a restaurant several miles from the hotel that featured Louisiana style food. All of the members and their families rode by chartered buses across town to have a special meal. When we arrived at the restaurant a delicious meal was served. It featured some type of fish with shrimp etouffee on top of it. I felt like I was back home it was so good, but many of the members had never eaten anything like that. To them it was just some type of casserole, appetizer, or such and they weren't impressed at all. Quite a few of them ate all their salad, took a bite of the fish and etouffee and decided they didn't like it. They waited for the next course, which they expected to be steak. As it turned out, there was no next course, except for dessert. When we got back on the bus many were complaining about still being hungry, and they did not care anything about the food. One of the members, who was a multimillionaire, made an announcement that he was gonna make sure everybody had something to eat. He then ordered the bus driver to take us to the nearest McDonald's where he and the driver went in and ordered about 100 hamburgers and distributed them to everyone on the bus.

After we came back home I started to get my legs in shape for my next mountain hunt and also made sure that we had the right kind of equipment for Loretta, DeVan and I to use. We flew from New Orleans to Seattle, Washington, then on to Anchorage, Alaska where Keith Johnson met us at the airport. We spent a day in Anchorage before leaving to go out to the place where we were going to hunt. Keith had a young guide hired to take DeVan to the Sheep hunting area, but first we flew to a lake where he had a cabin. Loretta and I stayed there with our shotguns to shoot ducks and ptarmigan and our fishing rods to fish for grayling and lake trout. We also had my spotting scope and binoculars to observe caribou, moose, and other wildlife that were in the area. On the flight in Keith's four passenger bush plane we spotted a grizzly bear and some wolves below us as well as many caribou who had just started their annual migration. After we were dropped off at the cabin, DeVan and the young guide flew with Keith into the high mountains where they landed on a glacier and set up sheep camp. They hunted for about four or five days but weren't successful in locating a trophy ram.

In the meantime, while DeVan was up on the mountain, Loretta and I took a boat and went up the lake and started catching fish. The lake was full of grayling and lake trout that were approximately 3 pounds apiece. Every time we threw a bait we would get a bite and most of the time catch a fish. At home when we were fly fishing for bream, it wasn't unusual to catch 50 to 100 fish in a morning. I would bring those fish home and we would eat all we wanted, probably no more than 10 or 15, and give the others away to our neighbors.

I don't know what I was thinking about when we were up in Alaska. There were no neighbors, and before we knew it we had caught and put probably 15 fish in the boat. I realized that there was no way we could eat more than 3 or 4 of them, and here we were with all these other fish. Well, the problem was quickly solved. All around that lake were bald eagles. We watched them soaring high in the sky, and lighting in little trees around the lake. Their main food was fish. Every morning we watched them flying around the lake and diving to catch fish. When I set up my spotting scope outside the cabin, so I could glass the surrounding area, I noticed a stone ledge about 150 yards up the mountain, where several eagles perched between their fishing expeditions. After we got back to the cabin I took those extra fish we caught, climbed up the mountain and put them on that ledge. Within an hour there were two eagles perched on the ledge eating the fish. After that, every day Loretta and I went fishing, we always caught some extra ones for the birds.

There were lots of ducks on the lake. This was late August and the ducks were still in family groups prior to their getting ready for the migration south. At that time of the year they did not have their mating plumage, and all of them were rather drab looking. We shot a few which I cleaned, and Loretta cooked with Louisiana seasoning and they were delicious. We also killed ptarmigan, which were grouse like birds feeding on wild berries, on the slopes of the mountain near the cabin. We watched a moose swimming across the lake, and caribou moving through the area every day. After three or four days DeVan and his guide came back off the mountain. Keith picked Loretta and I up and flew us to a Lodge on a large lake, where Loretta stayed while DeVan and I hunted for moose.

When he arrived at the cabin Keith told me he had seen a wolf, so I got in the plane with him and we went wolf hunting. I had never shot anything out of a plane before and didn't know how the aerodynamics would affect the shots. Keith didn't explain anything to me before we got started except to make sure I didn't hit the propeller when I shot. I was in the seat directly behind him and the plane was built in such a way that as we flew I could let the door down and lean out of it to aim and shoot. Keith had a shotgun in the plane loaded with buckshot, but it only had three shells in the gun. We flew along and spotted the wolf below us as he was trying to catch a caribou calf. Keith made a run at that wolf like a dive bomber and when we got close enough he told me to shoot. I aimed ahead of the wolf and shot, but the wolf merely changed his course and kept running. I couldn't figure out why I missed that wolf. We made another circle around and came back again and I sighted again, and I missed the second time. I asked Keith what the hell was the matter. He asked me where I was aiming. I told him I'm aiming right in front of his head. He told me the way we're coming in, with the speed of the plane and all, you have to aim at the tip of his tail, so the shot will actually hit him in the head and upper body. Well, what I didn't know was the last shotgun shell was not buckshot, but number 6 shot Keith used for hunting birds. When we made the next run, I aimed at the wolf's tail. When I shot he crumbled up and went spinning away. I thought I had killed him, but when we looked around the wolf got up and ran off unhurt and reached a den in a bunch of rocks. There was no place to land within a couple of miles of the place we last saw the wolf and since he was not dead it wasn't important for us to go look for him. The fine shot that hit the wolf certainly didn't kill him or hurt him very badly because it would not penetrate his thick winter coat and tough skin.

When we got to the lodge and left Loretta, DeVan and I and the two young guides flew out to another lake where we were going to hunt for moose. They had a rule in Alaska that you could not hunt the day that you flew. When we flew to the new lake we spotted two Bull Moose feeding in the scrub willows, so we knew right about where they were. It would not have been ethically correct to land on that lake and go directly to those moose where we probably would've killed them. Instead we had to camp out overnight and then go hunt for the moose the next day. They were a couple of miles from where we landed and set the camp up at the lower end of the lake. The camp consisted of a couple of tents with all of our gear for cooking and other necessities. We got up the next morning and walked to the other end of the Lake where the guides felt there would be a chance to find a moose that we could kill. We were fortunate in coming on a good bull, which was in the middle of the rut. This meant that he was going to be very very hard to kill. I shot that moose with my 300 Weatherby rifle and it took about three shots to actually kill him. He was tremendous, his antler spread was almost 60 inches which made him a true trophy. First, we caped out the moose and got the antlers, the cape, and cut out the two loins, which really are like beef tenderloins, and we started our trek back to our camp. DeVan carried guns, I carried 40 to 50 pounds of tenderloins over my shoulders. One of the two guides carried the antlers, which probably weighed close to 100 pounds and the other guide carried the cape, which also weighed close to 100 pounds. We left the rest of the meat where the animal fell.

We got back to the tent camp after dark and had a good night's sleep. In the middle of the night I got up to take a leak and walked outside. The full moon was turning a reddish color, and I realized that the moon was going into a total eclipse, which I watched from that Alaskan mountainside. It was a beautiful sight with the mountains in the background.

The next morning Keith came back with the plane and brought DeVan and I, our tenderloins, the antlers, and the cape back to the Lodge. The two guides went back to the location of the kill to butcher and pack out the rest of the meat which they brought to the campsite where Keith could land the plane and pick them up. There was a rule in Alaska and Canada that required hunters to butcher any animal they kill and bring the meat back with them rather than just let it go to waste.

Normally when moose hunting, if you have a bear tag, which I had, I would have tried to kill a grizzly by setting up at a place where I could clearly see the gut pile of the moose I shot. The ideal place to do this would be for me to get on a high hill, or side of the mountain where I could see the bear coming to feed on the moose. I needed to be at least 150 yards away because when you shoot a bear, and the bullet doesn't hit just right, that bear could run 200 yards and get you before he died even though the bullet would go through his lungs and heart and eventually kill him, When I shot the moose, it fell in a thicket and there was no clear way to see the gut pile at a distance of more than 50 yards. It was just too dangerous to try to hunt a grizzly under those circumstances.

On the flight back from the lake to the Lodge we saw beautiful sights with all the leaves changing colors. Winter was coming on and in one days' time, I actually saw the weather change from bright sunshine to clouds, to misty rain, to light snow, and back to clear again. All this occurred in a period of about 18 hours, which was how long the sun was out that time a year. We flew back with the Moose antlers tied to a wing of the plane since they were too large to fit inside with the rest of us. We stayed at the Lodge for a day or so and had a very good meal which was listed on the menu as a cheeburger and oley. It was really a cheeseburger with a lot of different types of condiments to go with it, french fries, and an Olympia beer. It was delicious, after two days of freeze-dried camp food and Dinty Moore canned stew.

We next flew back to the cabin where Loretta and I had seen the Eagles, shot the ducks, and caught the fish. We were hoping DeVan would have a chance to kill a caribou while we were there, and they were still in full migration. Each morning for the next couple of days DeVan and his guide would go across the lake, climb a small mountain, and set up the spotting scope so they could glass around several miles, and observe the caribou as they came by. They saw probably 100 caribou in those two days, but none were really big bulls that DeVan wanted. The second day after he had not killed anything we decided we would go to the other end of the lake from where they had been hunting and see if he could find a caribou there. Loretta and I took our shotguns to try to kill some ptarmigan while DeVan and his guide started off to a high point to try to hunt caribou. As luck would have it, while we were walking towards the high point the guide spotted to 2 caribou bulls on another mountain that were coming our way. The guide told us he thought the caribou would come behind a small ridge and should come out into view about 100 or so yards away. I had a movie camera with a zoom lens, so I could get a video of DeVan shooting his caribou. Imagine my surprise when the caribou popped out from behind that ridge about 50 yards away. DeVan immediately set up and shot the biggest bull. I looked for the animal in the viewfinder of the camera and all I could see was its hide. Before I could take the camera off zoom, DeVan had one Bull on the ground. The animal was starting to get up so, he did like I would have done, and both of us had done while hunting Whitetail deer, he shot again. The problem was, when he had knocked one down, the other one had stepped behind a rock, and what he thought was the first bull getting up was the second bull as it stepped back out. He shot that one also. Fortunately, he had his Dall sheep tag as well as a caribou tag and you could use the Dall sheep tag on any lesser animal such as a moose or caribou. We harvested both caribou and came back to the cabin where we stayed for another day until Keith came back and got us in the plane.

The cabin had a meat pole near it, which was merely a pole suspended between two posts where you could hang the meat from the animals you killed. This is where I hung the tenderloins from the moose. The first morning when I came out to cut some steaks for breakfast, I noticed some black and white magpies as well as some grey colored whiskey jays, which are different types of birds, sitting on top of the meat pole picking at the meat that was hanging there. The pole served as our icebox, the meat was off the ground so no critter or anything could get it, but I wasn't counting on the birds flying up there and picking on it from the top. I remedied that real quick with a plastic bag tied to the top of the meat, so the birds couldn't get at it.

When we got ready to leave we discovered we had too much gear to take off from the lake. Keith was a very experienced bush pilot and didn't take any chances about anything, so he took Loretta and I first to another larger lake a few miles away where we landed at a cabin where a couple he knew lived. He left us there while he flew back to get DeVan, the meat, antlers of the caribou, and other gear. He then flew back to the lake where he had left us. We boarded the plane where he had a longer distance to taxi, so he could get up before we ran out of water. The lake was like a sheet of glass that morning, with no wind blowing, and he knew he didn't want to take any chances of not being able to get the plane up. He taxied down the lake before we took off and then started going back and forth across the lake creating waves so when he taxied back and made his run up the lake we hit the waves which gave the plane more lift, so we could get up and leave the water before we reached the bank.

The rest of the trip back to Anchorage was uneventful except for a portion of the way where we flew over the Alaskan pipeline which was still under construction at that time. We got to Anchorage just about dark and landed at the busy airport where jet airplanes were taking off and landing. We spent another day or so in Anchorage exploring the city, where we went to an area along the harbor which had been partially destroyed by an earthquake a few years before and had not been completely rebuilt. I also got my first taste of sushi at a Japanese

408

Seafood Market which specialized in raw fish. Loretta declined to join me while I tasted it, but I thought it was delicious.

Alaska Moose

Loretta, DeVan and Hobart Pardue
Alaska Caribou

Alaska Lake Trout

Mount Denali, Alaska

Alaska Pipeline

Chapter 16. 1980's Duck Hunt - Laguna Madre

In the early 1980s I subscribed to a publication called The Hunting Report which gave information about opportunities to hunt game around the world. There were two editions one catering big-game hunters and the other to bird hunters. After I had killed all four of the North American wild sheep as well as elk and moose I mainly concentrated on duck hunting.

The bird hunting report furnished information on guides, accommodations, species of game, and bag limits. The authors of the articles traveled to different locations in the United States, Canada, South America, Europe, and Africa and wrote about their experiences with different outfitters who had hunts for sale.

I had hunted elk, mule deer, and bighorn sheep in southern Colorado and observed small flocks of redhead ducks in the mountain lakes but had never killed any. The ducks were beautiful, and I wanted one or two for my trophy room.

The hunting reports were published every few months and were mailed to subscribers. When I received my report one year I read an article about hunting redhead ducks with an outfitter named Charlie Veigh from Brownsville, Texas who conducted hunts in the Laguna Madre near San Fernando Mexico.

I had hunted white wing doves in the area and fished for largemouth bass in nearby Lake Guerrero in the past. I contacted Mr. Veigh and booked a hunt with him for my friend Tom Kent Stewart and I and our wives to hunt ducks in the Laguna and bobwhite quail in the surrounding countryside. He also arranged for a hunt to a freshwater lake to hunt whistling tree ducks.

We flew to Brownsville Texas where we met our outfitter, and he took us to the hunting camp which consisted of several cabins located at the edge of the water. Each cabin was painted a different bright color with a large kitchen and dining area nearby.

Before daylight the next morning we boarded two air boats and were taken several miles down the Laguna which contained many islands in the shallow open waters behind the main barrier island next to the Gulf of Mexico. The guides dropped us off at two primitive blinds made of small sticks of driftwood with buckets to sit on. The blinds were about three quarters of a mile apart had large decoy spreads of redhead and pintail ducks.

The redhead ducks were mainly mute, but I had my pintail whistle with me. Air boats and guides sped away into the open bay and we observed large flocks of ducks that were rafted up in the middle start to fly as the air boats approached them. Soon small flocks of ducks began to break away from the others and some spied our decoys and approached our blind. Loretta and I quickly killed several redheads and I waded in the knee-deep water to pick them up.

The action was fast and furious for the first hour or so as more and more rafts of ducks were disturbed by the air boats and I called several small flocks of pintails to our blind. We had killed about 15 ducks a piece when the morning flight ended, and I walked across the barrier island to the open surf of the Gulf of Mexico.

The vacant beach was strewn with seashells and other flotsam from a recent storm and I picked up a couple of large conch shells and a bright orange crab trap float with Spanish language marked on it.

The shells and float with its short rope attached are in my trophy room next to other shells and another crab trap float I picked up on the beach at Kitty Hawk North Carolina several years later when I was hunting sea ducks and swans.

When the air boats returned to pick us up we observed many small wooden platforms in the shallow waters of the lagoon. Each one had weirs extending several yards from the platform which contained a seat for a Mexican child to catch shrimp with a dip net as they migrated along the shore. The weirs acted as a funnel to concentrate shrimp under the platform. We were told the children usually fished at night with a bright light extended over the water which also attracted the shrimp.

The lagoon also had flocks of white pelicans which were sitting in the water as we passed on our way back to the camp. The guides drove the air boats through the pelicans who did not move until the air boats were only a few feet away from them and we could almost reach out and touch the large birds.

That afternoon we were taken to a ranch where we spread out and walked up coveys of bobwhite quail to shoot. The next morning, we returned to the lagoon and shot more ducks.

The following morning, we left very early in the guides vehicles and traveled about 75 miles to a man-made freshwater lake that had been built to irrigate farmland. It contained flooded timber in the nearby creek bottoms. We were taken in boats into the flooded timber and stood in shallow water awaiting flights of whistling ducks which fed in the grain fields at night.

All the ducks I ever hunted flew right at daylight or just before dark and the flights usually lasted only a few hours. The guides told us that the whistling ducks fed in grain fields at night and only left their feeding grounds several hours after daylight to return to the lake where they roosted in trees during the middle of the day.

When the ducks began to arrive, we could hear their whistle like calls before we could see them. The call was somewhat similar to a wood duck, and I immediately began to imitate the whistles that they made with my pintail whistle. I discovered the different calls the ducks were making that would attract them to my location and soon had several that could be mounted for my trophy room. I had never seen this species of duck in Southeast Louisiana but had heard they were rarely found in Southwest Louisiana near the Gulf Coast next to the Texas border. Now some 30 years later they are fairly common all-over South Louisiana.

Red Head Ducks and Blind at Laguna Madre, Mexico

417

Hunting Camp at Laguna Madre, Mexico

Fulvous Whistling Ducks – Hobart Pardue and Guide

Chapter 17. Duck and Deer Hunting in Tangipahoa Parish, Louisiana

I made one deer hunt in the swamp below Ponchatoula, Louisiana in the early 1960s before interstate 55 was completed. The cypress timber had been logged out by the early 1950's. The method used by the loggers was to build railroads through the swamp on dummy lines and the logs were pulled by cable several hundred yards to the railroad lines, loaded on trains and moved to the sawmill at Ponchatoula. We hunted in the cut over where young Cypress and Tupelo had grown after the harvest of the big trees. To make this hunt we traveled down Highway 51 which was a two-lane highway running south towards New Orleans. A canal was dredged alongside the highway through the swamp. We crossed the canal in boats then walked down the old dummy line in the swamp and took our stands. A driver would go further down the canal, then walk into the swamp with the dogs then turn them loose and drive toward the stand line. I was in the swamp for several hours and never saw a deer and no other hunters killed any. The men who I hunted with would shoot any deer they saw even though you could only legally kill bucks.

If a doe deer was killed it was skinned and butchered in the swamp and the meat was divided among the hunters to put in backpacks and bring back to the boat. One of those hunters, Spec Gatlin, a small man who worked occasionally as a bartender in one of the local joints and specialized in shooting loaded dice in illegal crap games, was a regular on these hunts. He had killed a spike buck on a hunt several weeks before the hunt I was on and he had cut the deer's head off. Every day he went hunting he would bring that deer head in his sack in the hopes that someone would kill a doe. If he got caught by the game warden, he would say the meat came from that buck. The old deer head lost all its hair, but Spec still carried it back and forth through the swamp. Luckily no game warden ever checked it out.

Years later in the late 1970s and early 1980s a group of men from South Tangipahoa Parish formed a hunting club and leased several hundred acres in the same area where I had hunted deer. I was invited to make a couple of hunts for ducks by Tom and Gordon Anderson who were members of the club and had been my guests at my deer hunting club in Southwest Mississippi.

The Anderson brothers each had air boats which would transport three or four hunters through the swamps. They, with the other club members, had cut air boat runs through the swamp and had mapped out various areas where different hunters would go each morning. These air boat runs were built through the swamp before the hunting season by cutting trails and removing logs, so the air boats could speed 30 or 40 mph on the way to the hunting areas without danger of hitting obstacles.

I met the other hunters about an hour before daylight in Ponchatoula where I left my car and went with them to the place where we launched the boats across the canal from the air boat runs. I was given a pair of earmuffs to wear for protection against the roar of the air boat engine and sat in front and at the feet of Gordon who operated the air boat. The air boat run was about 12 feet wide and the boat itself was about 6 feet wide. The operator had a Q beam light that clearly lit up the run in front of the boat. As we sped along Coots would try to take to the air to escape being hit by the boat, and often they would dive underwater to avoid us. Gordon knew exactly where he was going, and he rarely slowed down to turn into connecting channels on the way to the location where we hunted.

It was still pitch black when we arrived at a small pond surrounded by second growth Cypress and Tupelo trees and parked the boat near some bushes. The air boat itself was covered with camouflage netting and strips of Spanish moss and brush. When the engine was shut off for a few minutes there was silence, then the sound of ducks calling in the surrounding swamp got louder until it almost became a roar. We put out about a dozen Mallard decoys and waited for legal shooting time one half hour before sunup.

We were all dressed in camouflage coats and gloves and had head masks or camouflage paint on our faces. I was using my favorite 12gauge Remington automatic shotgun, but I had also brought my 10gauge Ithaca that I used to hunt wild turkeys. I left the Ithaca in its case in the boat and didn't tell any of the other hunters about it. Gordon and I were in one boat and Bobby Moran, and a young man who was his guest were in another. Bobby, a local banker, was an excellent duck caller but was extremely greedy, as most bankers are, and he would do anything to try to kill the most ducks.

As the darkness faded we could hear the ducks calling in the swamp around us then begin to hear the whistling wings of unseen ducks as they flew over us. Time seemed to crawl while we waited for the legal shooting hour to arrive, and finally a shot rang out from another group of hunters who couldn't wait any longer. At the sound of the shot ducks begin flying everywhere. We started calling and soon got lots of shots ourselves. As the morning progressed we would spy flocks of ducks in the distance and call them to us. They were usually flying very high and had to be coaxed down by our calls and the decoys to get them in range. As the ducks would circle, invariably the young man in Bobby Moran's boat would shoot before they got close enough and none of us would kill a duck. After this happened a couple times I put my Remington down and got my Ithica that had a range of about 80 yards using 3 ½ inch long Magnum shotgun shells.

The other hunters including Gordon did not see me change guns and I said nothing about the others shooting too soon and at too great a distance. Another group of ducks approached us and this time no shots were fired until they were in range. I let the others take the first shots and a couple of ducks fell. The other ducks frantically flew up and away to escape the shots that continued to be fired at them by my companions. Only then did I shoot with my Ithaca and killed two ducks that were clearly out of range for the other hunters. After that I would wait until the others had finished shooting and then would kill a duck or two.

A few days later Gordon and I made another hunt in the same area. I brought my Chesapeake Bay retriever with us to pick up the ducks that we killed. After a while we had almost taken our limits, and after counting the ducks we determined we could kill two more. We then decided to go to another area to try to fill our limits. We stopped the boat at a small pond surrounded by marsh and as we sat talking I was looking at my dog, Chief, who was facing me. I saw him moving his head and knew he saw something behind me. I spun around with my gun to my shoulder and saw three green head drakes coming in to light about 25 yards away. I aimed just ahead of the first duck. When I squeezed the trigger all three collapsed. We now had one duck over the limit. So, we put him in the bottom of the boat under some gear and decided to take the chance that no game warden would show up to check us and luckily no one did.

Hurricanes that brought in saltwater to the swamps around the lakes have killed the cypress and tupelo and the swamp is turning into marsh. Invasive non-native vegetation has choked the ponds and climate change has altered the migration of mallard ducks. The practice of short stopping the ducks in northern states by providing feed during the coldest part of the winter has changed the hunting opportunities I used to have, on my last hunt I traveled all the way to Tennessee during the very late season to try to shoot some mallards. In the Mississippi Delta close to the mouth of the river that used to hold mallards, very very few are killed and if you are going to hunt ducks there now mostly you shoot only gadwall and teal.

Chapter 18. Goose Hunting Hudson's Bay

I first heard about goose hunts near Hudson's Bay in Ontario, Canada while reading articles in hunting magazines as a boy. The distance from South Louisiana and the cost made it an impossible dream. In college, I read about the tremendous height of the tides in the Bay of Fundy area of Canada, but I never connected them to the tundra area surrounding Hudson's Bay.

In the early 1970s I made a hunt for Dall sheep in Yukon Territory, Canada. On my way home from Whitehorse I met some hunters from California. While on the jet flying to Seattle Washington we talked about our hunting experiences. They were interested in waterfowl hunts in South Louisiana, and I gave them some information on guides and locations in the Lake Arthur, Louisiana area.

They told me of hunting Canadian and light geese in the tundra adjoining Hudson's Bay with Cree Indian guides who called Geese with their natural voices. The limit was five per day and the cost for a three-day hunt was about $1500 plus airfare. This was comparable to what I paid for a mule deer hunt. I knew that I could hunt geese in Southwest Louisiana at a cost of about $125 per day with almost no expense to drive the 120 miles to the hunting location. The Cajun food served at that lodge was worth the entire cost of the hunt, and the bag limit was the same except for Canada geese which were unavailable in Louisiana.

My friend, Dr. Herbert Plauché, who hunted ducks with me at my camp in Mississippi a few years after my first sheep hunt, made a trip to Canada with some of his friends to hunt geese. When he returned he told me of the thousands of geese he had seen, the liberal limits they had taken, and the trout fishing they had done on pristine rivers flowing into Hudson's Bay. He explained that they flew from New Orleans to northern Minnesota, crossed the Canadian border at International Falls, then flew north to Fort Seven where they hunted.

I had never killed a Canadian goose and very few blue and snow geese. Herb was very interested in making a return trip and had all the information we needed to book the hunt. I called the outfitter and was told he had openings for a group of hunters in early September when the geese were concentrating into large flocks in preparation for their migration.

In the 1950's, during the Cold War, the Canadian government had built bases in cooperation with the United States Defense Department to set up early warning radar sites across northern Canada to protect against missile attacks by the Soviet Union. By the time we made our hunts the United States and Canada had developed satellite technology which allowed them to observe Russian missile sites from space and the Hudson's Bay facility became obsolete.

The outfitter got permission from the Canadian government to rent the barracks, mess hall, and other facilities formerly used by the Canadian soldiers as a hunting lodge. The barracks were different than the ones we used when I was in the Army, where 30 or 40 men slept in one large building. At Fort Seven there were several buildings each sleeping 6 to 8 men that had no bathrooms. If we had to take a leak at night, we walked outdoors where we could see the surrounding wilderness in the glow of the northern lights. It was an eerie feeling because there were polar bears in the vicinity that would be attracted to garbage from the camp. At the time I didn't realize that the bears were still on the ice flows miles away from us hunting seals and they only came ashore where we were staying after the ocean froze.

The outfitter had chartered a propeller driven cargo plane to fly his group of hunters from an airport right across the United States border to a gravel airstrip on the banks of a large river that flowed into Hudson's Bay. The airstrip had previously been used to service the military base and continued to serve a Cree Indian village with weekly flights.

The airplane was identical to the MATS flights that I traveled on when I flew from North Africa to Charleston, South Carolina while serving in United States Army in 1957. The seats were movable to different areas of the plane, which also carried cargo consisting of supplies for the Indian village, the hunting operation, and all our gear, guns, and ammunition. There were no separate compartments for passengers and baggage and cargo. Our gear was secured by netting attached to the airplane's interior.

Normally the outfitter would have several small groups of hunters from all over the United States and Canada to make a total of about 30

425

men. I contacted about 15 of my friends and organized the hunt with about two dozen members. I collected hunting fees for our members and obtained brochures for each. Herb had the information on the flights we needed to take to and from New Orleans and I made the reservations for the trip.

We met at the airport prior to our departure about 7 AM. In New Orleans. The lounge at the airport never closed and most off us enjoyed a Bloody Mary before we boarded. We flew to St. Louis Missouri and changed planes for the flight to Hibbing Minnesota and on to International Falls, where we deplaned and were loaded into a chartered bus to cross the border. Before crossing we stopped at a liquor store and each purchased two cases of beer and several bottles of liquor.

No liquor could be purchased at the Cree Indian village which was our destination, and we were told not to give or sell any liquor to the Indians. If you did you would not only be violating Canadian law, your Indian guide would quickly get drunk and not show up the next morning for your hunt.

I, being experienced in Livingston and Tangipahoa Parish politics, decided that I would buy several ½ pint bottles of cheap whiskey as well as some vodka and Jack Daniels for myself. I had no intention of giving the Indians any whiskey during the time we were hunting, but rightly figured they would rather have a ½ pint than $50 as a tip for their services to be awarded upon our departure.

We were met at the landing strip by the outfitter and a group of Cree Indians who had a large wagon attached to a pickup truck to transport our gear through the village to a boat landing. We were then transported in large skiffs across a large tidal river to the old army base a couple of miles away. The river was very muddy because of the daily fluctuation of the tide which was as much as 25 feet. I had brought my fly rod at Herb's suggestion so that we could get some trout fishing in the afternoon after a hunt. When I asked the outfitter how we could catch fish in such muddy water, he told me he would fly us in a small floatplane to a nearby river with flowing clear water.

A large meal was prepared for us at the mess hall that night and we talked to the outfitter and his two assistants about the availability of geese for the next morning's hunt while partaking in some of the drinks we had brought with us. They told us that we had arrived at the prime time to hunt as the geese which remained in small family flocks were beginning to concentrate into large staging groups in preparation for the upcoming migration. When we asked about limits they told us that each man could kill five or six birds a piece and the same number for each Cree guide.

The next morning, we were awakened a couple of hours before daylight and quickly dressed in our camouflage gear. We had an early breakfast and hot coffee at the mess hall where sandwiches and thermos bottles of coffee had been prepared to take with us on the hunt. We divided into groups of four men and two guides and got in a boat for the 20-minute ride to the hunting area. As we sped through the darkness we had no idea where the guides were taking us. We left the main river, proceeded through several channels of its Delta and stopped at the bottom of the 30-foot-high grass covered bank. When we got out of the boat and climbed up to the top of the bank one of the guides was carrying a long rope attached to the boat. I thought it strange that he didn't tie the rope to a small tree where we landed and instead tied off at the top of the bank. The mystery was revealed after we returned five or six hours later to find the tide had risen about 25 feet and the boat was floating near where it had been tied.

As we walked from the boat across the tundra, which was covered with grasses and intermediate bogs that were several inches deep, inter spaced with low willow bushes, we could hear the sound of geese brought to us on the wind as the sky began to brighten.

About a half-mile from the boat we divided into two groups with Shorty Rogers and I going with one Cree guide and Tom and Gordon Anderson going with the other. About a quarter of a mile further we found some willow bushes that were high enough for us to make a blind. While we were working on the blind the Indian took some newspapers from a bag he was carrying and placed four or five papers in three separate groups near us to use for decoys.

It was a cold, cloudy, windy morning and as the sun rose we could see small flocks of geese starting to rise across the horizon in all directions over the flat tundra. A group of geese approached from several hundred yards away and the Indian begin to call with his mouth,

427

sounding like a whole flock of geese. When the geese heard the call, they turned and came directly to us flying about 25 feet above the ground. I was using my 10gauge Ithaca automatic shotgun with number two shot. Shorty, who had never been hunting geese before had borrowed a 12gauge shotgun from his brother and had purchased shotgun shells at a local sporting goods store before we left.

When the geese got in range I killed two and Shorty shot three times without killing any. When the next group came in I killed another and Shorty again shot three times without any success. Later another group of geese approached and this time I did not shoot until Shorty had shot three more times and then I killed another.

When Shorty first started missing the geese I figured it was due to his inexperience, but many of these birds were first-year hatchlings who had never been shot at before and came into point-blank range. I told him to let me see his shotgun shells and when I looked at them I saw they were number seven and one half shot which were bouncing off the heavy feathers of the geese. After that each time a flock approached we would take turns shooting with my gun and Shorty begin to knock them down.

We mainly killed light geese, blues and snows, but we also killed several Canadian geese whose calls are entirely different from the snow geese. It was amazing to me to hear the Indians change from one call to another as the different species approached us in the wind. I only wanted to bring home specimens of the two types of Canadian geese that I killed, small cackling geese slightly larger than a mallard and other very large ones. Except for their size, their colors and markings were identical. We had more than our limits by the time the Indian told us it was time to go and I asked him what he was going to do with all those geese. He told me that he and his friends would come back and pick up the extra geese which they froze for their winter meat.

After the next morning's hunt, Herb, his brother Tommy, Tom Kent Stewart and I got our rods and boarded the floatplane for the short ride to the trout river. We fished for a couple of hours in the crystal-clear water of the shallow stream flowing through the boreal forest of small Aspen and spruce trees. The fish we caught weighed about 2 pounds and had beautiful red spots on their dark brown bodies. They were still biting as it started to get late in the evening but when we came across some fresh bear tracks in the sand we decided to return to the camp.

That night we saw a spectacular display of the northern lights, but at that season of the year the only color was white. We were told in late winter the lights often would turn green and red also. The next year Tom Kent Stewart and I, along with our wives, saw the Southern Cross in the predawn sky when we were hunting Magellan geese in the Patagonia region of Argentina.

Hobart Pardue – Canadian Geese –
Hudson's Bay Quebec, Canada

Hobart Pardue and Tom Anderson
Hudson's Bay

Shorty Rogers Hudson's Bay

Trout Fishing near Hudson's Bay

Chapter 19. Argentina Goose and Duck Hunting

In 1982 my friend Tom Kent Stewart told me about an article he read in a magazine about goose hunting in Argentina. I remembered our conversation about the Argentina hunting and invited he and his wife to accompany Loretta and I on a hunting trip to that country the next year.

The magazine article gave the name of the outfitter that arranged the hunts, Frontiers Travel Agency, so I contacted them and booked a hunt. The people at Frontiers told me that the only shotgun shells available in Argentina were Italian made and not very reliable, but we could expect to kill dozens of geese every day as well as ducks, pigeons, perdiz and grain eating parrots. I contacted my friend Billy Abels who operated a sporting goods store in Hammond Louisiana and had him order me a dozen cases of three-inch Magnum Winchester shotgun shells to shoot geese and ducks.

We booked a hunt for early August which was midwinter in South America. Frontiers had set up hunts for us in Patagonia near the Chilean border and in Entre Rios Province in central Argentina with two different outfits. We flew from New Orleans to Miami and boarded an Argentine Airlines jet to Buenos Aries, with a stop at Rio de Janeiro, Brazil. We left at midnight and arrived the next afternoon where we were met by our tour guide and taken to a large hotel.

I had read about the food in Argentina which is famous for its beef. The Frontiers agent had recommended a restaurant within walking distance of the hotel. When we entered the restaurant there was a fire burning near a large window that contained several pigs that were roasting, and an open grill fueled with charcoal along one side of the dining room where steaks were being cooked.

Our waiter, a man named Washington could speak excellent English. We ordered martinis and some excellent red wine. We started the meal with an appetizer, a meat pie that reminded me of those made in Natchitoches, Louisiana. When we ordered our meal, the waiter did not bring us a menu. Instead he brought a platter of raw steaks sliced very thick and we chose the steak we wanted them to cook, either a T-bone, ribeye, or filet.

When we were served, Tom Kent and I finished our steaks before our wives, Mary Ann and Loretta. I pushed my empty plate aside and the waiter poured me another glass of wine. I was expecting him to suggest a dessert, when to my surprise he placed another steak before me and one for Tom Kent. When I asked the waiter what this was all about he told me that a standard order was two steaks per person. Our wives, who were still eating their first steak quickly canceled the second ones. The cost of the meal was approximately 10% of the cost of a steak dinner at one of the most expensive restaurants in Louisiana.

The next morning, we boarded a jet for our flight to the tip of South America not far north of the Strait of Magellan, and a few miles from the eastern border of Chile. We were taken to a chalet containing two bedrooms and living room where we changed into our hunting clothes, stored our gear and boarded a vehicle for a short drive to the hunting area.

We were on a high plateau that resembled eastern Colorado where the white capped Andes mountains could be seen in the distance. Our guides took us to a pasture a couple of miles from a large river that was flowing out of the mountains, where we were lined up behind a fence about 40 yards apart. Tom Kent and I were standing next to each other with our wives on either side of us when geese begin flying from the fields where they had been feeding toward the river.

These geese, which were a mixture of Magellan and ashy headed geese did not have a call like the geese in North America. The Magellan's call was Ka, ka, ka, ka, Ka, ka, ka, ka. The ashy headed geese were mute.

The male Magellan was a large white bird with black specks on its feathers, the female was brown and white. They were about the size of snow geese in North America. The ashy head geese had brown and white bodies and their heads were ashy gray. They were smaller than the Magellan's, about the size of a mallard duck.

When the geese begin flying towards us you could hear them calling. I found it easy to mimic their calls and the approaching geese flew lower towards us. When they came in range we all began shooting, and every time I knocked down a bird Tom Kent would shout "I got him". We killed about 20 or 30 birds that afternoon before returning to the village where we were taken to a very good restaurant for dinner.

The next morning, I told our guide to make sure he put me at least a half-mile away from Tom Kent Stewart because I did not want him to continue to claim the birds that I shot. When we arrived at the place we were going to hunt it was bitterly cold, probably 10 to 15° below zero and our wives decided they were going to stay in the truck where they could keep warm rather than go with us to shoot geese.

The area we hunted that morning was open pasture land interspersed with groves of large cottonwood trees with small dry creek beds extending from the trees into the pastures. When we left the truck, I slipped a couple of dollars into the guide's hand and he sent Tom Kent on one side the road into a pasture where his only cover was a fencepost. A teenage bird boy led me on the other side of the road to a grove of trees several hundred yards away where I stood next to the pasture.

I was wearing my camouflaged coat, cap, and face mask but the bird boy was wearing bright colored clothing. When the geese began to approach me, they began to flare just out of range, so I moved the boy behind a large tree where they couldn't see him. The geese were flying about 10 to 15 feet off the ground and as they approached the trees they flew higher into the air making them more difficult for me to hit. I saw a shallow dry creek bed about 4 feet deep and 6 feet wide extending out into the pasture, so I followed it about 150 yards away from the trees. I cut some short bushes and tall grasses near the creek bank and placed them around me so when I sat in the bed of the creek on a bucket the geese could not see my head and shoulders protruding from the bank due to the grass and brush.

I took the plug out of my shotgun, so I would have five shots before I had to reload. As the flocks of geese approached me they were flying very low and I waited until they were no more than 20 or 30 yards away coming straight at me before I shot. Out of every flock I killed from one to five geese. As soon as I started killing those geese the bird boy would run pick them up then place them 10 or 15 yards in front of me to act as natural decoys. Within 30 or 40 minutes I was surrounded by the dead geese which resembled a feeding flock. The more geese I killed the larger my decoy spread grew. After couple of hours the morning flight

436

ended and the guide and one of his men came to the place my bird boy and I were hunting.

I walked back to the truck while they started picking up the dead geese and tying them together, so they could be brought back to the truck. When they had tied about 12 geese together they hung them on a pole which two of them carried back to the truck.

When I got to the truck Tom Kent was standing next to it with the geese he had killed laid out on the ground in front of it. I counted his geese and he had 14. My guide and bird boys were out of sight picking up my birds when Tom Kent asked me how many I killed. I told him only a few. He told me that since he had killed so many we should take a picture together and I could say that I killed part of them. I told him that my bird boys were bringing in my geese and when they got there we could get a picture of all of them. But first I took a picture of him and his pile of geese.

When my bird boys arrived, they had 12 geese on their pole which they dropped to the ground and started back for more. Tom Kent counted my geese, so he had more than I did and insisted we take a picture of us and the two piles of geese while he bragged about killing more than I had. I refused to take a picture and told him I thought my bird boys had missed picking up some of my geese. I said I was certain they would be bringing another three or four when they came back to the truck, which would show I shot about the same amount of geese that he did.

When the bird boys came back with another 15 geese and dropped them in my pile Tom Kent knew that I had bested him, but he had no idea how many I had actually killed. After three more trips my bird boys had delivered 78 geese that I had shot, and I told him he needed to borrow one of my Remington shotguns instead of using his Browning. I also told him I would be happy to give him instructions on how to shoot so he could kill a few more birds.

He got swollen up like a toad frog and told me that I had bribed his guide to put him out in the middle of the pasture behind a single fence post, so the geese could see him and wouldn't come close enough for him to shoot. I laughed and admitted that it only cost me two dollars, which was a cheap payback for him claiming the birds that I had killed the day before. The guides gave the geese to a local hospital where they were gratefully accepted. A day or so later we flew to Entre Rios where the first morning we killed over 100 geese.

At that location we also killed several species of South American ducks and Argentine perdiz, a bird that resembles sharp tailed grouse that I had hunted in Nebraska, North and South Dakota.

The outfitter at that area, Chille, was a wealthy landowner who owned several cattle ranches and apple orchards as well as herds of sheep. There were few natural predators of the sheep, but occasionally huge wild boar would kill and eat sheep, sometimes killing many animals. When that happened the sheep herders would contact Chille to have him come and kill the boars.

When I was a boy in South Louisiana one of my uncles owned free ranging hogs which we caught with dogs. We would turn three or four dogs loose in the woods and when the dogs found the hogs they would bay them. The dogs would surround the hogs who would back up to a fallen tree or stump and face the dogs who would bite the ears of the hogs and hold them, so they couldn't use their razor-sharp tusks to cut either the dogs or the hunters.

While the dogs held the hogs, we would approach them from the rear, grab their hind feet and tie them up. The hogs we caught rarely weighed more than 100 pounds and were often moved to pigpens where they could be fattened before being slaughtered. Any large boars were usually shot, but you had to be very careful not to shoot a dog that was trying to fight the hog.

In Argentina, our outfitter Chile, used two dogs that were specially bred to hunt hogs. They were huge, weighing more than 120 pounds and snow white, with the features of a cross between a pitbull and mastiff.

When hunting a sheep killing boar Chili did not use a gun even though the hog might weigh several hundred pounds because he did not want to take a chance of killing or injuring his dogs. Instead, he used an 18-inch-long dagger. When the dogs caught the boar, with one holding each ear, he would approach the animal from its rear and stab it through the heart with his dagger.

When we visited his home for dinner one evening he showed us his trophy room with one wall completely covered with the skulls of huge wild boars that he had killed.

Loretta and Hobart Pardue and Mary Ann and Tom Kent Stewart, Patagonia, Argentina

Argentina Goose Blind – Mary Ann Stewart

Argentina Gaucho

How to Order a Steak
Argentina Steak House

Magellan and Ashy Head Geese
In Argentina

Goose Hunt near the
Andes Mountains

Chapter 20. Trip to Mexico to Hunt Ocellated Turkey

The Oceola was the last of the four-turkey species I took in the United States. I killed my last one in Florida in 1985, and I had already decided to hunt the Ocellated Turkeys in Mexico. That breed of turkey is different from any other turkey, but he does make a racket during mating season in the spring. The hens don't make a yelp, their call is a peep peep peep. he male doesn't say gobble gobble gobble he makes a different kind of call entirely. I had killed all the other species of turkeys in North America, except the Gould turkey in Northwest Mexico, and I wanted to go ahead and kill the ocellated turkey, which was a jungle bird. I got a hold of my buddies Chaney Phillips and Charlie Abels who had hunted turkeys with me all over the United States and set up a hunt in the Spring of 1985, at a place in the Yucatan peninsula where we could hunt that kind of turkey.

Very, very few people in the world had ever killed that kind of turkey and fewer still had killed all the rest of them. I was trying to be the first to do all that, but I knew even if I didn't do all that I'd still be the first son of a gun from Livingston Parish, or the state of Louisiana and probably from most of the south that ever did it. And for that reason, I and my buddies that hunted with me all the time, wanted to be in on the deal. And that was all good too.

I set up the hunt with an outfitter whose headquarters was on the Bay of Campeche in Mexico. The guy's name was Jorge' but when you spelled out his name in English, it was George. He had an outfit where he mainly took people fishing for Snook and Tarpon in the Bay of Campeche and in the river Campeche which was a saltwater estuary that flowed into the Bay. The Snook and the Tarpon congregated there at certain times of the year after the rainy season, but some remained year-round. Jorge' had a little hotel/motel right on the Bay where the river came into the Gulf of Mexico. He fed us gourmet food which was mainly seafood, often cooked in lime juice and it was gourmet, I guarantee you.

He found out there was some crazy people like me and other hunters that wanted to try to kill an Ocellated turkey which is smaller than any other wild turkey and has tail feathers that look like a peacock. He correctly figured they would pay good green dollars to go to the border of Guatemala in the Mexican jungle to hunt that kind of trophy bird. Since I had already killed all those others in the states, I decided I had to get this one also. My buddies had not killed all of them either but had killed most of them, and they wanted to get this one too.

We took off on our hunt in early April 1985 and flew down to the city of Merida, in the Yucatan Peninsula, Mexico, and had a layover there before we caught the van that was provided for us to go to Campeche. Naturally we got there in the afternoon and spent the evening in Merida. At the airport we ran into a Mexican that had lived in the United States for a time, before he got shipped back to Mexico from Florida. He apparently had been deported after engaging in some of his nefarious violations of laws of the United States and the State of Florida. He could speak very good English, and he knew a little bit about the way the world went around. He also knew a whole lot about the city of Merida, such as the best restaurants, the best places to stay, the nightlife, the day life, and everything else.

We told him about our plans to go on up the coast, meet our guides, then go back into the jungle and make our hunt. We told him when we finished we were coming back to Merida and would need some more guiding in the city before we came back to the United States. His name was Carlos and, he was a very intelligent fellow who could speak very good English that we could understand. The next morning, we caught our taxi van up to Campeche and met Jorge' at the Snook Inn, named after the illusive snook fish that was a trophy in a lot of places for people that caught exotic fish.

The next morning, we all loaded up in vehicles and headed out to the jungle to go hunt turkeys. The outfitter had a deuce and a half truck, which is a two-and-a-half-ton vehicle like to ones I rode in when I was in the army in Turkey in 1957. They hauled equipment, supplies, soldiers and such between the capitol of Ankara Turkey and the Province of Sinop where we had a radar base, to spy on the Russians when they were launching the Sputnik satellites.

The deuce and a half that Jorge' had was loaded down with gourmet food, Ice, generators, cots, mosquito nets, and everything we needed to be as comfortable as you can get in a jungle setting, where malaria was a

446

real threat and the comforts of home were far away. We left the Snook Inn that morning in two convertibles that resembled Volkswagens but were built right after WWII and were kind of semi armored. They were 4-wheel drive and would go through all kind of jungle trails to get to the place we were going to hunt. As we rode along through the jungle we could observe all kinds of plants, animals, birds, insects and everything else that was not readily available to be seen anywhere else.

The deuce and a half truck either followed or was ahead of us at various times as we traveled through the jungle roadways. I remember it got stuck in the middle of the night in a slough as we were heading south, and it took a long time for the Mexicans to get it unstuck and get us through the mud hole. During that time, I heard some of the most hideous sounds I had ever heard in my life. It was like terrific screams that made you think that animals or people were being attacked. The Mexicans payed no attention to it and of course I couldn't speak Spanish and they couldn't speak good English. I finally found one that could talk a little bit of English and asked him what the hell all of this racket was, and he said it was frogs. Apparently, it was frogs, cause as soon as we got out of the bog, and back on high land and moved further in the jungle we didn't hear any more of it. That is, until we got to the hunting area, set up camp and went into our tents just before daylight. We had started off at probably about 7 or 8 o'clock in the morning and the trip lasted from that time until we arrived. At daylight the next morning we awoke to the sound of things awakening in the jungle. It wasn't as hideous as the frogs screaming like banshees, but it was quite a roar. There was no way to sleep through it and when I asked them what the hell this was, we were informed it was monkey's, birds, insects, and all kind of things that made the jungle come alive at daylight in the morning. It calmed down later but for the first hour or two in the morning the noise was everywhere.

We went back to bed and tried to get a little sleep after the uproar from the daylight passed, and a couple of hours later, we got in the vehicles with our guides, and started riding through the jungle to try to locate some wild turkeys. Chaney went with his guide one way; Charley and his guide went a different way and my guide, and I went another. I saw my first Ocellated turkey cross the narrow dirt road and my guide

447

marked the place. We came on back to the camp, and after lunch and a siesta, we went back out to try to roost the turkey before dark. My guide and I went to the area where I had seen the turkey earlier. I had my gun ready and was determined to shoot him if I could. Just before dark, that gobbler started cutting up, not with a gobble gobble gobble, but with a Wee Woo Waa Waa How kind of noise, a crazy kind of sound. He was very loud and very close to us, but the jungle was so thick I couldn't see through it. I know that turkey walked within 25 steps of me at least 3 times that evening but I couldn't get a shot.

The technique for killing a turkey in that area was to shoot them off a limb, because there was no way I could call him to me through the jungle and get a shot before he saw me. We tried that, and it didn't work, but we managed to get close to him before he flew up to roost. Those jungle turkeys did not act like a turkey in Louisiana, Mississippi, Texas, or anywhere in the United States and northern Mexico that I had hunted before. In those places, turkeys will fly up and light on a large limb and roost right close to the tree truck. The turkeys in the jungle fly up to a limb, then move down it until they get to a point where the weight of the bird causes it to swing up and down, before they go to sleep. This is a survival action the turkey uses when sleeping.

There were several different kinds of jungles cats in the area. Not only big jaguars, although those will catch a turkey also, but smaller ones the size of a house cat. They will crawl out on the limb to try to kill that turkey while he's asleep. When this happens, the turkey who's way out on the end of the limb, will feel it shaking, wake him up and he can haul his ass and fly away.

My goal was to try to get close enough to see the turkey fly up, watch him as he moved out on that limb, and hope to be able to shoot him before it got too dark to see him. Now that may not sound very sporting, but the challenge I faced was much greater than calling a turkey to me in the United States. The turkey is calling, then flies up and lands on a limb and continues to call. At the time he flies up it is twilight, and twilight in the jungle doesn't last but about 4 to 5 minutes from the time the sun drops down until dark. During that 4 to 5-minute time you have got to move from where you first saw him fly up and get close enough to shoot before it gets black dark and you can't see him.

Jorge' gave his guides a spotlight to use so they could bull eye that turkey if it got too black, and the hunter could shoot him in the dark. I figured it was bad enough not to give him much of a sporting chance and shoot him off a limb, but I damn sure didn't want to take advantage of him to the point that I had to bull eye him in the dark and shoot him.

Anyway, this particular turkey flew, and I saw him when he went up. I'd been hunting him for probably an hour and a half, listening to him call and cutup, but I only got one fleeting glimpse of him as he moved through the thick jungle, giving me no chance for a shot. When he finally flew up my guide used his machete to cut a little path in that thick jungle for us to get a little bit closer on him, so I could shoot him. This type of turkey, when he starts calling after reaching the limb, shuts his eyes. He might repeat his call several times, with his eyes shut, but when he hits that last call, his eyes are gonna open up again, and he's gonna be looking to see if there's any son of a bitch around trying to get him, which I was sure trying to do. When he started calling on the limb, we started moving. When he stopped making his call my guide, who was just ahead of me stopped using the machete to cut the path and stopped moving. I had to stop moving instantly to keep from making any kind of movement that he could see and cause him to fly the heck off. During the stalk, at least three times I got caught with one foot in the air and one foot down, and I couldn't move the foot in the air down to the ground before he started to make his call again, As we got closer I saw him on the end of that limb, and I shot him while it was still light enough to see him against the fading light of the sky, just before it got dark enough to use a light to bull eye that bird. He was one of the greatest trophies I have ever taken.

Well, I was the first out of our three to be successful, kill my turkey, and come on back in. The next morning, before daylight, Chaney and Charley had to get up and go out looking for turkey's again. I had the luxury of sleeping in which lasted until about 5 minutes after daylight, when all the howler monkeys, and all the damn birds, and insects, and everything else that made the jungle come alive and roar took place. Since I got woke up, I went over to the cook shack where the cooks were fixing breakfast, had some coffee and explored the campsite. When we first arrived, it was after midnight. And the next morning I went off hunting just like everybody else. That night I came back to camp after I killed my turkey, arriving after dark. We had a sumptuous gourmet meal, foods including shrimp, cracked crabs, pompano, and snook, just the best seafood in the world with all the seasonings and all the drinks and everything else you wanted to go with it. This was a hundred miles away from the coast and in the middle of the jungle. My partners were all in the jungle trying to catch up to me and kill a turkey, so I sat around being bored for a while.

It was then I realized that before we left the United States, I had bought a couple of Penthouse Magazines, and I quickly remembered the reason I bought them was to see what I could do to play some tricks on my friends. So, I spent the day taking the pictures of the naked women in various poses out of the magazines, while my friends were in the jungle. I did not say anything about this to Charlie and Chaney as we dined on grilled turkey breast, seafood dishes, exotic vegetables, fruit and wine that evening. Later on, I listened to their stories of the days hunt over Jack Daniels, and Scotch Whiskey.

I told them when they came in after not killing any turkey's that I wasn't going to wait for them any longer. I was leaving the next morning with one of the vehicles and a Mexican to carry me back to civilization, and I would wait for them a couple of days on the coast to see if they could kill anything and come on and join me. They didn't like it, of course, but there wasn't a damn thing they could do about it, so before daylight the next morning they took off to the jungle again. I got up bright and early, made sure I had my driver, and all my supplies to get me back to the coast ready to go, but before I left I took all the pictures of those naked women and I went to the thatched roof bunkhouse where my friends slept. I made sure that if they laid down in their bed, which was a folding cot inside a mosquito net draped facility that kept them from getting ate up by mosquitos, and they looked straight up in the air they would see pictures of beautiful naked women hung from the bottom of the bunk above them. I also made sure when they got up to go to the shower, which had a thatched straw roof and walls, with primitive type of levers to pull to unleash water from a cistern to wash themselves, they would see the pictures of undressed beautiful women. When they had to answer the call of nature and go to the crapper which also had a thatched

450

roof and grass walls; While they were sitting, they would see unadorned beautiful women. Naturally I didn't say anything or sign my name or give any kind of indication of where all these beautiful floral images came from.

I left out of the camp probably about 10:30 in the morning and I made it back to the place where we got off the jungle trail to a gravel road. Shortly after we reached a paved road which led to a village. We arrived about 3:00 p.m., had lunch and cold beers, and got back to the Snook Inn on the Bay of Campeche before dark.

When My friends got back to camp from the jungle and saw what I had left them, they were pissed off, but not surprised. I received many many derogatory statements from them not only during the time when we first saw each other again at the Snook Inn, but also before we got back on a plane to head back home. For many years thereafter, they talked about how a brown eyed son of a bitch did it to them again.

Anyway, Charley and Chaney did wind up killing Ocellated turkeys. Charlie also killed a collared peccary pig and a long tailed black bird called a great black grackle and made sure he brought the long tail feather back to me. He told me I needed to put it in my hat because it looked pretty damn much like a buzzard feather and that it would suit me better than having a turkey feather.

By the time they finally came out, I had waited 2 or 3 days for my friends. During that time, I caught snook in the river where I saw small flocks of rare wild Muscovy ducks, and shot doves in the afternoons with wealthy Mexican hunters who were hunting Brocket deer in the mornings. My companions finally came out of the jungle with their trophies and we headed back to Merida before returning to the United States.

When we arrived at Merida we contacted the Mexican cab driver who had gave us our ride to Campeche when we first got there, and he gave us a tour of the town. He took us to some of the great cathedrals and the best restaurants in the town where we had some of the most exotic food I have ever eaten. It was nothing like Mexican food you find on the border or in Louisiana. He made sure we had the best accommodations and gave us directions to where we could find other entertainment.

451

In those days in most parts of Mexico, and especially along the border, prostitutes were restricted to areas around large cities called boys towns. These are a series of bars and strip clubs, usually displaying strings of colored Christmas tree lights. When we hit Merida after coming out of the jungle there were no boys' towns, because there had been a police crackdown. Our friend and guide told us there had been with a high-profile murder case which resulted in the demolition of some of the boy's town facilities. After that if you wanted to find prostitutes there were certain areas of town they were restricted to. You could catch a cab, ride down the streets where dozens of young women would be congregated at each intersection, waiting for customers.

The day we arrived at Merida we went to a restaurant accompanied by our guide. He told us the food there was wonderful, but don't go over across the street to the sweet shop and eat any type of dessert such as, ice cream, cakes, cookies, brownies, or sweet rolls, because it was not as clean as we were used to. Well knowing us, we had a few drinks at the restaurant. We ate our food, and it was wonderful. Afterward we were walking around where we visited a large church while sightseeing, and we came on one of the sweet shops. They had ice cream, gelato, and all kinds of different desserts. I'm a sucker for desserts, and I was very tempted but when I started to reach to get a sweet dessert I had to knock off the flies before I could pick it up. I looked around and there were flies everywhere, so and I said the hell with this, and didn't eat anything. Charley Abels saw what happened, and he passed up the desserts also. Chaney Phillips, who was with us also, probably had his damn eyes shut, because he went ahead and grabbed some sort of a damn treat and just ate it. We all went back to the hotel for a siesta and about dark we decided we were gonna go out and look for some entertainment. By that time the only one's walking were me and Charley Abels because Chaney had contacted Montezuma's revenge. Charley and I told Chaney we would go find him some entertainment, and he told us to bring him one back. We got our cab driver and went for a ride. It took Charley and I about an hour and a half to pick one out for Chaney because we made individual inspections of all the candidates. Finally, we found one that we figured he would be interested in. I though we made an excellent choice for Chaney and when we brought her to him he was sitting on the

452

commode where he had been all evening. We let him know that we had found him a treat, and he came bounding off the damn commode and met One Tittie Annie. She was a girl who unfortunately had either been born with only one breast or lost one to surgery. We did not let him live that down for many years afterward.

Charlie Abels and Chaney Phillips Turkey and Peccary

Hobart Pardue, Guide and Ocellated Turkey

Bay of Campeche

Mexican Jungle Vehicle

Mexican Jungle Camp

Mexico – Jungle Camp Shower

Chapter 21. Ecuador Duck Hunt

By the mid-1980s I had collected most of the ducks in North America and others in Argentina and Mexico. On my trip to the Yucatán peninsula where I collected my Ocellated Turkey, I had spent a couple of days fishing for snook on the Campeche River. Early one morning I spied a flock of wild Muscovy ducks flying up the river near the coast. These ducks are very rare, and they may have been protected in Mexico at that time.

A couple of years later I was reading The Bird Hunting Report and saw an article on hunting ducks in Ecuador. The guide and outfitter was a young man who was attending LSU at the time. I looked him up, invited him to my home and showed him my trophy room with its collection of ducks. He told me about several species that were available in his country, including Bahama Pintail, and Wild Muscovy.

These ducks were non-migratory and could be hunted at any time of the year. If you wanted high-volume shooting, blue winged Teal were available in December and January. I told him I was interested in taking a wild Muscovy, and any other species I didn't already have. We set up a hunt in the early spring for my wife and I.

We flew to Guayaquil, the second largest city in Ecuador, which is located on the coast of the Pacific Ocean. The land was flat in this area and contained several small rivers and lakes. We were taken to a villa about 40 miles from the town and prepared to go hunting the next morning. The young man we were hunting with was not a professional guide but was familiar with the area where he had hunted since he was a boy. The first morning we went to some small ponds surrounded by small trees resembling mangroves which prevented us from approaching the edge of the water except in one or two places. There were no blinds and we had to been told not to bring any camouflage clothing since some revolutionaries wore it when they were attacking government soldiers in other parts of the country.

There were several flocks of ducks on the ponds, so we walked as close to the water as we could and stood at the edge of the small trees while our guide and his helpers walked around the ponds and flushed the ducks. When the ducks flew around by us we got some passing shots and discovered they were South American Ruddy Ducks. I had killed a few of the North American species, but none of them had mating plumage when I shot them in November and December.

The ducks in Ecuador were in full mating plumage with the drakes having feathers that were rusty red on their backs, black on their head and neck, and white on their cheeks, which contrasted with their sky-blue bills. The problem was each small flock consisting of 4 to 10 birds had only one drake in it. The rest were all drab colored females or juveniles, and the only Drake I knocked down fell in the thick mangrove type trees and the guides could not find it.

That afternoon we were taken to another area and killed some teal in open ponds. We were then taken to an adjoining swampy area where we were told Muscovy ducks came into roost after feeding in the banana trees during the day. We split up with Loretta staying near the edge of a swamp with one guide and I and my guide walking several hundred yards away to another area. Just before dark a few ducks came in to roost and we each managed to kill a young Muscovy.

These ducks are solid black as juveniles, but their colors change to black-and-white when they mature. They feed almost exclusively on bananas which are grown in plantations in the low lands of Ecuador. As we traveled near those plantations I observed workers putting plastic covering filled with insecticide over the banana stems when the fruit was small. This kept ducks and other birds from destroying the crop when it ripened.

The next morning, we went to a different area with shallow lakes where sticks were stuck in the mud to make blinds. Some larger pieces of wood were placed inside the blinds for us to stand on to keep from sinking in the mud. At daylight the sky was filled with Bahama Pintails which came to the handful of decoys placed around us. There were no limits and we quickly killed about two dozen. Some of the birds were molting and could not fly so we watched them swim away. After the hunt the guides set up a grill near the side of the lake and we had grilled duck, fresh fruit and vegetables for lunch.

That afternoon we started up the highway to Quito, the capital city whose elevation is 9350 feet in the Andes Mountains. We arrived at a small hotel after midnight and when we went to bed, I could not sleep due to the lack of oxygen. I had experienced this before when sheep hunting in British Columbia at a similar elevation, and I knew in a day or two we would be used to it. The next day we explored the city and I dined on grilled guinea pig which reminded me of the big Fox squirrels we killed at home. The next morning, we went to a large lake in the mountains that had lots of ducks in the middle, but we had no boats to get to them. I did manage to kill a Grebe that had different coloring than the ones at home for my trophy room. The next day our guides took us about 100 miles along a road through the mountains where we passed several volcanoes which were emitting smoke from their tops.

After spending the night at a small hotel, we drove away from the paved highway and proceeded toward the summit of a large inactive volcano in search of perdiz, a small grouse like bird about the size of a chuckar partridge. I had hunted them before in Argentina were hunters would line up and walk through the short grass and bushes to flush them. The altitude on those hunts were about 5000 or 6000 feet and I had no problem breathing.

We had been in the mountains of Ecuador for several days and as long as I was riding in an automobile or walking around the lake and in the city, I had no problems. What I didn't realize was the change in elevation as we drove up the mountain on the narrow gravel road. As we rounded a curve we saw a couple of birds cross the road about 50 yards in front of us. We stopped the car and I got out with my shotgun and started walking toward the place I had last seen the birds, which was in a little dip in the road. I was puffing to get my breath as I walked down the slope. When I turned to climb higher I took about three steps and had to stop and sit down because I couldn't breathe. I called the guide and told him to bring the car to me because I couldn't hunt at that altitude which had to be over 11,000 feet.

We returned to the hotel and ate supper with the guide who told us we could take a different route back to Quayaquil where we could shop at a small town for some leather goods where they were made by hand. When we arrived there the next day we spent a couple of hours and we purchased coats, gloves and other goods for about 10% of what they would've cost in the United States.

As we traveled down the mountain roads we passed terraced fields where grain and vegetables were planted. We stopped at a small restaurant that featured a spicy stew made from llama meat and vegetables, including grains of corn as large as my thumb which we washed down with local beer. The road was narrow and winding and we passed many buses and trucks along the way on our long slow journey. When we reached the foothills where banana plantations began our guides stopped at a roadside stand and bought a stem of small sweet bananas which we consumed on the rest of the ride.

As we were approaching the city, a small truck with wooden crates in the back pulled out in front of us. I asked the guide what was in the crates and he told me it was land crabs. I asked him if he knew how to boil crabs like we do in Louisiana where he went to school, and he said yes. I then got him to stop the truck and buy a couple of bushels which we brought with us for supper. The crabs which lived on land except when they deposited their eggs in the water at the seashore looked like our blue crabs and were delicious.

Andes Mountain Farm Land - Ecuador

Bahama Pintails Ducks
Ecuador

Wild Mascovy Ducks - Ecuador

Ecuador Fruit Stand

Chapter 22. 1993 Western Hunt

In 1990 Loretta and I made the spring turkey hunt that took us to northern California, Oregon, Washington, Idaho, Montana, Wyoming, South Dakota, and Nebraska. We pulled a camper trailer and were on the road for more than a month. On that trip we saw mule deer and pronghorn antelope in Wyoming and lots of pheasants, grouse, and waterfowl in Montana and the Dakotas.

I had never taken a pronghorn nor a Sandhill Crane, so we decided to return to hunt those species as well as other types of game in the fall of 1993. I prepared for this trip by reading hunting reports in the periodicals I had subscriptions from, "The Hunting Report and The Bird Hunting Report". Subscribers can receive copies of recent years publications that are limited to specific types of game and specific areas in which to hunt. In addition to the articles written by professionals, reports are also written by hunters who have actually hunted with the guides mentioned in the articles.

I personally have written critiques about hunts I made for different types of game, in these periodicals, and then received telephone calls from other hunters requesting more specific information about my hunts. In my research for this trip I talked to a Crow Indian outfitter near Plentywood, Montana about hunting sage grouse and waterfowl and a guide who specialized in goose hunts in Steel, North Dakota about hunting Sandhill Cranes.

I booked hunts with both of these outfitters and planned my trip to include self-guided hunts for pronghorn antelope, waterfowl, and mule deer in Buffalo Wyoming. On this trip we decided to stay in motels and the facilities provided by the guides instead of pulling a camper trailer, so I made reservations in small towns along the way.

We arrived in Buffalo a couple days before the hunting season opened and I drove to an area where I had observed antelope while turkey hunting in 1990. As we approached that location I saw herds of pronghorn antelope on both sides of the highway and when I reached a driveway leading to a ranch house I turned and drove in. The owner, a middle-aged woman, told me that she had leased the mule deer hunting rights to another group, but agreed to let me hunt pronghorn on her property when the season opened the next day. She also agreed to show me the best place for me to hunt. I expected to return the next morning before daylight, but she told me she drove a school bus and that I needed to meet her later in the morning after she had completed her route.

The next morning Loretta and I drove back to the ranch in my pickup truck, where I got into the owner's vehicle to ride across the prairie toward the pronghorn's. She told me we needed to use her truck because the animals were used to seeing it and we could get close enough for a shot without having to walk several miles from my truck, which would frighten them.

We saw several groups of pronghorns and I looked them over with my spotting scope, which I attached to the window of the truck to determine the largest buck. After driving several miles, we spotted a large buck with a group of does about 600 yards away and was able to drive a couple of hundred yards closer where I got out of the truck. I crawled to the top of a small hill and managed to get a shot when the animal was quartering about 300 yards away. It immediately disappeared down the slope and when I reached the place it had been I could find no blood.

My guide drove up in her truck and we slowly drove across the prairie searching for the buck. As we reached the top of a rolling prairie hill other animals ran away and we saw my buck trailing them with a broken leg. I quickly dispatched him with another shot.

We loaded the animal in the truck and returned to the ranch where I hung him in a shed and skinned him out and removed the entrals. It was quite cold that morning and the ranch owner allowed me to leave the animal hanging overnight.

The next day I returned and butchered the animal then took it to a meat processing facility where it was wrapped and frozen for shipment home. I then went to the Chamber of Commerce in Buffalo and was given the name and telephone number of several ranchers who allowed hunters to hunt mule deer on their property for a daily fee. I got a quadrangle map of the property, paid my fee and drove to the area in preparation for the next morning's hunt. That night at the motel I went over the map and planned the route I would take on roads along streambeds in search of deer.

The next morning, we arrived on the property before daylight and drove on a ranch road to a high point where I could glass for deer with my spotting scope while sitting in the truck with Loretta. There was an icy wind blowing from the west as the stars faded and the sky brightened. A dry creek bed ran parallel to the road on my left with a high, treeless ridge behind it. After closely examining the terrain for about 45 minutes and seeing no animals we moved further down the road to another high point and repeated the process.

After a few minutes I saw movement several hundred yards away on the other side of a canyon containing a dry creek bed. I focused on the spot with my spotting scope and observed two mule deer feeding in the brush. At that distance I could tell one was a buck but couldn't count the points on his antlers. As the light got stronger I could see it was a small buck, but big enough to shoot.

I did not expect to find a large trophy class animal in that area, in fact when I talked to the people at the Chamber of Commerce and other hunters I met in a restaurant they all told me that they went further west in the high mountains to hunt large mule deer.

I didn't see any other deer and had just about made up my mind to try to get close to the one I was looking at. The only trouble was that deer was a long way from the road and on the other side of the fairly deep canyon. I knew if I killed him it would probably take me a half a day to pull him to my truck. I decided that I would proceed down the road and try to find a place where I could cross the canyon with my truck and double back to the deer.

We slowly drove down the winding road and in a few hundred yards came around a bend where I spied another young buck a couple of hundred yards away. The deer was standing right next to the road, so I quickly got out of the truck and shot him.

When I drove up to the animal and loaded it into the back of my truck I realized there were no trees to hang it where I could easily skin and butcher it. I didn't want to take it to a game processing plant and pay someone a hundred and fifty dollars to prepare it for shipment, so we continued down the road searching for place to hang the deer.

We had passed several oil wells in the area the day before, and about a mile and a half down the road I found an abandoned one that had a wooden gate with a timber nailed to the top of two posts. I backed up to the gate climbed up in the truck and using a come a long hoisted the deer to the timber where I quickly skinned it out and disemboweled it. It was very cold that morning, and while Loretta and I drank coffee in the warm truck the deer quickly cooled enough for me to quarter it. After about another half hour of cooling, I was able to debone the meat and place it in Ziploc bags, so it could be frozen for shipment.

We then returned to the meat processing facility and had them freeze and box the venison along with the pronghorn I had killed and ship it to my son in Louisiana. We then proceeded toward Montana to hunt for birds.

I had obtained quadrangle maps of areas along the Montana – Canadian border near the town of Plentywood. We scouted the area from my pickup truck and got permission to hunt some potholes from several landowners. The next couple of mornings I waded along the banks of the potholes before daylight and set up a small spread of decoys near some tall grass which gave me the cover of a natural blind, where I collected a mixed bag of ducks.

The next day we traveled east to Steel, North Dakota and met the outfitter who I had contacted about hunting for Sandhill cranes. He had converted a small abandoned schoolhouse into a makeshift camp for goose hunts, where Loretta and I slept in a classroom.

That afternoon the outfitter took us to several fields were flocks of Sandhill cranes were feeding. There was no way to get to the birds since they were in the middle of large pastures and cut over grain fields. We didn't disturb them and when they went to roost in a shallow river several miles away the outfitter told me they would probably return to the same fields the next day, and I needed to get there before they arrived.

The next morning, I parked my truck about a half-mile from the field and walked to the area where the birds had been the day before. It was very cold, and the grass was covered with hoar frost when I walked into the field. I had traveled about 300 yards from the edge of the field and sat down in a small depression near the location I expected the birds to return to.

After daylight flocks of birds approached my location but flared and lit several hundred yards away from me. More birds continued to arrive but all of them joined the others on the ground. I couldn't figure out why these birds were avoiding my location since I was well camouflaged with my clothing as well as some blind material I had brought with me. Finally, I gave up the hunt and started back to my truck. Then I saw what had spooked the birds. When I walked through the hoar frost I had left a distinct trail that the birds could see from the air. They probably figured the trail was made by a coyote or other predator, and this caused them to avoid me.

That afternoon we drove around the countryside looking for other places to hunt. With my binoculars and spotting scope I was able to locate several other flocks of Sandhills and determined what their flight plan would be going to or coming back from their roost. One flock was feeding in a field that had several large piles of rocks on its edges that farmers had picked up when they were preparing the land for cultivation.

I drove to a nearby farmhouse and asked for permission to hunt there the next morning. The owner gave me permission to hunt Sandhill cranes, but not pheasants. I told him that I only wanted to kill a couple of cranes for my trophy room and he readily agreed.

The next morning, I left my truck in a grove of cottonwood trees a few hundred yards from the field and made certain that I did not walk through the field and leave a trail in the hoar frost that the birds could see. After walking around the outside of the field in heavy brush I approached a large pile of boulders near its border. I then climbed into the pile of rocks, made myself a seat and wrapped up in my gray camouflaged blind material which perfectly matched the boulders.

I had my 10gauge Ithaca shotgun that I used to hunt turkeys in the spring. It had a longer-range than my 12gauge that I usually used to hunt waterfowl. Not long after daylight I began to hear approaching flights of cranes, and soon they began to light in the field about 100 yards in front of me. I was sitting between the feeding birds and their roost as more small flocks flew over my location.

Most of them were out of range when they passed me, but after a while about a dozen birds dropped to about 40 yards high as they prepared light with the others. When this happened, I knocked two of them out of the sky. One crumpled and fell dead and the other hit the ground with a broken wing.

I had read about crippled Sandhill cranes blinding dogs with their sharp pointed beaks when they tried to catch them, so I had left my Chesapeake Bay retrievers in the truck with Loretta. Without a dog to help me I chased the crippled bird several hundred yards before I was able to get close enough to dispatch it.

After the shooting, the remaining birds moved away, and I returned to the schoolhouse camp with my trophies. The outfitter told me that Sandhill cranes, unlike cranes that inhabited the swamps of Louisiana, ate only grain, and were excellent table fare. I prepared one bird for mounting and cooked the other on my charcoal smoker for our supper.

The next morning, we began our long trek home from North Dakota through South Dakota, Nebraska, Iowa, Missouri, Tennessee, and Mississippi which took three days.

Sandhill Cranes, Steel, North Dakota

Badlands, South Dakota

South Dakota Pheasants - Otis Ratcliff, Hobart
Pardue and Tom Kent Stewart

South Dakota Pheasants

South Dakota Mule Deer

Rocky Mountain Bighorn Sheep
Villa Grove, Colorado

Hobart Pardue, Jim Richardson, Guide, Dickie
Abels, Charlie Abels and Mike Drude
Saquache, Colorado

Idaho Black Bear with Bow and Arrow

Idaho Bear Hunt

Hobart Pardue and Retrievers
Wyoming

Petrified Forest, Wyoming

Prong Horn Antelope
Buffalo, Wyoming

After the Hunt
Hobart Pardue, Herb Plauche` and
Tom Kent Stewart

Grand Slam of Rams

World Grand Slam Of Turkey's

Loggerhead Turtle

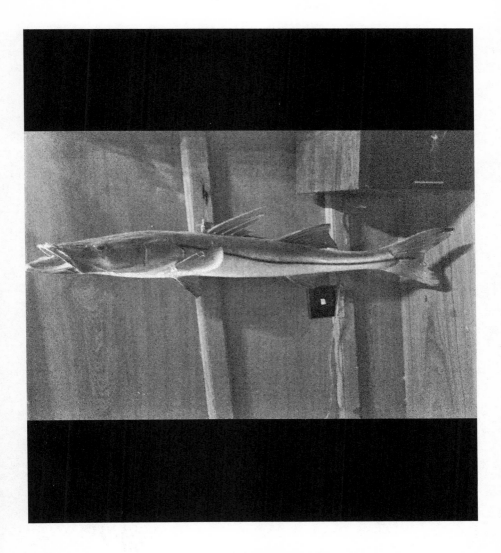

Mexican Snook

Author Hobart O. Pardue, Jr.